Jane's GUNS

RECOGNITION GUIDE

Ian Hogg

Rob Adam

HarperCollins*Publishers*

Acknowledgements:

Text and photos (except where noted below): Ian Hogg
Text and photos for pp 10-12, 50-54, 57, 105, 135-36, 162-4, and 192-99: Rob Adam
Thanks to the MoD Pattern Room, the Infantry Museum, Edgar Brothers, the Royal Military College of Science and the West
Midlands Constabulary for their invaluable assistance in providing access to and photography of various weapons in their care.

Cover photograph: David Hendley
Design: Rod Teasdale

HarperCollinsPublishers
PO Box, Glasgow G4 0BN

First published 1996

Reprint 10 9 8 7 6 5 4 3 2 1

© Jane's Information Group 1996

ISBN 0 00 4709799

Printed in Italy by Amadeus S.p.A. Rome

DISCLAIMER

Contents

PISTOLS

AMT Hardballer	10
AMT On Duty	11
AMT Automag II	12
Astra 300	13
Astra 400	14
Astra Model F	15
Astra Falcon	16
Astra A-50	17
Astra A-70	18
Astra A-75	19
Astra A-80	20
Astra A-90	21
Astra A-100	22
Beholla	23
Beretta Model 1915	24
Beretta Model 1915/19	25
Beretta Model 1923	26
Beretta Model 1931	27
Beretta Model 1934	28
Beretta M951	29
Beretta M951R	30
Beretta Model 84	31
Beretta Model 92	32
Beretta Centurion	
models	33
Beretta Model 93R	34
Bernardelli P-018	35
Bernardelli Mod. USA	36
Bergmann-Bayard	37
Browning 1900	38
Browning 1903	39
Browning 1910/22	40
Browning High-Power Model 1935	41
Browning BDA9	42
Browning BDA 380	43
Calico M950	44
China Type 54	45
China Type 64	46
China Type 67	47
China Type 80	48
Colt M1911/M1911A1	49
Colt Delta Elite	50
Colt MkIV Series 80	51
Colt Combat Commander	52
Colt Officer's ACP, Colt Officer's ACP LW	53
Colt Government Model .380	54
Colt Double Eagle	55
Colt 2000	56
Coonan	57
CZ27	58
CZ38	59
CZ50	60
CZ52	61
CZ75	62
CZ83	63
Daewoo DP 51	64
Dreyse	65
Eibar automatic pistol	66
Frommer 'Stop'	67
Frommer M1929	68
Frommer M1937	69
Glisenti	70
Glock 17	71
Glock Model 18	72
Glock Models 20, 21, 22, 23	73
Heckler & Koch HK4	74
Heckler & Koch P9/P9S	75
Heckler & Koch VP70	76
Heckler & Koch P7	77
Heckler & Koch P7K3	78
High Standard	79
FEG FP9	80
Imbel M973/MD1	81
Jericho 941	82
Kirrikale	83
Lahti L-35	84
Langenhan	85
Le Francaise 'Military'	86
Liberator	87
Llama Model IX	88
Llama Ruby	89
Llama M82	90
MAB PA-15	91
Makarov	92
Mannlicher M1900/1905	93
Mauser 1910 and 1934	94
Mauser Military (c/12)	95
Mauser HSc	96
Mauser Model 80SAV	97
Mauser Model 90DA	98
MAS Mle 1935S	99
MAS Mle 1950	100
Type 64	101
Type 68	102
Parabellum P'08	103
Parabellum 'Long '08'	104
Para Ordnance P14	105
Poland P-64	106
PSM	107

CONTENTS

Radom 108
Roth-Steyr 109
Ruger P-85 110
Ruger Standard 111
Sauer M1914 112
Sauer M30 'Behorden modell' 113
Sauer M38H 114
Savage 115
SIG P210 116
SIG P220 117
SIG P225 118
SIG P226 119
Smith & Wesson Model 39 120
Smith & Wesson Model 59 121
Smith & Wesson Third Generation Pistols 122
Spitfire 123
Springfield P9 124
Star Super B 125
Star Model MD 126
Star 30M 127
Star M40 Firestar 128
Star Megastar 129
Stechkin 130
Steyr 1909 131
Steyr 1912 132
Steyr GB 133

Tanfoglio TA90 134
Taurus PT 52 S 135
Taurus PT 92/99 AF 136
Tokagypt 137
Tokarev 138
Walther P38 139
Walther PP 140
Walther PPK 141
Walther P5 142
Walther P88 143
Webley & Scott 144
Zastava M57 145
Zastava M88 146

REVOLVERS

Arminius Model 10 148
Astra Model 960 149
Astra Cadix 150
Astra 357 Police 151
Llama Ruby Extra 152
Bodeo M1889 153
Bulldog revolvers 154
Cebra .38 revolver 155
Charter Arms Pathfinder 156
Colt New Navy/Army/ Marine Revolvers 157
Colt Detective Special 158

Colt Pocket Positive 159
Colt New Service revolver 160
Colt Model 1917 revolver 161
Colt Python 162
Colt King Cobra 163
Colt Anaconda 164
Em-Ge Model 323 'Valor' 165
Enfield Pistol, Revolver, No2 Mk1 or Mk1* 166
Escodin Model 31 167
Forehand & Wadsworth .38 Hammerless 168
Harrington & Richardson .38 Auto Ejector 169
Hopkins & Allen .38 Safety Police 170
Iver Johnson Safety Automatic 171
Harrington & Richardson Defender 172
Korth Combat Magnum 173
Llama Comanche 174
Manurhin MR73 175
Miroku .38 Special Police 176

Modele d'Ordonnance Mle 1892 (Lebel) 17?
Nagant: Russian Model 1895 178
Orbea .38 Revolver 179
Rast & Gasser revolver 180
Rohm .22 RG-34 18?
Ruger Security Six 18?
Ruger Police Service Six 18?
RUGER GP 100 184
Smith & Wesson Hand Ejector 18?
Smith & Wesson Safety Hammerless 18?
Smith & Wesson Pocket Safety Hammerless (2nd Model) 18?
Smith & Wesson Military & Police (Model 10) 18?
Smith & Wesson New Century Hand Ejector 18?
Smith & Wesson US Model 1917 19?
Smith & Wesson .38/200 British service revolver 19?
Smith & Wesson

CONTENTS

Model 29 & 629   192
Smith & Wesson
  586/686   193
Smith & Wesson 625   194
Smith & Wesson Model
  60   195
Smith & Wesson 36
  'Chiefs Special'   196
Taurus 76   197
Taurus 669   198
Taurus 441   199
Webley .320 Pocket
  Hammerless   200
Webley .38 Pocket
  Pistol No 3   201
Webley Mark IV
  service revolver   202
Webley Mark 5 service
  revolver   203
Webley Mark 6 service
  revolver   204
Webley .38 Mark IV
  service revolver   205
Webley RIC revolver   206
Webley .455 WG
  model   207
Webley-Wilkinson   208
Webley-Fosbery
  automatic revolver   209
Weihrauch HW-9   210

SUB-MACHINE GUNS

AKSU-74   212
Austen Mk I   312
Beretta 1938A   214
Beretta Model 38/42   215
Beretta Model 38/44   216
Beretta Model 3   217
Beretta Model 12   218
Beretta Model 12S   219
Bergmann MP18   220
Bergmann MP28   221
BRAZIL MD2A1   222
BXP   223
Calico M-960A   224
Carl Gustaf 45   225
China Type 64   226
China Type 79   227
Colt   228
Cristobal   229
CZ Model 25   230
Danuvia 39M   231
Danuvia M43   232
DUX   233
Erma EMP   234
FBP   235
FMK Mod 2   236

FN P-90   237
Franchi LF-57   238
H&K MP5   239
H&K HK53   240
Hyde-Inland M2   241
Ingram Model 6   242
Ingram Model 10   243
Japan 100/44   244
Labora   245
Lusa A2   246
Lanchester   247
Madsen Models 1946
  and 1951   248
MAS 38   249
MAT 49   250
MEMS 52/58   251
Mendoza HM-3   252
MGP-15   253
MGP-79A   254
MGP-87   255
MP38   256
MP40   257
MP41   258
Orita   259
Owen   260
Poland pz-63   261
PPD-1940   262
PPS-43   263
PPSh-41   264
Reising 50   265

Rexim-Favor   266
SAF   267
Sanna 77   268
SIG MP310   269
Skorpion   270
Socimi Type 821   271
Sola Super   272
Spectre   273
Star Si35   274
Star Z-62   275
Star Z-84   276
Sten Mark I   277
Sten Mk II   278
Sten Mk IIS   279
Sten Mk III   280
Sten Mk V   281
Sten Mk VI   282
Sterling   283
Steyr MPI69   284
Steyr AUG Para   285
Steyr TMP   286
Steyr-Solothurn MP34   287
Suomi M1931   288
Suomi M1944   289
Thompson M1928   290
Thompson M1   291
TZ-45   292
United Defense M42   293
US M3   294
Uzi   295

CONTENTS

Vietcong K-50M   296
Vigneron   297
Walther MPK and MPL   298
Zastava M85   299
ZK-383   300

BOLT ACTION RIFLES

Accuracy International
  L96A1   304
Arisaka 38th Year rifle   305
Arisaka Type 99 short
  rifle   306
Boys   307
Beretta Sniper   308
De Lisle silent carbine   309
Enfield Rifle No 2
  (Pattern '14)   310
Enfield US service rifle
  M1917 (Pattern '17)   311
Enfield Enforcer   312
FN 30-11 Sniping rifle   313
GIAT FR-F1, FR-F2   314
Krag-Jorgensen rifles   315
Lebel M1886 rifle   316
Lebel-Berthier
  1907/15 rifle   317

Lee-Enfield Carbine,
  Magazine, Mk 1   318
Lee-Enfield, Rifle,
  Short, Magazine,
  MkIII   319
Lee-Enfield; Rifle No 4   320
Lee-Enfield: Rifle No 5   321
McMillan M87R   322
Mannlicher turnbolt
  rifles   323
Mannlicher straight-
  pull bolt rifles   324
Mannlicher-Carcano TS
  Carbine M1891   325
Mannlicher-Carcano
  M1938 rifle   326
Mannlicher-Schoenauer
  Greek M1903 rifle   327
MAS Mle 1936   328
Mauser Gewehr 98   329
Mauser Karabiner 98k   330
Mauser SP66   331
Mauser 86   332
Mosin-Nagant rifles   333
Parker-Hale M82   334
Parker-Hale M83   335
Parker-Hale 85   336
Ross rifles   337
Ruger M77   338
Sako TRG   339

Schmidt-Rubin M1889
  rifle   340
Schmidt-Rubin M1911
  rifle   341
Schmidt-Rubin M1931
  carbine   342
SIG SSG-2000   343
SIG SSG-3000   344
Springfield US M1903
  rifles   345
Steyr-Mannlicher SSG-
  69   346
US M40A1 Sniper   347
Vapensmia NM149S   348

AUTOMATIC RIFLES

Armalite AR-18   350
Barrett 'Light Fifty'
  M82A1   351
Barrett M82A2   352
Beretta BM59   353
Beretta AR 70/.223   354
Beretta AR 70/90   355
Bofors AK5   356
Calico M-900   357
Chinese Type 56

carbine   358
Chinese Type 56
  assault rifle   359
Chinese Type 68 rifle   360
Colt Commando   361
CZ52   362
CZ58   363
Daewoo K2   364
Gepard M3   365
Dragunov   366
Enfield L85A1   367
FAMAS   368
FARA 83   369
FG 42   370
FN 1949   371
FN FAL   372
FN CAL   373
FN FNC   374
Galil   375
Heckler & Koch G3   376
Heckler & Koch PSG1   377
Heckler & Koch
  MSG90   378
Heckler & Koch HK33E   379
Heckler & Koch G41   380
Heckler & Koch G11   381
IMBEL MD2   382
Japan Type 64   383
Japan Type 89   384
Johnson M1941   385

CONTENTS

Kalashnikov AK47 and
  variants 386
La France M16K 388
Ljungman AG42 389
MAS-49 390
MP 44 391
Ruger Mini-Thirty 392
Ruger Mini-14 393
Sako M90 394
Santa Barbara CETME
  Model L 395
SIG SG510-4 (Stgw
  57) 396
SIG SG540 (SG542)
  series 397
SIG SG 550/551
  (Stgw 90) 398
Simonov SKS 399
Simonov AVS-36 400
Singapore SR88 401
Singapore SR88A 402
Steyr-Mannlicher AUG 403
Stoner SR-25 404
Taiwan Type 65 405
Tokarev SVT38 406
US M1 Rifle (Garand) 407
US M1/M2 Carbine 408
US M4 Carbine 409
M14 Rifle 410
US M16 rifle 411

VAL Silent Sniper 412
Valmet M76 413
Valmet M78 414
Vektor R4 415
Zastava M59/66 416
Zastava M70B1 417
Zastava M76 418
Zastava M80 419
ZH-29 420

MACHINE GUNS

AAT-F1 422
Alfa 423
Ameli 424
Armalite AR-10 425
Beretta M70/78 426
Besa 427
Breda Model 30 428
Breda Model 37 429
Bren 430
Browning M1917 431
Browning M1919 A4 432
Browning M1919 A6 433
Browning M2HB .50 434
Browning Automatic
  Rifle (BAR) 435

Chatellerault
  M1924/29 436
Chatellerault M1931 437
Chauchat 438
CZ Model 52/57 439
Darne 440
Degtyarev DP 441
Degtyarev DPM 442
Degtyarev DT and DTM 443
Enfield L86 444
Fiat-Revelli M1914 445
Fiat-Revelli M1935 446
FN BAR Type D 447
FN MAG 448
FN Minimi 449
Furrer M25 450
Goryunov SG43 451
Heckler & Koch HK13 452
Heckler & Koch HK21 453
Hotchkiss M1909 454
Hotchkiss M1914 455
Hotchkiss M1922/26 456
Japanese Type 11 457
Japanese Type 96 458
Japanese Type 99 459
Johnson M1941 and
  1944 460
Knorr-Bremse 461
Lewis Mark 1 (Ground) 462
Lewis Mark 2 (Air) 463

Madsen 464
Madsen-Saetter 465
Marlin 466
Maxim MG08 467
Maxim 08/15 468
Maxim 1910 469
Mendoza RM-2 470
MG13 471
MG 15Na Bergmann 472
MG34 473
MG42 474
Neuhausen KE7 475
Parabellum MG17 476
St Etienne 07/16 477
Schwarzlose 478
NSV 479
PK 480
RPK 481
RP-46 482
RPK-74 483
DShK 484
Ultimax 485
Vickers 486
Vickers-Berthier 487
VZ-26 488
VZ-37 489

BRAND NAMES

BRAND NAMES 490

FOREWORD

The object of this book is to enable police, customs officers and others who may be confronted with strange firearms to identify them with a reasonable degree of accuracy. I say 'a reasonable degree' because there are degrees in identification; the manufacturers of the Parabellum pistol recognised about a dozen different models, but collectors divide and sub-divide this into a hundred or more 'variations'. This is doubtless valid in the context of collecting, but for basic identification purposes it is unnecessary; what the makers consider different is sufficient for our purpose. There is also sufficient information to allow anyone unfamiliar with the weapon to ensure that it is unloaded and in a safe condition.

In order to keep the book within reasonable bounds, it has been necessary to use some guidelines in selecting the weapons. Firearms rarely wear out; provided that suitable ammunition is available, firearms of over one hundred years of age can be fired and are lethal, even if their rifling is worn away and their safety is marginal. The criteria for inclusion are, broadly, that:

1. The weapon is a military or para-military design.

2. Ammunition is currently made or has been available within the past twenty years.

3. It is possible to be found in criminal or terrorist hands.

Markings quoted have been taken from actual examples; experience shows that they may vary. Later production may differ from the original, and weapons made to specific contracts may bear different markings. Some discretion must be used where markings do not agree exactly.

Warning

This book deals with the examination and identification of firearms.

Firearms are designed to kill.

Therefore:

1. Never pick up, accept or hand over a firearm without removing any magazine or emptying any cylinder, and opening the action so as to expose the chamber and demonstrate that the weapon is empty. If you do not know how to do this, leave the weapon alone or ask someone else to do it for you.

2. If circumstances dictate that you must hand over a loaded firearm, make sure that the safety catch is applied and inform the recipient without any ambiguity: "This weapon is loaded. The safety catch is on." If there is no safety catch, ensure the recipient knows.

3. Always assume any firearm to be loaded until you have positively proved that it is not. No matter how old, corroded, rusted, obsolete, decrepit or dirt-covered a firearm may be, it is still possible that it is loaded. And that goes for muzzle-loaded antiques as well.

4. Always use an unloading box if one is available, and always point the firearm in a safe direction while unloading it.

5. Do not be overawed by 'experts' who decry these rules; you will outlive them.

PISTOLS

AMT Hardballer USA

A faithful stainless steel copy of the full sized Colt Government 1911A1 pistol with a magazine capacity of 7 rounds of .45 ACP. Also available in a 'long slide' version with a 178mm barrel and weight of 1303g.

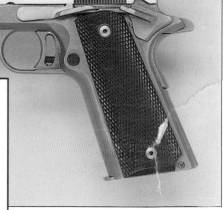

Specification & Operation

Cartridge:
.45 ACP

Dimensions:
Length o/a: 216mm
Barrel: 127mm
Weight: 1076g
Rifling: 6 grooves rh
Magazine capacity: 7

In production: 1977 -

Markings:
HARDBALLER , AMT with circle AUTOMATIC CALIBER .45 on left of slide, STAINLESS - MADE IN USA on right of slide, AMI and serial number on right of frame.

Safety:
Manual safety catch lever on top left of frame at the rear. UP for safe, DOWN for fire. A grip safety is incorporated into the rear of the frame which blocks trigger movement unless the butt is gripped correctly.

Unloading:
Magazine catch at left side of butt behind trigger, pressed in to release magazine. Remove magazine; pull back slide to eject any round in the chamber; inspect chamber through ejection port. Release slide, pull trigger.

AMT On Duty USA

A new design pistol making extensive use of machined Aluminium (frame) and steel investment castings (trigger group and internal parts) as well as a stamped sheet metal slide. Based on the .40 S&W cartridge with a 9mm Parabellum version also produced that is slightly heavier. Both models used double column high capacity magazines. Both are available in two versions, 'double action only' and 'decocker' (see safety operation above).

Specification & Operation

Cartridge:
9mm Parabellum, .40 S&W

Dimensions:
Length o/a: 203mm
Barrel: 114mm
Weight: 840g
Rifling: 6 grooves rh
Magazine capacity: 15 (9mm), 11 (.40 S&W)

In production: 1991 -

Markings:
AMT Motif, ON DUTY (9mm), or AMT Motif, ON DUTY CAL .40 S&W (.40 S&W) on left of slide, IRWINDALE CA on left of frame, MADE IN USA on right of slide, serial number and AMT motif on right of frame.

Safety:
There are two versions of the AMT On Duty. The 'decocker' model has a manual decocking lever at rear of the left hand side of the frame which is pushed UP to decock. The 'double action only' can only be fired by trigger cocking. The safety lever at rear of the left hand side of the frame is pushed DOWN for fire or UP for safe which locks the hammer down. Both versions have a trigger released firing pin block.

Unloading:
Magazine catch at left side of butt behind trigger, pressed in to release magazine. Remove magazine; pull back slide to eject any round in the chamber; inspect chamber through ejection port. Release slide.

Gas-assisted action, stainless steel self loading pistol in an unusual pistol calibre, .22 WMR made by Arcadia Machine & Tool, Inc in California. The Automags model were briefly branded IAI (Irwindale Arms Inc) in 1990. Three

models are made with varying length slides and barrels. The shortest pistol also has a cropped grip and a magazine capacity of 7 rounds. A number of larger calibre 'Automag' pistols are also made with calibres up to .50 Action Express.

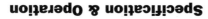

Specification & Operation

Cartridge:
.22 WMR

Dimensions: with 153mm barrel

Length o/a: 235mm
Barrel: 153mm (114mm & 86mm barreled models available)
Weight: 907mm
Rifling: 6 grooves rh
Magazine capacity: 9

In production: 1986 -

Markings:

AMT Motif, AUTOMAG II, .22 RIMFIRE MAGNUM on left of slide, IRWINDALE CA. on left of frame, STAINLESS – MADE IN USA, PAT PENDING on right of slide, serial number on right of frame.

Safety:

Thumb operated safety lever on left of slide at the rear, UP for fire, DOWN for safe.

Unloading:

Magazine catch at bottom of butt, pressed back to release magazine. Remove magazine; pull back slide to eject any round in the chamber; inspect chamber through ejection port. Release slide.

ASTRA 300 SPAIN

Smaller version of the Astra 400 introduced in 1922 for Spanish Prison Service; in 7.65mm and 9mm in 1923 for commercial sales. Adopted by Spanish Navy in 9mm in 1928. Total of 85,390 (both calibres) supplied to German Army in 1939-44; these will have German property marks (WAA and Nazi eagle). Manufacture ceased in 1947, 171,300 having been made.

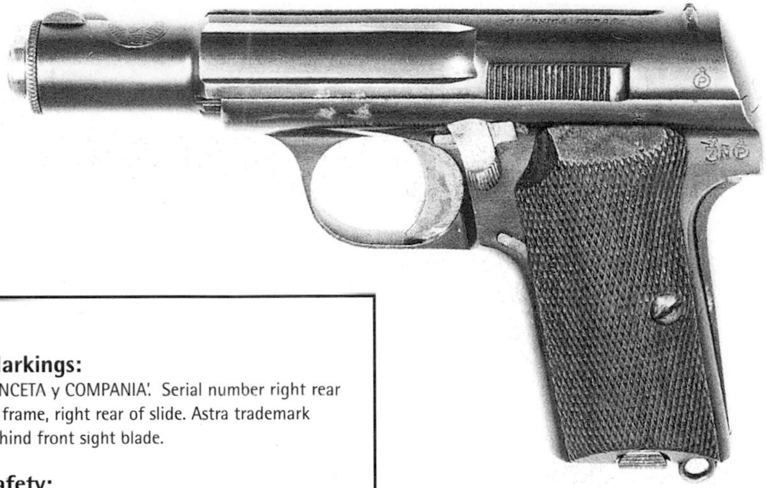

Specification & Operation

Cartridge:
9mm Short (1922-); 7.65mm ACP (1923-)

Dimensions:
Length o/a: 165mm
Barrel: 90mm
Weight: 560g
Rifling: 6 grooves, rh
Magazine capacity: 7 rounds

In service dates: 1922-50

Markings:
'UNCETA y COMPANIA'. Serial number right rear of frame, right rear of slide. Astra trademark behind front sight blade.

Safety:
Manual, above trigger; UP for safe, DOWN for fire. Magazine safety. Grip safety.

Unloading:
Magazine catch at heel of butt. Remove magazine; pull back slide to eject any round in the chamber; inspect chamber through ejection port. Release slide, pull trigger.

ASTRA 400 SPAIN

Spanish service pistol 1921-50, sold commercially, also used by French Army in 1920s. Total production 106,175. Based on an earlier Campo-Giro model which it resembles in its tubular receiver and barrel. Copies of this pistol were made during the Spanish Civil War and may be found marked 'F. ASCASO TARRASA' or simply 'RE'(Republica Espana). Although chambered for the 9mm Largo cartridge, these pistols, when

in good condition, would chamber and fire 9mm Parabellum, 9mm Steyr, 9mm Browning Long and .38 Super cartridges. It is not recommended in worn pistols. Pistols in 7.65mm and 7.63mm calibres are known but extremely rare and were probably only made as samples.

Specification & Operation

Cartridge:
9mm Largo (Bergmann-Bayard); 7.65mm ACP (rare); 7.63mm Mauser (rare)

Dimensions:
Length o/a: 235mm
Barrel: 150mm
Weight: 880g
Rifling: 6 grooves, rh
Magazine capacity: 8 rounds

In service dates: 1921-50

Markings:
'UNCETA Y COMPANIA' on slide top; Astra trademark behind front sight. Serial number right rear of frame.

Safety:
Manual behind trigger, UP for safe; DOWN for fire. Magazine safety. Grip safety.

Unloading:
Magazine catch at heel of butt. Remove magazine; pull back slide to eject any round in the chamber; inspect chamber through ejection port. Release slide, pull trigger.

ASTRA MODEL F SPAIN

A 903 (see p95) in 9mm Largo calibre to meet requirements of Spanish Civil Guard. Entering service on the eve of the Spanish Civil War, it was used by both sides, but faded from the scene after World War II.

Specification & Operation

Cartridge:
9mm Largo (Bergmann-Bayard)

Dimensions:
Length o/a: 330mm
Barrel: 180mm
Weight: 1530g
Rifling: 6 grooves, rh
Magazine capacity: 10 or 20 rounds

In service dates: 1935-45

Markings:
'ASTRA AUTOMATIC PISTOL CAL 7.63MM / PATENTED JULY 17 1928 / Unceta y Compania GUERNICA (Espana)' on left side of frame. Serial number on left side of frame behind trigger.

Safety:
Manual alongside hammer; forward for FIRE, back for SAFE. Rotary switch on right side of frame selects single shots or automatic fire.

Unloading:
Cock hammer, retract bolt and continue until all rounds in magazine are removed.

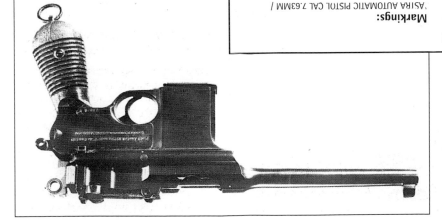

► Astra Falcon SPAIN

The Falcon is the last example of the 'water-pistol' style which characterised Astra pistols from 1920 onwards and it is little more than a scaled-down version of the Astra 400. Chambered for relatively weak rounds it handles them well and is a simple and robust design.

Specification & Operation

Cartridge:
9mm Short (.380 Auto)

Dimensions:
Length o/a: 164mm
Barrel: 98.5mm
Weight: 646g
Rifling: 4 grooves, rh
Magazine capacity: 7

In service dates: 1956-

Markings:
'ASTRA Mod Falcon 9m/m Guernica Spain' on top rear of slide. The butt grips may be marked 'MODEL 4000 FALCON'. Serial number right side of frame.

Safety:
Manual safety catch on left side of frame, above trigger; UP for safe.

Unloading:
Magazine catch is a push-button at heel of butt. Remove magazine; pull back slide to eject any round in the chamber; inspect chamber through ejection port. Release slide, pull trigger.

Astra A-50 SPAIN

This is an updated version of an earlier model known as the 'Constable' and in spite of its appearance is a simple single-action design of fixed-barrel blowback. It can also be found chambered for the 7.65mm Browning cartridge.

Specification & Operation

Cartridge:
9mm Short (.380 Auto)

Dimensions:
Length o/a: 168mm
Barrel: 89mm
Weight: 650g
Rifling: 6 grooves, rh
Magazine capacity: 7

In service dates: 1960-

Marking:
'ASTRA UNCETA CIA Guernica Spain Mod A-50' on left side of slide. Serial number right side of frame.

Safety:
Manual safety catch at left rear of frame. UP for safe.

Unloading:
Magazine catch at left side of butt behind trigger. Remove magazine; pull back slide to eject any round in the chamber; inspect chamber through ejection port. Release slide, pull trigger.

A new style of pistol for Astra, this chunky weapon appears to have been inspired by the SIG-Sauer designs, though the mechanism is entirely different. This is a single-action pistol of relatively small size and fires two potent cartridges; it is intended for the police and military market.

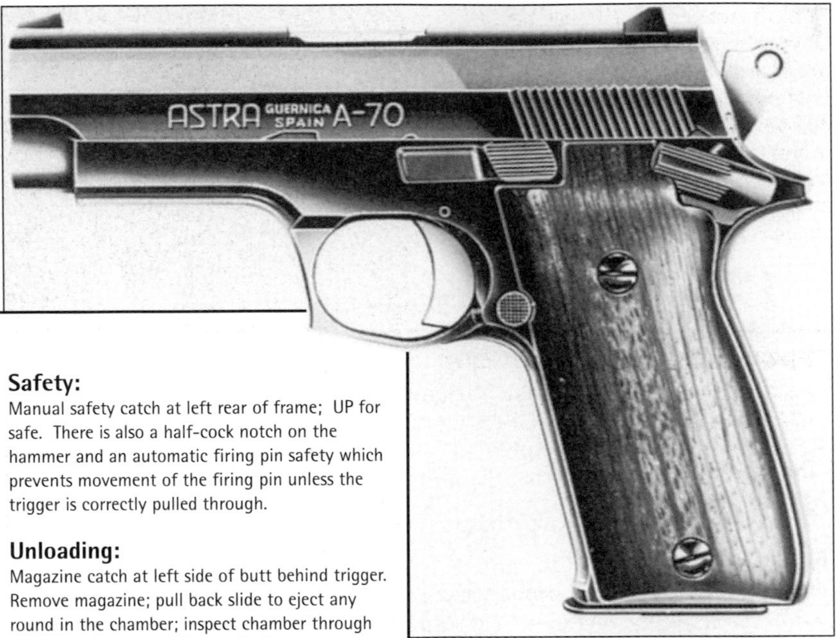

Specification & Operation

Cartridge:
9mm Parabellum or .40 S&W

Dimensions:
Length o/a: 166mm
Barrel: 89mm
Weight: 840g
Rifling: 6 grooves, rh
Magazine capacity: 8 (9mm) or 7(.40)

In service dates: 1992-

Markings:
'ASTRA GUERNICA SPAIN A-70'on left of slide;
Serial number right of frame.

Safety:
Manual safety catch at left rear of frame; UP for safe. There is also a half-cock notch on the hammer and an automatic firing pin safety which prevents movement of the firing pin unless the trigger is correctly pulled through.

Unloading:
Magazine catch at left side of butt behind trigger. Remove magazine; pull back slide to eject any round in the chamber; inspect chamber through ejection port. Release slide, pull trigger.

18

Astra A-75 SPAIN

This is more or less a double-action version of the A-70, a compact and robust weapon firing a pair of potent cartridges. Primarily intended for police and military use it has seen some success in the commercial market. In 1994 an aluminium-framed version was announced and a version in .45ACP chambering is expected in late 1995.

Specification & Operation

Cartridge:
9mm Parabellum or .40 S&W

Dimensions:
Length o/a: 166mm
Barrel: 89mm
Weight: 880g
Rifling: 6 grooves, rh
Magazine capacity: 8 (9mm) or 7 (.40)

In service dates: 1993-

Markings:
'ASTRA GUERNICA SPAIN A-75' on left side of slide; serial number on right side of frame.

Safety:
Manual safety catch at left rear of frame; UP for safe. Half-cock notch on the hammer, and automatic firing pin safety device.

Unloading:
Magazine catch at left side of butt behind trigger. Remove magazine; pull back slide to eject any round in the chamber; inspect chamber through ejection port. Release slide, pull trigger.

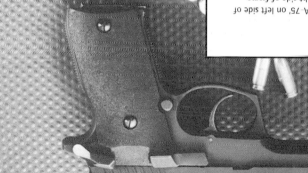

ASTRA A-80 SPAIN

This has a distinct look of having been inspired by the square-cut lines of the SIG pistols, and the de-cocking lever might well have also come from that direction. Nevertheless, this is a sound and well-built pistol and has been taken into military and police service in several countries as well as being sold commercially.

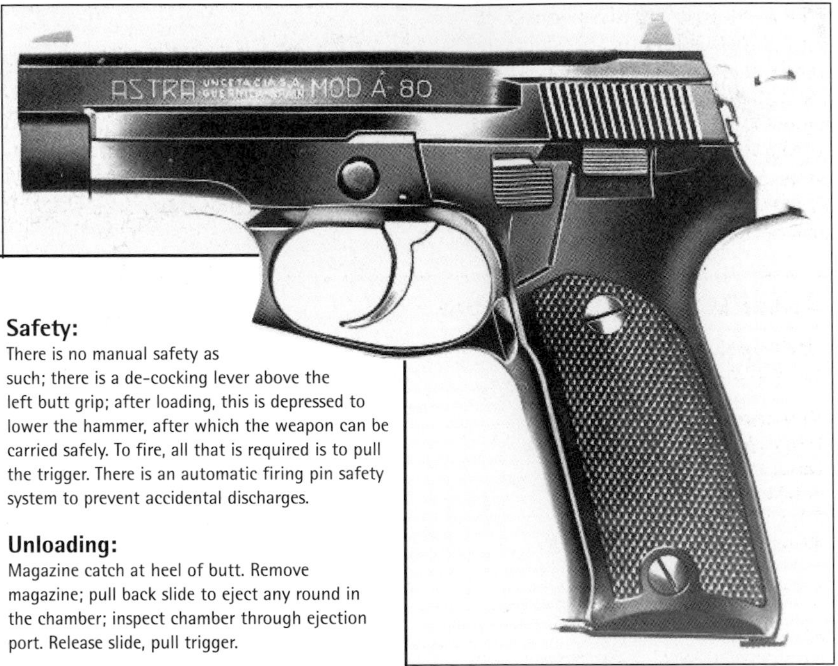

Specification & Operation

Cartridge:
9mm Parabellum, 9 x 23mm Steyr, 38 Super Auto, .45 ACP or 7.65mm Parabellum

Dimensions:
Length o/a: 180mm
Barrel: 96.5mm
Weight: 985g
Rifling: 6 grooves, rh
Magazine capacity: 15

In service dates: 1982-

Markings:
'ASTRA UNCETA CIA SA GUERNICA SPAIN MOD A80' on left side of slide. Serial number right side of frame.

Safety:

There is no manual safety as such; there is a de-cocking lever above the left butt grip; after loading, this is depressed to lower the hammer, after which the weapon can be carried safely. To fire, all that is required is to pull the trigger. There is an automatic firing pin safety system to prevent accidental discharges.

Unloading:

Magazine catch at heel of butt. Remove magazine; pull back slide to eject any round in the chamber; inspect chamber through ejection port. Release slide, pull trigger.

ASTRA A-90 SPAIN

The A-90 is an improved version of the A-80 with adjustable sights, greater magazine capacity and, for those who distrust modern innovations, a manual safety catch in addition to the existing automatic safeties. As with the earlier models it was aimed at the police/military market but seems to have done better on the commercial market.

Specification & Operation

Cartridge:
9mm Parabellum or .45 ACP

Dimensions:
Length o/a: 180mm
Barrel: 96.5mm
Weight: 985g
Rifling: 6 grooves, rh
Magazine capacity: 17 (9mm); 9 (.45)

In service dates: 1985-

Markings:
'ASTRA UNCETY CIA SA GUERNICA SPAIN MOD A90' on left side of slide. Serial number right side of frame.

Safety:
Manual safety catch at left rear of slide which rotates a portion of the two-piece firing pin out of the path of the hammer. A de-cocking lever above the left grip will drop the hammer safely, irrespective of the position of the manual safety catch. There is also an automatic firing pin safety system.

Unloading:
Magazine catch at heel of butt. Remove magazine; pull back slide to eject any round in the chamber; inspect chamber through ejection port. Release slide, pull trigger.

21

With the introduction of the A-90, the A-80 was discontinued, but there was still a demand for a pistol without manual safety. In addition, overseas markets preferred the magazine release in the butt, behind the trigger. The A-100 attended to these requirements, improved the safety mechanisms and introduced the .45 chambering. It also adopted the larger magazine of the A-90.

Specification & Operation

Cartridge:
9mm Parabellum or .45 ACP

Dimensions:
Length o/a: 180mm
Barrel: 96.5mm
Weight: 985g
Rifling: 6 grooves, rh
Magazine capacity: 15 (9mm); 9 (.45)

In service dates: 1990-

Markings:
'ASTRA UNCETA CIA SA GUERNICA SPAIN MOD A-100', on left side of slide. Serial number on left side of frame.

Safety:
No manual safety is provided; there is a de-cocking lever and an automatic firing pin safety, allowing the pistol to be carried loaded with the hammer down and fired by simply pulling the trigger.

Unloading:
Magazine catch at left side of butt behind trigger. Remove magazine; pull back slide to eject any round in the chamber; inspect chamber through ejection port. Release slide, pull trigger.

BEHOLLA SPAIN

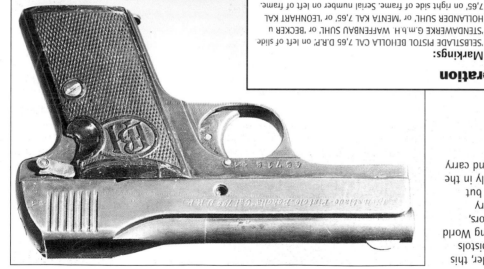

Designed by Becker & Hollander, this was one of the 15 or more pistols issued to the German army during World War I. Made by various contractors, Wartime models will have military acceptance marks on the frame, but numbers were made commercially in the 1920s by Leonhardt and Menz and carry only their trade names.

Specification & Operation

Cartridge:
7.65mm ACP

Dimensions:
Length o/a: 140mm
Barrel length: 75mm
Weight: 640g
Rifling: 6 grooves, rh
Magazine capacity: 7 rounds

In service dates: 1915-18

Markings:
'SELBSTLADE PISTOL BEHOLLA CAL 7,65 D.R.P.' on left of slide. 'STENDAWERKE G.m.b.H. WAFFENBAU SUHL' or 'BECKER u HOLLANDER SUHL' or 'MENTA KAL 7,65' or 'LEONHART KAL 7,65' on right side of frame. Serial number on left of frame.

Safety:
Manual catch on left rear of grip.

Unloading:
Magazine catch at heel of butt. Remove magazine; pull back slide to eject any round in the chamber; inspect chamber through ejection port. Release slide, pull trigger.

Differs from all other Beretta pistols in having two-thirds of the slide top solid. Internal hammer. WARNING: The 9mm version will chamber the standard 9 x 19mm Parabellum cartridge, but this is more powerful than the designed Glisenti cartridge and should NOT be fired.

Specification & Operation

Cartridge:
9mm Glisenti or 7.65mm ACP (rare).

Dimensions:
Length o/a: 149mm
Barrel length: 85mm
Weight: 570g
Rifling: 6 grooves, rh
Magazine capacity: 7 rounds

In service dates: 1915-45

Markings:
'PIETRO BERETTA-BRESCIA-CASA FONDATA NEL 1680 CAL 9M.-BREVETTO 1915' on left of slide.

Serial number on left rear end of slide. Police issue pistols will be marked 'PS' (Publica Sicurezza) , military issues 'RE' (Regia Esercito). Serial numbers left rear of frame and left rear of slide.

Safety:
Left of slide above trigger. UP for fire, DOWN for safe.

Unloading:
Magazine catch at heel of butt. Remove magazine; pull back slide to eject any round in the chamber; inspect chamber through ejection port. Release slide, pull trigger.

24

BERETTA MODEL 1915/19 ITALY

Differs from the Model 1915 in having two thirds of the slide top cut away and a simpler safety catch, and has sheet metal grip plates instead of wood. As with the Model 1915, it will chamber 9mm Parabellum cartridges, but these must NOT be fired from this gun.

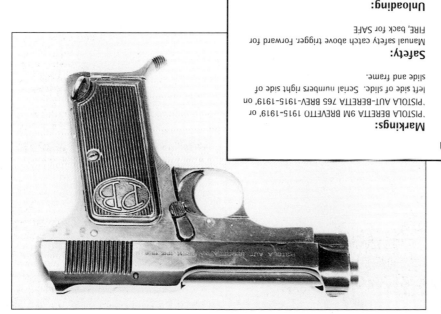

Specification & Operation

Cartridge:
9mm Glisenti

Dimensions:
Length o/a: 145mm
Barrel length: 85mm
Weight: 670g
Rifling: 6 grooves, rh
Magazine capacity: 7 rounds

In service dates: 1919-45. Commercially manufactured 1923-31

Markings:
'PISTOLA BERETTA 9M BREVETTO 1915-1919' or 'PISTOLA AUT-BERETTA 765 BREV-1915-1919' on left side of slide. Serial numbers right side of slide and frame.

Safety:
Manual safety catch above trigger. Forward for FIRE, back for SAFE

Unloading:
Magazine catch at heel of butt. Remove magazine; pull back slide to eject any round in the chamber; inspect chamber through ejection port. Release slide, pull trigger.

BERETTA MODEL 1923 ITALY

The Model 1923 is simply a larger, 9mm version of the M1915-19 with an external hammer. Uncommon; easily recognised because the butt is long and the butt-plates short, leaving a prominent space between the bottom of the plates and the bottom of the butt. As with other Glisenti-chambered pistols, DO NOT attempt to fire 9mm Parabellum cartridges from this pistol.

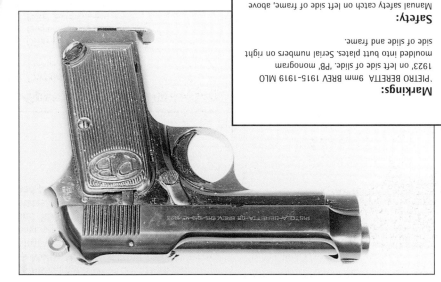

Specification & Operation

Cartridge:
9mm Glisenti

Dimensions:
Length o/a: 150mm
Barrel length: 85mm
Weight: 100g
Rifling: 6 grooves rh
Magazine capacity: 8 rounds

In service dates: 1924-45

Markings:
'PIETRO BERETTA 9mm BREV 1915-1919 MLO 1923' on left side of slide. 'PB' monogram moulded into butt plates. Serial numbers on right side of slide and frame.

Safety:
Manual safety catch on left side of frame, above trigger. Forward for SAFE, rearward for FIRE.

Unloading:
Magazine catch at heel of butt. Remove magazine; pull back slide to eject any round in the chamber; inspect chamber through ejection port. Release slide, pull trigger.

Beretta Model 1931 ITALY

This is an improved version of the Model 1915 with an external hammer. Most were issued to the Italian Navy and have a silver monogram of an anchor and 'RM' let into the wooden butt plates. A few were sold commercially and had plastic grips with 'PB' embossed.

Specification & Operation

Cartridge:
7.65mm ACP

Dimensions:
Length o/a: 152mm
Barrel length: 88mm
Weight: 700g
Rifling: 6 grooves, rh
Magazine capacity: 8 rounds

In service dates: 1931-45

Markings:
'PISTOLA BERETTA 7.65 BREV 1915-1919 Mo 1931' on left side of slide. Serial numbers right side of frame and slide.

Safety:
Manual safety catch on left side, above trigger. Forward for SAFE, rearward for FIRE.

Unloading:
Magazine catch at heel of butt. Remove magazine; pull back slide to eject any round in the chamber; inspect chamber through ejection port. Release slide, pull trigger.

Beretta Model 1934 ITALY

Probably the most common of the small Berettas, having been widely issued to the Italian armed forces during WWII. Similar to the Model 1931 and best identified by its marking. The year mark in Roman figures indicates the year of the Fascist regime.

Specification & Operation

Cartridge:
9mm Short/.380 Auto

Dimensions:
Length o/a: 150mm
Barrel length: 88mm
Weight: 750g
Rifling: 6 grooves rh
Magazine capacity: 7 rounds

In service dates: 1934-45

Markings:
'P BERETTA CAL 9 CORTO Mo 1934 BREVETTATO GARDONE V.T. 1937 - XVI' (or other year) on left side of slide. Serial number right side of slide and frame. 'PB' monogram bottom of butt-plates.

Safety:
Manual safety catch on left side, above trigger. Forward for SAFE, rearward for FIRE.

Unloading:
Magazine catch at heel of butt. Remove magazine; pull back slide to eject any round in the chamber; inspect chamber through ejection port. Release slide, pull trigger.

Beretta M951 ITALY

Recognisably Beretta by the cut-away slide top, this was their first locked-breech military pistol. It was also adopted by the Egyptian and Israeli armies, the Nigerian police forces and others.

Specification & Operation

Cartridge:
9mm Parabellum

Dimensions
Length o/a: 203mm
Barrel length: 114mm
Weight: 870g
Rifling: 6 grooves, rh
Magazine capacity: 8 rounds

In service dates: 1953-1982 (Italian forces)

Markings:
`P BERETTA - CAL 9m/m MOD 1951 - PATENT GARDONE VT ITALIA' (Italian service models); `HELWAN CAL 9 m/m U.A.R.'(Egyptian versions). Serial number on right side of slide

Safety:
The safety device is a push-through button at the top of the grip; push to the LEFT for safe, to the RIGHT for fire.

Unloading:
The magazine catch is a button at the lower left of the grip; push in and remove magazine. Pull back slide to eject round in the chamber; examine breech; release slide, pull trigger.

Beretta M951R ITALY

This is basically the same pistol as the M951 above, but modified to permit automatic fire. The barrel extends in front of the slide, and a wooden front grip is attached to the front end of the frame to give better control in automatic fire. It was originally issued to Italian special forces and anti-terrorist units.

Specification & Operation

Cartridge:
9mm Parabellum

Dimensions:
Length o/a: 203mm
Barrel length: 125mm
Weight: 1350g
Rifling: 6 grooves, rh
Magazine capacity: 10 rounds

In service dates: 1955-80

Markings:
'P BERETTA - CAL 9m/m MOD 1951R - PATENT GARDONE VT ITALIA' left side of slide. Serial number right side of frame.

Safety:
The safety device is a push-through button at the top of the grip; push to the LEFT for safe, to the RIGHT for fire. In addition, there is a fire selector switch at the top right of the grip; when pressed UP, the pistol delivers full-automatic fire at about 750 rds/minute. When pressed DOWN the pistol fires in the conventional semi-automatic mode.

Unloading:
The magazine catch is a button at the lower left of the grip; push in and remove magazine. Pull back slide to eject round in the chamber; examine breech; release slide, pull trigger.

Beretta Model 84 ITALY

The Model 84 represents Beretta's unlocked-breech blowback design in modern form and is accompanied by several variant models. The Model 81 is the same pistol but in 7.65mm ACP calibre; both are double-action pistols and use double-row magazines with a slot in the rear face which allows the contents to be checked. The Models 81BB, 82BB, 83F, 84BB, 84F, 85F, 87BB and 87BB/LB are all variants which differ

Specification & Operation

Cartridge:
9mm Short (.380 Auto)

Dimensions:
Length o/a: 172mm
Barrel length: 97mm
Weight: 660g
Rifling: 6 grooves, rh
Magazine capacity: 13 rounds

In service dates: 1976-

Markings:
'PIETRO BERETTA GARDONE V.T.' left side of slide.
'MODEL 84 9m/m' right side of slide; serial number left front of frame.

Safety:
Manual safety catch at left rear of frame; UP for safe.

Unloading:
Magazine catch at left side of butt behind trigger. Remove magazine; pull back slide to eject any round in the chamber; inspect chamber through ejection port. Release slide, pull trigger.

in the following ways: the BB models have a smaller magazine, a single-column type allowing a thinner butt, a loaded chamber indicator and improved safety by using an automatic firing pin safety system. F models have all the BB features but also have a de-cocking mechanism which allows the hammer to be dropped safely on a loaded chamber.

Beretta Model 92 ITALY

The Beretta 92, adopted by the US Army as the M9 is offered in many different versions, each denoted by a suffix. The 92S has a decocking lever; the B has an ambidextrous decocking lever; the C is a compact version 197mm long; the F has the trigger guard modified for two-handed grip; the G has no manual safety, just a decocker on the slide. The 92D is double-action only: the hammer cannot be single-action cocked and after each shot the hammer follows

Specification & Operation

Cartridge:
9mm Parabellum

Dimensions:
Length o/a: 217mm
Barrel length: 125mm
Weight: 850g
Rifling: 6 grooves, rh
Magazine capacity: 15

In service dates: 1976–

Markings:
'Pist Mod 92 Cal 9 Para BERETTA' left side of slide. Serial number left front of frame.

Safety:
Manual or other safety depends upon model; see below.

Unloading:
Magazine catch at left side of butt behind trigger. Remove magazine; pull back slide to eject any round in the chamber; inspect chamber through ejection port. Release slide, pull trigger.

the slide back and falls to a safe position. The DS is similar, but without manual safety. The 92M is stainless steel, with a thinner butt and smaller magazine capacity. The Beretta 96 series is a .40 S&W version of the same family and uses the same suffixes.

Beretta Centurion models ITALY

The Centurion series is a further variant on the Model 92. These weapons use the frame of the 92FS or the Model 96 (according to calibre) with the reduced length of slide and barrel of the Compact models. The variations noted under D, DS and G in the remarks on the Model 92 are also applied to the Centurion series, but these models are confined to sale in Europe. The data given above is for the Model 92FS Centurion.

Specification & Operation

Cartridge:
9mm Parabellum or .40 S&W

Dimensions:
Length o/a: 197mm
Barrel length: 109mm
Weight: 940g
Rifling: 6 grooves. rh
Magazine capacity: 15 (9mm) or 10 (.40)

In service dates: 1993-

Markings:
'PIETRO BERETTA GARDONE V.T. MADE IN ITALY'

on left side of slide. Serial number on left front of frame. Model number on right side of frame.

Safety:
Manual catch at left rear of slide, acting as a de-cocking lever in some models. UP for safe. The Centurion 92D has no manual safety devices.

Unloading:
Magazine catch at left side of butt behind trigger. Remove magazine; pull back slide to eject any round in the chamber; inspect chamber through ejection port. Release slide, pull trigger.

Beretta Model 93R ITALY

This is a selective-fire pistol with a
selector switch allowing automatic
fire at about 1100 rounds per minute in
three-round bursts for each pressure of
the trigger. There is a fold-down grip in
front of the trigger-guard and an
extendible steel shoulder stock which
can be attached to the rear of the butt.
The basic design is that of the Model 92

Specification & Operation

Cartridge:
9mm Parabellum

Dimensions:
Length o/a: 240mm
Barrel length: 156mm incl muzzle brake
Weight: 1129g
Rifling: 6 grooves, rh
Magazine capacity: 15 or 20

In service dates: 1986-

Markings:
'PIETRO BERETTA GARDONE V.T. Cal 9 Parabellum'
on left side of slide. Serial number on right side of
frame.

Safety:
Manual safety catch behind trigger. Fire selector
lever above left grip: one white dot = single shots,
three white dots = three-round burst fire.

Unloading:
Magazine catch at heel of butt. Remove magazine;
pull back slide to eject any round in the chamber;
inspect chamber through ejection port. Release
slide, pull trigger.

but with an extended barrel with a
muzzle brake. The alternative 20-round
magazine extends some distance below
the bottom of the butt when fitted.

Bernardelli P-018 ITALY

A conventional double-action semi-automatic. There is also a 'compact' version 109mm long with a 102mm barrel and with a 14-shot magazine. Although specifically designed for police and military use it appears to have had more success on the commercial market.

Specification & Operation

Cartridge:
9mm Parabellum

Dimensions:
Length o/a: 213mm
Barrel length: 122mm
Weight: 998g
Rifling: 6 grooves, rh
Magazine capacity: 15

In service dates: 1986-

Markings:
'VINCENZO BERNARDELLI SpA Gardone V.T. Made in Italy' left side of slide. 'Mod P-018 9 Para' left side of frame. Serial number right side of frame and on the barrel, visible in the ejection opening.

Safety:
Manual safety catch at left rear of frame; UP for safe.

Unloading:
Magazine catch at heel of butt. Remove magazine; pull back slide to eject any round in the chamber; inspect chamber through ejection port. Release slide, pull trigger.

Bernardelli Mod. USA ITALY

This first appeared in 1961 as the Model 60, a modernisation of an earlier 'Pocket Model'. After the US Gun Control Act of 1968, which laid down various criteria for imported weapons, it was given a slide-mounted safety catch which locked the firing pin and lowered the hammer safely. These were in addition to the existing frame-mounted safety catch and magazine safety.

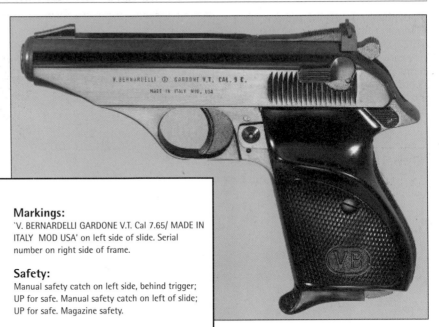

Specification & Operation

Cartridge:
9mm Short, 7.65mm ACP or .22 Long Rifle

Dimensions:
Length o/a: 165mm
Barrel length: 90mm
Weight: 690g
Rifling: 6 grooves rh
Magazine capacity: 7 rounds

In production: 1968-

Markings:
'V. BERNARDELLI GARDONE V.T. Cal 7.65/ MADE IN ITALY MOD USA' on left side of slide. Serial number on right side of frame.

Safety:
Manual safety catch on left side, behind trigger; UP for safe. Manual safety catch on left of slide; UP for safe. Magazine safety.

Unloading:
Magazine catch at the heel of the grip; remove magazine. Pull back slide to eject any round in the chamber; release slide, pull trigger.

Bergmann-Bayard GERMANY

Adopted by the Danish and Spanish armies; the Spanish abandoned it c.1922, but the Danes used it until 1945. Very early models were made in Germany but these are rare; they can be identified by the rifling using 4 grooves and by the markings.

Specification & Operation

Cartridge:
9mm x 23 Bergmann-Bayard (9mm Largo)

Dimensions:
Length o/a: 254mm
Barrel length: 102mm
Weight: 1020g
Rifling: 6 grooves, rh
Magazine capacity: 6 or 10 rounds

In service dates: 1910-45

Markings:
'ANCIEN ETABLISSMENTS PIEPER / HERSTAL-LIEGE / BERGMANN'S PATENT' and 'BREVETE S.G.D.G.' on left side of the receiver. The magazine housing carries an engraved mounted knight with lance and the word 'BAYARD'. Danish Army models will also be marked 'M 9m/m' on the left of the receiver, below and ahead of the Pieper markings and do not have the Bayard badge.

Safety:
Manual safety catch along side the hammer. FORWARD for fire, back and DOWN for safe.

Unloading:
Press in catch in the front edge of the trigger guard to release the magazine. Grasp the two round buttons at the rear of the bolt and pull the bolt back to eject any round in the chamber. Release bolt, pull trigger.

Browning 1900 BELGIUM

The first successful blowback pocket pistol, over a million were made by 1912 and production continued for several years thereafter. The shape is unique, but it has been widely copied (in cheap materials) in India and China; these can easily be identified by the poor finish and unintelligible markings.

Specification & Operation

Cartridge:
7.65mm Browning (.32 ACP)

Dimensions:
Length o/a: 172mm
Barrel length: 102mm
Weight: 625g
Rifling: 6 groove, rh
Magazine capacity: 7 rounds

In service dates: 1900-

Markings:
'FABRIQUE NATIONALE HERSTAL LIEGE / BREVETE S.G.D.G' on left side of slide. Serial number on right of slide, frame and rear sight mounting. Details of markings have differed slightly over the years of production.

Safety:
Manual safety catch at rear left side of frame; UP for safe, DOWN for fire.

Unloading:
Magazine catch at the heel of the grip; remove magazine. Pull back slide to eject any round in the chamber; release slide, pull trigger.

Browning 1903 BELGIUM

Designed by John Browning, who sold the rights to Colt for the USA and FN for the rest of the world. Colt produced it as a home defence pistol in 7.65mm, FN as a military pistol in 9mm Browning Long calibre. Widely copied in Spain from 1905 onward and in various calibres - most 1905-35 cheap Spanish

Specification & Operation

Cartridge:
9x 20SR Browning Long, or 7.65mm Browning (.32 ACP)

Dimensions:
Length o/a: 205mm
Barrel length: 127mm
Weight: 10g
Rifling; 6 grooves, rh
Magazine capacity: 7 rounds (9mm) or 8 rounds (7.65mm)

In service dates: 1903 -

Markings:
'FABRIQUE NATIONALE D'ARMES de GUERRE HERSTAL BELGIQUE / BROWNING'S PATENT / DEPOSE' on left side of slide. Serial number on right side of frame (Belgian model). 'COLT'S PT FA MFG CO HARTFORD CT USA / PATENTED APR 20 1897 DEC 22 1903' on left side of slide. Serial number left side of frame. 'COLT AUTOMATIC / CALIBER .32 RIMLESS SMOKELESS' on right side of slide (US model).

Safety:
Safety catch at left rear of frame; UP for fire, DOWN for safe. Grip safety in rear edge of butt, must be squeezed in to release the firing mechanism. A magazine safety is fitted.

Unloading:
Magazine catch in heel of butt. Remove magazine. Pull back slide to eject any round in the chamber and inspect the chamber through the ejection port. Release slide, pull trigger.

automatic pistols are copies of this weapon due to its simple design and manufacture.

Browning 1910/22 BELGIUM

An improved version of the M1903, in which the recoil spring is placed around the barrel instead of beneath it, giving the unique tubular appearance to the slide. It was copied in Spain in the 1920-35 period, though not to the extent of the M1903, and also in Germany as the 'Rheinmetall' and 'DWM' pistols, easily distinguished by their

Specification & Operation

Cartridge:
7.65mm Browning (.32 ACP)

Dimensions:
Length o/a: 152mm
Barrel length: 88mm
Weight: 600g
Rifling: 6 grooves, rh
Magazine capacity: 7 rounds

In service dates: 1910-

Markings:
'FABRIQUE NATIONALE D'ARMES de GUERRE HERSTAL BELGIQUE / BROWNING'S PATENT DEPOSE' on left side of slide. 'CAL 7m/m.65' on barrel, visible through ejection opening. Serial number on right side of frame, right side of slide and on barrel. On the 1922 model it is also on the slide extension.

Safety:
Safety catch at left rear of frame. UP for safe, DOWN for fire. Grip safety in rear of pistol grip which must be depressed to permit firing. A magazine safety is also fitted; the pistol cannot be fired if the magazine is withdrawn.

Unloading:
Magazine catch at heel of butt. Remove magazine, pull back slide to eject any round in the chamber. Release slide. The pistol will remain cocked and the trigger cannot be pressed unless the emptied magazine is replaced.

markings. In 1922 it was given a longer barrel and the slide lengthened by a bayonet-jointed extension, remaining otherwise the same.

Browning High Power Model 1935 BELGIUM

Originally produced by FN Herstal in 1935. Wartime German High Powers have approval marks and 'Pist. 640(b)' stamped on the slide. Canadian-made High Powers are marked 'J Inglis'. After 1945 production began again under FN Herstal, and the design was adopted by over 50 armies around the world. The two most innovatory features were the large-capacity magazine and the use of a shaped cam rather than a pinned

Specification & Operation

Cartridge:
9mm Parabellum

Dimensions:
Length o/a: 200mm
Barrel length: 118mm
Weight: 882g
Rifling: 6 grooves, rh
Magazine capacity: 13

In service dates: 1935-

Markings:
'FABRIQUE NATIONALE HERSTAL BELGIUM

BROWNING'S PATENT DEPOSE FN (Year)' on left side of slide. Military models may have the NATO stock number.

Safety:
Manual at left rear of frame; recent models have it duplicated on both sides of the frame. UP for Safe.

Unloading:
Magazine catch at left side of butt behind trigger. Remove magazine; pull back slide to eject any round in the chamber; inspect chamber through ejection port. Release slide, pull trigger.

swinging link to lower the rear end of the barrel during recoil; both these feaures have been widely copied on other designs since 1935. Mark 2 and Mark 3 (illustrated above) versions appeared in the late 1980s. The Mk3 has an automatic firing pin safety device.

Browning BDA9 BELGIUM

This is derived from the High Power Model 35 above, but uses a double-action lock mechanism and has a de-cocking lever on each side of the frame instead of a safety catch. The magazine catch can be fitted to either side of the grip, and the trigger guard is shaped for two-handed firing. Mechanically, it is the same as the Model 35, operates and strips in the same way except that the slide needs to be pressed back about 1mm to permit removal of the slide stop pin.

Specification & Operation

Cartridge:
9mm Parabellum

Dimensions:
Length o/a: 200mm
Barrel length: 118mm
Weight: 875g
Rifling: 6 grooves, rh
Magazine capacity: 14

In service dates: 1993-

Markings:
'FABRIQUE NATIONALE HERSTAL BELGIUM FN (year)' left side of slide. Serial number right side of frame.

Safety:
Both sides of frame at rear; UP for safe.

Unloading:
Magazine catch at left side of butt behind trigger. Remove magazine; pull back slide to eject any round in the chamber; inspect chamber through ejection port. Release slide, pull trigger.

Browning BDA 380

This is little more than a Beretta 84 with a Belgian accent. FN wanted a blowback pistol for the police market, and since they owned a piece of Beretta it made sense to take an existing successful design, make a few minor cosmetic changes. The most obvious difference is the plastic grip plate with the `FN` monogram.

Specification & Operation

Cartridge:
9mm Short (.380 Auto) or 7.65mm ACP

Dimensions:
Length o/a: 173mm
Barrel: 96mm
Weight: 640g
Rifling: 6 grooves, rh
Magazine capacity: 13 (9mm) or 12 (7.65mm)

In service dates: 1980-

Markings:
`FABRIQUE NATIONALE` or `FN HERSTAL SA` on left side of slide. `BDA-380` and Serial number left side of frame. If made in the Beretta Factory will have `PB` monogram on right side of slide.

Safety:
Manual safety catch at left rear of slide, which acts as a de-cocking lever. Press down to make safe, when the hammer will be released to fall safely on a loaded chamber.

Unloading:
Magazine catch at left side of butt behind trigger. Remove magazine; pull back slide to eject any round in the chamber; inspect chamber through ejection port. Release slide, pull trigger.

Calico M950 USA

Although classed as a pistol in the USA it is doubtful whether such classification will be agreed to in several other countries. This is a semi-automatic, shortened version of a submachine gun design using a unique helical 50-shot magazine which fits on top of the rear of the receiver and adds 810 grammes to the weight of the weapon. A 100 round magazine also can be used, though this makes the weapon somewhat cumbersome.

Specification & Operation

Cartridge:
9mm Parabellum

Dimensions:
Length o/a: 356mm with magazine
Barrel: 152mm
Weight: 1000g
Rifling: 6 grooves, rh
Magazine capacity: 50 or 100

In service dates: 1988-

Markings:
'CALICO M-950' on left sideof magazine mounting. Serial number on left side of frame

Safety:
Manual safety catch on left side of frame, behind trigger; UP for safe.

Unloading:
The magazine release is part of the magazine, a serrated catch upon the left side. Depress, remove magazine. Then pull back cocking lever, inspect chamber, release cocking lever and pull trigger.

China Type 54 CHINA

This is a direct copy of the Soviet Tokarev TT-33 manufactured under licence in China. It is distinguishable from other Tokarevs and copies by having a number of narrow vertical grooves on the slide, for gripping the slide in order to load; Soviet and Polish pistols have alternating narrow and wide grooves, while other pistols using narrow grooves (Hungarian and Yugoslavian) can be identified by other markings.

Specification & Operation

Cartridge:
7.62mm Soviet Pistol (or 7.63mm Mauser)

Dimensions:
Length o/a: 195mm
Barrel: 115mm
Weight: 890g
Rifling: 4 grooves, rh
Magazine capacity: 8

In service dates: 1954–

Markings:
Chinese ideographs on slide and frame.

Safety:
No manual safety device other than a half-cock notch on the hammer.

Unloading:
Magazine catch at heel of butt. Remove magazine; pull back slide to eject any round in the chamber; inspect chamber through ejection port. Release slide, pull trigger.

China Type 64 CHINA

A n unusual silenced pistol, easily recognised by the bulbous integral silencer. The breech slide can be locked closed to prevent ejection of the spent case after firing, which could make more noise than the shot itself. Alternatively, it can be unlocked, when the weapon operates in the normal blowback self-loading mode. Note that the cartridge

Specification & Operation

Cartridge:
7.65x 17mm rimless

Dimensions:
Length o/a: 222mm
Barrel: 95mm
Weight: 1810g
Rifling: 4 grooves, rh
Magazine capacity: 9

In-service dates: 1964–

Markings:
'64' with factory number in an oval and serial number on left of slide.

Safety:
Manual safety catch at top of left butt grip; UP for safe. A cross-bolt in the upper part of the slide will lock the slide to the barrel and prevent self-loading action and thus prevent any mechanical noise after firing a silent shot.

Unloading:
Magazine catch at heel of butt. Remove magazine; pull back slide to eject any round in the chamber; inspect chamber through ejection port. Release slide, pull trigger.

for this weapon is peculiar to it; it will NOT chamber the 7.65mm ACP, which is otherwise of similar dimensions, because the ACP round is semi-rimmed and will prevent the breech closing.

China Type 67

An improved version of the Model 64, this has a rather less clumsy silencing system which fits better into a holster and gives the weapon better balance. There is no provision for locking the breech closed on this model, normal blowback operation being the only option. Note also that not only

Specification & Operation

Cartridge:
7.62 x 17mm Type 64 rimless

Dimensions:
Length o/a: 226mm
Barrel: 89mm
Weight: 1050g
Rifling: 4 grooves, rh
Magazine capacity: 9

In service dates: 1968-

Markings:
Factory identifying number in oval; '67' followed by Chinese character; serial number; all on left side of slide.

Safety:
Manual safety catch at top of left butt grip; UP for safe. A cross-bolt in the upper part of the slide will lock the slide to the barrel and prevent self-loading action and thus prevent any mechanical noise after firing a silent shot.

Unloading:
Magazine catch at heel of butt. Remove magazine; pull back slide to eject any round in the chamber; inspect chamber through ejection port. Release slide, pull trigger.

does this weapon not fire the 7.65mm ACP cartridge, it is not intended to fire the same 7.65mm rimless round used with the Model 64 but needs a special low-powered 7.62mm round known as the Type 64.

China Type 80 CHINA

This is a near-copy of the long-obsolete Mauser Model 712 Westinger machine pistol, made from 1932 to 1936. It was popular with Chinese warlords of the time and was thus probably more common in China than anywhere else. Some improvements have been made; the magazine angle is sloped, rather than vertical beneath the frame, and the grip is flatter and bulkier than the familiar Mauser 'broomhandle' grip. There is a folding detachable shoulder stock available, and also a

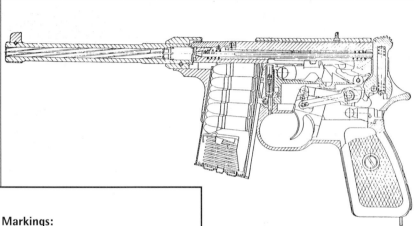

Specification & Operation

Cartridge:
7.62mm Soviet pistol (or 7.63mm Mauser)

Dimensions:
Length o/a: 300mm
Barrel: 140mm
Weight: 1100g
Rifling: 4 grooves rh
Magazine capacity: 10 or 20

In service dates: 1932-

Markings:
 Not known

Safety:
Manual safety catch at left rear of frame.

Unloading:
Magazine catch in front of trigger-guard; remove magazine. Pull back bolt to eject any round in the chamber, inspect chamber to ensure it is empty, release bolt, pull trigger.

bayonet. The mechanical operation is the same as the original Mauser, using a prop-up lock to hold the breech block closed.

Colt M1911/M1911A1 USA

Also made commercially, when it will carry the Colt name and 'prancing pony' badge. There are many look-alikes: the Spanish Llama and Star, Argentine Hafdasa and Mexican Obregon can be confused with this pistol; the easiest method of distinguishing is to look at the markings. The Norwegian forces used a modified version, made under license, and

Specification & Operation

Cartridge: .45 ACP

Dimensions:
Length o/u: 216mm
Barrel: 127mm
Weight: 1105g
Rifling: 6 grooves, lh
Magazine capacity: 7 rounds

In service dates: 1911-90

Markings:
'MODEL OF 1911 U.S.ARMY PATENTED APRIL 29 1907 COLT'S PAT FA MFG CO'
'M1911A1 U.S.ARMY ITHACA GUN CO INC ITHACA N.Y.'
'REMINGTON RAND INC SYRACUSE N.Y. U.S.A.'

'M1911A1
U.S.ARMY U.S.& S.CO SWISSVALE PA USA'
All models will also be marked 'UNITED STATES PROPERTY'. Serial number right side of frame.

Safety:
Grip safety. Manual safety catch at left rear of frame; UP for safe, DOWN for fire. The hammer may be drawn to the half-cock position.

Unloading:
Magazine catch on left side, behind trigger; press in to release magazine. Remove magazine, pull back slide to eject any round in the chamber; inspect chamber through ejection opening in slide; release slide, pull trigger.

marked 'Mo 1912'; the slide release catch (on the left side of the frame above the trigger) is longer. A model marked 'RAF' or 'ROYAL AIR FORCE' may be found; this is chambered for the .455 Webley & Scott cartridge NOT interchangeable with .45 ACP!

Colt Delta Elite USA

Colt's Government model re-chambered for the powerful 10mm Auto cartridge with a small internal modification to the frame above the slide stop and a recoil absorbing polymer recoil spring guide. Produced in blued carbon steel and stainless steel.

Specification & Operation

Cartridge:
10mm Auto

Dimensions:
Length o/a: 216mm
Barrel: 127mm
Weight: 1077g
Rifling: 6 grooves lh
Magazine capacity: 8

In production: 1987 -

Markings:
DELTA ELITE, COLT AUTO and 'Delta' triangle with 10MM inside on the left of the slide;
GOVERNMENT MODEL on right of slide;
COLT PT. F. A MFG. CO, HARTFORD, CONN, U.S.A

and serial number on the right of the frame.

Safety:
Manual safety catch lever on top left of frame at the rear. UP for safe, DOWN for fire. A grip safety is incorporated into the rear of the frame which blocks trigger movement unless the butt is gripped correctly. A firing pin safety also blocks firing pin movement unless the trigger is pulled fully rearwards.

Unloading:
Magazine catch at left side of butt behind trigger, pressed in to release magazine. Remove magazine; pull back slide to eject any round in the chamber; inspect chamber through ejection port. Release slide.

Colt MkIV Series 80 USA

A continuation of the powerful .45 ACP Colt 1911/1911A1 pistol line with the inclusion of a firing pin block safety. Available in .38 Super with a higher magazine capacity and 28 grams greater weight. Models have been manufactured from blued carbon steel and stainless steel. A low priced, matte

Specification & Operation

Cartridge:
.45 ACP, .38 Super

Dimensions:
Length o/a: 216mm
Barrel: 127mm
Weight: 1076g
Rifling: 6 grooves lh
Magazine capacity: 8 (.45), 9 (.38 Super)

In production: 1983 -

Markings:
COLT MK IV - SERIES 80 - on left of slide, GOVERNMENT MODEL on right of slide, COLT'S PT.F.A. MFG. CO. HARTFORD, CONN, U.S.A. and serial number on right of frame.

Safety:
Manual safety catch lever on top left of frame at the rear. UP for safe, DOWN for fire. A grip safety is incorporated into the rear of the frame which blocks trigger movement unless the butt is gripped correctly. A firing pin safety also blocks firing pin movement unless the trigger is pulled fully rearwards.

Unloading:
Magazine catch at left side of butt behind trigger, pressed in to release magazine. Remove magazine; pull back slide to eject any round in the chamber; inspect chamber through ejection port. Release slide.

finish, carbon steel version was introduced in 1993 as the model 1991 with slightly different markings, most notably COLT M1991 A1 on the left of the slide.

51

Colt Combat Commander USA

A variation of the Colt Mk IV Series 80 Government Model with a 19mm shorter slide and barrel but the same magazine capacity. The Lightweight Commander has an Aluminium alloy frame and carbon steel slide and is only chambered for .45 ACP. The Combat Commander is produced in carbon steel

Specification & Operation

Cartridge:
.45 ACP, .38 Super

Dimensions:
Length o/a: 197mm
Barrel: 146mm
Weight: 1020g std, 779g Lightweight
Rifling: 6 grooves rh
Magazine capacity: 8 (.45), 9 (.38 Super)

In production: 1983 -

Markings:
COLT MK IV - SERIES 80 - on left of slide, GOVERNMENT MODEL on right of slide, COLT'S PT.F.A. MFG. CO. HARTFORD, CONN, U.S.A. and serial number on right of frame.

Safety:
Manual safety catch lever on top left of frame at the rear. UP for safe, DOWN for fire. A grip safety is incorporated into the rear of the frame which blocks trigger movement unless the butt is gripped correctly. A firing pin safety also blocks firing pin movement unless the trigger is pulled fully rearwards.

Unloading:
Magazine catch at left side of butt behind trigger, pressed in to release magazine. Remove magazine; pull back slide to eject any round in the chamber; inspect chamber through ejection port. Release slide.

and stainless steel chambered for .45 ACP and is stainless steel only in .38 Super. A low priced, matte finish, carbon steel version was introduced in 1993 as the model 1991 with slightly different markings, most notably COLT M1991 A1 on the left of the slide.

Colt Officer's ACP, Colt Officer's ACP LW USA

A very compact version of the .45 ACP Colt Mk IV Government Model with a 37.5mm shorter slide and 10mm shorter frame. The standard models are produced in carbon steel and stainless steel with the lightweight version having an aluminium alloy frame which reduces the weight by 203g. This makes for a

Specification & Operation

Cartridge:
.45 ACP

Dimensions:
Length o/a: 184mm
Barrel: 88.9mm
Weight: 963g std, 680g Lightweight
Rifling: 6 grooves lh
Magazine capacity: 6

In production: 1985 -

Markings:
COLT MK IV - SERIES 80 - on left of slide, OFFICERS ACP right of slide, COLT'S PT.F.A. MFG. CO. HARTFORD, CONN, U.S.A. and serial number on right of frame.

Safety:
Manual safety catch lever on top left of frame at the rear. UP for safe, DOWN for fire. A grip safety is incorporated into the rear of the frame which blocks trigger movement unless the butt is gripped correctly. A firing pin safety also blocks firing pin movement unless the trigger is pulled fully rearwards.

Unloading:
Magazine catch at left side of butt behind trigger, pressed in to release magazine. Remove magazine; pull back slide to eject any round in the chamber; inspect chamber through ejection port. Release slide.

potent combination: extremely light and concealable yet still chambered for a major calibre round.

Colt Government Model .380 USA

Derived from the .45 ACP Colt Government Model with a similar barrel locking system, the Government .380 is built with a much smaller frame, slide and barrel. The characteristic Model 1911 grip safety is not fitted. A number of variations of the Model .380 are made: with a shorter slide (Mustang Plus II) or shorter slide and frame (.380 Mustang). In addition aluminium alloy

Specification & Operation

Cartridge:
.380 Auto (9mmK)

Dimensions:
Length o/a: 152.4mm
Barrel: 82.6mm
Weight: 730g
Rifling: 6 grooves lh
Magazine capacity: 7

In production: 1983 -

Markings:
COLT MKIV SERIES 80, GOVERNMENT MODEL .380 AUTO on left of slide, serial number on left of frame, COLT'S PT. F .A. MFG. CO. HARTFORD, CONN, U.S.A. on right of frame.

Safety:
Manual safety catch lever on top left of frame at the rear. UP for safe, DOWN for fire. A firing pin safety also blocks firing pin movement unless the trigger is pulled fully rearwards.

Unloading:
Magazine catch at left side of butt behind trigger, pressed in to release magazine. Remove magazine; pull back slide to eject any round in the chamber; inspect chamber through ejection port. Release slide.

framed versions are available with the suffix 'Pocketlite', the heaviest of which weighs only 418g.

Colt Double Eagle USA

(114mm barrel) and also available in .40 S&W calibre, and an 'Officers Model' with an 89mm barrel available only in .45 calibre.

This is based on the Government Model M1911A1 but has the added feature of double-action firing. The shape is slightly different, being more 'streamlined' and with a reverse-curved trigger guard for two-handed firing. Variations include the 'Combat Commander'; version, more compact

Specification & Operation

Cartridge:
10mm Auto or .45 ACP

Dimensions:
Length o/a: 216mm
Barrel: 127mm
Weight: 2205g
Rifling: 6 grooves, lh
Magazine capacity: 8 rounds

In production: 1990-

Markings:
'COLT DOUBLE EAGLE/ MK II SERIES 90' on left side of slide. Serial number on right side of frame.

Safety:
Safety and de-cocking lever behind the left grip. Pressing down secures the safety pin and drops the hammer, after which pulling the trigger will cock and fire.

Unloading:
Magazine catch on left side, behind trigger; press in to release magazine. Remove magazine, pull back slide to eject any round in the chamber; inspect chamber through ejection opening in slide; release slide, pull trigger.

the trigger 'feel' of a double-action revolver. Unfortunately for Colt it failed to attract interest and production ended in 1994.

Specification & Operation

Cartridge:
9mm Parabellum

Dimensions:
Length o/a: 197mm
Barrel: 114mm
Weight: 808g
Rifling: 6 grooves, lh
Magazine capacity: 15

In production: 1991-94

Markings:
'COLT ALL AMERICAN MODEL 2000' on left side of slide, with Colt pony badge. 'COLT DOUBLE ACTION 9mm' on right side of slide. Serial number underneath the front end of the frame.

Safety:
There are no manual safety devices on this pistol. Like a double-action revolver, it is necessary to pull the trigger in order to cock the firing mechanism and then release the striker.

Unloading:
Magazine catch at either side of butt behind trigger. Remove magazine; pull back slide to eject any round in the chamber; inspect chamber through ejection port. Release slide, pull trigger.

The Model 2000 was to be the Colt for the 21st century; designed by Reid Knight and Eugene Stoner, it broke away from the familiar dropping barrel system of breech locking and adopted a rotating barrel. The trigger mechanism was self-cocking, the object being to duplicate

Coonan USA

A limited number were produced to order with a 153mm bull varrel and standard slide. Other options included a shortened and cropped Cadet model.

An all stainless steel pistol built on the Colt Government pattern but lengthened and internally modified to accommodate the rimmed .357 Magnum revolver cartridge. Approximately 5000 made in the first ten years of production, mainly with the 'B' series linkless barrel.

Specification & Operation

Cartridge:
.357 Magnum

Dimensions:
Length o/a: 222 mm
Barrel: 127mm
Weight: 1190g
Rifling: 6 grooves rh
Magazine capacity: 7

In production: 1980 -

Markings:
COONAN .357 MAGNUM AUTOMATIC on left of slide, serial number on right of frame.

Safety:
Manual safety catch lever on top left of frame at the rear. UP for safe, DOWN for fire. A grip safety is incorporated into the rear of the frame which blocks trigger movement unless the butt is gripped correctly.

Unloading:
Magazine catch at left side of butt behind trigger, pressed in to release magazine. Remove magazine; pull back slide to eject any round in the chamber; inspect chamber through ejection port. Release slide.

CZ27 CZECHOSLOVAKIA

A simplified version of the Model 24, doing away with the unecessary breech locking system. To distinguish it, the grip grooves at the rear of the slide are vertical. Note the three phases of manufacture (1) original Czech, (2) under German occupation and (3) postwar Czech.

Specification & Operation

Cartridge:
9mm Browning Short (.380 Auto)

Dimensions:
Length o/a: 165mm
Barrel: 97mm
Weight: 710g
Rifling: 6 grooves, rh
Magazine capacity: 8 rounds

In service dates: 1927-55

Markings:
`CESKA ZBROJOVKA A.S. v PRAZE' on top of slide. Last two digits of year of manufacture on left rear of slide. (Czech manufacture pre-1938). `BOHMISCHE WAFFENFABRIK AG in PRAG' on top of slide. `PISTOLE MODELL 27  KAL 7,65' on right aide of slide. (German contract manufacture 1938-45). `CESKA ZBROJOVKA NARODNY PODNIK' on top of slide (1945-1951 Czech manufacture). Serial number on left side of frame in all models.

Safety:
Lever in front edge of left grip; pressed DOWN for safe. When pressed down it locks in place and is released to fire by pressing the button underneath.

Unloading:
Magazine catch at heel of butt. Remove magazine, pull back slide to eject any round in the chamber; inspect chamber through ejection opening; release slide, pull trigger.

CZ38 CZECHOSLOVAKIA

A dangerous and clumsy weapon. The catch on the left side is for dismantling and will release the slide and barrel as a unit which is hinged to the front of the frame. Doing this with the weapon loaded could lead to accidents. The heavy trigger pull impairs accuracy.

Specification & Operation

Cartridge:
9mm Browning Short (.380 Auto)

Dimensions:
Length o/a: 206mm
Barrel: 118mm
Weight: 940g
Rifling: 6 grooves, rh
Magazine capacity: 8 rounds

In service dates: 1938-45

Markings:
'CESKA ZBROJOVKA AKC SPOL V PRAZE' on left side of slide. Serial number front left side of slide and frame.

Safety:
THERE IS NO SAFETY DEVICE ON THIS WEAPON. Pulling the trigger will cock and fire the firing pin at all times. BE CAREFUL.

Unloading:
Magazine catch at heel of butt. Remove magazine; pull back slide to eject any round in the chamber; inspect chamber through ejection port. Release slide, pull through on trigger to cock and release the firing pin.

⌐ CZ50 CZECHOSLOVAKIA

Intended for the Czech Army but the calibre was considered too small and it was adopted by the police and also made for commercial sale. Uses a double-action lock similar to that of the Walther PP.

Specification & Operation

Cartridge:
7.65mm Browning (.32 ACP)

Dimensions:
Length o/a: 167mm
Barrel: 96mm
Weight: 700g
Rifling: 4 grooves rh
Magazine capacity: 8 rounds

In service dates: 1950-65 (Czech police)

Markings:
'CESKA ZBROJOVKA PRAHA' with two 'CZ' monograms. Commercial models also have 'MADE IN CZECHOSLOVAKIA'. All markings on left side of slide. Serial number on right side of frame.

Safety:
Safety catch above left grip UP for safe; DOWN for fire.

Unloading:
Magazine catch at left top of butt, behind trigger. Press in to release magazine. Remove magazine, pull back slide to eject any round in the chamber; inspect chamber through ejection port. Release slide, press trigger.

CZ52 CZECHOSLOVAKIA

This replaced the M38 design; it is intended to fire the Czech M48 cartridge, which is more powerful than the normal 7.62mm Soviet pistol round, and thus it uses a complicated roller-locked breech. It can also fire 7.63mm Mauser pistol cartridges.

Specification & Operation

Cartridge:
7.62mm Czech M48 (7.62mm Soviet Pistol)

Dimensions:
Length o/a: 209mm
Barrel: 120mm
Weight: 860g
Rifling: 4 grooves rh
Magazine capacity: 8 rounds

In service dates: 1953-70

Markings:
Serial number on left side of frame. No other markings

Safety:
Safety catch at left rear of slide; UP for safe, DOWN for fire. This is a three-position switch; pointing DOWN, the pistol is ready to fire, pointing backward it is safe; and when pushed UP from this position it will drop the cocked hammer safely on to the rebound notch. The safety catch can then be moved to the FIRE position and the pistol can be quickly brought into use by thumbing back the hammer.

Unloading:
Magazine catch at the heel of the butt. Remove magazine, pull back slide to eject any round in the chamber, inspect chamber through the ejection port. Release slide, pull trigger.

derived design, using the same type of cam-dropped barrel as the Browning High-power. It is simply well put-together of good materials. The fully automatic model has a slightly longer barrel with the end formed into a compensator, and can fire at about 1000 rounds/minute. The CZ85, is similar to the 75 but has ambidextrous safety catch and slide stop.

O ne of the best designs to come out of Europe since 1945, the CZ75 has been widely distributed and even more widely copied. It has no unique features, using ideas obviously adopted from many designs; basically it is a Browning-

Specification & Operation

Cartridge:
9mm Parabellum

Dimensions:
Length o/a: 203mm
Barrel: 120mm
Weight: 980g
Rifling: 6 grooves, rh
Magazine capacity: 15 rounds

In service dates: 1975-

Markings:
`CZ MODEL 75 CAL 9 PARA' on left side of slide.
`MADE IN CZECHOSLOVAKIA' on left side of frame
Serial number right side of frame and slide.

Safety:
Manual safety catch at left rear of frame. UP for safe.

Unloading:
Magazine catch at left side of butt behind trigger. Remove magazine; pull back slide to eject any round in the chamber; inspect chamber through ejection port. Release slide, pull trigger.

CZ83 CZECHOSLOVAKIA

and has a few refinements such as an automatic firing pin safety system, ambidextrous safety catch and magazine release, and a trigger guard large enough to take a gloved hand. Note that in 7.65mm and 9mm short calibres the rifling is conventional, but in 9mm Makarov it is of the polygonal form - i.e. the barrel section resembles a circle which has been slightly flattened on four sides.

A conventional double-action blowback pocket automatic pistol which can be thought of as Czechoslovakia's answer to the Makarov. It fills the same niche in Czech services

Specification & Operation

Cartridge:
7.65mm ACP, or 9mm Short (.380 Auto) or 9mm Makarov

Dimensions:
Length o/a: 173mm
Barrel: 96mm
Weight: 650g
Rifling: 6 grooves, rh
Magazine capacity: 15 (7.65mm) or 13 (9mm)

In service dates: 1984-

Markings:
'CZ 033 CAL 7,65MM   MOD 83 MADE IN

CZECHOSLOVAKIA' on left side of slide. Serial number on right side of slide, repeated on barrel.

Safety:
Ambidextrous manual safety catch at rear of frame which locks hammer and trigger, plus an automatic firing pin safety system which locks the pin until the trigger is pressed.

Unloading:
Magazine catch at either side of butt behind trigger. Remove magazine; pull back slide to eject any round in the chamber; inspect chamber through ejection port. Release slide, pull trigger.

Daewoo DP 51 SOUTH KOREA

The DP51 is a semi-automatic pistol in 9mm Parabellum operating on a delayed blowback system. Designed for military and police use, it has a double-action trigger mechanism which is better than most, providing a relatively even trigger pull.

Specification & Operation

Cartridge:
9mm Parabellum,

Dimensions:
Length o/a: 190mm
Barrel: 105mm
Weight: 800g
Rifling: 6 grooves, rh
Magazine capacity: 13

In service dates: 1993-

Markings:
'DP51 9MM PARA DAEWOO' on left side of slide. Serial number on right side of frame.

Safety:
Manual safety catch at left rear of frame; UP for safe.

Unloading:
Magazine catch at left side of butt behind trigger. Remove magazine; pull back slide to eject any round in the chamber; inspect chamber through ejection port. Release slide, pull trigger.

Dreyse GERMANY

A pistol with a peculiar system of construction. There is a stud at the rear of the frame which, when pressed to the right, allows the entire barrel/breech assembly to hinge upwards for cleaning or dismantling. There is also a 6.35mm Dreyse pistol which, for all practical purposes is the same as the Browning 1903 design but smaller.

Specification & Operation

Cartridge:
7.65mm Browning (.32 ACP)

Dimensions:
Length o/a: 160mm
Barrel: 93mm
Weight: 710mm
Rifling: 4 grooves, rh
Magazine capacity: 7 rounds

In service dates: 1907 -19

Markings:
'DREYSE RHEINMETALL ABT SOMMERDA' on left sife of receiver. Serial numbers on top of frame, bottom of barrel housing and top of breech block.

Safety:
Manual safety catch at left rear of frame; forward for fire, back for safe.

Unloading:
Magazine catch at rear of butt; remove magazine. Grasp the obliquely grooved grip area above the muzzle and pull backwards; the breech block will emerge from the rear of the receiver and any round in the chamber will be ejected. Check the chamber by looking through the ejection port. Release the breech-block unit, press the trigger.

Eibar automatic pistol SPAIN

The 'Eibar' automatic pistol is peculiar to Spain and has been made by scores of firms, by the hundreds of thousands, in all three calibres noted above. Due to the peculiar Spanish patent regulations of the time, it became possible for Spanish gunmakers to copy the Browning M1903 and M1906 pistols without license. Some began as early as 1906, but most got into the business as sub-contractors to major manufacturers struggling to meet French and Italian

Specification & Operation

Cartridge:
7.65mm Browning (.32 ACP); 6.35mm Browning (.25 Auto); 9mm Short (.380 Auto).

Dimensions: (representative specimen – a 7.65mm Ruby)
Length o/a: 155mm
Barrel: 85mm
Weight: 665g
Rifling: 4 grooves rh
Magazine capacity: 7 rounds

In production: 1905-1936

Markings:
Various; see Remarks

Safety:
Manual safety catch on the left side of the frame, above the trigger, with a prominent hook to hold the slide back for dismantling. UP for safe.

Unloading:
Magazine catch in heel of butt. Remove magazine; pull back slide to eject any round in the chamber; inspect chamber via ejection port; release slide, press trigger.

orders in 1915-18. They stayed in business until the outbreak of the Spanish Civil War. Some were of reasonable quality, many were not.

Frommer 'Stop' HUNGARY

An extremely complicated, though reliable and proven pistol, this uses the 'long recoil' system of operation and a rotating bolt head to lock the breech - all quite unnecessary in these calibres. Do NOT be tempted to dismantle this pistol without expert guidance.

Specification & Operation

Cartridge:
7.65mm Browning (.32 ACP) or 9mm Browning Short (.380 Auto)

Dimensions:
Length o/a: 165mm
Barrel: 100mm
Weight: 610g
Rifling: 4 grooves, rh
Magazine capacity: 7 rounds

In service dates: 1912-45

Markings:
'FEGYVERGYAR BUDAPEST FROMMER PAT STOP

CAL 7,65mm (.32)' on left side of receiver. Serial number rear left side of frame.

Safety:
Grip safety let into the rear of the butt. Must be squeezed in to allow the trigger to function. There is NO manual safety catch. BE CAREFUL

Unloading:
Magazine catch at heel of butt. remove magazine. Grasp the grooved collar at the rear of the pistol and pull the bolt back. This will eject any cartridge in the chamber; inspect the chamber by looking through the ejection opening. Release the bolt, pull the trigger.

Frommer M1929 HUNGARY

This replaced the Frommer 'Stop' as the Hungarian service pistol; it is a simple blowback weapon more or less based on the Browning 1903 design, much easier to manufacture and maintain than the earlier model.

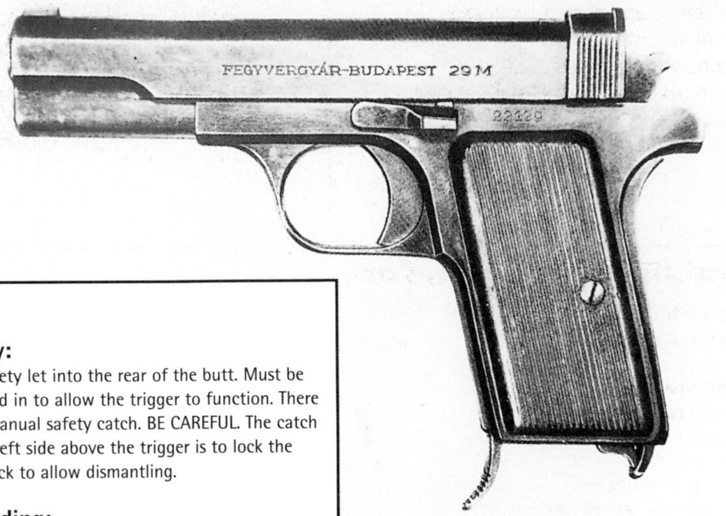

Specification & Operation

Cartridge:
9mm Browning Short (.380 Auto)

Dimensions:
Length o/a: 172mm
Barrel: 100mm
Weight: 750g
Rifling: 4 grooves, rh
Magazine capacity: 7 rounds

In service dates: 1930-45

Markings:
'FEGYVERGYAR - BUDAPEST - 29M' on left side of slide. Serial number on left side of frame, above grip.

Safety:
Grip safety let into the rear of the butt. Must be squeezed in to allow the trigger to function. There is NO manual safety catch. BE CAREFUL. The catch on the left side above the trigger is to lock the slide back to allow dismantling.

Unloading:
Magazine catch at heel of butt; remove magazine. Pull back slide to eject any round in the chamber; inspect chamber via ejection port; release slide, pull trigger.

Frommer M1937 HUNGARY

Little more than a tidied-up Model 29, a simple and robust blowback. Several tens of thousands were made, and these became widely distributed in the aftermath of the war. It is therefore a very common weapon in Europe.

Specification & Operation

Cartridge:
9mm Browning Short (.380 Auto)

Dimensions:
Length o/a: 182mm
Barrel:110mm
Weight: 770g
Rifling: 4 grooves, rh
Magazine capacity: 7 rounds

In service dates: 1937 -55

Markings:
'FEMARU FEGYVER ES GEPGYAR R.T. 37M' on left of slide (Hungarian models); 'P. Mod 37 Kal 7,65 jhv' on left of slide (German contract models; the year of manufacture will be found beneath the 'jhv' mark). Serial number on left of frame above grip, left front of slide and on barrel on all models.

Safety:
Original Hungarian models had NO manual safety, only a grip safety let into the rear of the butt. Those made for the German occupying forces were given an additional manual safety catch at the left rear of the frame: UP for SAFE, DOWN for FIRE

Unloading:
Magazine catch in heel of butt. Remove magazine; pull back slide to eject any round in the chamber; inspect chamber via ejection port; release slide, press trigger.

Although this pistol will chamber the 9mm Parabellum cartridge, it is dangerous to fire it. It should fire the weaker 9mm Glisenti, which is dimensionally similar. The construction (notably a removable side-plate on the left of the frame) is weak and firing too powerul ammunition could cause damage.

Specification & Operation

Cartridge:
9mm Glisenti

Dimensions:
Length o/a: 207mm
Barrel: 102mm
Weight: 850g
Rifling: 6 grooves, rh
Magazine capacity: 7 rounds

In service dates: 1910 -45

Markings:
`FAB' and year in circle, serial number, both on right side of receiver.

Safety:
Wing nut on the end of the bolt; this normally lies horizontal; when the pistol is cocked the wing nut can be turned anti-clockwise 45 degrees, locking the striker in the SAFE position. There is also a grip safety in the front edge of the grip which must be squeezed in to release the trigger.

Unloading:
Magazine catch in toe of butt. Remove magazine; grasp the end of the bolt and pull back to eject any round in the chamber. Inspect chamber via ejection port. Release bolt, press trigger.

Glock 17 AUSTRIA

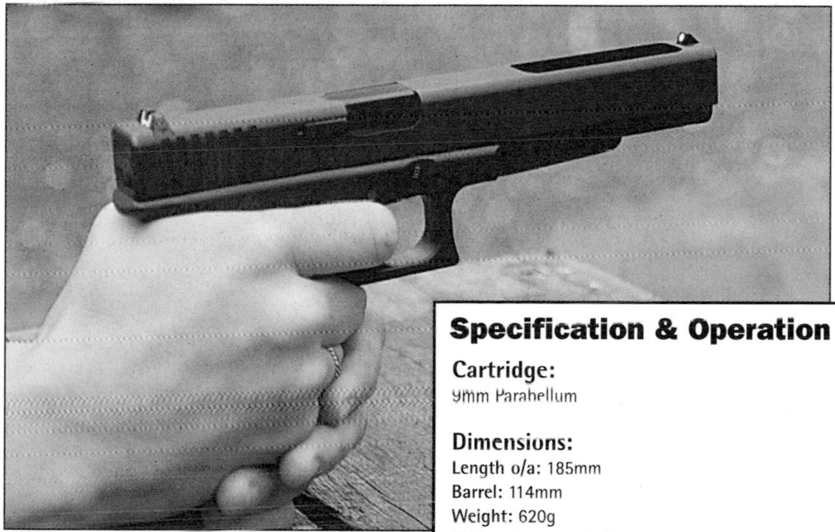

relying on the Browning tilting barrel. About 40% of the weapon is made of plastic materials. There are two variant models; the 17L (illustrated here) with a longer (153mm) barrel, giving an overall length of 225mm and a weight of 666g. The 19 is the same but in 'compact' form, barrel 102mm, overall 174mm, weight 595g.

This pistol appeared in 1983, winning a contract to supply the Austrian Army. Since then it has become enormously popular with police officers, particularly in the USA and has also seen military adoption in several countries. It is a self-cocking automatic using a locked breech

Specification & Operation

Cartridge:
9mm Parabellum

Dimensions:
Length o/a: 185mm
Barrel: 114mm
Weight: 620g
Rifling: hexagonal, rh
Magazine capacity: 17 rounds

In service dates: 1983-

Markings:
'GLOCK 17 AUSTRIA 9X19' Left side of slide.
Serial number right side of slide.

Safety:
There are no manual safety devices; a trigger safety bar protrudes from the trigger face and is automatically pressed in when taking pressure on the trigger. This unlocks an internal safety device, and further pressure on the trigger cocks the striker and then releases it.

Unloading:
Magazine catch at left side of butt behind trigger. Remove magazine; pull back slide to eject any round in the chamber; inspect chamber through ejection port. Release slide, pull trigger.

Glock Model 18 AUSTRIA

This was developed from the Model 17 and is a selective fire version which allows automatic fire at about 1300 rds/minute. Sold only to government bodies, several parts are designed so that it is impossible to convert a 17 to automatic fire by substitution of parts. Apart from this the Model 18 looks just like the 17 except when the 33-round magazine is fitted, since this protrudes well below the bottom of the butt grip.

Specification & Operation

Cartridge:
9mm Parabellum

Dimensions:
Length o/a: 185mm
Barrel: 114mm
Weight: 675g
Rifling: hexagonal, rh
Magazine capacity: 19 or 33

In service dates: 1986-

Markings:
'GLOCK 18 AUSTRIA 9X19' Left side of slide.
Serial number right side of slide.

Safety:
There are no manual safety devices; a trigger safety bar protrudes from the trigger face and is automatically pressed in when taking pressure on the trigger. This unlocks an internal safety device, and further pressure on the trigger cocks the striker and then releases it.

Unloading:
Magazine catch at left side of butt behind trigger. Remove magazine; pull back slide to eject any round in the chamber; inspect chamber through ejection port. Release slide, pull trigger.

Glock Models 20, 21, 22, 23 AUSTRIA

These four models are large-calibre variants of the 17 and 18 The 20 is in 10mm Auto calibre, the 21 in .45ACP, the 23 in .40 S&W. All are based on the 17 and differ slightly in dimensions. The 24 is in .40 S&W and is the 'compact' version, equivalent to the Model 18.

Specification & Operation

Cartridge:
10mm Auto (20,21) or .40 S&W (22,23)

Dimensions: (Model 22)
Length o/a: 185mm
Barrel: 114mm
Weight: 645g
Rifling: hexagonal, rh
Magazine capacity: 15

In service dates: 1990-

Markings:
'GLOCK XX (model number) AUSTRIA 9X19' Left side of slide. Serial number right side of slide.

Safety:
There are no manual safety devices; a trigger safety bar protrudes from the trigger face and is automatically pressed in when taking pressure on the trigger. This unlocks an internal safety device, and further pressure on the trigger cocks the striker and then releases it.

Unloading:
Magazine catch at left side of butt behind trigger. Remove magazine; pull back slide to eject any round in the chamber; inspect chamber through ejection port. Release slide, pull trigger.

Heckler & Koch HK4 GERMANY

This was Heckler & Koch's first firearm, and was based upon the pre-war Mauser HSc pistol. It was available with a kit of four interchangeable barrels, allowing the pistol to be converted to any of the four calibres - 9mm Short, 7.65mm ACP, 6.35mm or .22 rimfire. For the latter, an adjustment was provided to alter the strike of the firing pin.

Specification & Operation

Cartridge:
9mm Browning Short (.380 Auto) or 7.65mm browning (.32ACP)

Dimensions:
Length o/a: 157mm
Barrel: 85mm
Weight: 480g
Rifling: 6 grooves, lh
Magazine capacity: 7 rounds (9mm); 8 rounds (7.65, 6.35mm and .22)

In production: 1956 -90

Markings:
`HECKLER & KOCH GmbH OBERNDORF/N MADE IN GERMANY   Mod HK4' on left side of slide.
Safety:
Safety catch on left rear of slide; DOWN for SAFE, UP for FIRE.

Unloading:
Set the safety catch to safe. Press back the magazine catch at the heel of the butt and remove the magazine. Pull back the slide to eject any round in the chamber. On releasing the slide it will stay open. Inspect the chamber, then press the trigger; this will allow the slide to close, leaving the hammer cocked. Press the trigger again to drop the hammer.

Heckler & Koch P9/P9S GERMANY

Heckler & Koch's first locked-breech military pistol, this uses a complex roller-locked delayed blowback system similar to that used on the company's rifles and machine guns. The P9 pistol came first but was soon followed and then replaced by the P9S, the difference being that the P9 was single action only,

Specification & Operation

Cartridge:
9mm Parabellum

Dimensions:
Length o/a: 192mm
Barrel: 102mm
Weight: 880g
Rifling: Polygonal, 4 'grooves' rh
Magazine capacity: 9 rounds

In production: 1970 -90

Markings:
'HK MOD P9 HECKLER & KOCH GmbH OBERNDORF/NECKAR Made in Germany' on left side of slide. Serial number on left side of slide and right side of frame.

Safety:
Manual safety catch on left rear of slide, DOWN for SAFE, UP for FIRE. A lever beneath the left grip offers control of the hammer. When the hammer is down, pressing this lever will cock it; when the hammer is cocked, pressing this lever, then pulling the trigger, will allow the pressure on the lever to be gently released and the hammer safely lowered.

Unloading:
Magazine catch at the heel of the butt. Remover magazine. Pull back slide to eject any round from the chamber; inspect chamber through ejection port. Release slide; it will remain open; press down on the cocking lever under the left grip to release the slide; pull the trigger.

whereas the P9S was double action.

Heckler & Koch VP70 GERMANY

There are two models of the VP70; the VP70Z is the civil version and is a conventional blowback semi-automatic pistol. The VP70M is the Military version and, as a pistol, operates in the same way. But when an accessory shoulder-stock is fitted, this makes an internal adjustment to the firing mechanism which turns the weapon into a full-

Specification & Operation

Cartridge:
9mm Parabellum

Dimensions:
Length o/a: 204mm
Barrel: 116mm
Weight: 823g
Rifling: Polygonal, 4 'grooves' rh
Magazine capacity: 18 rounds

In production: 1972-86

Markings:
`HECKLER & KOCH GmbH OBERNDORF/N Made in Germany' on left side of slide.   `VP70' embossed into the lower part of the butt grips (Early models). `MOD VP 70Z [or 70M] 9mm x 19 HECKLER & KOCH GmbH OBERNDORF/N Made in Germany' on left side of slide (later models).

Safety:
On VP70Z model only; a crossbolt behind the trigger. Push to the RIGHT for FIRE. The VP70M has NO safety devices.

Unloading:
Magazine catch at heel of butt. Remove magazine; pull back slide to eject any round in the chamber; inspect chamber through ejection port; release slide. There is no need to pull the trigger as the firing pin does not cock as the slide closes but only when the trigger is pulled.

automatic submachine gun with a very high rate of fire (2200 rounds per minute). These were probably the first production pistols to make extensive use of plastic materials.

Heckler & Koch P7 GERMANY

Developed in response to a German police demand for a pistol which would be safe at all times but without needing to be set to fire before using it. It has a unique grip-catch in the front edge of the butt which, when gripped, engages the trigger with the cocking and firing mechanism. To fire, one simply grips the weapon and pulls the trigger, which then cocks and releases the firing

Specification & Operation

Cartridge:
9mm Parabellum, .40 S&W

Dimensions:
Length o/a: 171mm
Barrel: 105mm
Weight: 950g
Rifling: 4-groove polygonal
Magazine capacity: 8 rounds (P7M8) or 13 (P7M10)

In service dates: 1980-

Markings:
'HECKLER & KOCH GmbH Oberndorf/Neckar   US

Pat No 3,566,745   Made in Germany Serial Number'. All on left side of slide. Serial number also on left side of frame. 'P7M8' or 'P7M13' in a panel on the lower part of the butt grip.

Safety:
No applied safety, a grip control in the butt prevents firing unless the weapon is properly held.

Unloading:
Magazine catch at left side of butt behind trigger. Remove magazine; pull back slide to eject any round in the chamber; inspect chamber through ejection port. Release slide, squeeze grip and pull trigger.

pin. If the weapon is dropped, the grip is released and the weapon is instantly made safe. It uses an unusual gas piston delay system to slow down the opening of the breech after firing.

Heckler & Koch P7K3

A variation of the basic P7 design, the K3 does away with the gas-retardation system to become a simple fixed-barrel blowback weapon, since it is chambered for the 9mm Short cartridge which does not demand a locked breech. It is also possible to obtain conversion kits for this pistol to adapt it to fire either .22 Long Rifle rimfire cartridges or

Specification & Operation

Cartridge:
9mm Short (.380 Auto) (but see below under 'Remarks')

Dimensions:
Length o/a: 160mm
Barrel: 96.5mm
Weight: 750g
Rifling: 4-groove polygonal
Magazine capacity: 8 rounds

In service dates: 1987-

Markings:
'HECKLER & KOCH GmbH Oberndorf/Neckar   US Pat No 3,566,745   Made in Germany Serial Number'. All on left side of slide. Serial number also on left side of frame. 'P7K3' in a panel on the lower part of the butt grip.

Safety:
No applied safety; a grip control in the butt prevents firing unless the weapon is properly held.

Unloading:
Magazine catch at left side of butt behind trigger. Remove magazine; pull back slide to eject any round in the chamber; inspect chamber through ejection port. Release slide, pull trigger.

7.65mm Browning (.32ACP) cartridges. The kits consist of replacement barrels, magazines and recoil springs and are easily fitted in a few minutes.

High Standard USA

High Standard produced a wide range of models over the years, but they were all very similar in appearance, differing in sights, grips, barrel contours, finish and so forth but all to the same basic design. Only one was ever produced in a calibre other than .22, and that was the 9mm Short Model G of 1947. Recent information is that the design has been revived by the Mitchell

Specification & Operation

Cartridge:
.22 Long Rifle

Dimensions:
Length o/a: 279mm
Barrel: 171mm
Weight: 1135mm
Rifling: 6 grooves, rh
Magazine capacity: 10 rounds

In production: 1932-84

Markings:
'.22 LONG RIFLE' on left side of barrel. 'HIGH STANDARD' on left side of slide. 'SUPERMATIC CITATION' on left side of frame. Serial number on right side of frame.

Safety:
Manual safety catch on left rear of frame; UP for safe.

Unloading:
Magazine catch at toe of butt. Remove magazine; pull back slide to eject any round in the chamber; inspect chamber through ejection port. Release slide, pull trigger.

Arms Co of California and will enter production in 1995. The description and data provided here apply to the 'Olympic' model of 1950.

This is little more than a copy of the Browning Model 1935 Hi-Power, so close a copy that several parts will interchange with the Browning. The only major difference is that the Hungarian pistol has a ventilated rib above the slide, carrying the sights. It also weighs slightly less than the Belgian pistol, probably due to the use of different steel.

Specification & Operation

Cartridge:
9mm Parabellum

Dimensions:
Length o/a: 200mm
Barrel: 118mm
Weight: 950g
Rifling: 6 grooves rh
Magazine capacity: 13 rounds

In service dates: 1975-

Markings:
`PARABELLUM Cal 9mm MADE IN HUNGARY FEG-BUDAPEST' on left side of slide. Serial number right side of slide beneath the ejection port.

Safety:
Manual safety catch on left rear of slide; up for safe. There is also a magazine safety which prevents firing unless the magazine is in the pistol.

Unloading:
Magazine catch at left side of butt behind trigger. Remove magazine; pull back slide to eject any round in the chamber; inspect chamber through ejection port. Release slide, pull trigger.

Imbel M973/MD1 BRAZIL

though it is believed a number have gone to police and some army units. Most parts are interchangeable between all three pistols.

Specification & Operation

Cartridge:
.45 ACP, 9mm Parabellum or .38 Super Auto

Dimensions:
Length o/a: 216mm
Barrel: 128mm
Weight: 1035g
Rifling: 6 grooves, rh
Magazine capacity: 7 rounds (.45); 8 rounds (9mm); 9 rounds (.38 Super)

In production: 1973-

Markings:
'FABRICA ITJUBA BRASIL' on left side of slide. 'EXERCITO BRASILIERO' and serial number right side of slide. 'Pist 9 [or 45] M973' and serial number on right side of frame above trigger. Or 'Pist 38 MD1' and serial number on right side of frame

Safety:
Manual safety catch on left rear side of frame; UP for safe.

Unloading:
Magazine catch is a button in the front left side of the butt, behind the trigger. Press in, remove magazine. Pull back slide to eject any round in the breech, inspect chamber through ejection port, release slide. Pull trigger.

The M973 in its original form was simply a copy of the US Colt M1911A1 in .45 calibre. It was then reworked into 9mm Parabellum calibre but was still known as the M973. In 1990 it was again reworked, this time into .38 Super Auto calibre, primarily for the civil and export markets,

Jericho 941 ISRAEL

This originally appeared as a 'convertible' pistol in 9mm with a spare barrel, recoil spring and magazine for .41 Action Express cartridges. (The .41AE had the same rim dimensions as 9mm). However, it failed to gain much of a following, and later models dropped the '941' appelation and were

Specification & Operation

Cartridge:
9mm Parabellum or .41 Action Express

Dimensions:
Length o/a: 207mm
Barrel: 120mm
Weight: 1000g
Rifling: 6 grooves, rh, polygonal
Magazine capacity: 16 (9mm) or 12 (.40) rounds

In production: 1990-

Markings:
'JERICHO 941/ ISRAEL MILITARY INDUSTRIES' on left side of slide. 'MADE IN ISRAEL' on right side of frame. Serial number on right side of frame, right side of slide, and last four digits on barrel, visible

through the ejection opening.

Safety:
Manual safety catch/decocking lever at left rear of slide which locks the firing pin, disconnects the trigger and drops the hammer when applied. DOWN for Safe. Later models may have a plain safety catch on the frame or a safety catch/decocking lever on the slide; see below, under 'Remarks'.

Unloading:
Magazine catch is a button in the front left side of the butt, behind the trigger. Press in, remove magazine. Pull back slide to eject any round in the breech, inspect chamber through ejection port, release slide. Pull trigger.

convertible to .40 S&W calibre which also has the same rim dimensions but is shorter than the .41AE. There are variant models; the 'F' model has the safety on the frame, while the 'R' Model has it on the slide and uses it as a de-cocking lever.

Kirrikale TURKEY

This is a Turkish-made copy of the Walther PP and is almost identical to the German product. Kirrikale Tufek became Makina ve Kimya Endustrisi in 1952 and the final two years production carried the MKE badge. Frequently found with American dealer's name `FIREARMS CENTER INC VICTORIA, TEXAS' marked on left side of slide.

Specification & Operation

Cartridge:
7.65mm Browning or 9mm Short

Dimensions:
Length o/a: 168mm
Barrel: 95mm
Weight: 700g
Rifling: 6 grooves, rh
Magazine capacity: 7 rounds

In production: 1948-1954

Markings:
`Kirrikale Tufek FB Cap 7,65 [9]mm' on left side of slide. Serial number and year of manufacture on right side of slide. Late models marked `MKE MADE IN TURKEY' on left side of slide.

Safety:
Safety catch/decocking lever on left rear of slide; press DOWN to make safe and drop hammer.

Unloading:
Magazine catch at heel of butt. Remove magazine, pull back slide to eject any round in the chamber, release slide. Pull trigger.

Lahti L-35 FINLAND

Although resembling the Parabellum, the mechanism is totally different. These pistols were made in small batches which differed in minor details. The Swedish version also differs from the Finnish in minor details. A highly reliable pistol, it became available on the surplus market in the 1970s. DO NOT attempt to dismantle without expert guidance and a full toolkit.

Specification & Operation

Cartridge:
9mm Parabellum

Dimensions:
Length o/a: 245mm
Barrel: 107mm
Weight: 1220g
Rifling: 6 grooves, rh
Magazine capacity: 8 rounds

In service dates: 1939-85

Markings:
`VKT' inside a diamond on top of the receiver and moulded into the butt plates (Finnish).

`HUSQVARNA VAPENFABRIKS AB' on left side of receiver (Swedish).
Serial number left side of receiver and left side of frame, all models.

Safety:
Manual safety catch at left rear of frame.

Unloading:
Magazine catch at the toe of the butt. Remove magazine; grasp the end of the bolt and pull back to eject any round in the chamber. Inspect chamber via ejection port. Release bolt, press trigger.

Langenhan GERMANY

This pistol was developed for the German Army and never sold commercially, though thousands found their way on to the market after 1918. A dangerous weapon; the breech block is held in the slide by a stirrup and screw which can easily come loose during firing. Should this happen, and the stirrup free itself, the breech-block will be blown out of the slide and back at the firer.

Specification & Operation

Cartridge:
7.65mm Browning (.32 ACP)

Dimensions:
Length o/a: 168mm
Barrel: 105mm
Weight: 650g
Rifling: 4 grooves, rh
Magazine capacity: 8 rounds

In service dates: 1915-19

Markings:
'F.L. SELBSTLADER DRGM 825263 - 683251' on right side of breech-block. Serial number oin right side of frame behind trigger; last three digits on breech-block.

Safety:
Manual safety catch at left rear of frame;

Unloading:
Magazine catch at heel of butt. Remove magazine; pull back slide to eject any round in the chamber; inspect chamber through ejection slot. Release slide, pull trigger.

Le Francaise 'Military' FRANCE

Developed in 1929 for the French Army but relatively few were taken into service. Then sold commercially until 1939. Similar, but smaller, models in 6.35mm and 7.65mm were manufactured until the late 1950s. They all operate in the same way.

Specification & Operation

Cartridge:
9SR Browning Long

Dimensions:
Length o/a: 203mm
Barrel: 127mm
Weight: 1090g
Rifling: 6 grooves, rh
Magazine capacity: 8 rounds

In service dates: 1929-40

Markings:
`MANUFACTURE FRANCAISE D'ARMES ET CYCLES DE SAINT-ETIENNE' on right side of slide. `LE FRANCAISE TYPE MILITAIRE CAL 9 m/m BREVETTE S.G.D.G' on left side of slide. Serial number stamped into the right rear chamber area of the barrel and only visible when the barrel is opened by depressing the lever catch above the trigger or by removing the magazine.

Safety:
There is NO safety device on this weapon. BE CAREFUL

Unloading:
Magazine catch at toe of butt. Remove magazine. This will unlock the barrel and allow the breech to rise so that any cartridge in the chamber can be removed manually. Empty the magazine and replace it, close the barrel, pull the trigger.

Liberator USA

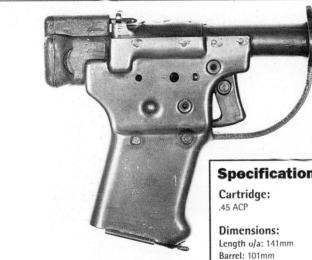

This was a mass-produced assassination pistol which was dropped to resistance groups and guerilla forces in various theatres of war in 1944-45. A short-range, single-shot weapon, a million were made and distributed freely, and will continue to turn up for years. Five loose cartridges can be carried in the hollow butt; ejection of the empty case must be done by using a pencil or some similar implement.

Specification & Operation

Cartridge:
.45 ACP

Dimensions:
Length u/a: 141mm
Barrel: 101mm
Weight: 445g
Rifling: None; smoothbore.
Magazine capacity: Nil; single-shot weapon

In service dates: 1942-45

Markings:
None.

Safety:
None.

Unloading:
Pull back the striker, at the rear end of the pistol, and turn through 90 degrees to lock. Lift the plate closing the rear end of the barrel and check that the chamber is empty. Replace the plate. Turn the striker back through 90 degrees. Press the trigger. Pull out the sliding plate at the bottom of the butt and check that there are no loose cartridges inside.

Llama Model IX SPAIN

As with all Llama pistols of the period, this is simply a slightly modified copy of the Colt M1911 design,. using the same method of locking the breech closed even in calibres which did not require it. Well made, of good material, they were among the best Spnaish pistols of their day and many are still in use.

Specification & Operation

Cartridge:
7.65mm Parabellum, 9mm Largo or .45ACP

Dimensions:
Length o/a: 215mm
Barrel: 127mm
Weight: 1075g
Rifling: 6 grooves, rh
Magazine capacity: 7 rounds

In service dates: 1936-54

Markings:
'GABILONDO y Cia ELGOIBAR (ESPANA) CAL [XX]m/m LLAMA' on left side of slide (pre-1945); 'LLAMA Gabilondo y Cia Elgoibar (Espana) Cal {xx}m/m' on left side of slide (post-1945). Serial number right side of frame.

Safety:
Manual safety catch left rear of frame; UP for safe, DOWN for fire.

Unloading:
Magazine catch is controlled by a button in the front left side of the butt, behind the trigger. Remove magazine; pull back slide to eject any round in the chamber; inspect chamber through ejection port. Release slide, pull trigger.

Llama Ruby SPAIN

This was the prototype of millions of cheap Spanish `Eibar' automatic pistols. A copy of the Browning 1903 pattern, it was first produced commercially in 1914 by Gabilondos, then in 1915 under contract for the French Army. Demand

Specification & Operation

Cartridge:
9mm Short (.380 Auto) or 7.65mm Browning (.32 ACP)

Dimensions:
Length o/a: 155mm
Barrel: 88mm
Weight: 661g
Rifling: 6 grooves, rh
Magazine capacity: 9 rounds

In service dates: 1914 -30

Markings:
`GABILONDOS y URRESTI - EIBAR - RUBY - CAL 7,65',
`GABILONDOS y URRESTI - ELGOIBAR - RUBY - CAL 7,65',
`915 PATENT "RUBY" CAL 7,65',
`MANUFACTURED IN SPAIN BY RUBY ARMS CO   PATENT 70724   CAL 7.65'.
Any of the above markings may be found on the left side of the slide, depending upon the period of manufacture.The serial number will usually be found on the right side of the frame, above the trigger or behind it.

Safety:
Manual safety catch, above and behind the trigger. UP for safe, DOWN for fire. The catch has a hook which engages in the slide as an aid to dismantling the pistol.

Unloading:
Magazine catch in heel of butt. Remove magazine; pull back slide to eject any round in the chamber; inspect chamber through ejection port. Release slide, pull trigger.

was so great that sub-contractors had to be employed, and these often went into business on their own account, pirating a pirated copy. So the Ruby and its imitators flooded the world from 1918-35.

Llama M82 SPAIN

This was adopted by the Spanish Army in 1987 but is also widely sold commercially. It is rather unusual in employing a dropping block system of locking the breech, copied from the Walther P38, rather than the more usual Browning dropping barrel system which has been used by Llama ever since the early 1920s. An enlarged version, with longer barrel and fully adjustable sights

Specification & Operation

Cartridge:
9mm Parabellum

Dimensions:
Length o/a: 209mm
Barrel: 114mm
Weight: 1110g
Rifling: 6 grooves, rh
Magazine capacity: 15 rounds

In production: 1986-

Markings:
'LLAMA Cal 9m/m Parabellum' on left side of slide. Serial number on right side of frame.

Safety:
Manual safety catch on left rear of slide; UP for fire. This is not a decocking lever; when applied, the trigger is disconnected and the firing pin locked.

Unloading:
Magazine catch is a button behind the trigger on the left side. Remove magazine; pull back slide to eject any round in the chamber; inspect chamber through ejection port. Release slide, pull trigger.

is known as the Llama M87 and is principally used for competition shooting.

MAB PA-15 FRANCE

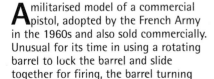

during recoil to release the slide. A long-barrel target model was also produced.

Specification & Operation

Cartridge:
9mm Parabellum

Dimensions:
Length o/a: 203mm
Barrel: 114mm
Weight: 1090g
Rifling: 6 grooves, rh
Magazine capacity: 15 rounds

In service dates: 1975-90

Markings:
'Pistol Automatique MAB Brevete SGDG' on left side of slide. 'MODELE PA-15' on right side of slide. Military models: 'P.A.P. Mle F1 Cal 9m/m' on right side of slide; 'MADE IN FRANCE' on right side of frame on both military and commercial models. Serial number on right side of frame above trigger.

Safety:
Manual safety catch left rear of frame.

Unloading:
Magazine release button on left side behind trigger. Remove magazine; pull back slide to eject any round in the chamber; inspect chamber through ejection port. Release slide, pull trigger.

A militarised model of a commercial pistol, adopted by the French Army in the 1960s and also sold commercially. Unusual for its time in using a rotating barrel to lock the barrel and slide together for firing, the barrel turning

Makarov RUSSIA

This is generally assumed to be based upon the Walther PP, though various other versions of its origin exist. The trigger mechanism is simpler than that of the Walther, paid for by a terrible double-action pull. The 9mm Makarov cartridge was designed to obtain the maximum performance from an unlocked breech pistol; though nominally the same size as the western

Specification & Operation

Cartridge:
9mm Makarov

Dimensions:
Length o/a: 161mm
Barrel: 93mm
Weight: 730g
Rifling: 4 grooves, rh
Magazine capacity: 8 rounds

In production: 1952-

Markings:
Serial number, factory identifying mark and year of manufacture on left side of frame.

Safety:
Manual safety catch/decocking lever at left rear of slide. Moved UP for safe, it places a block between the hammer and the firing pin, then releases the hammer.

Unloading:
Magazine release at heel of butt. Remove magazine; pull back slide to eject any round in the chamber; inspect chamber through ejection port. Release slide, pull trigger.

9mm Police round, the two are not interchangeable. Makarov copies were made in East Germany and China.

Mannlicher M1900/1905 AUSTRIA

Although this gun is almost a century old and virtually a collector's item, ammunition is still manufactured in South America and it could still turn up from that area, though it is now rarely seen in Europe. It has an unusual delayed blowback system of operation in which the hammer spring acts against a cam to exert pressure on the slide during its rearward movement. Models with various types of safety catch can be encountered, as it was a favourite with inventors of the period. The year of manufacture is always present, which leads to them being described as Models 1901, 1902, 1903 and so on.

Specification & Operation

Cartridge:
7.63 x 21mm Mannlicher

Dimensions:
Length o/a: 246mm
Barrel: 160mm
Weight: 910g
Rifling: 4 grooves, rh
Magazine capacity: 8 rounds

In production: 1901-15

Markings:
'MD [year] WAFFENFABRIK STEYR' on the left side of the slide; 'PATENT MANNLICHER' on the right.

Safety:
A thumb-piece on the end of the slide forces a bar down in front of the hammer.

Unloading:
This pistol has an integral magazine, from which the rounds will be ejected with some force. Holding the pistol by its grip, pull back the slide and hold it back; then press in the catch at the top of the right butt grip; this will withdraw a keeper and allow the magazine spring to eject the contents of the magazine. Inspect the magazine and chamber to ensure they are empty, release the slide and pull the trigger.

Mauser 1910 and 1934 GERMANY

An enlarged version of a design which appeared in 6.35mm calibre in 1910, this became an officer's pistol during the 1914-18 war and was then sold commercially as the Model 1914. In 1934 a small change in the shape of the butt and some other minor improvements brought the Model 1934 which was sold

Specification & Operation

Cartridge:
7.65mm Browning (.32 ACP)

Dimensions:
Length o/a: 153mm
Barrel: 87mm
Weight: 600g
Rifling: 6 grooves, rh
Magazine capacity: 8 rounds

In production: 1914-34; 1934-45

Markings:
'WAFFENFABRIK MAUSER A.G. OBERNDORF aN MAUSER'S PATENT' on left of slide; Mauser badge on left of frame. Serial number on left front of slide and rear of frame (1914). 'MAUSER-WERKE AG OBERNDORF aN' on left side of slide. 'CAL 7,65 DRPuAP' on right side of slide. Serial numbers on left front of slide and rear of frame (1934).

Safety:
Manual catch at front edge of left butt grip; UP for fire; when pressed DOWN for safe it locks in this position and can be released by pressing in the button beneath it, when it rises to the FIRE position.

Unloading:
Magazine catch at heel of butt. Remove magazine; pull back slide to eject any round in the chamber; inspect chamber through ejection port. Release slide, pull trigger.

commercially and then adopted by the German armed forces in 1939-45.

Mauser Military (c/12) GERMANY

There were several variations on the basic 'broomhandle' Mauser (so called because of its grip), but this M1912 model is probably the most commonly found and, apart from the safety catch, is representative of all models. Note that this model was also made in 9mm Parabellum calibre in 1914-18 and such

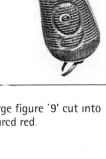

Specification & Operation

Cartridge:
7.63mm Mauser

Dimensions:
Length o/a: 318mm
Barrel: 140mm
Weight: 1250g
Rifling: 6 grooves, rh
Magazine capacity: 10 rounds

In service dates: 1912-45

Markings:
'WAFFENFABRIK MAUSER OBERNDORF A NECKAR' on right side of frame. Serial number in full on left side of chamber and rear of bolt; last two digits of the number on almost every removeable part.

Safety:
Safety lever alongside the hammer; UP for safe, DOWN for fire. NOTE - Earlier models worked in the opposite direction. BE CAREFUL

Unloading:
This pistol uses an integral box magazine ahead of the trigger which is charger-loaded.   Unlike Mannlicher and Roth designs, there is no short cut to unloading. Grasp the pistol and pull back the bolt, gripping the 'wings' at the rear end. This will eject any round from the chamber. Release the bolt to load the next round from the magazine, pull back to eject, and carry on loading and ejecting until the magazine is empty. Inspect magazine and chamber, release bolt and pull the trigger.

weapons have a large figure '9' cut into the grips and coloured red.

Mauser HSc GERMANY

Adouble-action weapon introduced in
response to Walther's PP model.
Most pre-1945 production was taken for
military use. Post-1964 production was
sold commercially, but in 1984 Mauser
ceased manufacture and licensed the
design to Renato Gamba of Italy; they
ran into difficulties and re-organised in
the early 1990s as Societa Armi

Specification & Operation

Cartridge:
7.65mm Browning (.32 ACP)

Dimensions:
Length o/a: 152mm
Barrel: 86mm
Weight: 600g
Rifling: 6 grooves, rh
Magazine capacity: 8 rounds

In production: 1937-45; 1964-85

Markings:
'MAUSERWERKE AG OBERNDORF aN Mod HSc
KAL 7,65mm' on left side of slide. Serial number
on front edge of butt.

Safety:
Manual safety catch on left rear of slide; UP for
safe, DOWN for fire. There is also a magazine
safety.

Unloading:
Magazine catch at heel of butt. Remove magazine
and empty it; pull back slide to eject any round in
the chamber; inspect chamber through ejection
port. Release slide, replace empty magazine, pull
trigger.

Bresciana (SAB) and again set about
putting the HSc back into production,
but few appear to have been made.

Mauser Model 80SAV GERMANY

This marked the return of Mauser to the pistol business after several years of absence but is not a Mauser product; it is, in fact, the Hungarian FEG FP9 without its ventilated rib and finished to a very high standard in the Mauser factory. It is thus a second cousin of the FN Browning High Power or Model 35 and the three pistols are difficult to tell apart from any distance.

Specification & Operation

Cartridge:
9mm Parabellum

Dimensions:
Length o/a: 203mm
Barrel: 118mm
Weight: 900g
Rifling: 6 grooves, rh
Magazine capacity: 14 rounds

In production: 1991-

Markings:
'MAUSER WERKE OBERNDORF GmbH' and Mauser banner on left side of slide. Serial number on right side of frame.

Safety:
Manual safety catch left rear of frame. UP for safe.

Unloading:
Magazine release button on left side behind trigger. Remove magazine; pull back slide to eject any round in the chamber; inspect chamber through ejection port. Release slide, pull trigger.

Mauser Model 90DA GERMANY

As with the Mauser 80SA, the Mauser 90DA is also a Hungarian product, finished off in the Mauser factory in Germany. It is the same as the Hungarian FEG P9R but without the ventilated sight rib and also without the option of a light alloy frame. The principal difference between this and the 80SA is that the 90DA is a double-action

Specification & Operation

Cartridge:
9mm Parabelum

Dimensions:
Length o/a: 203mm
Barrel: 118mm
Weight: 1000g
Rifling: 6 grooves, rh
Magazine capacity: 14 rounds

In production: 1991–

Markings:
'MAUSER Banner/ Modell 90 DA Kal 9mm Para/ Mauser-Werke Oberndorf GmbH D-728 Oberndorf' on left side of slide. Serial number on right side of frame.

Safety:
Manual safety catch/decocking lever at left rear of slide. Pressing down locks the firing pin, disconnects the trigger and releases the hammer.

Unloading:
Magazine release button on left side behind trigger. Remove magazine; pull back slide to eject any round in the chamber; inspect chamber through ejection port. Release slide, pull trigger.

mechanism, thus the trigger guard is larger and the safety catch doubles as a decocking lever. There is also a Model 90 Compact, the same design but 188mm overall with a 105mm barrel and weighing 950g.

MAS Mle 1935S FRANCE

This pistol fires an unusual cartridge unlikely to be found in any quantity outside France or ex-French colonies. There is an earlier model (the 1935A) which is the same weapon made to a better quality and with a better appearance. It is less common than the 1935S.

Specification & Operation

Cartridge:
7.65mm Longue

Dimensions:
Length o/a: 188mm
Barrel: 105mm
Weight: 790g
Rifling: 4 grooves, rh
Magazine capacity: 8 rounds

In service dates: 1936-50

Markings:
'MODELE 1935S CAL 7.65 L ' on right side of slide. 'M.A.S.' on left side of slide. Serial number on right side of frame.

Safety:
Manual safety catch at right rear of slide. UP for fire, DOWN for safe.

Unloading:
Magazine catch is a button behind the trigger on the left side. Remove magazine; pull back slide to eject any round in the chamber; inspect chamber through ejection port. Release slide, pull trigger.

MAS Mle 1950 FRANCE

This is a slightly modified version of the Mle 1935S but re-designed to use the 9mm Parabellum cartridge.

Specification & Operation

Cartridge:
9mm Parabellum

Dimensions:
Length o/a: 195mm
Barrel: 112mm
Weight: 860g
Rifling: 4 grooves, rh
Magazine capacity: 9 rounds

In service dates: 1950-88

Markings:
`M.A.S.' or `M.A.C.' on left side of slide; `MODELE 1950 9mm' on right side of slide. Serial number on right side of frame.

Safety:
Manual safety catch on left rear of slide.

Unloading:
Magazine catch is a button behind the trigger on the left side. Remove magazine; pull back slide to eject any round in the chamber; inspect chamber through ejection port. Release slide, pull trigger.

Type 64 NORTH KOREA

This is a copy of the Browning Model 1900, and nobody has ever found a convincing explanation for why the North Koreans chose to copy this design sixty-odd years later. There are many other designs which are easier to make, but the 1900 has always had a peculiar fascination for that part of the world; the only Browning 1900 forgeries and copies ever seen have all been from China or Manchuria. Note that in spite of being marked '7,62' it is actually 7.65mm, as was the original Browning.

Specification & Operation

Cartridge:
7.65mm Browning

Dimensions:
Length o/a: 170mm
Barrel: 102mm
Weight: 650g
Rifling: 6 grooves, rh
Magazine capacity: 7 rounds

In production: 1964–

Markings:
Year of manufacture and '7,62' on left side of slide or frame.

Safety:
Manual safety catch at left rear side of frame. UP for safe.

Unloading:
Magazine release at heel of butt. Remove magazine; pull back slide to eject any round in the chamber; inspect chamber through ejection port. Release slide, pull trigger.

Type 68 NORTH KOREA

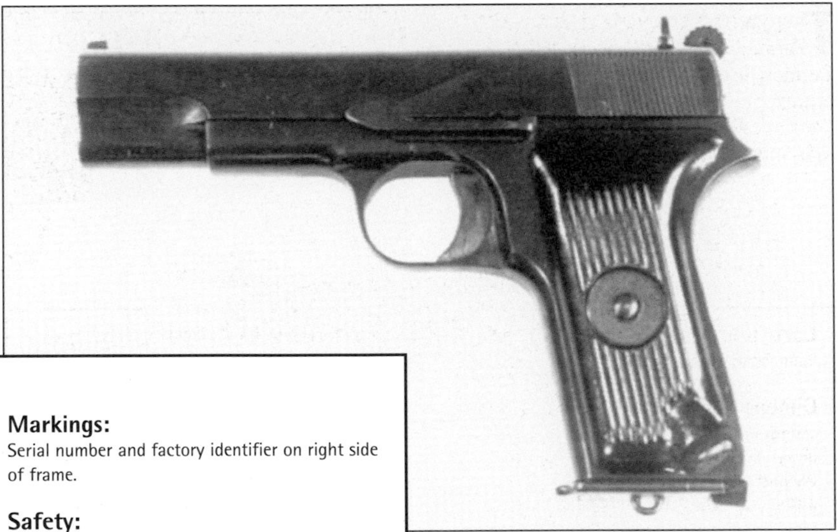

This is a modified and improved copy of the Soviet Tokarev TT-33; it generally resembles the Tokarev but is shorter and more bulky. Internal differences include the use of a cut-out cam below the chamber to drop the barrel, instead of the swinging link of the TT-33, retention of the firing pin by a plate instead of a cross-pin, a much stronger slide stop pin, and the positioning of the magazine release at the bottom of the butt. Tokarev

Specification & Operation

Cartridge:
7.62mm Soviet Pistol

Dimensions:
Length o/a: 185mm
Barrel: 108mm
Weight: 795g
Rifling: 4 grooves, rh
Magazine capacity: 8 rounds

In production: 1969-

Markings:
Serial number and factory identifier on right side of frame.

Safety:
There is no safety device other than a half-cock notch on the hammer.

Unloading:
Magazine release at heel of butt. Remove magazine; pull back slide to eject any round in the chamber; inspect chamber through ejection port. Release slide, pull trigger.

magazines will fit and work in this pistol, but not vice-versa.

Parabellum P'08 GERMANY

There are several variations on the Parabellum (Luger) pistol but the German Army pistole '08 can be taken as representative of the type. Foreign (Persian, Finnish, Portuguese etc) markings can also be found.

Cartridge:
9mm Parabellum

Dimensions:
Length o/a: 223mm
Barrel: 102mm
Weight: 850g
Rifling: 8 grooves, rh
Magazine capacity: 8 rounds

In service dates: 1908-45

Markings:
Maker's name `DWM-ERFUR-KRIEGHOFF-SIMSON' or identifying code `-S/42-42-byf-' engraved on toggle. Year of manufacture engraved over the chamber, Mauser pistols of 1934 and 1935 are marked 'K' and 'G'. Serial number on left side of the barrel extension. Note: these can be duplicated; each of three factories making this pistol used the same numbering system, relying on the factory marking to distinguish them. Each year saw the start of a fresh series of numbers, distinguished by a prefix or suffix letter. It is therefore quite possible to have six pistols all bearing the number 1234, but they would be distinguished by having a letter behind the number and by the maker's mark. Figures stamped on the front end of the barrel extension beneath the rear end of the barrel are the actual (as opposed to the nominal) diameter of the bore across the grooves. Why the makers thought this important enough to stamp on the pistol is a mystery.

Parabellum 'Long '08' GERMANY

This is simply the standard pistol '08 with a long barrel, introduced for support troops in place of the normal artillery or engineer carbines. They were also used by the German Navy. The 'snail' magazine was not entirely effective and is now rarely encountered with these pistols.

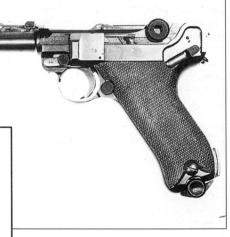

Specification & Operation

Cartridge:
9mm Parabellum

Dimensions:
Length o/a: 313mm
Barrel: 200mm
Weight: 1060g
Rifling: 6 grooves, rh
Magazine capacity: 8 rounds box or 32-round 'snail' magazine

In service dates: 1913-45

Markings:
Maker's name - `DWM' or `Erfurt' - on the forward toggle link.
Serial numbers on left side of barrel extension, and the last three or four digits will be found repeated on almost every removeable part.

Safety:
Manual safety catch at left rear of frame; UP for safe, DOWN for fire.

Unloading:
Magazine catch is a push-button behind the trigger on the left side. Remove magazine. Pull up and back on the two grips on the breech toggle. This will eject any round in the chamber. Inspect the chamber, release the toggle, pull the trigger.

Para Ordnance P14 CANADA

A high-capacity Canadian-made version of the Colt Government pistol with a double column magazine and supported chamber barrel. The company originally produced aftermarket high capacity frame kits in aluminium and later carbon steel. Complete pistols are available with aluminium alloy or steel frames. Compact models are also listed (P13-45

Specification & Operation

Cartridge:
.45 ACP

Dimensions:
Length o/a: 216mm
Barrel: 127mm
Weight:
Rifling: 6 grooves rh
Magazine capacity: 13

In production: 1991 -

Markings:
PARA-ORDNANCE on left of slide, P-14-45 on right of slide, PARA-ORDNANCE INC, FT.

LAUDERDALE FL, MADE IN CANADA and serial number on right of frame.

Safety:
Grip safety. Manual safety catch lever on top left of frame at the rear. UP for safe, DOWN for fire. A firing pin safety also blocks firing pin movement unless the trigger is pulled fully rearwards.

Unloading:
Magazine catch at left side of butt behind trigger, pressed in to release magazine. Remove magazine; pull back slide to eject any round in the chamber; inspect chamber. Release slide.

and P12-45) along with a similar sized range in .40 S&W with slightly higher capacities. The combination of high capacity and powerful cartridges makes a formidable if weighty pistol with the steel frame.

Poland P-64 POLAND

Yet another Walther PP derivative, with elements of the Makarov thrown in, notably the simplified double-action firing mechanism. Like the Makarov, the double-action trigger pull is not very smooth or crisp, but in this type of pistol it is not critical.

Specification & Operation

Cartridge:
9mm Makarov

Dimensions:
Length o/a: 155mm
Barrel: 84mm
Weight: 635g
Rifling: 4 grooves, rh
Magazine capacity: 6 rounds

In production: 1964-84

Markings:
'9mm P-64' on left side of slide. Serial number on right side of frame.

Safety:
Manual safety catch/decocking lever on left rear of slide. Press DOWN to make safe; the firing pin is blocked, the trigger disconnected and the hammer is allowed to fall safely.

Unloading:
Magazine release on heel of butt. Remove magazine; pull back slide to eject any round in the chamber; inspect chamber through ejection port. Release slide, pull trigger.

PSM RUSSIA

This is a simple blowback pistol which has been made as slim as possible and without any surface excrescences so that it can be easily concealed. It fires an unusual bottle-necked cartridge at an unremarkable velocity, and yet some reports claim that it has remarkable penetrative powers against certain specific types of body armour. Although intended strictly as an issue pistol for Soviet security forces, it has become readily available on the black market in

Specification & Operation

Cartridge:
5.45mm Soviet Pistol

Dimensions:
Length o/a: 160mm
Barrel: 85mm
Weight: 460g
Rifling: 6 grooves, rh
Magazine capacity: 8 rounds

In production: 1980-

Markings:
Factory identifier and serial number on left side of slide.

Safety:
Manual safety catch at the left rear of slide. Pull back to safe.

Unloading:
Magazine release in heel of butt. Remove magazine; pull back slide to eject any round in the chamber; inspect chamber through ejection port. Release slide, pull trigger.

Central Europe and might be expected to turn up anywhere in the future.

Radom POLAND

An excellent combat pistol, made for the Polish army pre-1939; during the German occupation it was made for German use but the quality gradually deteriorated. It was reported in late 1994 that it is being put back into production in Poland.

Specification & Operation

Cartridge:
9mm Parabellum

Dimensions:
Length o/a: 211mm
Barrel: 115mm
Weight: 1050g
Rifling: 6 grooves, rh
Magazine capacity: 8 rounds

In service dates: 1936-45

Markings:
`F.B. RADOM [year] [Polish eagle] VIS Mo 35 Pat Nr 15567' on left side of slide (Polish models), `F.B. RADOM VIS Mod 35 Pat Nr 15567 / P. 35(p)' on left side of slide (German occupation models). Serial number on right side of frame above trigger.

Safety:
The only safety device on this weapon is a grip safety let into the rear of the butt; this must be pressed in before the pistol can be fired. The catch at the left rear of the slide is a de-cocking lever; when depressed it will withdraw the firing pin into a safe position and allow the hammer to fall safely. The weapon can then be readied by simply thumbing back the hammer.

Roth-Steyr AUSTRIA-HUNGARY

adopted by a major power, being taken into use by the Austro-Hungarian cavalry in 1907.

Specification & Operation

Cartridge:
8mm Roth-Steyr

Dimensions:
Length o/a: 233mm
Barrel: 131mm
Weight: 1030g
Rifling: 4 grooves, rh
Magazine capacity: 10 rounds

In service dates: 1907-42

Markings:
'FEGYVERGYAR BUDAPEST' or 'WAFFENFABRIK STEYR' on top of the barrel; serial number right side of frame above butt. Invariably have a brass disc inlet into the butt with regimental identity marks.

Safety:
There is NO safety device on this pistol. BE CAREFUL. Safety is ensured by having a self-cocking trigger which first pushes back the striker to the full cock position and then releases it.

Unloading:
This pistol has an integral magazine loaded by a charger. To unload, prepare a receptacle to catch the ejected ammunition. Pull back the bolt and, while holding it open, press down the catch on the left side of the frame above the butt. This withdraws a keeper and allows the magazine spring to eject the contents of the magazine with some force. Inspect the magazine and chamber to ensure no ammunition remains, release the bolt and press the trigger.

A complex design using a rotating barrel and a telescoping bolt, and one which should not be dismantled without expert advice. Still common in Central Europe and the Balkans, and ammunition is still manufactured. This was the first automatic pistol ever to be

Ruger P-85 USA

This first appeared as the P-85, but since then the model number has changed periodically with the year as minor improvements have been made. There are now several variations on the basic design, offering single action, double action, double-action only, and de-cocker models in which the safety catch also releases the hammer. Models

Specification & Operation

Cartridge:
9mm Parabellum

Dimensions:
Length o/a:
Barrel:
Weight:
Rifling:
Magazine capacity:

In production: 1987-

Markings:
`RUGER P[XXX]' (according to model number) on left side of slide. Serial number on right side of frame. `BEFORE USING THIS GUN READ

WARNINGS IN INSTRUCTION MANUAL AVAILABLE FREE FROM STURM, RUGER & Co INC' on right side of frame. `STURM, RUGER & CO INC/SOUTHPORT CONN USA' on right side of slide.

Safety:
Ambidextrous safety catch at rear of slide. When pressed DOWN it secures the firing pin, interposes a block between hammer and pin, and disconnects the trigger.

Unloading:
Magazine release latch on both sides behind trigger. Remove magazine; pull back slide to eject any round in the chamber; inspect chamber through ejection port. Release slide, pull trigger.

in .45 ACP and .40 S&W chambering are also available, differing only slightly from the basic model's dimensions, and there is also a 'convertible' model which allows changing the calibre to 7.65mm Parabellum.

Ruger Standard USA

by target models with longer barrels, and a 'bull barrel' model with a heavier cylindrical barrel replacing the normal tapered barrel. The 'Government Target Model Mark 2' has a heavy 175mm barrel.

This was the pistol which founded Ruger's business and it has been in constant production since 1949. A Mark 2 introduced in 1982 has some small improvements, including a hold-open latch and a new magazine catch, a new safety catch and a modified trigger system. Both pistols were supplemented

Specification & Operation

Cartridge:
.22 Long Rifle rimfire

Dimensions:
Length o/a. 222mm
Barrel: 120mm
Weight: 1020g
Rifling: 6 grooves, rh
Magazine capacity: 9 rounds

In production: 1949-

Markings:
'RUGER .22 CAL AUTOMATIC PISTOL MARK 1' on left side of receiver. 'STURM, RUGER & CO

SOUTHPORT CONN USA' and serial number on right side of receiver.

Safety:
Sliding button on the left rear side of the frame; push UP for safe. Note that this only works when the gun is cocked. The safety catch can also be used to hold the bolt to the rear.

Unloading:
Magazine release at heel of butt. Push backwards to remove magazine; pull back bolt, using the 'wings' at the rear end of the receiver, to eject any round in the chamber; inspect chamber through ejection port. Release bolt, pull trigger.

Sauer M1914 GERMANY

Widely used by European police forces until the end of World War II and also sold commercially. Similar to the M30 model (below).

Specification & Operation

Cartridge:
7.65mm Browning (.32ACP)

Dimensions:
Length o/a: 144mm
Barrel: 75mm
Weight: 570g
Rifling: 6 grooves, rh
Magazine capacity: 7 rounds

In service dates: 1914–45

Markings:
`J.P.SAUER & SOHN SUHL` on top of slide; `PATENT` on left side of slide; `CAL 7,65 [CAL 6,35]` on right of slide. `SAUER Cal 7,65 [or 6,35]` moulded into left butt-grip; `S & S` moulded into right butt grip. Serial number left side of frame above grip.

Safety:
Manual safety catch left side of frame, behind trigger; UP for safe, DOWN for fire.

Unloading:
Magazine catch at heel of butt. Remove magazine; pull back slide to eject any round in the chamber; inspect chamber through ejection port. Release slide, pull trigger.

Sauer M30 'Behorden modell' GERMANY

Differs from the 1914 model (above) by having a more rounded butt and a small safety plate let into the front edge of the trigger.

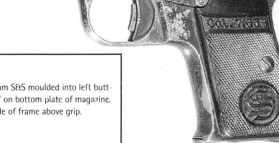

Specification & Operation

Cartridge:
7.65mm Browning (.32 ACP)

Dimensions:
Length o/a: 146mm
Barrel: 77mm
Weight: 620g
Rifling: 6 grooves, rh
Magazine capacity: 7 rounds

In service dates: 1930-45

Markings:
`J.P.SAUER & SOHN SUHL' on top of slide; `PATENT' on left side of slide; `CAL 7,65' on right of slide. `Cal 7,65' and a monogram S&S moulded into left butt-grip.`S & S CAL 7,65' on bottom plate of magazine. Serial number left side of frame above grip.

Safety:
Manual safety catch left side of frame, behind trigger; UP for safe, DOWN for fire. There is a signal pin which protrudes from the rear cap when a cartridge is in the chamber.

Unloading:
Magazine catch at heel of butt. Remove magazine; pull back slide to eject any round in the chamber; inspect chamber through ejection port. Release slide, pull trigger.

Sauer M38H GERMANY

A modernised version of the M30, of more streamlined appearance and with a double-action trigger.

Specification & Operation

Cartridge:
7.65mm Browning (.32 ACP)

Dimensions:
Length o/a: 171mm
Barrel: 83mm
Weight: 720g
Rifling: 4 grooves, rh
Magazine capacity: 8 rounds

In service dates: 1938-45

Markings:
`J.P.SAUER & SOHN SUHL CAL 7,65' on left side of slide; `PATENT' on right side of slide; `S&S' monogram on left butt-grip. `S&S Cal 7,65' on magazine bottom plate. Serial number on rear of frame.

Safety:
Manual safety catch on left rear of slide; UP for safe, DOWN for fire. A cocking/de-cocking lever lies behind the triggger on the left side of the frame; when the pistol is cocked, pressure on this lever releases the hammer so that it can be lowered safely on to a loaded chamber. When the pistol is uncocked, pressure on this lever will cock the hammer.

Savage USA

All Savage pistols look similar, though there are three different models: the 1907 with large grip serrations on the slide and a serrated hammer; the 1915 with similar slide serrations, a grip safety and no hammer; and the 1915 with thinner grip serrations, a spur hammer and a wedge-shaped grip. An American commercial product, numbers of 1915 models were bought by the Portuguese

Specification & Operation

Cartridge:
7.65mm Browning (.32 ACP) or 9mm Short (.380 Auto)

Dimensions:
Length o/a: 167mm
Barrel: 96mm
Weight: 625g
Rifling: 6 grooves, rh
Magazine capacity: 10 rounds

In production: 1907-28

Markings:
'SAVAGE' on left side of frame or top of slide.

1917 models have 'Savage 1917 Model' on left side of frame. All have company trade-mark (an Indian head) with 'Savage Quality' around it moulded into the butt grips.

Safety:
Manual safety catch left rear of frame; UP for safe.

Unloading:
Magazine catch at toe of butt. Remove magazine; pull back slide to eject any round in the chamber; inspect chamber through ejection port. Release slide, pull trigger.

Army and passed on to the Guarda Nacional de Republica, being sold off in the 1950s, so that they are rather more common in Southern Europe than might otherwise be expected.

SIG P210 SWITZERLAND

One of the world's finest pistols, this was developed during WWII by SIG and was adopted by the Swiss Army in 1949, and by the Danish Army shortly afterward. Widely sold, particularly in target versions, further military adoption has evaded it due to the high price. The slide runs in rails inside the frame, one of the first production pistols to use this system, which contributes to its renowned accuracy and reliability. There are several variations; the P-210 has a

Specification & Operation

Cartridge:
9mm Parabellum

Dimensions:
Length o/a: 215mm
Barrel: 120mm
Weight: 900g
Rifling: 6 grooves, rh
Magazine capacity: 8 rounds

In production: 1949-

Markings:
SIG badge, model number (eg P-210-2) and serial number on right side of slide.

Safety:
Manual safety catch on left side, behind trigger. UP for safe.

Unloading:
Magazine release at heel of butt. Remove magazine; pull back slide to eject any round in the chamber; inspect chamber through ejection port. Release slide, pull trigger.

polished finish and wooden grips; P-210-2 sand-blasted finish and plastic grips; P-210-4 was a special model for the West German Border Police; and P-210-5 and -6 are target models, the -5 having an extended barrel.

SIG P220 SWITZERLAND

Sales of the SIG P-210 suffered because of its high price, due to the design and method of manufacture, so the company set about simplifying these attributes, resulting in the P220. Even so, the quality is still outstanding. This, and subsequent models, are properly known as 'SIG-Sauer' pistols because SIG collaborated with JP Sauer of Germany, so enabling them to sell Swiss-designed

Specification & Operation

Cartridge:
9mm Parabellum

Dimensions:
Length o/a: 198mm
Barrel: 112mm
Weight: 750g
Rifling: 6 grooves, rh
Magazine capacity: 9 rounds
In production: 1975-

Markings:
'SIG SAUER' on left forward area of slide. P220 and serial number on right side of slide. Serial number on right side of frame.

Safety:
There is a de-cocking lever in the left side of the butt, with its thumb-piece just behind the trigger. Pressing DOWN on this will drop the hammer into a safety notch. There is an automatic firing pin safety. Note that the catch above the left grip is a slide lock, used when dismantling the pistol, and not a safety device.

Unloading:
Magazine release at heel of the butt. Remove magazine; pull back slide to eject any round in the chamber; inspect chamber through ejection port. Release slide, pull trigger.

but German-made pistols to the rest of the world, something not permitted had the pistols been made in Switzerland. Swiss companies are only permitted to sell weapons to people who do not want them.

SIG P225 SWITZERLAND

This model, which is more or less a compact version of the P220, was developed in response to a German police demand in the mid-1970s for a 9mm pistol which could be safely carried but brought into action without the need to set or operate any safety devices. It relies on the same automatic firing pin safety and de-cocking lever as do the other SIG

Specification & Operation

Cartridge:
9mm Parabellum

Dimensions:
Length o/a: 180mm
Barrel: 98mm
Weight: 740g
Rifling: 6 grooves, rh
Magazine capacity: 8 rounds

In production: 1978-

Markings:
`SIG SAUER' on left forward area of slide. P220 and serial number on right side of slide. Serial number on right side of frame.

Safety:
There is a de-cocking lever in the left side of the butt, with its thumb-piece just behind the trigger. Pressing DOWN on this will drop the hammer into a safety notch. There is an automatic firing pin safety which locks the pin at all times except during the last movement of the trigger when firing. Note that the catch above the left grip is a slide lock, used when dismantling the pistol, and not a safety device.

Unloading:
Magazine release at heel of the butt. Remove magazine; pull back slide to eject any round in the chamber; inspect chamber through ejection port. Release slide, pull trigger.

models, which was sufficient to meet the German requirement, and it was adopted by a number of Swiss and German police forces.

SIG P226 SWITZERLAND

The P226 was developed in late 1980 as an entrant for the US Army's pistol contest and came within an ace of winning it, being beaten solely on price. In effect, it was the P220 with an enlarged magazine and an ambidextrous magazine release in the forward edge of the butt, behind the trigger, instead of at the base of the butt. About 80 percent of

Specification & Operation

Cartridge:
9mm Parabellum

Dimensions:
Length o/a: 196mm
Barrel: 112mm
Weight: 750g
Rifling: 6 grooves, rh
Magazine capacity: 15 rounds

In production: 1981-

Markings:
'SIG SAUER' on left forward area of slide. `P226' and serial number on right side of slide. Serial number on right side of frame.

Safety:
There is a de-cocking lever on the left side of the butt, with its thumb-piece just behind the trigger. Pressing DOWN on this will drop the hammer into a safety notch. There is an automatic firing pin safety which locks the pin at all times except during the last movement of the trigger when firing. Note that the catch above the left grip is a slide lock, used when dismantling the pistol, and not a safety device.

Unloading:
Magazine release at heel of the butt. Remove magazine; pull back slide to eject any round in the chamber; inspect chamber through ejection port.

the parts are from the P220 and P225 pistols. Although turned down by the US Army, several US Federal agencies have purchased this pistol and it has been sold widely in the commercial market, almost half a million having been made by 1995.

119

Smith & Wesson Model 39 USA

Smith & Wesson's first modern automatic pistol, this was accompanied by the Model 44, essentially similar but single-action only. It was the progenitor of several similar improved models which followed it. Numbers were taken into service by the US Navy and Special Forces.

Specification & Operation

Cartridge:
9mm Parabellum

Dimensions:
Length o/a: 188mm
Barrel: 101mm
Weight: 750g
Rifling: 6 grooves, rh
Magazine capacity: 8

In service dates: 1954-80

Markings:
`SMITH & WESSSON MADE IN U.S.A.   MARCAS REGISTRADAS   SMITH & WESSON SPRINGFIELD

MASS' and S&W monogram on left side of slide. Serial number left side of frame above trigger.

Safety:
Magazine safety. Manual safety catch at rear left of slide which retracts the firing pin and lowers the hammer when applied.

Unloading:
Magazine catch at left side of butt behind trigger. Remove magazine; pull back slide to eject any round in the chamber; inspect chamber through ejection port. Release slide, pull trigger.

Smith & Wesson Model 59 USA

Basically the same pistol as the Model 39 but with a larger magazine; can be quickly distinguished because the rear edge of the butt is straight, and not curved as is that of the Model 39.

Specification & Operation

Cartridge:
9mm Parabellum

Dimensions:
Length o/a: 189mm
Barrel: 101mm
Weight: 785g
Rifling: 6 grooves, rh
Magazine capacity: 14 rounds

In service dates: 1954–80

Markings:
'SMITH & WESSSON MADE IN U.S.A. MARCAS REGISTRADAS SMITH & WESSON SPRINGFIELD MASS' on left side of slide. Serial number left side of frame above trigger.

Safety:
Magazine safety. Manual safety catch at rear left of slide which retracts the firing pin and lowers the hammer when applied.

Unloading:
Magazine catch at left side of butt behind trigger. Remove magazine; pull back slide to eject any round in the chamber; inspect chamber through ejection port. Release slide, pull trigger.

Smith & Wesson Third Generation Pistols USA

This series appeared in 1989 and consists of models in 9mm Parabellum, 10mm Auto, .40 Smith & Wesson and .45 ACP calibres. They are identified by a numbering system, the first two digits indicating the calibre, the third indicating features such as compact size or the presence of a decocking lever, and the final figure the material and finish. Thus the 4043 is a

Specification & Operation

Cartridge:
9mm Parabellum, 10mm Auto, .40 Smith & Wesson or .45 ACP

Dimensions: (Model 4000)
Length o/a: 190.5mm
Barrel: 101.6mm
Weight: 1091g
Rifling: 6 grooves, rh
Magazine capacity: 11 rounds

In production: 1989-

Markings:
`SMITH & WESSON SPRINGFIELD MA. USA' on left side of slide. `MOD 40XX' and serial number left side of frame.

Safety:
Ambidextrous safety catch on both sides of the slide at the rear. UP for safe. There are also an automatic firing pin safety system and a magazine safety system. Some models may have a de-cocking lever, some may be double-action only.

Unloading:
Magazine catch at left side of butt behind trigger. Remove magazine; pull back slide to eject any round in the chamber; inspect chamber through ejection port. Release slide, pull trigger.

.40 S&W with double-action only and an alloy frame with stainless steel slide. The Model 1076 was a special 10mm model developed for the FBI.

Spitfire UK

John Slough, designer and maker of this pistol, was the British agent for the ITM AT84 pistol in the mid-1980s and he decided to redesign the CZ75 copy into something more to the expressed desires of various British military forces. The Spitfire is of cast stainless steel finished to very fine tolerances and is equally efficient as a combat pistol or a target pistol, though for the latter role there are special variant models. It has been sold widely

Specification & Operation

Cartridge:
9mm Parabellum, 9mm IMI or .40 S&W

Dimensions:
Length o/a: 180mm
Barrel: 94mm
Weight: 1000g
Rifling: 6 grooves, rh
Magazine capacity: 15 rounds

In production: 1990-

Markings:
'SPITFIRE 9MM' on left side of slide. Serial number left side of frame.

Safety:
Ambidextrous safety catch on both sides of the frame above the butt. UP for Safe.

Unloading:
Magazine catch at left side of butt behind trigger. Remove magazine; pull back slide to eject any round in the chamber; inspect chamber through ejection port. Release slide, pull trigger.

and adopted by a number of European police forces, but military adoption by a major force has not yet taken place.

Springfield P9 USA

This was actually the Czech CZ75 pistol made for Springfield Armory (a private company, not the government establishment, which had closed in1975). There were some slight differences, such as the adoption of a ring hammer instead of the spur type used on the CZ75, and some changes in the frame contours, and it was available in three calibres, and in compact and longslide versions too.

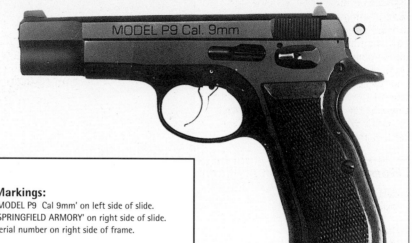

Specification & Operation

Cartridge:
9mm Parabellum

Dimensions:
Length o/a: 206mm
Barrel: 120mm
Weight: 1000g
Rifling: 6 grooves, rh
Magazine capacity: 16 rounds

In production: 1989-93

Markings:
`MODEL P9 Cal 9mm' on left side of slide.
`SPRINGFIELD ARMORY' on right side of slide.
Serial number on right side of frame.

Safety:
Manual safety catch on left side of frame above butt. UP for Safe.

Unloading:
Magazine catch at left side of butt behind trigger. Remove magazine; pull back slide to eject any round in the chamber; inspect chamber through ejection port. Release slide, pull trigger.

Star Super B SPAIN

Based on the Colt M1911A1 design and using the same Browning dropping barrel system of locking, but having a simplified method of dismantling. By rotating a locking lever on the right side of the frame the barrel and slide assembly can be slid forward and off the S frame. The Super A in 9mm Largo, Super M in .38 Auto and Super P in .45ACP were similar except for their calibres and magazine capacities.

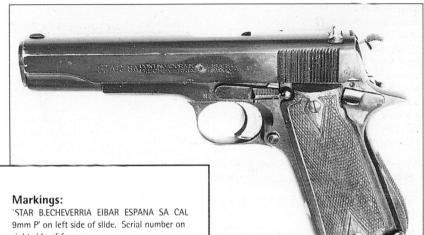

Specification & Operation

Cartridge:
9mm Parabellum

Dimensions:
Length o/a: 215mm
Barrel: 122mm
Weight: 1085g
Rifling: 4 grooves rh
Magazine capacity: 9 rounds

In service dates: 1946-65 (Spanish Army & Navy)

Markings:
'STAR B.ECHEVERRIA EIBAR ESPANA SA CAL 9mm P' on left side of slide. Serial number on right side of frame.

Safety:
Manual safety catch at left rear of frame; UP for safe.

Unloading:
Magazine catch at left side of butt behind trigger. Remove magazine; pull back slide to eject any round in the chamber; inspect chamber through ejection port. Release slide, pull trigger.

Star Model MD SPAIN

This is basically a Model B to which a selective-fire switch has been added, allowing full-automatic fire. It was provided with a shoulder-stock and extended magazines in order to convert it into something approximating to a sub-machine gun, and which helped to control it during automatic fire. About 8000 were made and they were exported to Central and South America and the

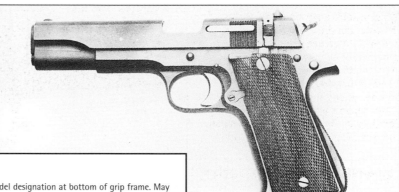

Specification & Operation

Cartridge:
9mm Largo

Dimensions:
Length o/a: 215mm
Barrel: 122mm
Weight: 695g
Rifling: 6 grooves rh
Magazine capacity: 8, 16 or 25 rounds

In service dates: 1930-60

Markings:
`STAR B.ECHEVERRIA EIBAR ESPANA SA CAL 9mm' on left side of slide.  Serial number and model designation at bottom of grip frame. May have `MILITARY MODEL' or `MODELO MILITAR' on right side of frame.

Safety:
Manual safety catch at left rear of frame; UP for safe. Manual fire selector at right rear of slide; UP for semi-automatic fire, DOWN for full automatic.

Unloading:
Magazine catch at left side of butt behind trigger. Remove magazine; pull back slide to eject any round in the chamber; inspect chamber through ejection port. Release slide, pull trigger.

Far East, while Thailand built a factory to manufacture them under license in 1938. Other models of pistol were similarly converted, and thus the design can be met in 9mm Parabellum, 9mm Largo, .38 Auto or .45 calibres. The original models fired at about 1400 rounds per minute, which was virtually uncontrollable, and after 1934 a rate reducer was added to bring the rate down to a slightly more controllable 1000 rpm.

Star 30M SPAIN

This pistol is a developed version of an earlier design, the Model 28, the principal difference being in the idiosyncratic safety catch. It is unusual in having the slide running inside the frame, rather than the more common outside system. This generally gives better support and aids accuracy. Certainly this is a very accurate weapon, and was adopted by the Spanish Army

Specification & Operation

Cartridge:
9mm Parabellum

Dimensions:
Length o/a: 205mm
Barrel: 110mm
Weight, empty: 1140g
Rifling: 6 grooves, rh
Magazine capacity: 15 rounds

In service dates: 1990-

Markings:
'STAR B.ECHEVERRIA EIBAR SPAIN SA Caliber
9mm' on right side of slide. 'MOD 30M'and Serial number on left side of slide.

Safety:
Ambidextrous manual safety catch at rear of slide; note that all this does is withdraw the firing pin to a safe position and lock it; it is still possible to pull the trigger and cock and drop the hammer, so that 'dry-firing' can be done with a loaded gun.

Unloading:
Magazine catch at left side of butt behind trigger. Remove magazine; pull back slide to eject any round in the chamber; inspect chamber through ejection port. Release slide, pull trigger.

soon after it first appeared. The Model 30M is entirely of steel; there is also a Model 30PK which has a light alloy frame but is otherwise identical.

Star M40 Firestar SPAIN

An extremely compact pistol for this calibre, the M40 is slimmer than a comparable revolver and smaller than most automatics of this power. It is easily concealed. It also has the slide running in internal rails in the frame, which helps reliability and accuracy and was among the first of the new generation Star pistol to have this feature. There is also an M45 Firestar,

Specification & Operation

Cartridge:
.40 S&W

Dimensions:
Length o/a: 165mm
Barrel: 86mm
Weight   : 855g
Rifling: 6 grooves, rh
Magazine capacity: 6 rounds

In production: 1993-

Markings:
`STAR EIBAR ESPANA' on left side of slide. Serial number on right side of frame.

Safety:
Manual safety catch on both sides of the frame above the butt; UP for safe. If the hammer is down, applying this catch locks both hammer and slide. If the hammer is cocked, only the hammer is locked and the slide can be withdrawn to check on the chamber. There is also an automatic firing pin safety, a magazine safety and a half-cock notch on the hammer.

Unloading:
Magazine catch at left side of butt behind trigger. Remove magazine; pull back slide to eject any round in the chamber; inspect chamber through ejection port. Release slide, pull trigger.

which is the same pistol but chambered for the .45ACP cartridge; the only noticeable difference lies in the slide; the M45 slide is the same width end to end, while the M40 slide has the front section rebated. However the .45 model is some 5mm longer and weighs 1025g.

Star Megastar SPAIN

This is a full-sized heavy calibre weapon which has an unusually large magazine capacity; the data for the .45 version is given above, and the 10mm holds 14 rounds and is fractionally heavier. As with the Firestar models, the slide runs inside the frame, giving it good support and contributing to the accuracy.

Specification & Operation

Cartridge:
.45 ACP or 10mm Auto

Dimensions:
Length o/a: 212mm
Barrel: 116mm
Weight: 1360g
Rifling: 6 grooves rh
Magazine capacity: 12

In production: 1993-

Markings:
'STAR EIBAR ESPANA' on left side of slide. Serial number on right side of frame.

Safety:
Manual safety catch/de-cocking lever on both sides of slide at rear. UP for fire, DOWN for safe, and a continued downward movement will lock the firing pin and release the hammer. When the lever is released it moves back to the safe position. There is also a magazine safety.

Unloading:
Magazine catch at left side of butt behind trigger. Remove magazine; pull back slide to eject any round in the chamber; inspect chamber through ejection port. Release slide, pull trigger.

Stechkin RUSSIA

This could be considered as an overgrown Walther PP modified to permit selective full-automatic fire; the cyclic rate is about 850 rds/min, though the practical rate is more like 80 rds/min, fired in short bursts. It was issued to officers and NCOs of various Soviet units and also exported to some countries. It was claimed to be an effective submachine gun, but like all such conversions it was difficult to control

Specification & Operation

Cartridge:
9mm Makarov

Dimensions:
Length o/a: 225mm
Barrel: 140mm
Weight: 1030g
Rifling: 4 grooves, rh
Magazine capacity: 20 rounds

In service dates: 1951-1975

Markings:
The serial number and the factory identifying number are stamped on left side of slide.

Safety:
A safety/selector lever is on the left side of the slide; it has three positions - safe (np), semi-automatic (OA) and full automatic (ABT). When set at safe the slide cannot be retracted.

Unloading:
Magazine catch at heel of butt. Remove magazine; move selector lever off safe, pull back slide to eject any round in the chamber; inspect chamber through ejection port. Release slide, pull trigger.

and was withdrawn in the 1970s when the AKSU shortened version of the AK47 rifle appeared. Terrorists tend to regard it with some favour, and it is likely to appear for a long time to come.

Steyr 1909 AUSTRIA

A licensed copy of a Belgian design, the Steyr pistols were made until well into the 1930s and widely distributed in Europe. Well made, many are still perfectly serviceable and relatively common.

Specification & Operation

Cartridge:
7.65mm Browning (.32 ACP)

Dimensions:
Length o/a: 162mm
Barrel: 92mm
Weight: 630g
Rifling: 6 grooves, rh
Magazine capacity: 7 rounds

In production: 1909-39

Markings:
'WAFFENFABRIK GES STEYR' on left side of receiver. 'PAT NO 9379-05 U 25025-06' on the upper left side of the barrel unit. 'PAT + 40335' on the right upper side of the barrel unit. 'N. PIPEPER PATENT' on the right side of the receiver. Models made after 1911 have an additional patent 'NO 16715-08' added to the left side of the barrel. The last digits of the year of manufacture are stamped into the barrel unit just ahead of the frame on the left side.

Safety:
Manual safety catch left rear of frame. Forward for safe, back for fire.

Unloading:
Magazine catch at heel of butt. Remove magazine. Press down lever on the left side above the trigger, thus releasing the barrel and allowing the breech to rise so that any round in the chamber can be removed. Close the barrel. There is no need to press the trigger since the weapon did not cock during this action.

Steyr 1912 AUSTRIA

One of the most robust and reliable service pistols ever made, it was hampered by being chambered for a unique cartridge. When Austria was assimilated into the Third Reich in 1938 the service pistols were re-barrelled for the 9mm Parabellum cartridge, and will be found marked ' P-08' on the left side of the slide to indicate their conversion. 9mm Steyr ammunition is still made.

Specification & Operation

Cartridge:
9mm Steyr or 9mm Parabellum

Dimensions:
Length o/a: 216mm
Barrel: 128mm
Weight: 1020g
Rifling: 4 grooves, rh
Magazine capacity: 8 rounds
In service dates: 1912-45

Markings:
'STEYR' [date of manufacture] (Austrian)
'STEYR MOD 1912' (Hungarian)
'OESTERREICHISCHE WAFFENFABRIK STEYR M1911 9m/m' (commercial)
'EJERCITO DE CHILE' (Chilean) The serial number is on the left of the slide and left of the frame in all models.

Safety:
Manual safety: forward for safe, DOWN for fire.

Unloading:
Pull back the slide and press the catch on the right side of the pistol. This retracts a keeper and allows the magazine spring to push out all the cartridges. Once the magazine is empty release the slide; if it does not close, depress the cartridge catch again. Then pull the trigger.

Steyr Pi18/GB AUSTRIA

A high quality pistol using a gas pressure system to delay the opening of the breech. It originally appeared in the 1974 as the Pi18 and a poor-quality license-built version appeared in the USA as the P18. Steyr revoked the license and improved the pistol with a view to meeting an Austrian Army demand; but the Army chose the Glock and apart from moderate commercial sales the GB failed to find a market due to its cost.

Specification & Operation

Cartridge:
9mm Parabellum

Dimensions:
Length o/a: 216mm
Barrel: 136mm
Weight: 845g
Rifling: 4 grooves, polygonal, rh
Magazine capacity: 18

In production: 1974-88

Markings:
'Mod GB [Steyr Monogram] 9mm Para' on left side of slide; 'MADE IN AUSTRIA' on right side of slide. Serial number right side of frame and slide.

Safety:
Manual safety catch/de-cocking lever on left side of slide. When depressed, it locks the firing pin and releases the hammer.

Unloading:
Magazine catch at left side of butt behind trigger. Remove magazine; pull back slide to eject any round in the chamber; inspect chamber through ejection port. Release slide, pull trigger.

Military use was restricted to a handful of Special Forces units that took it on trials. Manufacture ceased in 1988.

Tanfoglio TA90 ITALY

This began more or less as a license-built CZ-75 but improvements have been made and variations introduced, and it is now an independent and original design. The standard model came first; the combat model differs only in its safety arrangements which allow it to be carried 'cocked and locked'. There are also 'Baby Standard' and 'Baby Combat' models which are

Specification & Operation

Cartridge:
9mm Parabellum

Dimensions:
Length o/a: 202mm
Barrel: 120mm
Weight: empty: 1015g
Rifling: 6 grooves, rh
Magazine capacity: 15 rounds

In service dates: 1983-

Markings:
'Fratelli Tanfoglio SpA Gardone V.T. Italy Mod TA-90 Cal 9mm Parabellum' on left side of slide.

Safety:
Standard models have a manual safety catch on left side of slide which locks firing pin and drops hammer. Combat models have a manual safety catch on left side of frame above butt which simply locks the trigger; there is also an automatic firing pin safety which holds the firing pin locked until the trigger is correctly pulled through.

Unloading:
Magazine catch at left side of butt behind trigger. Remove magazine; pull back slide to eject any round in the chamber; inspect chamber through ejection port. Release slide, pull trigger.

some 25mm shorter and use 9-round magazines. In addition to 9mm parabellum, these pistols are available in 9mm IMI, .40 S&W, .41AE, 10mm Auto and .45ACP chamberings.

134

Taurus PT 52 S BRAZIL

A compact straight blowback pistol modelled on the larger PT 92 AF with identical control levers and takedown. Like the larger 9mm pistols the PT 52 S is available with a stainless steel or carbon steel slide/barrel assembly on an Aluminium frame.

Specification & Operation

Cartridge:
.380 Auto (9mmK)

Dimensions:
Length o/a: 180mm
Barrel: 102mm
Weight: 800g
Rifling: 6 grooves rh
Magazine capacity: 12

Markings:
TAURUS on left of slide along with TAURUS BRASIL in circle with bull's head motif inside, serial number on left of frame, FORJAS TAURUS S.A., MADE IN BRAZIL along with PT 52 S, .380 ACP on right of slide. Earlier models did not have any reference to Int Mfg Miami Fl on the slide.

Safety:
Manual safety catch/de-cocking lever on both sides of the frame at rear. UP for safe which will lock the hammer in the cocked and uncocked position. DOWN for fire and a continued downward movement releases the hammer to fall onto an intercept notch. When the lever is removed it returns to the fire position. In addition there is a trigger released firing pin block

Unloading:
Magazine catch at left side of butt behind trigger,

Taurus PT 92/99 AF BRAZIL

An obvious copy of the 9mm Italian Beretta 92 (M9) series, the Taurus PT 92 AF(fixed sights) and PT 99 AF(adjustable sights) are produced with a blue carbon steel barrel/slide or stainless steel barrel/slide on an Aluminium alloy frame. A compact version (Model PT 92 C, fixed sights) has a 19mm shorter barrel and magazine capacity of 13 rounds. Full sized .40 S&W models PT

Specification & Operation

Cartridge:
9mm Parabellum

Dimensions:
Length o/a: 215mm
Barrel: 124mm
Weight: 949g
Rifling: 6 grooves rh
Magazine capacity: 15

Markings:
TAURUS INT. MFG. INC. MIAMI, FL on left of slide along with TAURUS BRASIL in circle with bull's head motif inside, serial number on left of frame, FORJAS TAURUS S.A., MADE IN BRAZIL along with

PT 92 AF CAL 9MM PARA on right of slide. Earlier models did not have 'Int Mfg Miami Fl' on the slide.

Safety:
Manual safety catch/de-cocking lever on both sides of the frame at rear. UP for safe which will lock the hammer in the cocked and uncocked position. DOWN for fire and a continued downward movement releases the hammer to fall onto an intercept notch. When the lever is removed it returns to the fire position. In addition there is a trigger released firing pin block

Unloading:
As Beretta 92.

100 AF (fixed sights) and PT 101 AF (adjustable sights) have a magazine capacity of 11 rounds. The high magazine capacity coupled with the high reliability of the Beretta/Taurus design and low cost has made these models very popular.

Tokagypt EGYPT

This is a copy of the Soviet Tokarev TT-33 but firing the 9mm Parabellum cartridge, a worthwhile and sensible modification produced in Hungary for the Egyptian Army in the 1960s. For some reason or other the Army didn't like it and most were taken by the Egyptian police, the surplus being sold off commercially into West Germany under various names.

Specification & Operation

Cartridge:
9mm Parabellum

Dimensions:
Length o/a: 194mm
Barrel: 114mm
Weight: 910g
Rifling: 6 grooves rh
Magazine capacity: 7 rounds

In service dates: 1958-

Markings:
'TOKAGYPT 58/Cal 9mm Para [badge] Made in Hungary/ FEG [year]'
Serial number left side of frame behind trigger

Safety:
Manual catch at left rear of frame; UP for fire, DOWN for safe.

Unloading:
Magazine catch at heel of butt. Remove magazine; pull back slide to eject any round in the chamber; inspect chamber through ejection port. Release slide, pull trigger.

Tokarev RUSSIA

First produced in 1930, this uses the Browning dropping barrel system of locking and was unusual in having the hammer and its spring and other components in a removable module in the back edge of the butt. It also has the magazine lips machined into the frame, so that slight malformation of the actual magazine does not interfere with feeding. In 1933 the design was modified to have the locking lugs on the

Specification & Operation

Cartridge:
7.62mm Soviet Pistol(also fires 7.63mm Mauser)

Dimensions:
Length o/a: 196mm
Barrel: 116mm
Weight: 840g
Rifling: 4 grooves RH
Magazine capacity: 8 rounds

In service dates: 1930-

Markings:
Serial number on frame or slide; may have a

factory number but generally not.
Copies made in other countries can usually be identified by the badge moulded into the butt grips.

Safety:
No manual safety; only a half-cock notch on the hammer

Unloading:
Magazine catch at heel of butt. Remove magazine; pull back slide to eject any round in the chamber; inspect chamber through ejection port. Release slide, pull trigger.

barrel all around it, rather then simply on top, a change which speeded up manufacture and became the TT-33 model It was not in use in large numbers during WWII, but replaced the Nagant revolver thereafter and was widely exported to fellow-Communist countries.

Walther P38 GERMANY

Became the German Army official sidearm in 1938 to replace the Luger; was re-adopted when the Bundeswehr reformed in the 1950s, now known as the P1. As with the other Walther pistols, there are slight dimensional differences betwen the pre- and post-1945 models. There is also a short-barrel model known

Specification & Operation

Cartridge:
9mm Parabellum

Dimensions:
Length o/a: 213/218mm
Barrel: 127/124mm
Weight: 840/772g
Rifling: 6 grooves rh
Magazine capacity: 8 rounds
(first figure pre-1945; second figure current production)

In service dates: 1938 -

Markings:
Pre-1945: (a) 'WALTHER (banner)/Waffenfabrik Walther Zella Mehlis (Thur)/ Walther's {Patent Kal 9m/m/ Mod P38' on left side of slide (very early production); (b) '480 P-38' (late 1939 production) (c) 'ac P-38' (1939-45 production) (d) 'WALTHER (banner)/ Carl Walther Waffenfabrik Ulm/Do / P-1' (current production) Serial number left side of slide and left side of frame ahead of trigger guard.

Safety:
Safety catch on left rear of slide. UP for fire; DOWN for safe, when it locks the safety pin and drops the cocked hammer.

Unloading:
Magazine catch at heel of butt. Remove magazine; pull back slide to eject any round in the chamber; inspect chamber through ejection port. Release slide, pull trigger.

as the P38K, though this is uncommon. It was the first locked-breech pistol to use the double-action lock, allowing the firer to carry the weapon loaded with the hammer down and then pull through on the trigger to fire the first shot. Surprisingly, the P38 has never ever been copied elsewhere.

Walther PP GERMANY

Introduced as a pistol for uniformed police, it was the first successful application of the double-action principle which Walther then adapted to the P38. There is no significant mechanical difference between pre- and post-war models, though the postwar

Specification & Operation

Cartridge:
7.65mm Browning or 9mm Short

Dimensions:
Length o/a: 162/173mm
Barrel: 85/99mm
Weight: 710/682g
Rifling: 6 grooves, rh
Magazine capacity: 8 rounds
(first figure pre-1945; second figure current production)

In service dates: 1929-

Markings:
`WALTHER (banner)/Waffenfabrik Walther Zella-Mehlis (Thur)/ Walther's PatentCal 7.65m/m/ Mod PP' on left side of slide (Pre-1945). `WALTHER

(banner)/ Carl Walther Waffenfabrik Ulm/Do / Model PP Cal 7.65mm' left side of slide, post-1945. Serial number right side of frame behind trigger. May also be found bearing the `MANURHIN' name; this French company made these pistols under license from abouit 1948 to 1956.

Safety:
Safety catch on left rear of slide. UP for fire; DOWN for safe, when it locks the safety pin and drops the cocked hammer.

Unloading:
Magazine catch at heel of butt. Remove magazine; pull back slide to eject any round in the chamber; inspect chamber through ejection port. Release slide, pull trigger.

weapons are a few millimetres longer and slightly lighter, and the design has been widely copied, with and without benefit of licence.

Walther PPK GERMANY

This was simply the PP scaled-down for use by plain-clothes police; there are some fundamental design differences in the frame, but mechanically the two work the same way. As with the PP, the post-war models are slightly larger. Easily recognised by the finger-extension on

Specification & Operation

Cartridge:
6.35mm Browning, 7.65mm Browning, 9mm Short

Dimensions:
Length o/a: 148/155mm
Barrel: 80/83mm
Weight: 580/590g
Rifling: 6 grooves, rh
Magazine capacity: 7 rounds
(first figure pre-1945; second figure current production)

In service dates: 1930-

Markings:
'WALTHER (banner)/Waffenfabrik Walther Zella-Mehlis (Thur)/ Walther's PatentCal 7.65m/m/ Mod PPK' on left side of slide (Pre-1945). 'WALTHER (banner)/ Carl Walther Waffenfabrik Ulm/Do / Model PPK Cal 7.65mm' left side of slide, post-1945. Serial number right side of frame behind trigger. May also be found bearing the 'MANURHIN' name; this French company made these pistols under license from about 1948 to 1956.

Safety:
Safety catch on left rear of slide. UP for fire; DOWN for safe, when it locks the safety pin and drops the cocked hammer.

Unloading:
Magazine catch at heel of butt. Remove magazine; pull back slide to eject any round in the chamber; inspect chamber through ejection port. Release slide, pull trigger.

the bottom of the magazine to give a better grip for the hand. A hybrid model, the PPK/S used the slide and barrel of the PPK and the frame of the PP in order to circumvent the US Gun Control Act of 1968 by increasing its depth dimension, and was restricted to sales in the USA. .

Walther P5 GERMANY

This another one of the designs which appeared in response to a German police requirement in the early 1970s for a safe but fast-acting pistol. To achieve this the firing pin of the P5 normally lies lined up with a recess in the hammer; if the hammer falls, it hits the slide but does not touch the firing pin. Only at the instant of hammer release, with the trigger drawn fully back, does a pawl push the entire firing pin up and align it

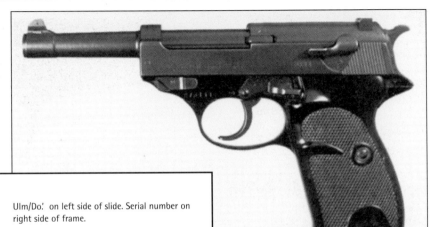

Specification & Operation

Cartridge:
9mm Parabellum

Dimensions:
Length o/a: 181mm
Barrel: 90mm
Weight: 795g
Rifling: 6 grooves, rh
Magazine capacity: 8 rounds

In production: 1975-

Markings:
`Walther Banner/ P5/Carl Walther Waffenfabrik

Ulm/Do! on left side of slide. Serial number on right side of frame.

Safety:
There is a de-cocking lever on the left side of the frame which, when pressed, drops the hammer safely on a loaded chamber. All other safety devices are automatic.

Unloading:
Magazine catch at heel of butt. Remove magazine; pull back slide to eject any round in the chamber; inspect chamber through ejection port. Release slide, pull trigger.

with the solid portion of the hammer. There is also a safety notch in the hammer and the trigger is disconnected from the firing mechanism unless the slide is fully forward.

Walther P88 GERMANY

The P88 marked Walther's move away from the wedge system of locking the breech introduced with the P-38 and continued in several other designs. This pistol uses a Browning dropping barrel, controlled by a cam and locking the squared-off area of the chamber into the ejection opening in the slide, a system easier and cheaper to manufacture. The safety system is the same as that adopted in the P5 pistol, described above, and relies upon a non-aligned firing

Specification & Operation

Cartridge:
9mm Parabellum

Dimensions:
Length o/a: 187mm
Barrel: 102mm
Weight: 900g
Rifling: 6 grooves, rh
Magazine capacity: 15 rounds

In production: 1988-

Markings:
'Walther Banner/ P88/ Made in Germany' on left side of slide. Serial number on right side of frame.

Safety:
An ambidextrous de-cocking lever is on both sides of the frame, above the butt. Depressing this allows the hammer to fall safely. All other safety devices are automatic.

Unloading:
Magazine catch on both sides of butt behind trigger. Remove magazine; pull back slide to eject any round in the chamber; inspect chamber through ejection port. Release slide, pull trigger.

pin; should the hammer accidentally fall, then the end of the firing pin is lined up with a recess in the hammer face. Only by pulling the trigger all the way through will the firing pin be lifted to line up with the solid portion of the hammer.

Webley & Scott UK

One of several pistols of similar outline, this was the British Navy's service pistol. Others, in 9mm Browning calibre, were used by South African Police, and they were also sold commercially in .455 and .38 Super calibres. Blowback models, in 6.35mm and 7.65mm calibre, were the same shape, but smaller, and were used by

Specification & Operation

Cartridge:
.455 Webley & Scott

Dimensions:
Length o/a: 216mm
Barrel: 127mm
Weight: 1130g
Rifling: 6 grooves, rh
Magazine capacity: 7 rounds

In service dates: 1915-50

Markings:
'WEBLEY & SCOTT Ltd Pistol Self-Loading .455 Mk 1 (year)' on left side of slide.

Safety:
Grip safety in the rear of the butt which has to be squeezed in to allow the trigger to contact the sear and thus operate the hammer. Some early models may have a manual safety catch on the hammer itself, but these are exceptionally rare. (The button above the left grip is the slide release; when the last shot in the magazine has been fired, the slide remains in the open position; after changing magazines, press this button to close the slide.)

Unloading:
Magazine catch in the rear edge of the butt. Remove magazine, pull back slide to eject any round in the chamber. Release slide, pull trigger.

some British police forces until about 1950. They were also sold commercially.

Zastava M57 YUGOSLAVIA

A Yugoslavian service pistol, this is another copy of the Soviet Tokarev TT-33. Originally produced in Soviet 7.62mm calibre, it was later re-designed and chambered for 9mm Parabellum calibre. A Model 70A was later produced, having a safety catch added to the slide; when operated this locks the firing pin. They were also exported fairly widely around the Middle East.

Specification & Operation

Cartridge:
7.62mm Soviet Pistol or 9mm Parabellum

Dimensions:
Length o/a: 200mm
Barrel: 116mm
Weight: 900g
Rifling: 4 grooves rh (7.62mm); 6 grooves rh (9mm)
Magazine capacity: 9 rounds

In service dates: 1957-

Markings:
'CRVENA ZASTAVA Kal 9mm [7.62mm] Mod 57' on left side of slide. Serial number right side of frame.

Safety:
Model 70 has no safety device other than a half-cock notch on the hammer. The Model 70A has a safety catch on the slide (see 'Remarks' below).

Unloading:
Magazine catch at heel of butt. Remove magazine; pull back slide to eject any round in the chamber; inspect chamber through ejection port. Release slide, pull trigger.

Zastava M88 YUGOSLAVIA

Although its appearance is more modern, this is actually little more than an improved Tokarev T-33, by way of the Zastava M57, which was the local Tokarev licensed copy. The changes consist of adding a safety catch, better-looking grips and a finger rest on the bottom of the magazine, but underneath the skin the mechanism is the same Tokarev version of the Browning dropping barrel. There is also an M88A model which is exactly the same

Specification & Operation

Cartridge:
9mm Parabellum

Dimensions:
Length o/a: 175mm
Barrel: 96mm
Weight: 780g
Rifling: 6 grooves, rh
Magazine capacity: 8 rounds

In production: 1988-

Markings:
'ZAVODI CRVENA ZASTAVA' on left side of slide.
M88 and serial number on right side of slide.

Safety:
Manual safety catch at left rear of frame, UP for safe. Disconnects trigger and locks hammer when applied.

Unloading:
Magazine catch at left side of butt behind trigger. Remove magazine; pull back slide to eject any round in the chamber; inspect chamber through ejection port. Release slide, pull trigger.

but has the safety catch on the rear of the slide instead of on the frame, where it blocks the firing pin as well as interrupting the trigger linkage.

REVOLVERS

Arminius Model 10 GERMANY

This is shown as an example of a wide range of cheap revolvers made by Friedrich Pickert of Zella St Blasii/Zella Mehlis, Germany, from the 1890s until 1945. Although cheap and simple, they were made of sound material and untold numbers survive in working order. They can be found in 'hammerless' (actually with a concealed hammer) or hammer

Specification & Operation

Cartridge:
7.65mm Browning

Dimensions:
Length o/a: 155mm
Barrel: 65mm
Weight: 460g
Rifling: 4 grooves, rh
Chambers: 5

In production: 1895-1945

Markings:
'F PICKERT DEUTSCHE INDUSTRIE' on top strap. 'Kal .380' on left side of barrel. Warrior's head trademark moulded into butt grips.

Safety:
Manual safety catch on left side of frame, above butt. Press forward to fire, back for safe. Locks hammer when applied and also disconnects it from the cylinder to permit unloading.

Unloading:
Apply the safety catch. Depress the latch on the right side beneath the barrel and pull out the ejector rod from the hollow cylinder axis pin. Swing the ejector about its hinge until it is aligned with the 'one-o-clock' chamber, then thrust out the empty case. Retract the ejector rod, turn the cylinder to the next chamber and repeat until the cylinder is empty.

designs, with varying barrel lengths, and in calibres of .22RF, 5.5mm Velo-Dog, 6.35mm ACP, 7.65mm ACP, .320, 7.5mm Swiss, 7.62mm Nagant and .380. Cylinders can be 5, 7 or 8 shot, according to calibre, and some models have no ejector rod but require the removal of the cylinder (by pulling out the axis rod) to unload.

Astra Model 960 SPAIN

This is a modern double action revolver for police or commercial use. It is a re-work of the earlier Cadix model (see below) to conform to the US 1968 Gun Control Act, the essential change being the adoption of a transfer bar mechanism to prevent the hammer striking the firing pin unless the trigger is correctly pulled through. The front sight has a larger ramp, the trigger-guard is somewhat more smoothly

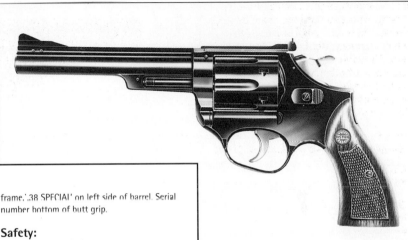

Specification & Operation

Cartridge:
.38 Special

Dimensions:
Length o/a: 241mm
Barrel: 102mm
Weight: 1150g
Rifling: 6 grooves, rh
Chambers: 6

In production: 1973-

Markings:
'ASTRA SPAIN' with badge, on right side of frame.'.38 SPECIAL' on left side of barrel. Serial number bottom of butt grip.

Safety:
There is no safety device on this revolver.

Unloading:
Press forward the thumb catch on the left side of the frame, behind the cylinder, and allow the cylinder to swing out to the left of the frame. Press in the ejector rod so as to force out the ejector plate and thus eject the contents of the chambers. Return the cylinder to the frame, ensuring the catch locks.

streamlined and the hammer was made larger. The back sight is adjustable and the mainspring can be regulated for strength of hammer blow. It can be found with a 152mm barrel.

Astra Cadix SPAIN

The Cadix is a double-action revolver with swing-out cylinder and can be found in the four calibres quoted below. The dimensions differing accordingly; data given here is for the .38 Special model. Models in .22 calibre have a 9-chambered cylinder, .32 models a 6-chambered cylinder. The ejector rod shroud and trigger guard have very distinctive shapes.

Specification & Operation

Cartridge:
.22LR, .22 Magnum, .32 S&W Long or .38 Special

Dimensions:
Length o/a: 229mm
Barrel: 102mm
Weight: 715g
Rifling: 6 grooves, rh
Chambers: 5

In production: 1958-73

Markings:
`ASTRA SPAIN' and badge on right side of frame above butt. Calibre at left front of ejector rod shroud beneath barrel. Serial number on left side of frame behind trigger. Astra badge on grips.

Safety:
There is no safety device on this revolver.

Unloading:
Press forward the thumb catch on the left side of the frame, behind the cylinder, and allow the cylinder to swing out to the left of the frame. Press in the ejector rod so as to force out the ejector plate and thus eject the contents of the chambers. Return the cylinder to the frame, ensuring the catch locks.

Astra 357 Police SPAIN

This replaced an earlier model, the 357, and has a stronger hammer, smoothed-out front sight which is less liable to snag in the holster, and a non-adjustable rear sight better adapted to instinctive shooting. The short barrel tends to deliver a good deal of muzzle blast due to the powerful cartridge.

Specification & Operation

Cartridge:
.357 Magnum

Dimensions:
Length o/a: 212mm
Barrel: 77mm
Weight: 1040g
Rifling: 6 grooves, rh
Chambers: 6

In production: 1980-

Markings:
'ASTRA SPAIN' and badge on right side of frame, above butt. '357 MAGNUM CTG' on left side of barrel. Serial number left side of frame behind trigger. Astra badges on grips.

Safety:
There is no safety device on this revolver.

Unloading:
Press forward the thumb catch on the left side of the frame, behind the cylinder, and allow the cylinder to swing out to the left of the frame. Press in the ejector rod so as to force out the ejector plate and thus eject the contents of the chambers. Return the cylinder to the frame, ensuring the catch locks.

Llama Ruby Extra SPAIN

The Ruby name, first used by Llama for an automatic pistol in the early 1900s, was revived in the 1950s for an economy line of revolvers. The Model 12, seen here, was in .38 calibre, the Model 13 was in .38 Special with a rounded butt, and the Model 14 was in .22RF or .32CF, and all had a variety of barrel lengths.

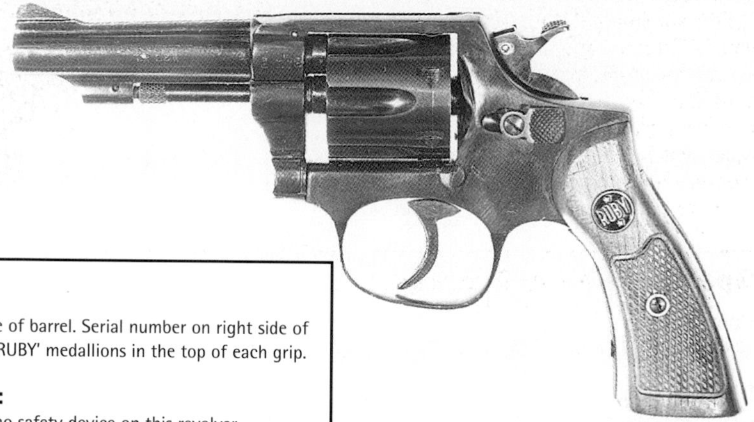

Specification & Operation

Cartridge:
.38 S&W

Dimensions:
Length o/a: 250mm
Barrel: 125mm
Weight: 816g
Rifling: 6 grooves, rh
Chambers: 6

In production: 1955-70

Markings:
'RUBY EXTRA'on an oval on the left side of the frame. 'GABILONDO y CIA ELGOEIBAR SPAIN' on right side of barrel. Serial number on right side of frame. `RUBY' medallions in the top of each grip.

Safety:
There is no safety device on this revolver.

Unloading:
Press forward the thumb catch on the left side of the frame, behind the cylinder, and allow the cylinder to swing out to the left of the frame. Press in the ejector rod so as to force out the ejector plate and thus eject the contents of the chambers. Return the cylinder to the frame, ensuring the catch locks.

Bodeo M1889 ITALY

Italian service revolver, widely distributed throughout the Mediterranean and Balkan regions and in Somalia, Ethiopia and adjoining areas. Two variant models; one has trigger guard and fixed trigger (most common) the other no trigger guard and folding trigger which unfolds when the hammer is cocked. Frames may be steel or brass and there are many minor variations in

Specification & Operation

Cartridge:
10.4mm Italian Ordnance

Dimensions:
Length o/a: 280mm
Barrel: 152mm
Weight: 965g
Rifling: 6 grooves lh
Cylinder: 6 chambers

In service dates: 1889-1945

Markings:
Various manufacturers, usually on left side of frame in front of cylinder: e.g. 'N & V CASTELLI BRESCIA' or 'GLISENTI BRESCIA'.
Serial number: right side above butt, with date: 'BS4567/1922'.

Safety:
No manual safety catch; the lever catch at the rear left side, above the butt, is actually a dismantling screw which releases the left side frame cover plate.

Unloading:
Hinged gate at right rear of cylinder allows loading one cartridge at a time when the hammer is half-cocked. Ejection through this gate by using the ejector rod beneath the barrel.

details due to different manufacturers. Little danger of confusion with any other revolver.

Bulldog revolvers UK

This is a class of revolver rather than a specific make. Originated by Webley as a small, heavy-calibre personal defence weapon, it was widely copied by European makers, especially in Belgium. All exhibit the same appearance, a solid frame double-action revolver with a large butt and short, stubby barrel, often oval in section, though round and octagonal barrels will be met. Usually in

Specification & Operation

Cartridge:
.44 or .45

Dimensions:
Length o/a: 159mm
Barrel: 64mm
Weight: 515g
Rifling: 7 grooves, rh
Chambers: 6
In production: 1878-1939

Markings:
Various. Original Webley designs have `WEBLEY PATENT' on the left side of the frame in front of the cylinder and may also have the Webley 'Winged Bullet' trademark.

Safety:
Not usually found on these revolvers, though some continental makes can be found with a safety catch on the left side of the frame above the butt.

Unloading:
Usually with a swinging ejector rod and a loading gate on the right side. Opening the loading gate will disconnect the hammer, allowing the cylinder to be rotated, and pushing the ejctor rod back will empty each chamber in turn. Cheaper models will have no ejector system and require the axis pin to be removed to allow the cylinder to drop out of the frame, after which the axis pin is used to punch the case out of each chamber.

.44 or .45, specimens in .380 are not uncommon, and some European versions may be found chambered for 10.6 German Ordnance and similar metric calibres.

Cebra .38 revolver SPAIN

This is basically a copy of the Colt Police Positive, though of somewhat lesser quality, and is typical of the product put out by a number of Spanish makers in the 1920s. Only the trademark on the butt identifies it; the maker was Arizmendi Zulaica & Co of Eibar, Spain, who also used the Cebra name on a 7.65mm automatic pistol during the same period.

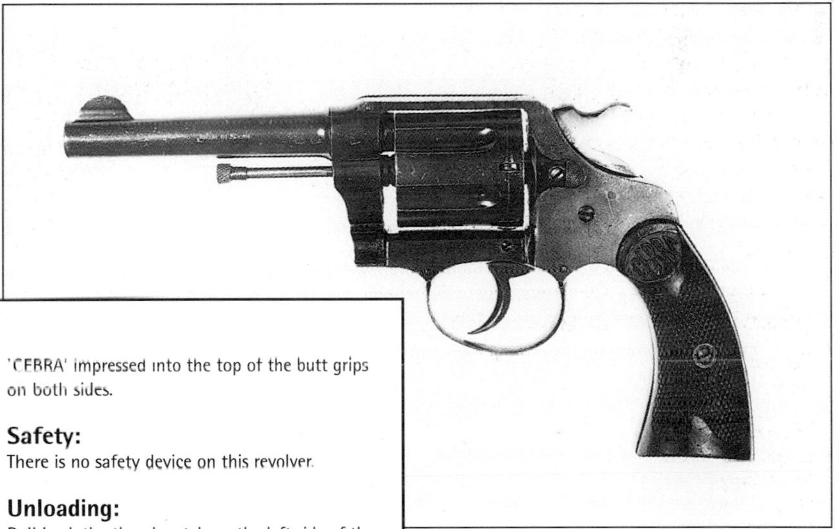

Specification & Operation

Cartridge:
.38 Special

Dimensions:
Length o/a: 222mm
Barrel: 100mm
Weight: 575g
Rifling: 6 grooves, rh
Chamber: 6

In production: 1920-25

Markings:
'MADE IN SPAIN' on the left side of the barrel.

'CEBRA' impressed into the top of the butt grips on both sides.

Safety:
There is no safety device on this revolver.

Unloading:
Pull back the thumb catch on the left side of the frame, behind the cylinder, and allow the cylinder to swing out to the left of the frame. Press in the ejector rod so as to force out the ejector plate and thus eject the contents of the chambers. Return the cylinder to the frame, ensuring the catch locks.

Charter Arms Pathfinder USA

This design is typical of a number of small revolvers made by Charter Arms in calibres from .22 to .44 under names such as 'Undercover', Undercoverette', 'Off Duty', 'Pathfinder' and 'Bulldog'. All were side-opening double-action weapons of high quality, intended for concealed carriage by police officers or for personal defence.

Specification & Operation

Cartridge:
.22LR

Dimensions:
Length o/a: 188mm
Barrel: 76mm
Weight: 525g
Rifling: 6 grooves, rh
Chambers: 6

In production: 1964–

Markings:
`PATHFINDER .22' on left side of barrel. `CHARTER ARMS CORP/BRIDGEPORT CONN' on left side of barrel. Serial number on right side of frame.

Safety:
There is no safety device on this revolver.

Unloading:
Press forward the thumb catch on the left side of the frame, behind the cylinder, and allow the cylinder to swing out to the left of the frame. Press in the ejector rod so as to force out the ejector plate and thus eject the contents of the chambers. Return the cylinder to the frame, ensuring the catch locks.

Colt New Navy/Army/Marine Revolvers USA

Three variant models; New Army has smooth walnut butt plates, New Navy has hard rubber; New Marine Corps has chequered walnut, slightly rounded butt. New Navy had five rifling grooves. Marine Corps chambered .38 Special cartridge instead of .38 Long Colt. All cylinders revolve anti-clockwise. Distinguishable from Smith & Wesson revolvers by the unsupported ejector rod.

Specification & Operation

Cartridge:
.38 Long Colt

Dimensions:
Length o/a: 280mm
Barrel: 152mm
Weight: 965g
Rifling: 6 grooves lh
Cylinder: 6 chambers

In service dates: 1889-1919

Markings:
'COLT .38 DA' left side of barrel; 'US ARMY/NAVY/MARINE CORPS' top of barrel. Serial number: bottom of butt frame.

Safety:
No manual safety devices but trigger will not operate unless cylinder is closed and locked.

Unloading:
Pull back the thumb catch on left side of frame, which releases cylinder to open to the left. Push back on ejector rod to eject cases; load chambers individually; swing chamber into frame.

Colt Detective Special USA

The Detective Special was simply a shortened version of the standard Police Positive Special revolver, designed to provide plain-clothes police with a concealable but powerful pistol. It is very similar to the 'Banker's Special' which appeared in 1928, the principal difference being that the Banker had a full-sized butt with squared-off end, whereas the Detective had a smaller butt

Specification & Operation

Cartridge:
.38 Special

Dimensions:
Length o/a: 171mm
Barrel: 54mm
Weight: 595g
Rifling: 6 grooves, lh
Chambers: 6

In production: 1927-86

Markings:
'.38 DETECTIVE SPECIAL' on left side of barrel. Colt 'Prancing Pony' badge on left side of frame.

Safety:
There is no safety device on this revolver.

Unloading:
Pull back the thumb catch on the left side of the frame, behind the cylinder, and allow the cylinder to swing out to the left of the frame. Press in the ejector rod so as to force out the ejector plate and thus eject the contents of the chambers. Return the cylinder to the frame, ensuring the catch locks.

with rounded end, again for better concealment. With something in the order of a million and a half of these two models made, they are relatively common.

Colt Pocket Positive USA

This was the continuance of an earlier mode, the New Pocket Model, but with the addition of the Positive Safety feature described under 'Police Positive'. Serial numbers continued, but any serial number above 30,000 has the Positive Safety device. These pistols can be found chambered either for the .32 Long Colt, or for the .32 Police Positive and .38 S&W Long cartridges. The chambers

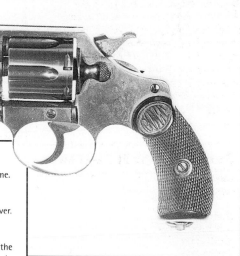

Specification & Operation

Cartridge:
.32 Long Colt

Dimensions:
Length o/a: 215mm
Barrel: 115mm
Weight: 455g
Rifling: 6 grooves, lh
Chambers: 6

In production: 1895-1943

Markings:
'POCKET POSITIVE/32 POLICE CTG' on left side of barrel. 'COLT'S PAT FA CO' on right side of barrel.

Colt 'Prancing Pony' badge on left side of frame.

Safety:
There is no applied safety device on this revolver.

Unloading:
Pull back the thumb catch on the left side of the frame, behind the cylinder, and allow the cylinder to swing out to the left of the frame. Press in the ejector rod so as to force out the ejector plate and thus eject the contents of the chambers. Return the cylinder to the frame, ensuring the catch locks.

differ slightly in order to obtain the optimum performance from each round; it is possible to interchange ammunition quite safely.

159

Colt New Service revolver USA

Developed in the 1890s primarily as a military revolver, it was not officially adopted until 1917 (see below) but then continued in production until 1944, some 360,000 being made. The greater part were in .45 Colt or .44 S&W Russian, though such odd calibres as .44/40 Winchester and .476 Eley were produced in small numbers.

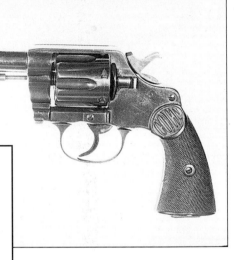

Specification & Operation

Cartridge:
.45 Colt and 17 other calibres

Dimensions:
Length o/a: 275mm
Barrel: 140mm
Weight: 1162g
Rifling: 6 grooves, lh
Chambers: 6

In service dates: 1898-1944

Markings:
`NEW SERVICE 45 COLT' [or other calibre] on left side of barrel. `Colt's Pat FA Co Hartford Conn'
and various patent dates on top of barrel. Serial number bottom of butt frame.

Safety:
There is no applied safety device on this revolver.

Unloading:
Pull back the thumb catch on the left side of the frame, behind the cylinder, and allow the cylinder to swing out to the left of the frame. Press in the ejector rod so as to force out the ejector plate and thus eject the contents of the chambers. Return the cylinder to the frame, ensuring the catch locks.

Colt Model 1917 revolver USA

In 1917 the US Army, short of pistols, called on Colt (and Smith & Wesson) to fill the gap using their stock heavy revolver but chambering it for the .45 Auto cartridge fired by the Colt automatic pistol which was the approved sidearm. The M1917 is therefore the New Service but with a shortened cylinder so that the rimless .45 ACP cartridge will load with the aid

Specification & Operation

Cartridge:
.45 ACP

Dimensions:
Length o/a: 273mm
Barrel: 140mm
Weight: 1134g
Rifling: 6 grooves, lh
Chambers: 6

In service dates: 1917-45

Markings:
'COLT D.A. 45' on left side of barrel. 'COLT'S PAT FA CO HARTFORD CONN' on top of barrel, with various patent dates. 'UNITED STATES PROPERTY' on right side of frame. Serial number bottom of butt.

Safety:
There is no applied safety device on this revolver.

Unloading:
Pull back the thumb catch on the left side of the frame, behind the cylinder, and allow the cylinder to swing out to the left of the frame. Press in the ejector rod so as to force out the ejector plate and thus eject the contents of the chambers. Return the cylinder to the frame, ensuring the catch locks.

of two three-shot clips, positioning the rounds in the chamber and giving the ejector something to push against. It remained in service throughout World War II.

Colt Python USA

Colt's premier double-action revolver in post war year with a fine reputation for accuracy with its 1:14 twist rifling. Early models were available with a nickel plated finish but this was dropped with the introduction of stainless steel to supplement the existing blued carbon steel models. A very limited number were made with 203mm (8") barrels and chambered for .38 S&W Special only.

Specification & Operation

Cartridge:
.357 Magnum (&.38 S&W Special)

Dimensions: With 203mm (8") barrel
Length o/a: 343mm
Barrel: 203mm (also available with 153mm (6") and 102mm (4") barrel)
Weight: 1360g
Rifling: 6 grooves rh
Magazine capacity: 6

In production: 1955 -

Markings:
PYTHON 357, 357 MAGNUM CTG on left of barrel, rampant Colt motif on left of frame, COLT'S PT. F. A. MFG. CO. HARTFORD, CONN, USA on right of barrel, serial number on frame under cylinder crane.

Safety:
Trigger retracted hammer block

Unloading:
The cylinder latch is on the left of the frame behind the cylinder. Pull cylinder latch to the rear, swing out the cylinder to the left, eject any live or spent cartridges by pushing the cylinder ejector rod to the rear.

Colt King Cobra USA

A budget double-action stainless steel revolver with two barrel lengths and adjustable sights introduced to succeed the Trooper series. Built on a rugged frame with extensive use of cast parts the Cobra was a competitor for the Ruger GP 100 and Smith & Wesson L frame .357 Magnum revolvers.

Specification & Operation

Cartridge:
.357 Magnum

Dimensions: With 153mm (6") barrel
Length o/a: 280mm
Barrel: 153mm (also available with 102mm (4") barrel)
Weight: 1300g
Rifling: 6 grooves lh
Magazine capacity: 6

In production: 1986 -

Markings:
KING COBRA and Cobra head motif on left of barrel, rampant Colt motif on left of frame, - 357 MAGNUM CARTRIDGE - & COLT'S PT. F. A. MFG. CO. HARTFORD, CONN, USA on right of barrel, serial number on frame under cylinder crane.

Safety:
Trigger retracted hammer block

Unloading:
The cylinder latch is on the left of the frame behind the cylinder. Pull cylinder latch to the rear, swing out the cylinder to the left, eject any live or spent cartridges by pushing the cylinder ejector rod to the rear.

Colt Anaconda USA

Colt's largest double-action revolver and made entirely from stainless steel. Chambered for the formidable .44 Magnum cartridge with 6" and 8" barrelled versions also produced chambered for .45 Colt.

Specification & Operation

Cartridge:
.44 Magnum

Dimensions: With 203mm (8") barrel
Length o/a: 346mm
Barrel: 203mm (also available with 153mm (6") and 102mm (4") barrel)
Weight: 1672g
Rifling: 6 grooves lh
Magazine capacity: 6

In production: 1990 -

Markings:
COLT ANACONDA 44 MAGNUM on left of barrel, rampant Colt motif on left of frame, DOUBLE-ACTION REVOLVER, COLT'S PT. F. A. MFG. CO. HARTFORD, CONN, USA on right of barrel, serial number on frame under cylinder crane.

Safety:
Trigger retracted hammer block

Unloading:
The cylinder latch is on the left of the frame behind the cylinder. Pull cylinder latch to the rear, swing out the cylinder to the left, eject any live or spent cartridges by pushing the cylinder ejector rod to the rear.

Em-Ge Model 323 'Valor' GERMANY

This is a cheap, but reasonably well made revolver which started life as a starting pistol firing .22 blank cartridges and was then improved into a .22 rimfire revolver and then to a .32 calibre centre-fire model. It can also be found with longer barrels. These were widely exported, particularly to the USA, where they were sold under the 'Valor' name in the middle 1960s until the 1968 Gun

Specification & Operation

Cartridge:
.32 S&W Long

Dimensions:
Length o/a: 155mm
Barrel: 45mm
Weight: 700g
Rifling: 6 grooves, rh
Chambers: 6

In production: 1965-

Markings:
'CAL 32 S&W lg' on left side of barrel. 'MADE IN GERMANY' and serial number right side of barrel. 'Gerstenberger & Eberwein Gersetten-Gussenstadt' on left side of frame. Serial number on right side of frame.

Safety:
There is no applied safety device on this revolver.

Unloading:
Draw back the hammer to half-cock. Open the loading gate on the right side of the frame, and push out the contents of the chambers one by one by using the ejector rod.

Control Act outlawed them. They are still widely found throughout Europe.

Enfield Pistol, Revolver, No2 Mk1 or Mk1* UK

A fter WWI the British Army decided to adopt a .38 revolver, easier for trainees to maste. Provided with a 200-grain bullet, it promised sufficient stopping power. Webley produced a design, but one from the Royal Small Arms Factory at Enfield was selected. It was, in fact, little more than a copy of

Specification & Operation

Cartridge:
.38 Mark 1 or 2 British service. Will also chamber .38 S&W, .38 Short Colt, .380 Revolver.

Dimensions:
Length o/a: 260mm
Barrel: 127mm
Weight: 780g
Rifling: 7 grooves, rh
Chambers: 6

In service dates: 1931-55

Markings:
'ENFIELD/ No 2 [crown] Mk I [or I*]/[year]' on right side of frame below hammer. These pistols were also made by the Albion Motor Company and may

be found marked 'ALBION' instead of Enfield. Parts may be found stamped SSM, indicating manufacture of these parts by the Singer Sewing Machine Company. Serial number on bottom of butt frame.

Safety:
There is no safety device on this revolver.

Unloading:
Press down the thumb-catch alongside the hammer to release the 'stirrup lock' above the standing breech, and hinge the barrel down to expose the cylinder. This will cause the extractor plate to come out of the cylinder and extract any rounds or cases. Once clear, raise the barrel until the top strap engages with the stirrup lock once more.

the Webley Mark VI revolver scaled down and with a slightly different trigger mechanism. The Mark I version had a conventional hammer with spur; this was inconvenient for tank crews, and the Mark I* had the hammer spur removed; most Mk I were converted to Mk I* on repair, so few originals remain.

Escodin Model 31 SPAIN

This is another one of the many Smith & Wesson look-alikes which appeared in Spain between 1920 and 1936. Made by Manuel Escodin of Eibar, the only means of positively identifying it with its maker is to dismantle it and look inside the frame for a small 'ME' stamp and a date mark. However, the ornate coat of arms, which may have been the Escodin trademark, is sufficient to identify it as

Specification & Operation

Cartridge:
.38 Special

Dimensions:
Length o/a: 250mm
Barrel: 125mm
Weight: 830g
Rifling: 6 grooves, rh
Chambers: 6

In production: 1924-36

Markings:
None other than an ornate coat of arms on the left side of the frame.

Safety:
There is no applied safety device on this revolver.

Unloading:
Press forward the thumb catch on the left side of the frame, behind the cylinder, and allow the cylinder to swing out to the left of the frame. Press in the ejector rod so as to force out the ejector plate and thus eject the contents of the chambers. Return the cylinder to the frame, ensuring the catch locks.

an Escodin product. He also made a similar revolver in .32 calibre.

As can be seen there is very little to distinguish this from the other popular 1890s pistols, the Smith & Wesson, Harrington & Richardson, Iver Johnson and Hopkins and Allen pocket ejectors. Apart from small details of the triggers and hammers, and perhaps a frame contour or two, they are as alike as peas in a pod. And fragile as they may

Specification & Operation

Cartridge:
.38 S&W

Dimensions:
Length o/a: 165mm
Barrel: 80mm
Weight:
Rifling: 6 grooves, lh
Chambers: 5

In production: 1890-1902

Markings:
'FOREHAND ARMS CO WORCESTER MASS' on barrel rib, together with various patent dates. Serial number bottom of butt.

Safety:
There is no applied safety device on this revolver. Like almost all so-called 'hammerless' revolvers it does have a hammer, concealed under a shroud.

Unloading:
Press on the hammer shroud to disengage it from the top strap, then hinged the barrel down; this will cause the central ejector plate to empty the chamber. Hinge the barrel back and ensure it snaps into place under the spring catch.

look, they are sufficiently robust to have lasted for a century and still work well. There must be tens of thousands of them out there.

Harrington & Richardson .38 Auto Ejector USA

Another of the popular pocket revolvers of the early years of the century, though this one lasted in production for longer than all its competitors and, with some changes in the butt contours, even re-appeared in post-1945 years. Commonly found nickel-plated, it can also be seen in .22 and .32 calibres and with barrels from 2 to 6 inches, though the 3.35 and 4 inch

Specification & Operation

Cartridge:
.38 S&W

Dimensions:
Length o/a: 187mm
Barrel: 83mm
Weight: 420g
Rifling: 5 grooves, rh
Chambers: 5

In production: 1897-1940

Markings:
'AUTO EJECTING .38 S&W' on left side of barrel.
'HARRINGTON & RICHARDSON ARMS COMPANY
WORCESTER MASS USA' and various patent dates on top of barrel rib. 'H&R' trademark, a pierced target, on both grips. Serial number on the left side of the butt frame, concealed by the grips.

Safety:
There is no applied safety device on this revolver.

Unloading:
Grasp the knurled ends of the spring catch above the standing breech, lift, and hinge the barrel down. This will cause the ejector plate to move out and eject the contents of the chambers. Close the barrel and ensure the spring catch engages.

barrels are most common since they are more pocketable.

Hopkins & Allen .38 Safety Police USA

Apart from the catch securing the barrel closed, there is little to distinguish this from any of its contemporaries, but the trigger action is unique; the hammer is mounted on an eccentric axis pin and if it is thumbed back and released it strikes the pistol frame and not the firing pin in the standing breech. Pulling the trigger rotates the axis pin and lowers the hammer so that it will strike the firing

Specification & Operation

Cartridge:
.38 S&W

Dimensions:
Length o/a: 185mm
Barrel: 83mm
Weight: 460g
Rifling: 6 grooves, rh
Chambers: 5

In production: 1907-14

Markings:
'HOPKINS & ALLEN ARMS CO NORWICH CONN'
and various patent dates on top barrel rib. Serial
number of butt frame beneath grips.

Safety:
There is no applied safety device on this revolver.

Unloading:
Squeeze together the two ribbed catches on each
side of the top strap to release, then hinge down
the barrel to eject the contents of the cylinder.
Return the barrel, ensuring that the spring catch
engages.

pin. It was this which inspired the 'Safety' portion of the name. It was a well-made and sound design, but is less common than the others shown here since it was only made for seven years.

Iver Johnson Safety Automatic USA

As with most revolvers of this period, the word 'automatic' means automatic ejection of the spent cases as the barrel is opened. Also as usual, the word 'hammerless' means a concealed hammer, though in this case the frame of the pistol is designed to conceal it, while other makers often used the frame of their hammer models and added a light metal shroud. The 'Safety' title comes from the Iver Johnson 'Hammer

Specification & Operation

Cartridge:
.32 S&W

Dimensions:
Length o/a: 191mm
Barrel: 76mm
Weight: 440g
Rifling: 5 grooves, rh
Chambers: 6

In production: 1894-1917

Markings:
'IVER JOHNSON'S ARMS & CYCLE WORKS FITCHBURG MASS USA' on left side of barrel. Serial number on butt frame beneath grips.

Safety:
There is no applied safety device on this revolver.

Unloading:
Grasp the knurled ends of the spring catch above the standing breech, lift, and hinge the barrel down. This will cause the ejector plate to move out and eject the contents of the chambers. Close the barrel and ensure the spring catch engages.

the Hammer' transfer bar system which prevents the hammer striking the frame-mounted firing pin unless the trigger is correctly pulled so as to slide a transfer bar between the two and thus transfer the blow. Dropping the pistol or letting the hammer slip during cocking could not cause the weapon to fire.

Harrington & Richardson Defender USA

Harrington & Richardson, as noted above, were prominent among the group producing those ribbed-barrel, hinged-frame revolvers of the 1890-1920 period, and after 1945 they completely revamped their range. They were still simple and inexpensive revolvers, and they leaned very heavily towards .22 rimfires, but the company

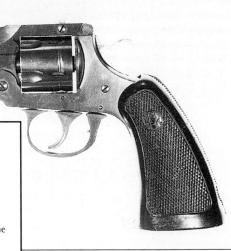

Specification & Operation

Cartridge:
.38 S&W

Dimensions:
Length o/a: 210mm
Barrel: 101mm
Weight: 878g
Rifling: 6 grooves, rh
Chambers: 6

In production: 1964-84

Markings:
'DEFENDER .38' on left side of barrel. 'H & R INC WORC. MASS. USA' on right side of frame. Serial number on right side of frame.

Safety:
There is no safety device on this revolver.

Unloading:
Grasp the two knurled heads at the top of the standing breech, in front of the hammer; pull back and up, so unlatching the frame. Swing the muzzle down and the cylinder will rise and the rear face will be exposed. A cam automatically forces a central ejector plate out, so pushing out all the cartridges in the chambers. Close the weapon by swinging the barrel up sharply so that the latch re-engages with the standing breech.

then produced a handful of heavier weapons of which this 'Defender' was probably the best. It stuck to the old hinged frame construction but allied it to a man-sized butt and a good reinforced barrel to produce a very sensible home defence revolver.

Korth Combat Magnum GERMANY

Probably the most expensive revolver in the world, and certainly one of the most carefully made, this would be unusual to find in the wrong hands. A conventional double-action revolver with ventilated rib, it has such refinements as an adjustable firing pin and adjustable trigger pull, and its automatic ejection feature is unique.

Specification & Operation

Cartridge:
.357 Magnum

Dimensions:
Length o/a: 230mm
Barrel: 100mm
Weight: 980g
Rifling: 6 grooves, rh
Chambers: 6

In production: 1975-

Markings:
'.357 MAGNUM' on left side of barrel. `KORTH' in a circle on the left side of the frame, above the butt.

Safety:
There is no applied safety device on this revolver.

Unloading:
Press the release catch alongside the hammer and the cylinder will swing out of the frame and automatically eject the contents of the chambers.

Llama Comanche SPAIN

A thoroughly conventional modern revolver, quite obviously based upon the Smith & Wesson design and none the worse for that. It is well made of good material and excellently finished, and it enjoys a wide sale throughout Europe as well as being widely exported. It can be met almost anywhere in the world. The company makes several similar revolvers which only differ in size and calibre.

Specification & Operation

Cartridge:
.357 Magnum

Dimensions:
Length o/a: 235mm
Barrel: 102mm
Weight: 1035g
Rifling: 6 grooves, rh
Chambers: 6

In production: 1970-

Markings:
'GABILONDO y CIA VITORIA ESPANA' on left side of barrel. 'LLAMA .357 MAG CTG' on right side of barrel. Serial number on bottom of grip frame.

Safety:
There is no applied safety device on this revolver.

Unloading:
Push forward the thumb catch on the left side of the frame, behind the cylinder, and allow the cylinder to swing out to the left of the frame. Press in the ejector rod so as to force out the ejector plate and thus eject the contents of the chambers. Return the cylinder to the frame, ensuring the catch locks.

Manurhin MR73 FRANCE

backbone. Though generally based on Smith & Wesson's pattern, it has a few features of its own such as a roller-bearing trigger system which gives a remarkably smooth action. There are various models - the 'Defense' is detailed above - for competition, sport and service use. They are widely sold in Europe and used by many French police forces.

Specification & Operation

Cartridge:
.357 Magnum

Dimensions:
Length o/a: 195mm
Barrel: 63mm
Weight: 880g
Rifling: 6 grooves, rh
Chambers: 6

In production: 1973-

Markings:
'MR 73 Cal 357 MAGNUM' on right or left side of barrel. Manurhin (MR) monogram badge let into grips.

Safety:
There is no applied safety device on this revolver.

Unloading:
Push forward the thumb catch on the left side of the frame, behind the cylinder, and allow the cylinder to swing out to the left of the frame. Press in the ejector rod so as to force out the ejector plate and thus eject the contents of the chambers. Return the cylinder to the frame, ensuring the catch locks.

Manurhin were primarily machinery manufacturers but took to making Walther automatic pistols under license after the 1939-45 war. In the early 1970s they began developing a line of revolvers of which the MR73 is the

Miroku .38 Special Police JAPAN

This appears to have been intended to attract Japanese police, who had been armed with revolvers during the US occupation after 1945. They preferred to return to automatics once they were given the chance, and Miroku therefore exported almost their entire output to the USA under the EIG and Liberty Chief badges. Cheap but serviceable, they

Specification & Operation

Cartridge:
.38 Special

Dimensions:
Length o/a: 195mm
Barrel: 64mm
Weight: 485g
Rifling: 6 grooves, rh
Chambers: 5

In production: 1967-1984

Markings:
Japanese markings unknown, but those exported carry either an `EIG' monogram on the left side of the frame or the name `LIBERTY CHIEF' on the left side of the frame over the trigger. `.38 SPECIAL CALIBER' on left side of barrel. Serial number on right side of frame.

Safety:
There is no applied safety device on this revolver.

Unloading:
Pull back the thumb catch on the left side of the frame, behind the cylinder, and allow the cylinder to swing out to the left of the frame. Press in the ejector rod so as to force out the ejector plate and thus eject the contents of the chambers. Return the cylinder to the frame, ensuring the catch locks.

survived for about twenty years. There was also a six-shot model, slightly larger, using the same names.

Modele d'Ordonnance Mle 1892 (Lebel) FRANCE

Sometimes called the 'Lebel', despite the fact that Lebel had nothing to do with it, this was the French service and police revolver for many years and a large number still survive. Ammunition is sometimes made in small batches, and some commercial .32 ammunition can be fired from it, though the practice is not recommended. The right-handed opening of the Mle 1892's cylinder is

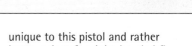

Specification & Operation

Cartridge:
8mm French Ordnance

Dimensions:
Length o/a: 238mm
Barrel: 114mm
Weight: 830g
Rifling: 4 grooves, lh
Chambers: 6

In service dates: 1892-1950

Markings:
'St Etienne' (arsenal) in script on left side of frame. Serial number on barrel, and last two digits on several other parts.

Safety:
There is no safety device on this revolver.

Unloading:
Pull back the large catch behind the cylinder on the right side. This will release the cylinder, which can then be swung out to the right. The ejector rod moves with it and can now be pushed back to eject all rounds in the cylinder. Allow the ejector rod to return to the forward position, swing the cylinder back into the frame and push the locking catch forward.

unique to this pistol and rather inconvenient for right-handed firers.

Nagant: Russian Model 1895 BELGIUM/RUSSIA

A solid-frame revolver which may be found as a single-action or double-action, the latter being the more common. An unusual weapon; as the hammer is cocked, the cylinder is pushed forward so that the mouth of the chamber engages around the rear of the

Specification & Operation

Cartridge:
7.62mm Russian Revolver

Dimensions:
Length o/a: 230mm
Barrel: 114mm
Weight: 750g
Rifling: 4 grooves, rh
Chambers: 7

In service dates: 1895-1950

Markings:
Russian inscription in an oval form, with the date of manufacture beneath on left side of frame prior to 1917. Under Soviet control a large star and factory number may be stamped anywhere on the weapon. Commercial models will be marked `L

NAGANT BREVETE LIEGE' with a date prior to 1902. Serial number on frame in front of cylinder and possibly on barrel; some commercial models also have it on the cylinder, trigger-guard and butt.

Safety:
There is no safety device on this revolver.

Unloading:
Open the loading gate on the right side, behind the cylinder; this will disconnect the hammer and allow the cylinder to be rotated freely by hand. Withdraw the ejector rod forward from its resting place in the axis of the cylinder, swing it to the right and then push back to eject the cartridge from the chamber. Repeat this for all chambers. Replace ejector rod, close loading gate.

barrel. This, together with a specially long cartridge with the bullet concealed inside the case, makes a gas-tight joint between cylinder and barrel. This revolver can be found all over Europe and in any other country which has been subjected to Soviet influence. Modern revolvers using the same principle are produced for target shooting in Russia and the Czech Republic, and ammunition is available in many countries.

Orbea .38 Revolver SPAIN

Another of the multitude of Smith & Wesson copies which filled Spain in the 1920s. This particular maker was rather more enterprising than most and supplied these revolvers with various barrel lengths and in .22LR, .32-30, 8mm French Ordnance and 5.56mm VeloDog calibres as well as the .38 Special shown here. Revolvers marked 'Orbea y Cia' date from after 1930 when the original

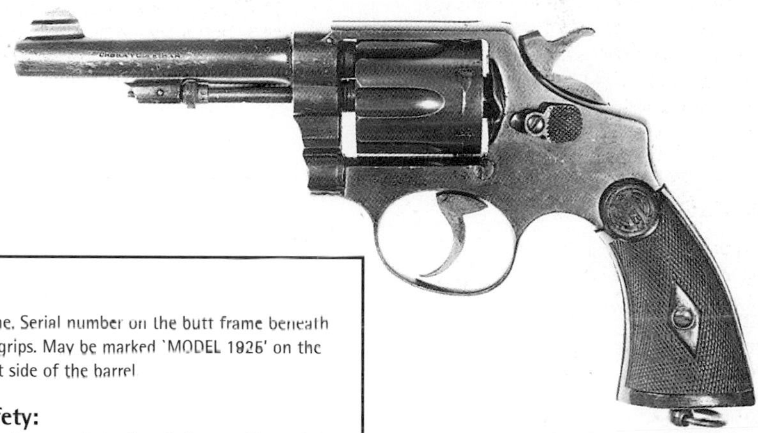

Specification & Operation

Cartridge:
.38 Special

Dimensions:
Length o/a: 248mm
Barrel: 122mm
Weight: 840g
Rifling: 6 grooves, rh
Chambers: 6

In production: 1925-35

Markings:
'ORBEA y CIA, EIBAR' on left side of barrel. May have an 'OH' monogram on the right side of the frame. Serial number on the butt frame beneath the grips. May be marked 'MODEL 1926' on the right side of the barrel

Safety:
There is no applied safety device on this revolver.

Unloading:
Press forward the thumb catch on the left side of the frame, behind the cylinder, and allow the cylinder to swing out to the left of the frame. Press in the ejector rod so as to force out the ejector plate and thus eject the contents of the chambers. Return the cylinder to the frame, ensuring the catch locks.

company, Orbea Hermanos, was reorganised under the new name.

Rast & Gasser revolver AUSTRIA

A solid-frame revolver which was the Austro-Hungarian army service issue from 1896 onwards. Numbers were given to the Italian Army as reparations in 1919 and hence were used by Italian troops until 1945. These, and similar civil and police models, were widely distributed in the Austro-Hungarian empire and the Balkan states and

Specification & Operation

Cartridge:
8mm Gasser

Dimensions:
Length o/a: 229mm
Barrel: 114mm
Weight: 935g
Rifling: 4 grooves rh, or 5 grooves lh (see Remarks)
Chambers: 8

In service dates: 1898-1945

Markings:
'PATENT/RAST & GASSER/ WIEN' on left side of frame below cylinder. Serial number on barrel and cylinder. May have a regimental number stamped on left side of frame.

Safety:
There is no safety catch, but the loading gate on the right side is linked to the hammer and when opened prevents the hammer moving during loading and unloading.

Unloading:
Open the loading gate on the right side behind the cylinder. This disconnects the hammer and allows the cylinder to be revolved by hand. Push back the ejector rod beneath the barrel to eject each round from its chamber. Close the loading gate.

ammunition is still available for them. Note that early models (prior to about 1914) were rifled with 4 grooves, right-hand twist, while later models (probably 1914-18 wartime production) can be found with 5 grooves left-hand twist rifling.

Rohm .22 RG-34 GERMANY

Rohm began in the 1950s by making starting and blank cartridge pistols, then progressed to cheap solid-frame .22 revolvers based on the starting pistols, and finally improved the design to something approximating a Smith & Wesson pattern. The cylinder lock is perhaps less robust, but sufficient for this calibre, and there are variant models with ventilated ribs, longer barrels and fully adjustable sights which make

Specification & Operation

Cartridge:
.22LR

Dimensions:
Length o/a: 273mm
Barrel: 150mm
Weight: 978g
Rifling: 8 grooves, rh
Chambers: 7

In production: 1960-

Markings:
`ROHM GmbH SONTHEIM-BRENZ/MOD 34 CAL .22LR' on left side of barrel. Serial number on right side of frame

Safety:
There is no applied safety device on this revolver.

Unloading:
Push forward the thumb catch on the left side of the frame, behind the cylinder, and allow the cylinder to swing out to the left of the frame. Press in the ejector rod so as to force out the ejector plate and thus eject the contents of the chambers. Return the cylinder to the frame, ensuring the catch locks.

reasonable beginner's target revolvers. Their cheaper weapons were exported to the USA in the 1960s under a variety of names - Burgo, Hy-Score, EIG, Liberty-21 and so forth - but the 1968 Gun Control Act put an end to most of them.

181

RUGER SECURITY SIX USA

Sturm, Ruger & Co got into the revolver business in the early 1950s, making single-action Western guns for the 'quick-draw' craze of the time. These were so popular that they persuaded Colt to restart making single action guns and many others joined in. Ruger then moved to the police market with this extremely sound and reliable revolver, since when, as they say, he has never

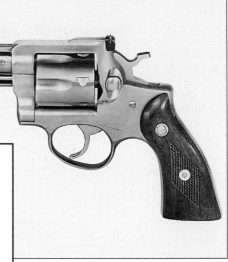

Specification & Operation

Cartridge:
.357 Magnum

Dimensions:
Length o/a: 235mm
Barrel: 102mm
Weight: 950g
Rifling: 6 grooves, rh
Chambers: 6

In production: 1968-

Markings:
`STURM RUGER & CO  INC SOUTHPORT CONN USA' on left side of barrel. `.38 SPECIAL CAL [or .357 MAGNUM CAL]' on right side of barrel. `RUGER SECURITY SIX' on right side of frame.

Safety:
There is no applied safety device on this revolver.

Unloading:
Press in the recessed catch on the left side of the frame, behind the cylinder, and allow the cylinder to swing out to the left of the frame. Press in the ejector rod so as to force out the ejector plate and thus eject the contents of the chambers. Return the cylinder to the frame, ensuring the catch locks.

looked back. The 'Speed Six' is the same pistol but with a rounded butt.

Ruger Police Service Six

sights deranged by careless insertion into the holster or other rough handling. A highly successful weapon, it was widely adopted by US police forces and sold for home defense.

This is simply the Security Six (above) with slightly modified grips and with a sighting groove in the backstrap instead of a separate rear sight, a modification intended to provide adequate sights for rapid combat firing at short range and avoid getting the

Specification & Operation

Cartridge:
.357 Magnum

Dimensions:
Length o/a: 254mm
Barrel: 102mm
Weight: 950g
Rifling: 6 grooves, rh
Chambers: 6

In production: 1969-87

Markings:
'STURM RUGER & CO INC SOUTHPORT CONN USA' on left side of barrel. '.38 SPECIAL CAL [or .357 MAGNUM CAL]' on right side of barrel 'RUGER POLICE SERVICE SIX' on right side of frame.

Safety:
There is no applied safety device on this revolver.

Unloading:
Push in the recessed catch on the left side of the frame, behind the cylinder, and allow the cylinder to swing out to the left of the frame. Press in the ejector rod so as to force out the ejector plate and thus eject the contents of the chambers. Return the cylinder to the frame, ensuring the catch locks.

RUGER GP 100 USA

The SP-100 replaced the Security Six as the standard police revolver in 1987 and incorporated a number of improvements which experience had suggested, such as the full-length ejector shroud to give a slight degree of muzzle preponderance and the construction of the trigger guard and mechanism as a separate inserted sub-assembly. It is a robust revolver and will be around for many years to come.

Specification & Operation

Cartridge:
.357 Magnum

Dimensions:
Length o/a: 238mm
Barrel: 102mm
Weight: 1247g
Rifling: 5 grooves, rh
Chambers: 6

In service dates: 1987-

Markings:
'STURM RUGER & CO INC SOUTHPORT CONN USA' on left side of barrel. 'RUGER GP 100 .357 MAGNUM CAL [or .38 SPECIAL CAL]' on right side of barrel. Serial number right side of frame.

Safety:
There is no applied safety device on this revolver.

Unloading:
Push in the recessed catch on the left side of the frame, behind the cylinder, and allow the cylinder to swing out to the left of the frame. Press in the ejector rod so as to force out the ejector plate and thus eject the contents of the chambers. Return the cylinder to the frame, ensuring the catch locks.

Smith & Wesson Hand Ejector USA

The .32 Hand Ejector was the first S&W revolver to employ the side-opening cylinder, and it went through three models, the second of which (shown here) adopted the innovations of the Military and Police such as the now-familiar push-catch for releasing the cylinder and the front anchorage for the

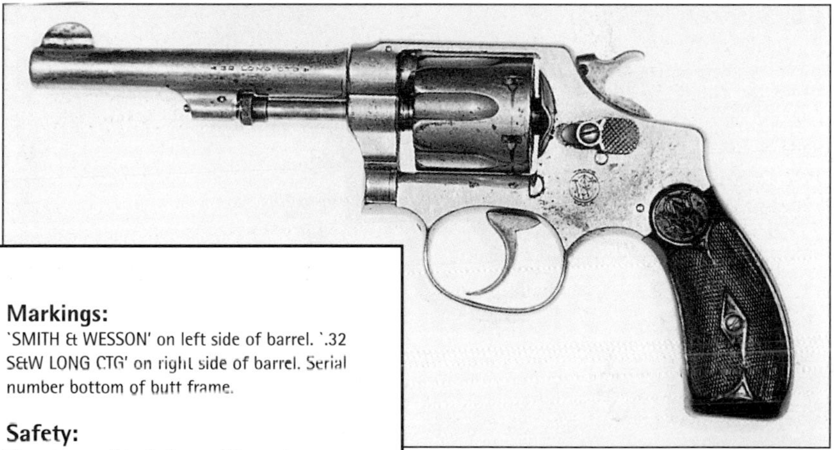

Specification & Operation

Cartridge:
.32 Smith & Wesson Long

Dimensions:
Length o/a: 190mm
Barrel: 82mm
Weight: 505g
Rifling: 5 grooves, rh
Chambers: 5

In production: 1896-1942

Markings:
`SMITH & WESSON' on left side of barrel. `.32 S&W LONG CTG' on right side of barrel. Serial number bottom of butt frame.

Safety:
There is no safety device on this revolver.

Unloading:
Press forward the thumb-catch on the left side of the frame, behind the cylinder. This releases the cylinder which can then be swung out to the left side on its crane. Push back on the ejector rod and a central ejector plate emerges from the cylinder to remove the cases from the chambers. Release the ejector rod, swing the cylinder back into the frame until it locks safe.

ejector rod. The third model added the safety hammer block and a few refinements to the trigger mechanism. It was a popular weapon, widely used by police forces and for home defence, over 300,000 of the three models being made.

Smith & Wesson Safety Hammerless USA

This is more or less the same revolver as the contemporary standard `Double Action' model but with the hammer concealed under a rise in the frame and with a grip safety bar let into the rear edge of the butt. It is not actually hammerless. A popular weapon, it went through a number of minor changes during its life, though it finalised in 1907 and remained unchanged until 1940.

Specification & Operation

Cartridge:
.38 Smith & Wesson

Dimensions:
Length o/a: 190mm
Barrel: 83mm
Weight: 510g
Rifling: 5 grooves rh
Chambers: 6

In production: 1887-1940

Markings:
`S&W' Monogram on right rear side of frame. `*.38 S&W CTG' on left side of barrel.

Safety:
Grip safety which must be depressed to unlock the hammer mechanism.

Unloading:
Grasp the two knurled buttons above the standing breech, pull back and up. This will unlock the frame latch and pivot the barrel/cylinder assembly about its pivot on the frame, so raising the rear of the cylinder. A cam forces out an extractor plate to empty the chambers. Once emptied, swing the barrel up with sufficient force to snap the frame latch into engagement.

Smith & Wesson Pocket Hammerless USA

described above. The 2nd and 3rd were almost identical, the principal visible difference being that the 2nd uses a pin to hold the foresight while the 3rd had the foresight made as part of the barrel forging. About 240,000 of all three models were made.

This was the .32 'pocket' version of the hammerless safety design and is sometimes referred to as the 'New Departure' model. Its full name is the Pocket Safety Hammerless (2nd model). Three versions were made; the first model used a press-stud on the top strap to unlock the frame; the 2nd and 3rd models used the two knurled studs

Specification & Operation

Cartridge:
.32 S&W

Dimensions:
Length o/a: 165mm
Barrel: 76mm
Weight: 400g
Rifling: 5 grooves, rh
Chambers: 5

In production: 1902-37

Markings:
'S&W' Monogram on right rear side of frame. '*.38 S&W CTG' on left side of barrel.

Safety:
Grip safety let into the backstrap of the butt which prevents movement of the hammer unless pressed in.

Unloading:
Grasp the two knurled buttons above the standing breech, pull back and up. This will unlock the frame latch and pivot the barrel/cylinder assembly about its pivot on the frame, so raising the rear of the cylinder. A cam forces out an extractor plate to empty the chambers. Once emptied, swing the barrel up with sufficient force to snap the frame latch into engagement.

Smith & Wesson Military & Police (Model 10) USA

This began production in 1899 and, with improvements and modifications, has continued to the present day. Prior to 1902 the ejector rod was unsupported at its front end; after that date the familiar socket was used, supporting the ejector rod at the front end. Production stopped in 1942, about 800,000 having been made, and

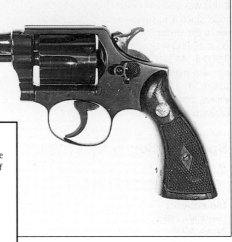

Specification & Operation

Cartridge:
.38 Special

Dimensions:
Length o/a: 235mm
Barrel: 101mm
Weight: 865g
Rifling: 5 grooves rh
Chambers: 6

In service dates: 1899-

Markings:
`MADE IN U.S.A./MARCA REGISTRADA/SMITH & WESSON/SPRINGFIELD MASS' on right side of frame. `S&W' monogram right side of frame

below hammer. `SMITH & WESSON' on right side of barrel. `.38 S&W SPECIAL CTG' on right side of barrel. Serial number on bottom of butt grip.

Safety:
There is no safety device on this revolver.

Unloading:
Press forward the thumb-catch on the left side of the frame, behind the cylinder. This releases the cylinder which can then be swung out to the left side on its crane. Push back on the ejector rod and a central ejector plate emerges from the cylinder to remove the cases from the chambers. Release the ejector rod, swing the cylinder back into the frame until it locks safe.

was resumed after the war as the `Model 10'. Various barrel lengths have been produced, from two to 6.5 inches, though four and five inches appear to have been the most popular. An `Airweight' model, with alloy frame, appeared in 1952 (Model 12) and a stainless model in 1970 (Model 64).

Smith & Wesson New Century Hand Ejector USA

The flagship of the S&W line in its day, this was also called the 'Triple Lock' model since it incorporated a third cylinder lock in the shroud beneath the barrel. About 20,000 were made in all, over 13,000 in .44 S&W calibre. Small numbers were also made in .45 Colt, .44 S&W Russian, .450 Eley and .44-40 Winchester calibres, and 5000 were made in .455 Webley for the British Army in 1915-17.

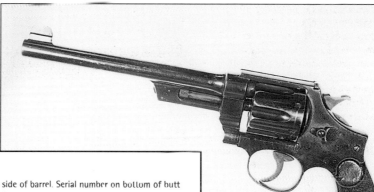

Specification & Operation

Cartridge:
.44 S&W Special and others (see remarks)

Dimensions:
Length o/a: 298mm
Barrel: 165mm
Weight: 1075g
Rifling: 5 grooves, rh
Chambers: 6

In production: 1907-15

Markings:
'SMITH & WESSON SPRINGFIELD MASS USA' and patent dates on top of barrel. 'S&W DA 44' on left side of barrel. Serial number on bottom of butt frame.

Safety:
There is no safety device on this revolver.

Unloading:
Press forward the thumb-catch on the left side of the frame, behind the cylinder. This releases the cylinder which can then be swung out to the left side on its crane. Push back on the ejector rod and a central ejector plate emerges from the cylinder to remove the cases from the chambers. Release the ejector rod, swing the cylinder back into the frame until it locks.

Smith & Wesson US Model 1917 USA

The Model 1917, like the similar Colt, was a standard S&W product (the .45 Hand Ejector) modified to accept the .45 automatic pistol cartridge for the sake of ammunition commonality. The cartridges were loaded into semi-circular clips, three at a time, and two clips loaded the cylinder. It is possible to load the cartridges without the clips, and they will chamber satisfactorily, being held at

Specification & Operation

Cartridge:
.45 Auto Colt

Dimensions:
Length o/a: 274mm
Barrel: 140mm
Weight: 1020g
Rifling: 6 grooves, rh
Chambers: 6

In service dates: 1917-45

Markings:
'SMITH & WESSON SPRINGFIELD MASS USA' and patent dates on top of barrel. 'S&W DA 45' on left side of barrel. Serial number on bottom of butt frame.

Safety:
There is no safety device on this revolver.

Unloading:
Press forward the thumb-catch on the left side of the frame, behind the cylinder. This releases the cylinder which can then be swung out to the left side on its crane. Push back on the ejector rod and a central ejector plate emerges from the cylinder to remove the cases from the chambers. Release the ejector rod, swing the cylinder back into the frame until it locks.

the correct point by a slight step in the chamber. But they will not eject without the clip. The pistol was released to the commercial market in the 1920s and a special cartridge with a thick rim, to reproduce the thickness of the clip and so fill the space between the cylinder and the standing breech, was made under the name `.45 Auto Rim', but this has been obsolete for many years.

Smith & Wesson .38/200 British service

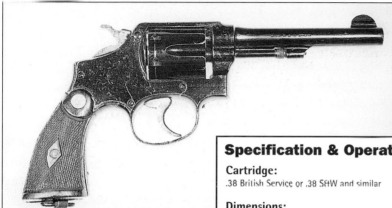

and early orders were filled with a mixture of 4, 5 and 6 inch barrel models. All were blued and polished, with chequered butts and S&W medallions. After April 1942 production was standardised on a 5 inch barrel, sand-blast blue finish and plain walnut butt grips.

Like the M1917, this was another standard commercial model (the Military & Police) modified to meet a British order. The only difference between it and the M&P is the dimensioning of the chamber for the British service .38 200-grain round; this dimension is such that the standard .38 S&W and .38 Colt New Police cartridges will also fit. About 890,000 were made,

Specification & Operation

Cartridge:
.38 British Service or .38 S&W and similar

Dimensions:
Length o/a: 258mm
Barrel: 127mm
Weight: 680g
Rifling: 5 grooves, rh
Chambers: 6

In service dates: 1940-54

Markings:
'SMITH & WESSON' on left side of barrel. 'UNITED STATES PROPERTY' on left side of top strap, above cylinder. Serial number at bottom of butt frame.

Safety:
There is no safety device on this revolver.

Unloading:
Press forward the thumb-catch on the left side of the frame, behind the cylinder. This releases the cylinder which can then be swung out to the left side on its crane. Push back on the ejector rod and a central ejector plate emerges from the cylinder to remove the cases from the chambers. Release the ejector rod, swing the cylinder back into the frame until it locks.

Smith & Wesson Model 29 & 629 USA

Smith & Wesson launched the carbon steel 'N' frame Model 29 as the first .44 Magnum revolver in 1955. In 1972 it won a awesome reputation as the 'Most Powerful Handgun In The World' following its discovery by Hollywood. The stainless steel equivalent, the Model 629 was first produced in 1979. Both models have been made in a number of styles

Specification & Operation

Cartridge:
.44 Magnum (& .44 Spl)

Dimensions: With 219mm (8.5/8" barrel) –
Length o/a: 353mm
Barrel: 219mm (also available with 153mm (6") and 102mm (4") barrel)
Weight: 1459g
Rifling: 6 grooves rh
Magazine capacity: 6

In production: 1955 - (Model 629 1979 -)

Markings:
SMITH & WESSON on left of barrel, 44 MAGNUM on the right of the barrel, Smith & Wesson motif on right of frame behind recoil shield, MADE IN USA, MARCAS REGISTRADAS SMITH & WESSON, SPRINGFIELD, MASS on right of frame below cylinder, model number and serial number on frame under cylinder crane.

Safety:
Trigger retracted hammer block.

Unloading:
The cylinder latch is on the left of the frame behind the cylinder. Push cylinder latch forwards, swing out the cylinder to the left, eject any live or spent cartridges by pushing the cylinder ejector rod to the rear.

and barrel lengths, the early versions only having a shrouded ejector rod. Recent production models designated the Model 629 Classic have the ejector rod shroud extended into a full length barrel under-lug. A lightweight barrel model known as the Mountain Gun has a 4" barrel.

Smith & Wesson 586/686 USA

The 'L' frame Smith & Wesson .357 Magnums in blued carbon steel (Model 586) and stainless steel (Model 686) have been among their fastest selling revolvers since their introduction and are available in a wide range of barrel lengths. Their heavy medium frame with heavy barrel lug have contributed to low recoil and good

Specification & Operation

Cartridge:
.357 Magnum (&.38 S&W Spl)

Dimensions: With 219mm (8.5/8" barrel) –
Length o/a: 351mm
Barrel: 219mm (also available with 153mm (6"), 102mm (4") and 63.5mm (2.1/2") barrels)
Weight: 1502g
Rifling: 6 grooves rh
Magazine capacity: 6

In production: 1981 -

Markings:
SMITH & WESSON on left of barrel, S.&W. 357

MAGNUM on the right of the barrel, Smith & Wesson motif on left of frame behind recoil shield, MADE IN USA, MARCAS REGISTRADAS SMITH & WESSON, SPRINGFIELD, MASS on right of frame below cylinder, model number and serial number on frame under cylinder crane.

Safety:
Trigger retracted hammer block.

Unloading:
The cylinder latch is on the left of the frame behind the cylinder. Push cylinder latch forwards, swing out the cylinder to the left, eject any live or spent cartridges by pushing the cylinder ejector rod to the rear.

reliability even when used continuously with full power ammunition.

clips reloading is extremely swift. The success of the 'Model of 1987' limited edition as a moderately powerful and reliable double-action revolver prompted Smith & Wesson to change the 625 to a catalogued product known as the Model of 1988.

The stainless steel 'N' frame Model 625 was introduced in 1987 as a limited edition of 5000 based on a carbon steel revolver made in 1917 for use with the rimless .45 ACP pistol cartridge. The ammunition is secured in 'half moon' three round clips or 'full moon' six round clips before inserting into the cylinder. With a quantity of prepared full moon

Specification & Operation

Cartridge:
.45 ACP

Dimensions:
Length o/a: 264mm
Barrel: 127mm
Weight: 1274g
Rifling: 6 grooves rh
Magazine capacity: 6

In production: 1987 -

Markings:
SMITH & WESSON on left of barrel, 45 CAL MODEL OF 1988 on the right of the barrel, Smith & Wesson motif on right of frame behind recoil shield, MADE IN USA, MARCAS REGISTRADAS SMITH & WESSON, SPRINGFIELD, MASS on right of frame below cylinder, model number and serial number on frame under cylinder crane.

Safety:
Trigger retracted hammer block.

Unloading:
The cylinder latch is on the left of the frame behind the cylinder. Push cylinder latch forwards, swing out the cylinder to the left, eject any live or spent cartridges by pushing the cylinder ejector rod to the rear.

Smith & Wesson Model 60 USA

The 'J' frame Smith & Wesson Model 60 was the first stainless steel revolver produced anywhere in the world. Designed to combat the corrosion found on blued carbon steel firearms which are carried close to the body, the Model 60 was based on the popular Model 36 'Chief's Special'.

Specification & Operation

Cartridge:
.38 S&W Spl

Dimensions: With 76mm (3") barrel
Length o/a: 191mm
Barrel: 76mm (also available with 63.5mm (2.1/2") barrel)
Weight: 694g
Rifling. 8 grooves rh
Magazine capacity: 5

In production: 1965 -

Markings:
SMITH & WESSON on left of barrel, .38 S&W SPL on the right of the barrel, Smith & Wesson motif on right of frame behind recoil shield, MADE IN USA, MARCAS REGISTRADAS SMITH & WESSON, SPRINGFIELD, MASS on right of frame below cylinder, model number and serial number on frame under cylinder crane.

Safety:
Trigger retracted hammer block.

Unloading:
The cylinder latch is on the left of the frame behind the cylinder. Push cylinder latch forwards, swing out the cylinder to the left, eject any live or spent cartridges by pushing the cylinder ejector rod to the rear.

Smith & Wesson 36 'Chiefs Special' USA

Smith & Wesson's steel framed Model 36 Chief's Special was the first of their small 'J' frame five-shot double-action revolvers. The name originated at a police officers' conference held in Colorado in 1950 where the revolver was first shown publicly. J frame Chiefs' Special derivatives include the shrouded hammer Model 38 Bodyguard Airweight and Model 49

Specification & Operation

Cartridge:
.38 S&W Spl

Dimensions: With 76mm (3") barrel
Length o/a: 191mm
Barrel: 76mm (also available with 63.5mm (2.1/2") barrel)
Weight: 694g
Rifling: 6 grooves rh
Magazine capacity: 5

In production: 1950 -

Markings:
SMITH & WESSON on left of barrel, .38 S&W SPL on the right of the barrel, Smith & Wesson motif on right of frame behind recoil shield, MADE IN USA, MARCAS REGISTRADAS SMITH & WESSON, SPRINGFIELD, MASS on right of frame below cylinder, model number and serial number on frame under cylinder crane.

Safety:
Trigger retracted hammer block.

Unloading:
The cylinder latch is on the left of the frame behind the cylinder. Push cylinder latch forwards, swing out the cylinder to the left, eject any live or spent cartridges by pushing the cylinder ejector rod to the rear.

Bodyguard along with the Model 40 and Model 42 enclosed hammer double-action only Centennials. In 1989 the J frame range were repackaged as 'LadySmith' revolvers and gained more barrel and grip options

Taurus 76 BRAZIL

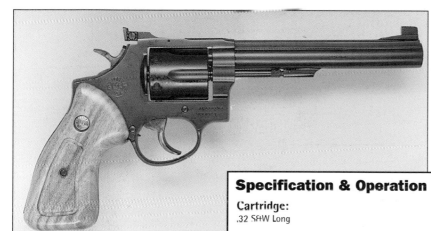

Primarily a target revolver with a Patridge frontsight and adjustable rearsight, the Taurus Model 76 is built on a medium frame the equivalent of Smith & Wesson's 'K' frame revolvers of which is an external copy. Internal parts of the trigger group are different however with a coil mainspring, floating firing pin and transfer bar safety.

Specification & Operation

Cartridge:
.32 S&W Long

Dimensions:
Length o/a: 284mm
Barrel: 155mm
Weight: 1190g
Rifling: 5 grooves rh
Magazine capacity: 6

Markings:
TAURUS BRASIL on left of barrel, .32 LONG on right of barrel, serial number and MADE IN BRAZIL on right of frame below front of cylinder, TAURUS BRASIL in circle with bull's head motif inside on right of frame behind recoil shield.

Safety:
Trigger operated transfer bar to transmit hammer force to floating firing pin.

Unloading:
The cylinder latch is on the left of the frame behind the cylinder. Push cylinder latch forwards, swing out the cylinder to the left, eject any live or spent cartridges by pushing the cylinder ejector rod to the rear.

Taurus 669 BRAZIL

M ade in two barrel lengths, each with a full length underlug, the Taurus Model 669 is built on a medium frame the equivalent of Smith & Wesson's 'K' frame revolvers of which is an external copy. Internal parts of the trigger group are different however with a coil mainspring, floating firing pin and transfer bar safety. A rugged, forged .357 Magnum double-action revolver with adjustable sights.

Specification & Operation

Cartridge:
.357 Magnum

Dimensions: With 155mm (6") barrel
Length o/a: 284mm
Barrel: 155mm (102mm (4") barrel also available)
Weight: 1190g
Rifling: 5 grooves rh
Magazine capacity: 6

Markings:
TAURUS BRASIL on left of barrel, .357 MAGNUM on right of barrel, serial number and MADE IN BRAZIL on right of frame below front of cylinder, TAURUS BRASIL in circle with bull's head motif inside on right of frame behind recoil shield.

Safety:
Trigger operated transfer bar to transmit hammer force to floating firing pin.

Unloading:
The cylinder latch is on the left of the frame behind the cylinder. Push cylinder latch forwards, swing out the cylinder to the left, eject any live or spent cartridges by pushing the cylinder ejector rod to the rear.

Taurus 441 BRAZIL

An unusual .44 S&W Special calibre double-action built on a medium frame the equivalent of Smith & Wesson's 'K' frame revolvers of which is an external copy. Internal parts of the trigger group are different however with a coil mainspring, floating firing pin and transfer bar safety. The medium frame size can only accommodate five rounds of .44 Special which has around half the

Specification & Operation

Cartridge:
.44 S&W Special

Dimensions: With 155mm (6") barrel
Length o/a: 284mm
Barrel: 155mm
Weight: 1140g
Rifling: 5 grooves rh
Magazine capacity: 5

In production: 1993 -

Markings:
TAURUS BRASIL on left of barrel, .44 SPECIAL on right of barrel, serial number and MADE IN BRAZIL on right of frame below front of cylinder, TAURUS BRASIL in circle with bull's head motif inside on right of frame behind recoil shield.

Safety:
Trigger operated transfer bar to transmit hammer force to floating firing pin.

Unloading:
The cylinder latch is on the left of the frame behind the cylinder. Push cylinder latch forwards, swing out the cylinder to the left, eject any live or spent cartridges by pushing the cylinder ejector rod to the rear.

muzzle energy of .44 Magnum but is still a very powerful and accurate cartridge.

Webley .320 Pocket Hammerless UK

In addition to being chambered for the .320 revolver cartridge, these pistols could also be chambered and regulated for the .32 Long or Short Colt or .32 Smith & Wesson cartridges if desired. Nickel plating and mother-of-pearl grips are also to be found. Although produced for several years, it is doubtful if more than 10,000 were made, but they still turn up quite regularly.

Specification & Operation

Cartridge:
.320 Revolver, or similar cartridges

Dimensions:
Length o/a: 178mm
Barrel: 76mm
Weight: 480g
Rifling: 7 grooves, rh
Chambers: 6

In production: 1901-36

Markings:
'WEBLEY'S PATENT' and serial number on right side of frame.

Safety:
A sliding manual safety catch is fitted over the hammer position. Sliding this back locks the hammer and exposes the word `SAFE'.

Unloading:
Press down the thumb catch on the left side of the frame, so withdrawing the stirrup lock and allowing the top strap to rise. Hinge down the barrel, and the ejector plate will be forced out, ejecting the contents of the chambers. Hinge the barrel back until the top strap locks beneath the stirrup catch once more.

Webley .38 Pocket Pistol No 3 UK

A popular weapon (it cost £3 when introduced) some 55,000 were made. Although primarily intended for commercial sale, numbers went to government and police agencies and various additional markings can be found. Longer barrels and adjustable sights could

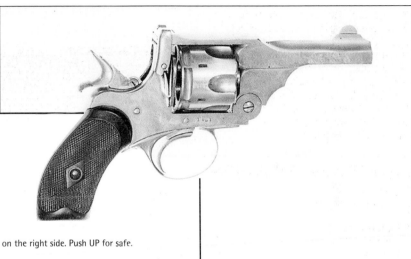

Specification & Operation

Cartridge:
.38 S&W

Dimensions:
Length o/a: 205mm
Barrel: 76mm
Weight: 540g
Rifling: 7 grooves, rh
Chambers: 6

In production: 1090-1939

Markings:
'WEBLEY'S PATENT' and serial number on right side of frame. 'MK III .38' on left side of top strap.

Safety:
An optional extra, in which case it is a small lever on the right side. Push UP for safe.

Unloading:
Press down the thumb catch on the left side of the frame, so withdrawing the stirrup lock and allowing the top strap to rise. Hinge down the barrel, and the ejector plate will be forced out, ejecting the contents of the chambers. Hinge the barrel back until the top strap locks beneath the stirrup catch once more.

also be provided, and there is also a rare variation with no trigger guard and a folding trigger. Small numbers of a version in .32 calibre were also made; this can be easily recognised by the cylinder having the front half of slightly smaller diameter than the rear half.

Webley Mark IV service revolver UK

This revolver was widely issued during the South African War and a total of 36,700 were made before production stopped in 1904. It was also sold on the commercial market, where it could be provided with 3, 5 or 6 inch barrels as well as the service 4 inch type. The changes between the earlier Mark III pistol and this one were small improvements found desirable by reports

Specification & Operation

Cartridge:
.455 British Service

Dimensions:
Length o/a: 235mm
Barrel: 102mm
Weight: 1020g
Rifling: 7 grooves, rh
Chambers: 6

In service dates: 1899-

Markings:
'MARK IV' on left side of top strap, above cylinder. '455/476' on left side of barrel lug in front of cylinder. 'WEBLEY PATENTS' and winged bullet trademark on left side of frame below cylinder. Serial number right side of frame above trigger.

Safety:
There is no safety device on this revolver.

Unloading:
Press down the thumb-catch alongside the hammer to release the 'stirrup lock' above the standing breech, and hinge the barrel down to expose the cylinder. This will cause the extractor plate to come out of the cylinder and extract any rounds or cases. Once clear, raise the barrel until the top strap engages with the stirrup lock once more.

from users, such as a lighter hammer, improved cylinder catch and locks and so on. It is still quite recognisably a Webley.

Webley Mark 5 service revolver

The Mark V differed from the Mark IV by having a slightly larger and stronger cylinder to withstand the additional force generated by smokeless powder cartridges; previous models had been developed around the existing black powder designs, but Cordite had been adopted during the life of the Mark IV pistol, and Webley's felt it better to be on the safe side. It is notable that many

Specification & Operation

Cartridge:
.455 British Service

Dimensions:
Length o/a: 235mm
Barrel: 102mm
Weight: 1005g
Rifling: 7 grooves, rh
Chambers: 6

In service dates: 1913-

Markings:
'WEBLEY/MARK V/PATENTS' on left side of frame below cylinder. 'MARK V' on left side of top strap

above cylinder. Serial number right side of frame above trigger.

Safety:
There is no safety device on this revolver.

Unloading:
Press down the thumb-catch alongside the hammer to release the 'stirrup lock' above the standing breech, and hinge the barrel down to expose the cylinder. This will cause the extractor plate to come out of the cylinder and extract any rounds or cases. Once clear, raise the barrel until the top strap engages with the stirrup lock once more.

earlier revolvers, on repair, were fitted with the Mark V cylinder, which necessitated machining away some of the frame to allow it to fit. These cylinders can be recognised by the rear edge being radiused, whereas previous cylinders had a sharp edge.

Webley Mark 6 service revolver UK

The last of the Webley service designs. It generally resembles earlier models but brought together various refinements. Main visual change is the square butt instead of the bird's head pattern of the Mark V pistol. Note that it is possible to find peculiar variants; in .450 or .45ACP calibre, Mark VI frames with Mark IV or V barrels, Mark V frames with Mark VI barrels and so forth. These

Specification & Operation

Cartridge:
.455 British Service

Dimensions:
Length o/a: 286mm
Barrel: 152mm
Weight: 1090g
Rifling: 7 grooves, rh
Chambers: 6

In service dates: 1915-45

Markings:
`WEBLEY/MARK VI/PATENTS.[year]'` on left side of frame below cylinder. `MARK VI'` on left side of top strap above cylinder. Serial number right side of frame above trigger.

Safety:
There is no safety device on this revolver.

Unloading:
Press down the thumb-catch alongside the hammer to release the 'stirrup lock' above the standing breech, and hinge the barrel down to expose the cylinder. This will cause the extractor plate to come out of the cylinder and extract any rounds or cases. Once clear, raise the barrel until the top strap engages with the stirrup lock once more.

were made by Webley to meet particular orders, or, in the case of the Mk V frame/Mk VI barrel combination, represented early production models. Although officially obsolescent after the introduction of the .38 Enfield revolver, many remained in use until well after World War Two.

Webley .38 Mark IV service revolver UK

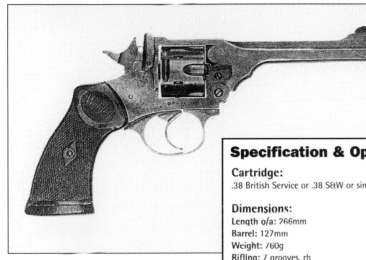

was based on the Webley design - only in its lockwork and some minor details, and the two can be easily confused at first glance. A target model, with adjustable backsight, was also sold commercially.

W eblcy developed this revolver to meet the British requirement for a .38 model, but the Army chose the Enfield design, and therefore Webley produced this commercially. But in World War Two over 100,000 were taken by the British Army and remained in use until 1956. It differs from the Enfield - which

Specification & Operation

Cartridge:
.38 British Service or .38 S&W or similar

Dimensions:
Length o/a: 266mm
Barrel: 127mm
Weight: 760g
Rifling: 7 grooves, rh
Chambers: 6

In service dates: 1929-56

Markings:
'MARK IV .38 145/200' on left side of top strap, above cylinder. Webley 'winged bullet' trademark or 'PAT 186131' on right side of frame, below

cylinder. Serial number on right side of frame below cylinder.

Safety:
There is no safety device on this revolver.

Unloading:
Press down the thumb-catch alongside the hammer to release the 'stirrup lock' above the standing breech, and hinge the barrel down to expose the cylinder. This will cause the extractor plate to come out of the cylinder and extract any rounds or cases. Once clear, raise the barrel until the top strap engages with the stirrup lock once more.

Webley RIC revolver UK

One of the most popular of Webley designs, this went through a number of changes in its long life, but the weapon was always a heavy calibre, short-barrel, heavy weapon with a good-sized grip, intended for official use. As well as its employment by the Royal Irish Constabulary, from which came its name,

Specification & Operation

Cartridge:
.442, .450, .455 .476

Dimensions:
Length o/a: 229mm
Barrel: 114mm
Weight: 850g
Rifling: 5 grooves, rh
Chambers: 6

In production: 1868-1939

Markings:
Crown and `RIC' on the chamber flat, left side in front of cylinder on official weapons.
'WEBLEY'S PATENT' on left side of frame, later models have the Winged Bullet trademark. Serial number on right or left side of frame.
Both service and commercial models will be found carrying the names of the gunmakers who sold the pistol; many police forces purchased locally and not directly from the factory.

Safety:
There is no applied safety device on these revolvers.

Unloading:
Open loading gate on right side, behind cylinder; withdraw ejector rod from its position inside the cylinder axis, swing the rod sideways to line up with the chamber and force it back to eject the contents. Repeat for each chamber in turn, revolving the cylinder by hand.

it was also used by many British and colonial police forces and enjoyed wide commercial sale. It was also widely copied in Belgium and Germany.

Webley .455 WG model UK

These revolvers were due to a new Webley designer, Michael Kautman, and his initials and a number are stamped on, largely to ensure that he got his royalties for every pistol. Many improvements which later became standard on other Webley designs first appear on this model, and it was widely

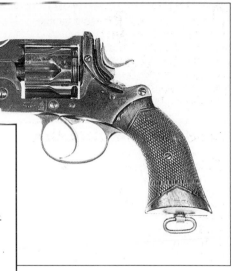

Specification & Operation

Cartridge:
.455 Webley

Dimensions:
Length o/a: 286mm
Barrel: 152mm
Weight: 1138g
Rifling: 7 grooves, rh
Chambers: 6

In service dates: 1885 - 1912

Markings:
'WEBLEY PATENTS' and Winged Bullet on left side of frame. Calibre of cartridge on left side of barrel assembly, in front of cylinder. Serial number on right side of frame. 'WG MODEL' and year on left side of top strap. The letters 'MK' in a triangle, together with a number will be found on the right side of the frame.

Safety:
There is no applied safety device on this revolver.

Unloading:
Press down the thumb-catch alongside the hammer to release the 'stirrup lock' above the standing breech, and hinge the barrel down to expose the cylinder. This will cause the extractor plate to come out of the cylinder and extract any rounds or cases. Once clear, raise the barrel until the top strap engages with the stirrup lock once more.

bought by British officers and travellers going to the wilder parts of the world in those days. The WG is generally held to mean 'Webley Government' model, though others say it means 'Webley-Green', Green being the original designer of the stirrup lock.

Webley-Wilkinson UK

The Wilkinson Sword Company had provided British officers with swords for years, and in the 1880s decided that the sword was on the way out and that revolvers were a better protection. They therefore asked Webleys to make them a superlative revolver to sell to officers who, under the regulations of the time, could purchase whatever they wanted so long as it fired the service .455 cartridge.

Specification & Operation

Cartridge:
.455 British Service or .450

Dimensions:
Length o/a: 289mm
Barrel: 152mm
Weight: 920g
Rifling: 7 grooves, rh
Chambers: 6

In production: 1884-1914

Markings:
'WILKINSON WEBLEY' on left side of top strap.
Cartridge type on barrel flat in front of cylinder.

Safety:
There is no applied safety device on this revolver.

Unloading:
Press down the thumb-catch alongside the hammer to release the 'stirrup lock' above the standing breech, and hinge the barrel down to expose the cylinder. This will cause the extractor plate to come out of the cylinder and extract any rounds or cases. Once clear, raise the barrel until the top strap engages with the stirrup lock once more.

The W-W went through a number of variations in its life - the model shown here is that of 1905 - but all are marked with the name and those sold commercially may be of other heavy calibres such as .450 or .476

Webley-Fosbery automatic revolver UK

The Webley-Fosbery was based on the standard Webley Mark V service revolver and operates on recoil; the cylinder and barrel unit recoil across the top of the butt frame, and a stud in the frame engages the zig-zag grooves in the cylinder to rotate it to the next chamber. The recoil movement also cocks the hammer. Apart from this, it is a

Specification & Operation

Cartridge:
.455 British Service

Dimensions:
Length o/a: 280mm
Barrel: 152mm
Weight: 1240g
Rifling: 7 grooves, rh
Chambers: 6

In production: 1901-15

Markings:
'WEBLEY-FOSBERY AUTOMATIC' on right side of top strap above cylinder. Webley winged bullet trademark and '.455 CORDITE ONLY' on left side of frame below cylinder.
Serial number on right side of frame above trigger.

Safety:
Manual safety catch on right side of frame above the butt grip. UP for safe.

Unloading:
Press down the thumb-catch alongside the hammer to release the 'stirrup lock' above the standing breech, and hinge the barrel down to expose the cylinder. This will cause the extractor plate to come out of the cylinder and extract any rounds or cases. Once clear, raise the barrel until the top strap engages with the stirrup lock once more.

conventional double-action revolver. Pleasant to fire, it was a notably accurate weapon, but proved to be too sensitive to mud and dirt for active service in France, and since it was never an officially-adopted weapon, production came to a stop in 1915 and was never resumed.

Weihrauch HW-9 GERMANY

This is actually a .38 frame carrying a .22 barrel, which makes for a heavy pistol of good accuracy. An inexpensive weapon, it and its various derivatives (different barrel lengths, sights and grips) are highly popular throughout Europe .

Specification & Operation

Cartridge:
.22LR

Dimensions:
Length o/a: 295mm
Barrel: 150mm
Weight: 1100g
Rifling: 8 grooves, rh
Chambers: 6

In production: 1970-

Markings:
Warrior's head trademark or `ARMINIUS' or both, and `HW9' on left side of frame. Serial number on right side of frame. `CAL .22 LR' on left side of barrel.

Safety:
There is no applied safety device on this revolver.

Unloading:
Grasp the sleeve surrounding the ejector rod beneath the barrel and pull it forward to unlock the cylinder, which will then swing out to the left on a crane. Push the ejector rod back so as to eject the contents of the chambers, then swing the cylinder back into the frame, where it will lock and the spring sleeve will re-engage.

SUB-MACHINE GUNS

AKSU-74 RUSSIA

This weapon first saw action in Afghanistan in 1982. It is simply a shortened version of the standard AK 74 rifle, intended for use by armoured troops, special forces and others requiring a more compact weapon. There is a bulbous muzzle attachment which compensates for firing a rifle cartridge in a much shorter barrel than that for which it was originally designed. The

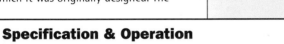

Specification & Operation

Cartridge:
5.45 x 39.5mm Soviet

Dimensions:
Length, stock extended: 730mm;
Length, stock retracted: 490mm
Barrel: 206.5mm
Rifling: 4 grooves, rh
Weight, empty: 2.70kg
Magazine capacity: 30 rounds
Rate of fire: 700 rds/min

In production: 1975-

Markings:
Factory identification, serial number and year of manufacture on left side of receiver.

Safety:
Manual safety catch/fire selector on right side of receiver; UP for safe, central for automatic fire, DOWN for single shots.

Unloading:
Magazine catch in front of trigger guard. Remove magazine, pull back cocking lever on right side of receiver to eject any round in the chamber, examine chamber through the ejection port, release cocking lever, pull trigger.

design has been copied in Yugoslavia, though chambered for the 5.56mm NATO cartridge and probably intended for export rather than for adoption by local forces.

Austen Mk I AUSTRALIA

Made In Australia between 1942 and 1945, about 20,000 total. Operation is blowback, the design being a combination of British Sten and German MP40; the folding stock, bolt and telescoping mainspring are from the MP40, the remainder from the Sten. An excellent weapon, it never achieved the popularity of the rival Owen and did not survive long after the war, though it remained in reserve until the mid-1950s.

Specification & Operation

Cartridge:
9mm Parabellum

Dimensions:
Length, stock extended: 732mm
Length, stock retracted: 552mm
Barrel: 198mm
Rifling: 6 grooves, rh
Weight, empty: 3.98kg
Magazine capacity: 28 rounds
Rate of fire: 500 rds/min

In production: 1952-55

Markings:
'AUSTEN' with serial number above chamber.

Safety:
To render this weapon safe the cocking handle is pulled to the rear and then turned up into a cut-out in the rear of the cocking handle slot in the receiver. A fire selector button above the trigger passes through the receiver. The right-hand end is marked 'AUTO' and when the button is pushed in, towards the left of the receiver, the weapon fires automatic. The left-hand end is marked 'SINGLE', and when this end is pushed in the weapon fires single shots.

Beretta 1938A ITALY

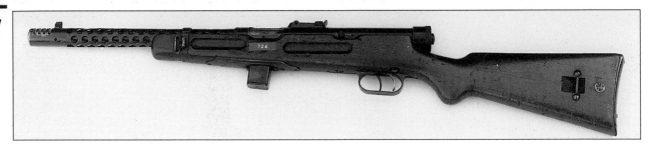

An excellent and well-made weapon, used by the Italian, German, Romanian and Argentine armies at various times. There are minor variations in the jacket slots, muzzle brake slots and presence or absence of the selector button on the trigger guard, but all are essentially the same. Two triggers are used; the front trigger fires single shots, the rear trigger gives automatic fire. Early models have a bayonet lug.

Specification & Operation

Cartridge:
9mm Parabellum

Dimensions:
Length o/a: 946mm
Barrel: 315mm
Weight, empty: 4.25kg
Rifling: 6 grooves, rh
Magazine capacity: 10, 20, 30 or 40 roundsRate of fire: 600 rds/min

In production: 1938-50

Markings:
MOSCHETTI AUT-BERETTA Mod 1938A BREVETTO No 828 428 GARDONE V.T. ITALIA and serial on top of receiver.

Safety:
Manual safety catch on left side, above trigger. Push forward to `F' for fire, rearward to `S' for safe. There is also a safety/selector button in the top rear of the trigger-guard: push in from left to lock the automatic-fire trigger and permit only single shots.

Unloading:
Magazine catch is in front of magazine housing. Remove magazine, pull back cocking handle to eject any round in the chamber. Inspect chamber, release cocking handle, pull trigger.

Beretta Model 38/42 ITALY

An improved version of the Model 38, dispensing with the barrel jacket and taking other manufacturing short-cuts for wartime manufacture. It was still a reliable and accurate weapon and was used extensively by German, Italian and Romanian forces during the war and remained in service with several armies for some years afterwards.

The Model 38/49 was similar but with the addition of a cross-bolt safety in the stock, and became very popular in the postwar period, being adopted by German border police and armies in the Middle and Far East.

Specification & Operation

Cartridge:
9mm Parabellum

Dimensions:
Length o/a: 798mm
Barrel: 210mm
Weight, empty: 3.25kg
Rifling: 6 grooves, rh
Magazine capacity: 20 or 40 rounds
Rate of fire: 550 rds/min
In production: 1943-75

Markings:
M.P. "BERETTA" Mod 38/42 Cal 9 and serial number stamped on top of receiver.

Safety:
Manual safety catch on the left side of the receiver, marked 'F' for fire and 'S' for safe. Move the catch to 'S' (rearwards) to make safe. Two triggers; front trigger for single shots, rear trigger for automatic fire.

Unloading:
Magazine catch on magazine housing. Remove magazine, pull back cocking handle to eject any round in the chamber. Inspect chamber, release cocking handle, pull trigger.

Beretta Model 38/44 ITALY

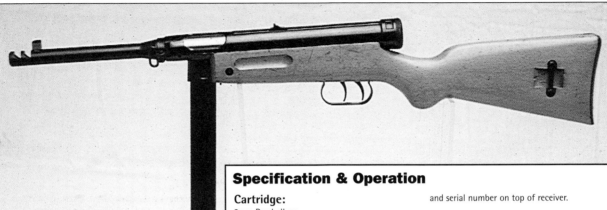

Specification & Operation

Cartridge:
9mm Parabellum

Dimensions:
Length o/a: 798mm
Barrel: 210mm
Weight, empty: 3.98kg
Rifling: 6 grooves, rh
Magazine capacity: 20 or 40 rounds
Rate of fire: 550 rds/min
In production: 1945-55

Markings:
MOSCH. AUTOM. BERETTA MOD 38/A44 CAL 9-

and serial number on top of receiver.

Safety:
Manual safety catch on the left side of the receiver, marked `F' for fire and `S' for safe. Move the catch to `S' (rearwards) to make safe. Two triggers; front trigger for single shots, rear trigger for automatic fire.

Unloading:
Magazine catch on magazine housing. Remove magazine, pull back cocking handle to eject any round in the chamber. Inspect chamber, release cocking handle, pull trigger.

This is a simplified model of the 38/42, differing in the size of the bolt and details of the mainspring. A visual distinction is the absence of the small spring housing which projects from the rear of the receiver in earlier models. This weapon was entirely exported, users being Pakistan, Syria, Costa Rica and Iraq among many others.

Beretta Model 3 ITALY

Although this weapon looks entirely different from the 1938 series which preceded it, the mechanism is the same. This redesign made the weapon cheaper and easier to make, but it was not the success that had been hoped. Its designer, Marengoni, who had designed all Beretta submachine guns from 1918 onwards, retired in 1956. It is not believed that production of the Model 3 reached great numbers. A Model 4, with a folding bayonet, was also developed.

Specification & Operation

Cartridge:
9mm Parabellum

Dimensions:
Length, stock extended: 711mm:
Length, stock retracted: 508mm
Barrel: 200mm
Rifling: 6 grooves, rh
Weight, empty: 3.47kg
Magazine capacity: 20 or 40 rounds
Rate of fire: 550 rds/min

In production: 1956-59

Markings:
P.M. BERETTA MOD 3 on top of receiver.

Safety:
There is no manual safety device; a grip safety in the pistol-grip must be pressed in, by grasping the grip, to release the bolt and permit it to be cocked or fired.

Unloading:
Magazine catch on right side of magazine housing. Remove magazine, grasp pistol grip so as to press in the grip safety, and pull back the cocking lever to eject any round in the chamber. Inspect the chamber through the ejection port, release the cocking handle, press trigger.

Beretta Model 12 ITALY

The Model 12 is considerably different to earlier Beretta submachine guns, due to the retirement of the designer Marengoni in 1956 and the appearance of a new designer, Salza. It is primarily made of metal stampings and uses a 'telescoping' or 'overhung' bolt which wraps around the barrel and thus reduces the length of the weapon. It has a front hand grip and the stock may be a

Specification & Operation

Cartridge:
9mm Parabellum

Dimensions:
Length, stock extended: 645mm
Length, stock folded: 418mm
Barrel: 200mm
Rifling: 6 grooves, rh
Weight, empty: 3.0kg
Magazine capacity: 20, 30, 40 rounds
Rate of fire: 550 rds/min
In production: 1959-78

Markings:
P.M. BERETTA Mod 12-Cal 9/m Parabellum and serial number on top of receiver

Safety:
There is a grip safety let into the rear of the pistol grip, which must be pressed in to unlock the bolt for either cocking or firing. A push-button safety catch above the grip on the left side, when pushed in, locks the grip safety in the safe position.

Unloading:
Magazine catch behind the magazine housing. Remove magazine, grasp the grip and press in the grip safety, pull back the bolt. Inspect the chamber, release the bolt, press the trigger.

hinged, tubular metal type folding around to the right side of the weapon, or a detachable wooden type. The Model 12 was adopted by the Italian forces in 1961 and by various South American and African countries. It has also been made under licence in Brazil and Indonesia.

Beretta Model 12S ITALY

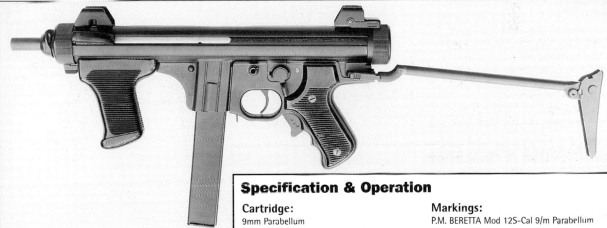

This is a 'product improved' version of the Model 12; the improvements consisted of altering the safety system to a more positive and somewhat easier arrangement, improving the sights, improving the attachment of the receiver rear cap and improving the mechanism of the folding stock. It superseded the Model 12 in Italian service and has been exported to several armies.

Specification & Operation

Cartridge:
9mm Parabellum

Dimensions.
Length, stock extended: 660mm.
Length, stock retracted: 418mm
Barrel: 200mm
Rifling: 6 grooves, rh
Weight, empty: 3.20kg
Magazine capacity: 20, 32 or 40 rounds
Rate of Fire: 550 rds/min

In production: 1978-

Markings:
P.M. BERETTA Mod 12S-Cal 9/m Parabellum and serial number on top of receiver.

Safety:
Manual safety catch on left side of receiver, above the pistol grip. UP for safe, intermediate for single shots, DOWN for automatic fire. There is also a grip safety as per the Model 12.

Unloading:
As for Model 12.

Bergmann MP18 GERMANY

The MP18 was the first submachine gun, developed by Schmeisser in 1916. In its original form it used the 'snail' magazine developed for the Parabellum Long '08 pistol, but in postwar years most were modified to take a straight 20 or 32-round magazine. It was forbidden to the German Army in the 1918-34 period but was extensively used by police and remained in concealed military reserve stocks, to re-appear during World War II.

Specification & Operation

Cartridge:
9mm Parabellum

Dimensions:
Length o/a: 815mm
Barrel: 200mm
Weight, empty: 4.18kg
Rifling: 6 grooves, rh
Magazine capacity: 32 (snail); 20 or 32 (box)
Rate of fire: 450 rds/min

In production: 1916-45

Markings:
`MP 18 I' above chamber. `SYSTEM SCHMEISSER' on straight-magazine modified models. `C.G.HAENEL WAFFENFABRIK SUHL' on left of receiver.

Safety:
Pull cocking handle to rear and turn up into a slot in the receiver cut-out.

Unloading:
Magazine release is a push-button on the magazine housing. Remove magazine, pull back cocking handle, inspect chamber through cocking-handle slot. Release cocking handle, pull trigger.

Bergmann MP28 GERMANY

An improved model of the MP18, this is simply the straight-magazine modification of the MP18 with a new tangent sight, a selector mechanism to allow single shots as well as automatic fire, and some minor internal improvements. Was also made under licence by Pieper of Belgium, copies were made in Spain, and it was widely exported to South America. Portugal had a special model chambered for the 7.65mm Parabellum cartridge, though these are thought to have all been scrapped.

Specification & Operation

Cartridge:
9mm Parabellum

Dimensions:
Length o/a: 812mm
Barrel: 200mm
Weight, empty: 4.0kg
Rifling: 6 grooves, rh
Magazine capacity: 20, 32 or 50 rounds
Rate of fire: 500 rds/min

In production: 1928-38

Markings:
'MP 28 II SYSTEM SCHMEISSER PATENT' over the chamber.

Safety:
Pull cocking handle to rear and turn up into a slot in the receiver cut-out.

Unloading:
Magazine catch on magazine housing. Remove magazine. Pull back cocking handle and make safe. Examine chamber. Release cocking handle from safety slot and press trigger.

BRAZIL MD2A1 BRAZIL

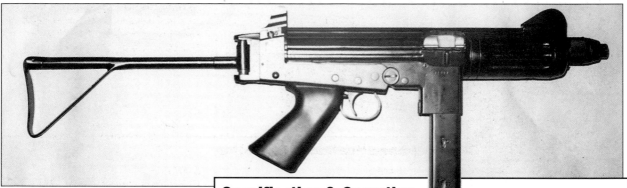

One of the objects behind this design was to produce a submachine gun using as many components of the FN FAL 7.62mm automatic rifle as possible, since that weapon was being produced in Brazil and using its parts would cut production costs. The appearance of the weapon bears this out, particularly the pistol grip and lower receiver; in fact, about 60 percent of the parts are common to the rifle. The design was considered, but not adopted by the Brazilian forces.

Specification & Operation

Cartridge:
9mm Parabellum

Dimensions:
Length, stock extended: 680mm.
Length, stock folded: 430mm
Barrel: 160mm
Rifling: 4 grooves, rh
Weight, empty: 3.18kg
Magazine capacity: 15 or 30 rounds
Rate of fire: 685 rds/min

In production: 1986-

Markings:
FABRICA DE ITAJUBA on right of receiver, IMBEL-MD2A1 9/mm on left.

Safety:
Selector lever on the left side of the receiver, above the pistol grip.   UP position for automatic, central for safe, DOWN for single shots.

Unloading:
Magazine release in magazine housing. Remove magazine, pull back cocking handle, inspect chamber, release cocking handle, pull trigger.

to wrap around that portion of the barrel which is inside the receiver, so that it has a full-length barrel even though only a part of it is visible.

A South African design, used by their army and police and which may yet find its way to other places. The BXP is a versatile weapon which can be fitted with a silencer, a grenade launching attachment, or various types of muzzle compensator. It is made from steel pressings, and the bolt is hollowed out

Specification & Operation

Cartridge:
9mm Parabellum

Dimensions:
Length, stock extended: 607mm.
Length, stock retracted: 387mmBarrel: 208mm
Rifling: 6 grooves, rh
Weight, empty: 2.50kg
Magazine capacity: 22 or 32 rounds
Rate of fire: 1000 rds/min

In production: 1988-

Markings:
G.D.P.S. and serial number on top of receiver.

Safety:
Manual safety catch on the left and right sides of the receiver, above the pistol grip. UP (green dot) for safe, DOWN (red dot) for fire. There is no fire selector; pulling the trigger to its first stop gives single shots; pulling it beyond this point produces automatic fire. There is a safety notch on the bolt which will catch the sear should the bolt be jarred back or should the hand slip during cocking.

Unloading:
Magazine catch in pistol grip. Remove magazine, pull back cocking handle (top of receiver) to eject any round in the chamber. Inspect the chamber through the ejection port. Release cocking handle, pull trigger.

Calico M-960A USA

Specification & Operation

Cartridge:
9mm Parabellum

Dimensions:
Length, stock extended: 835mm.
Length, stock retracted: 647mm
Barrel: 330mm with compensator
Rifling: 6 grooves, rh
Weight, empty: 2.17kg
Magazine capacity: 50 or 100 rounds
Rate of fire: 750 rds/min

In production: 1990-

Markings:
'CALICO M-900' on left side of magazine mounting. Serial number on left side of frame.

Safety:
Selector in the front edge of the trigger guard, with levers on both sides of the weapon. When to the rear, and projecting into the trigger guard, the system is safe. Pushed forward one notch permits single shots, all the way for automatic fire. Safety can be set by using the outside levers, removed by pressing forward with the trigger finger.

Unloading:
Magazine catch on top of receiver. Squeeze in, then remove magazine by withdrawing back and up. Pull back cocking lever to remove any round in the chamber, inspect chamber via the ejection slot, release cocking handle, pull trigger.

One of several similar weapons in the Calico range, the M960A is known as the 'Mini Sub Machine Gun'; there is also a 'Light' model with a solid butt-stock and a 'Concealable' model in which the barrel does not extend beyond the fore-end. All use the same receiver and the same helical-feed magazines. The 50 round magazine is shown here; the 100 round is similar but longer, stretching over the rear end of the receiver.

Carl Gustav 45 SWEDEN

One of the oldest submachine guns still in service, the Carl Gustav is a robust weapon which is likely to last a long time. The original models had no magazine housing and used a drum magazine, but in 1948 a box magazine was developed, leading to all guns being modified by having a magazine housing added. The Carl Gustav is used by the Swedish, Irish and Indonesian armies and was also made under licence in Egypt as the 'Port Said'. A highly modified version, with an integral silencer replacing the usual barrel, was used by US Special Forces in Vietnam.

Specification & Operation

Cartridge:
9mm Parabellum

Dimensions:
Length, stock extended: 808mm.
Length, stock retracted: 552mm
Barrel: 213mm
Rifling: 0 grooves, rh
Weight, empty: 3.90kg
Magazine capacity: 36 rounds
Rate of fire: 600 rds/min

In production: 1945-

Markings:
Serial number on top of receiver.

Safety:
Pull back the cocking handle and turn it up into a notch in the cocking handle slot. When the bolt is forward, it can be locked in place by pushing the cocking handle into the bolt so that its other end passes through the bolt and into a hole in the receiver.

Unloading:
Remove the magazine, pull back the cocking handle. Inspect the chamber, release the cocking handle and press the trigger.

China Type 64 CHINA

The Type 64 has an integral silencer and uses a special cartridge based on the 7.63mm Mauser but with a pointed, heavy bullet fired at subsonic velocity. The mechanism combines the blowback action and bolt of the Soviet PPS-43 submachine gun, the trigger mechanism of the Czech ZB26 machine gun and the silencer is a classical Maxim pattern full of baffles and with a perforated barrel. With the special cartridge it is reasonably silent, but with standard full-charge pistol ammunition it is almost as noisy as an unsilenced weapon.

Specification & Operation

Cartridge:
7.62 x 25mm Type P Subsonic

Dimensions:
Length, stock extended: 843mm.
Length, stock retracted: 635mm
Barrel: 244mm
Rifling: 4 grooves, rh
Weight, empty: 3.40kg
Magazine capacity: 30 rounds
Rate of fire: 1300 rds/min

In production: 1966-

Markings:
Factory identifier and serial on top of receiver.

Safety:
Safety catch on the right side of the receiver: a hinged plate which moves up to block the bolt.

Unloading:
Magazine catch behind magazine. Remove magazine, press down safety plate, pull back cocking handle to eject any round in the chamber. Inspect the chamber via the ejection port, release bolt, press trigger.

China Type 79 CHINA

A somewhat unusual weapon of which full details are not yet known, this is gas operated, using a short-stroke tappet above the barrel which forces back an operating rod to drive a rotating bolt; the system is broadly that of the AK series of rifles, as are the outer controls such as the safety and pistol grip, making it easier to train soldiers already familiar with the rifle. It is remarkably light for a submachine gun, no doubt due to the rotating bolt system which removes the need for the heavy bolt needed in a simple blowback weapon.

Specification & Operation

Cartridge:
7.62 x 25mm Soviet Pistol

Dimensions:
Length, stock extended: 740mm.
Length, stock folded: 470mm
Barrel: 225mm
Rifling: unknown
Weight, empty: 1.9kg
Magazine capacity: 20 rounds
Rate of fire: 650 rds/min

In production: 1980-

Markings:
Factory identifier and serial on top of receiver.

Safety:
Manual safety catch/fire selector on right side of receiver; UP for safe, central for automatic fire, DOWN for single shots.

Unloading:
Magazine catch at front of magazine housing. Remove magazine, pull back cocking lever to eject any round in the chamber. Inspect chamber via ejection port, release cocking lever, press trigger.

Colt USA

indicate which mechanism is in place. It is also possible to have a purely semi-automatic model with no automatic or burst-fire capability.

This is based upon the well-known M16 rifle configuration, so that the training time is greatly reduced when soldiers already familiar with the rifle are given this weapon. The butt-stock is telescoping, and the only outward difference between this and various short M16 type rifles is the thin and long magazine. Note that purchasers had the option of full automatic fire or three-round bursts, and the fire selector switch marking will

Specification & Operation

Cartridge:
9mm Parabellum

Dimensions:
Length, stock extended: 730mm
Length, stock retracted: 650mm
Barrel: 260mm
Weight, empty: 2.59kg
Rifling: 6 grooves, rh
Magazine capacity: 20 or 32 rounds
Rate of fire: 900 rds/min

In production: 1990-

Markings:
Colt 'prancing pony' trademark, `COLT' in script form, `SMG' and serial number on left side of magazine housing.

Safety:
Selector switch on left side above the pistol grip. When the switch is to the rear and its associated pointer to the front, the weapon is safe. With the switch forward and the pointer to the rear, the weapon is set for either automatic fire or three-round bursts. The intermediate position, with the switch down, gives single shots.

Unloading:
Magazine release on both sides of the weapon, a shrouded button on the right and a hinged tab on the left. Press either to remove magazine. Pull back the cocking handle (`wings' at the base of the carrying handle) inspect the chamber via the ejection slot, release bolt, press trigger.

Cristobal DOMINICAN REPUBLIC

The appearance of this weapon is largely due to the Dominican Republic's arms manufacture having been set up by refugee technicians from Italy and Hungary in the post-war period of the late 1940s. Externally it resembles the Beretta 1938 model; internally it has the two-piece bolt and folding magazine of the Danuvia 39M, while it fires the US .30 carbine cartridge which was doubtless easy to come by in that part of the world, even if not notably effective as a combat round.

Specification & Operation

Cartridge:
.30 US Carbine (7.62 x 33)

Dimensions:
Length o/a: 945mm
Barrel: 410mm
Weight, empty: 3.51kg
Rifling: 6 grooves, rh
Magazine capacity: 25 or 30
Rate of fire: 550 rds/min
In production: 1962-70

Markings:
Dominican national badge over chamber. Serial number on right side of receiver.

Safety:
Manual safety catch on left side of receiver, above triggers. Pull to the rear to make safe; this locks the triggers and bolt. The front trigger gives single shots, the rear trigger gives automatic fire.

Unloading:
Magazine release at rear of magazine housing. Remove magazine, place safety catch forward, pull back cocking handle to eject any round in the chamber. Release cocking handle, pull trigger. Apply safety. The magazine can be folded forward, beneath the barrel by pressing a release concealed under the fore-end.

CZ Model 25 CZECHOSLOVAKIA

This is one of a family of four similar weapons; the Model 23 (bottom right) has a wooden stock, the Model 25 (right) a folding stock, and both fire the 9mm Parabellum cartridge. The Model 24 has a wooden stock, the Model 26 a folding stock, and both fire the 7.62mm Soviet pistol cartridge, and will usually fire the 7.63mm Mauser pistol cartridge.

Specification & Operation

Cartridge:
9mm Parabellum

Dimensions:
Length, stock folded: 445mm
Length, stock extended: 686mm.
Barrel: 284mm
Rifling: 6 grooves, RH
Weight, empty: 3.09kg
Magazine capacity: 24 or 40 rounds.
Rate of fire: 600 rds/min

In production: 1949-68 (Czech Army)

Markings:
`ZB 1949 she' with serial number on left side of receiver behind pistol grip.

Safety:
A metal switch inside the trigger guard behind the trigger. Push to the RIGHT to lock the bolt open or closed. Push to the LEFT to fire. For single shots, press the trigger to the first resistance; for automatic fire press the trigger as far as possible.

Unloading:
Press the magazine catch, in the bottom of the pistol-grip, and remove the magazine. Pull back the cocking handle in the top of the receiver to eject Release the bolt, press the trigger.

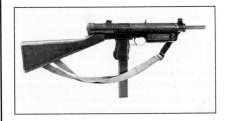

They were produced in large numbers, liberally supplied to revolutionaries and will be found anywhere in the world.

Danuvia 39M 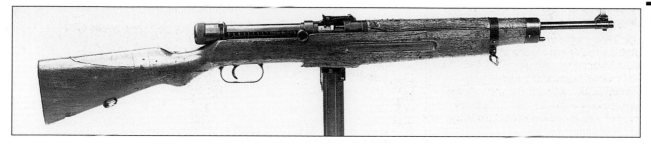HUNGARY

An unusual submachine gun, this looks more like a rifle, particularly when the magazine is folded forward into a recess in the fore-end. It fires the 9mm Mauser cartridge, a powerful round, and with its long barrel has a range and accuracy far greater than any other submachine gun. The mechanism is a delayed blowback using a two-part bolt, very similar to the system used in the current FAMAS 5.56mm rifle. There is an uncommon variation of this weapon which has the wooden butt-stock hinged to fold forward alongside the receiver.

Specification & Operation

Cartridge:
9 x 25mm Mauser 'Export'

Dimensions:
Length o/a: 1048mm
Barrel: 500mm
Rifling: 6 grooves, rh
Weight, empty: 3.40kg
Magazine capacity: 40 rounds
Rate of fire: 750 rds/min

In production: 1938-45

Markings:
'39M' and serial number on left side of chamber.

Safety:
A manual safety catch/fire selector in the form of a knurled ring at the rear of the receiver. Turn the marker to the letter 'Z' on the receiver to make the weapon safe. Turn to 'E' for single shots and to 'S' for automatic fire.

Unloading:
Magazine release on right side of magazine housing. Remove magazine, pull back cocking handle to eject any round in the chamber. Inspect chamber via ejection port, release cocking handle, pull trigger. The lever behind the magazine housing releases the magazine to fold forward into a slot in the fore-end.

Danuvia M43 HUNGARY

This is the same weapon as the Danuvia 39M described above, but with a shorter barrel and a folding stock. The magazine is angled forward, instead of being at right-angles to the receiver, and, as with the 39M, folds forward into a recess; at the same time a spring-loaded cover closes the bottom of the receiver. This version is rather more common than the 39M since more were produced.

Specification & Operation

Cartridge:
9 x 25mm Mauser 'Export'

Dimensions:
Length, stock extended: 953mm
Length, stock folded: 749mm
Barrel: 424mm
Rifling: 6 grooves, rh
Weight, empty: 9.8lb
Magazine capacity: 40 rounds
Rate of fire: 750 rds/min
In production: 1943-45

Markings:
`42M' and serial number on left side of chamber.

Safety:
A manual safety catch/fire selector in the form of a knurled ring at the rear of the receiver. Turn the marker to the letter `Z' on the receiver to make the weapon safe. Turn to `E' for single shots and to `S' for automatic fire.

Unloading:
Magazine release on right side of magazine housing. Remove magazine, pull back cocking handle to eject any round in the chamber. Inspect chamber via ejection port, release cocking handle, pull trigger. The lever behind the magazine housing releases the magazine to fold forward into a slot in the fore-end.

DUX SPAIN

This weapon resembles the Soviet PPS-43, largely because it began life as a design for a Finnish submachine gun copied from it. In 1945 the designer fled to Spain and gave the drawings to a friend at the Spanish arsenal of Oviedo. He sold the idea to the West German Border Police, who ordered 1000. The German army was keen, but doubts over the manufacturing rights caused the army to shy away, and that was the end of the Dux.

Specification & Operation

Cartridge:
9mm Parabellum

Dimensions:
Length, stock extended: 825mm
Length, stock folded: 615mm
Barrel: 250mm Rifling: 6 grooves, rh
Weight, empty: 3.49kg
Magazine capacity: 50 rounds
Rate of fire: 500 rds/min

In production: 1954-65

Markings:
'DUX 53' on left side of receiver, in front of magazine aperture. Serial number right side of receiver.

Safety:
Manual safety catch in front edge of trigger guard. Push backwards to make the weapon safe by locking the bolt in either its rear or forward position. There is no fire selector; the weapon fires only at full automatic.

Unloading:
Magazine catch under the receiver behind the magazine aperture. Remove magazine, pull back bolt to eject any round in the chamber. Inspect chamber through ejection port, release bolt, pull

Erma EMP GERMANY

The last of a series of Erma designs before they developed the MP38, the EMP was produced in some numbers. Although most generally recognised by the unique wooden fore-end grip, small numbers of a model without this grip were produced in about 1935, as well as a limited contract for Yugoslavia which had a longer barrel and mounted a bayonet. As with most designs by Vollmer, the Erma designer, this uses the telescoping mainspring casing which became better known in the MP38. A close copy of the EMP was produced by Poland in 1937-39 in limited numbers and might possibly be encountered.

Specification & Operation

Cartridge:
9mm Parabellum

Dimensions:
Length o/a: 892mm
Barrel: 250mm
Rifling: 6 grooves, rh
Weight, empty: 4.15kg
Magazine capacity: 20 or 32
Rate of fire: 500 rds/min

In production: 1934-45

Markings:
`EMP' and serial number on the rear receiver cap.

Safety:
Pull back the cocking handle and turn it upwards into a recess cut in the receiver slot. Some models may have an additional safety in the form of a thumb-catch on the top right of the receiver, behind the magazine housing. Switch to `S' for safe, `F' for fire. There is a fire selector lever on the right side of the stock, above the trigger. Move to `E' for single shots, `D' for automatic fire.

Unloading:
Magazine release on top of magazine housing. Remove magazine, pull back bolt to eject any round in the chamber. Inspect chamber via ejection port, release bolt, pull trigger.

FBP PORTUGAL

improved version of this weapon will be found marked as the M63 pattern, and this was superseded by the M1973 model which a perforated barrel jacket. All are mechanically almost identical.

A Portuguese service weapon, developed in Portugal and based upon features of other designs, combining the stock and firing mechanism of the US M3 and the bolt and general construction of the German MP40. A reliable and robust weapon, it was widely used in Africa and many found their way into the hands of insurgents of one sort and another. It could also turn up in the Far East, due to its use in Portuguese Timor. A slightly

Specification & Operation

Cartridge:
9mm Parabellum

Dimensions:
Length, stock extended: 813mm
Length, stock folded: 625mm
Barrel: 250mm
Rifling: 6 grooves, rh
Weight, empty: 3.77kg
Magazine capacity: 32 rounds
Rate of fire: 500 rds/min

In production: 1948-55

Markings:
'FBP M/48' and serial number on left side of magazine housing.

Safety:
Pull back cocking handle and turn up into a cut-out in the receiver slot to lock it in the rear position. When the bolt is forward, pushing the cocking handle in will lock the inner end into a cut in the receiver wall and thus lock the bolt forward.

Unloading:
Magazine catch on side of magazine housing. Remove magazine, pull back cocking handle to eject any round in the chamber. Release cocking handle, press trigger.

FMK Mod 2 ARGENTINA

An Argentine army weapon, this was originally called the 'PA3(DM)' for Pistola Ametralladora 3, Domingo Matheu factory. It replaced the earlier PA2(DM), which was simply a copy of the US M3A1 gun, in the early 1970s and is still in production. There is also a version with a solid wooden butt. The FMK is reliable and well-balanced; it can be fired quite easily single-handed.

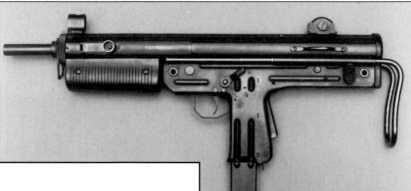

Specification & Operation

Cartridge:
9mm Parabellum

Dimensions:
Length, stock extended: 693mm
Length, stock retracted: 523mm
Barrel: 290mm
Weight, empty: 3.40kg
Rifling: 6 grooves, rh
Magazine capacity: 25 rounds
Rate of fire: 650 rds/min
In production: 1974-

Markings:

FMK 2 CAL 9MM FABRICA MILITAR DE ARMAS PORTATILES ROSARIO ARGENTINA and serial on right of receiver. Serial repeated on bolt.

Safety:
Grip safety with selector on the left side of the receiver; UP p for safe; midway for single shots, DOWN for automatic fire.

Unloading:
Remove magazine, squeeze in the grip safety, pull back the cocking handle to eject any round in the chamber. Inspect the chamber through the ejection port, release the bolt, press the trigger.

FN P-90 BELGIUM

It is unlikely that the P-90 will turn up in the wrong hands for some years yet, as production only got underway in the early 1990s and the entire output is destined for military use. Of unconventional appearance but entirely conventional internal blowback operation, the magazine is unique in

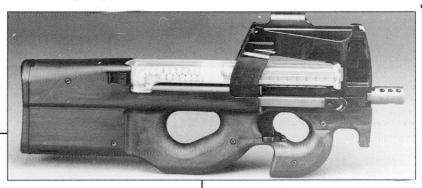

Specification & Operation

Cartridge:
9mm Parabellum

Dimensions:
Length o/a: 500mm
Barrel: 263mm
Rifling: 6 grooves, rh
Weight, empty: 2.54kg
Magazine capacity: 50 rounds
Rate of fire: 900 rds/min

In production: 1990-

Markings:
`P-90 Cal 5.7 X 28' and serial number on left side of sight mount. `FN HERSTAL SA BELGIUM' on left side of receiver.

Safety:
A manual safety in the form of a serrated catch In the rear edge of the trigger guard. Push forward for fire, back for safe.

Unloading:
The magazine catch is at the rear of the magazine, which lies on top of the receiver. Squeeze in, and remove the magazine by drawing the rear end up and back. Pull back the cocking lever to eject any round in the chamber; repeat to be sure, since the chamber cannot be examined through the ejection port. Release the cocking handle, press trigger.

lying above the weapon with the cartridges at 90 degrees. The penetrative power of the bullet is formidable. Empty cases are ejected downward through the hollow pistol grip.

Franchi LF-57 ITALY

An early example of excellent pressed-metal design and construction, the LF-57 also features an overhung bolt, with the greater part of its mass riding in the receiver above the barrel so as to give the maximum length of barrel in the shortest overall length. A sound design, it was adopted by the Italian Navy but failed to gain much more

Specification & Operation

Cartridge:
9mm Parabellum

Dimensions:
Length, stock folded: 420mm;
Length, stock extended: 680mm.
Barrel: 206mm
Rifling: 6 grooves, rh
Weight, empty: 3.32kg
Magazine capacity: 20 or 40 rounds
Rate of fire: 500 rds/min

In production: ca 1960-80

Markings:
`S p A   LUIGI FRANCHI - BRESCIA - CAL 9P - Mod 57' on left side of receiver. Serial number on left of receiver above pistol grip.

Safety:
A grip safety in the front edge of the pistol grip, which must be squeezed in to permit the bolt to move.

Unloading:
Magazine release on left side of magazine housing. Remove magazine. Pull back cocking handle to eject any round in the chamber, inspect chamber via ejection port. Release cocking handle, pull trigger.

success in the open market and after retaining the production machinery for some years Franchi finally took it out of their catalogue in the early 1980s. A similar model, with longer barrel and only semi-automatic firing, was marketed in the USA in the 1960s with some success.

H&K MP5 GERMANY

There are a number of variant models of the basic MP5, and details have changed from time to time, but they are all basically the same weapon, using a two-part, roller-delayed bolt and firing from a closed chamber. From 1992 models in .40 Smith & Wesson (lower

Specification & Operation

Cartridge:
9mm Parabellum

Dimensions:
Length, stock extended: 660mm.
Length, stock retracted: 490mm
Barrel: 225mm
Rifling: 6 grooves, rh
Weight, empty: 2.55kg
Magazine capacity: 15 or 30 rounds
Rate of fire: 800 rds/min

In production: 1965-

Markings:
'MP5 Kal 9mm x 19 serial number (month/year)' along top rib of receiver. 'Kal 9mm x 19' on left side of magazine housing.

Safety:
A manual safety catch/ fire selector is of the left side of the receiver, above the pistol grip. As a general rule the uppermost position is the safe position; the other positions vary with the model; most have single shot fire at the mid position and full automatic at the bottom position, but recent models have a fourth selection, three or two-round bursts for a single pressure of the trigger, in a second-from-top position. All are clearly marked, either by letters or bullet symbols.

Unloading:
The magazine catch is behind the magazine housing. Remove magazine, pull back cocking handle to clear any round from the breech, inspect the chamber via the ejection port, release cocking handle, pull trigger.

picture) have been made, which use straight magazines. MP5s had straight magazines until 1977 when the current curved variety were introduced.

H&K HK53 GERMANY

'**S**ub machine gun' means different things to different people; several countries classify the Kalashnikov rifle as a submachine gun, while most people consider that firing a pistol cartridge is the sole entree to the class. True, it is hard to say where a weapon in this calibre ceases to be a compact assault rifle and becomes a submachine gun, but

Specification & Operation

Cartridge:
5.56 x 45mm NATO

Dimensions:
Length, stock extended: 755mm.
Length, stock retracted: 563mm
Barrel: 211mm
Rifling: 6 grooves, rh
Weight, empty: 3.05kg
Magazine capacity: 25 rounds
Rate of fire: 700 rds/min

In production: 1975-

Markings:
`MP53 Kal 5.56mm x 45 serial number

(month/year)' along top rib of receiver. `Kal 5.56mm x 45' on left side of magazine housing.

Safety:
Manual safety catch/fire selector on left side of receiver, above trigger. UP for safe, central for single shots, DOWN for automatic fire.

Unloading:
The magazine catch is behind the magazine housing. Remove magazine, pull back cocking handle to clear any round from the breech, inspect the chamber via the ejection port, release cocking handle, pull trigger.

if the makers classify as such, then we can only follow suit. Certainly a number of armies and security forces have adopted the HK53 and appear to be happy with it. It has to have a very efficient flash suppressor to satisfy the demands of firing a rifle cartridge in a 211mm barrel.

Hyde-Inland M2 USA

Designed by Hyde, develpment by the Inland Division of General Motors and made by Marlin Firearms Co, this was approved for service as the US M2 submachine gun in 1942. Marlin had problems getting production under way, and the M3 submachine gun was approved and went into production before the M2 got started. The contracts were terminated and probably less than 500 Hyde-Inland guns were ever made.

Specification & Operation

Cartridge:
.45ACP

Dimensions:
Length o/a: 815mm
Barrel: 303mm
Weight, empty: 4.12kg
Rifling: 4 grooves, rh
Magazine capacity: 20 or 30 rounds
Rate of fire: 525 rds/min
In production: 1942-43

Markings:
US Submachine gun M2 and serial above chamber.

Safety:
A manual safety catch on the left side of the pistol grip. UP for safe, DOWN for fire. There is also a fire selector lever on the left side of the magazine housing; forward for automatic fire, rear for single shots.

Unloading:
Magazine catch button on right side of magazine housing. Remove magazine, pull back cocking handle to eject any round in the chamber. Inspect chamber via the ejection port, release cocking handle, press trigger.

Ingram Model 6 USA

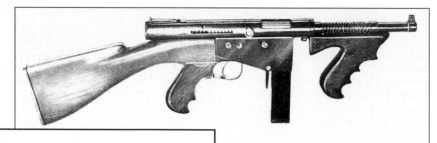

Something like 10,000 of these guns were produced and supplied to US police forces, US Army, Cuba and Peru, and it was also made under licence in Peru. Most were in .45 ACP calibre, though some were also made in 9mm Parabellum and in .38 Super Auto chambering. Two improved models, the

Specification & Operation

Cartridge:
.45 ACP

Dimensions:
Length o/a: 750mm
Barrel: 225mm
Weight, empty: 3.27kg
Rifling: 6 grooves, rh
Magazine capacity: 30 rounds
Rate of fire: 600 rds/min

In production: 1949-52

Markings:
'INGRAM 6 POLICE ORDNANCE CO LOS ANGELES CALIF. U.S.A.' above the chamber. Serial number on right side of chamber

Safety:
Pull back cocking handle and turn it up into a recess in the cocking handle slot. Some later models are said to have a manual safety catch on the left side of the receiver. Fire selection is done by the trigger; first pressure produces single shots, more pressure brings automatic fire.

Unloading:
The magazine catch is behind the magazine housing. Remove magazine, pull back cocking handle to clear any round from the breech, inspect the chamber via the ejection port, release cocking handle, pull trigger.

Model 7 which fired from a closed bolt, and the Model 8 which had a long fore-end rather than a forward pistol grip, were developed but it is doubtful if many of either type were made. Thailand bought the design of the Model 8 and invited the designer to assist in setting up a factory, but there is no record of any production.

INGRAM Model 10 USA

After designing the Models 6,7 and 8 for the Police Ordnance Company, Ingram moved on and developed the M10 in 1965-67. This was intended as a compact weapon for urban use, and for use with a silencer, for which reason Ingram developed the Model 11 in .380 Auto (9mm Short) calibre to provide a subsonic bullet. He then, to his cost,

Specification & Operation

Cartridge:
9mm Parabellum

Dimensions:
Length, stock extended: 548mm.
Length, stock retracted: 270mm
Barrel: 146mm
Rifling: 6 grooves, rh
Weight, empty: 2.84kg
Magazine capacity: 30 rounds

In production: 1970-75

Markings:
'INGRAM M10 CAL .45 Auto; MILITARY ARMAMENT CORP. POWDER SPRINGS GA USA serial number' all on right side of the receiver.

Safety:
Manual safety device is a sliding catch inside the trigger guard. Push forward for fire, back for safe. A fire selector switch on the left side of the receiver allows single shots or automatic fire.

Unloading:
Magazine catch in heel of butt. Remove magazine. Pull back cocking handle to eject any round in the chamber, inspect chamber via ejection port. Release cocking handle, press trigger.

became involved with various US government agencies in Vietnam; the gun was put into production; new management took over, disputes occurred and bankruptcy arrived in 1975. About 10,000 guns were made, but relatively few have ever been used by regular military forces.

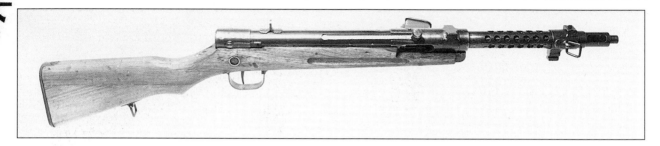

Submachine guns were not widely used by the Japanese forces during World War II. This model superseded a 1940 design which was very similar, this one being strengthened and simplified. It has a bayonet lug beneath the perforated barrel jacket and also an odd form of compensator on the muzzle which delivers more gas to the right side in order to cure the tendency to swing right in automatic fire. There is no provision for single shots other than agility with the trigger.

Specification & Operation

Cartridge:
8mm Nambu

Dimensions:
Length o/a: 900mm
Barrel: 230mm
Weight, empty: 3.85kg
Rifling: 6 grooves, rh
Magazine capacity: 30 rounds
Rate of fire: 800 rds/min

In production: 1944-45

Markings:
Japanese ideographs for 'Type 100' and serial number on rear of receiver.

Safety:
A manual safety catch in the form of a sliding catch in the underside of the receiver, in front of the trigger guard. Forward for safe, backward for fire.

Unloading:
Magazine catch on rear of magazine housing. Remove magazine, pull back cocking handle to eject any round in the chamber. Inspect chamber via ejection port, release cocking handle, press trigger.

Labora SPAIN

Specification & Operation

Cartridge:
9 x 23mm Bergmann-Bayard (9mm Largo)

Dimensions:
Length o/a: 794mm
Barrel: 260mm
Weight, empty: 4.38kg
Rifling: 4 grooves, rh
Magazine capacity: 36 rounds
Rate of fire: 750 rds/min

In production: 1936-38

Markings:
`LABORA [year]` on left side of receiver above trigger. Spanish crown and serial number on right side of receiver.

Safety:
Pull cocking handle to rear and turn the handle up into a notch in the receiver slot.
Selection of automatic fire or single shots is made by a cross bolt selector in the rear of the trigger guard. When pushed from right to left, automatic fire; when pushed from left to right, single shots.

Unloading:
Magazine catch on rear of magazine housing. Remove magazine, pull back cocking handle to eject any round in the chamber. Inspect chamber via ejection port, release cocking handle, press trigger.

This weapon was made in Spain during the Civil War and was made to a very high standard, being machined from solid steel and assembled by screws and pins. The recoil spring is exceptionally stiff, to compensate for a small and light bolt and keep the rate of fire down to a manageable level.

Lusa A2 PORTUGAL

This weapon was developed by the Portuguese INDEP company to replace the earlier FBP models. A robust and compact design, is has an unusual double-cylinder form of receiver, with the bolt and barrel in the lower section and the overhung section of the bolt, together with its recoil spring, in the

Specification & Operation

Cartridge:
9mm Parabellum

Dimensions:
Length, stock extended: 585mm
Length, stock folded: 458mm
Barrel: 160mm
Rifling: 6 grooves, rh
Weight, empty: 2.85kg
Magazine capacity: 30 rounds
Rate of fire: 900 rds/min

In production: 1992-

Markings:
`INDEP LUSA A2 [year] serial number' on right side of receiver.

Safety:
A combined safety catch and fire selector lever is mounted on the left side of the receiver, above the pistol grip. This is marked `0' for safe, `1' for single shots, `3' for three-round bursts and `30' for automatic fire.

Unloading:
Magazine catch on left side of receiver, behind magazine housing. Remove magazine. Pull back cocking handle to eject any round in the chamber, inspect chamber via the ejection port. Release cocking handle, press trigger.

top. The fire selector gives the full choice of options, and there are such things as sound suppressors and laser sighting aids provided as accessories.

Lanchester UK

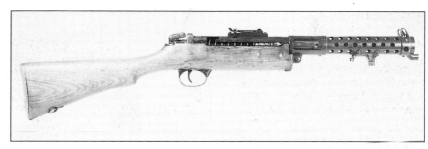

Made by the Sterling company, the Lanchester (named for its 'designer') was an unabashed copy of the Bergmann MP28 with a few typically British additions, such as a bayonet boss and a solid brass magazine housing which could be polished to a blinding finish. Production was mooted in 1940 when there was a desperate need for weapons to defend airfields. By the time

Specification & Operation

Cartridge:
9mm Parabellum

Dimensions:
Length o/a: 751mm
Barrel: 200mm
Weight, empty: 4.34kg
Rifling: 6 grooves, rh
Magazine capacity: 50 rounds
Rate of fire: 600 rds/min

In production: 1940-42

Markings:
LANCHESTER MARK I and serial on mag. housing

Safety:
Pull back cocking handle and turn it up into a notch in the receiver slot. There was originally a selector switch in front of the trigger guard which selected automatic fire or single shots, but the later production had this omitted and early models were generally converted by having it removed so as to fire automatic only.

Unloading:
Magazine catch on magazine housing. Remove magazine, pull back cocking handle to eject any round in the chamber. Inspect chamber via ejection port, release cocking handle, press trigger.

production had been organised the Sten had appeared and was in production, so the Lanchesters went almost all to the Royal Navy, who kept them in service until the 1960s. A veritable Rolls-Royce of submachine guns, it was totally the wrong weapon for the desperate days of 1940.

Madsen Models 1946 and 1951 DENMARK

The first of a series of Madsen designs which are all very similar. The receiver is made of two pressings, hinged down the back, and by removing the barrel retaining nut and barrel it is possible to open the receiver up like a book, exposing all the parts inside. The cocking handle on this model is actually a plate

Specification & Operation

Cartridge:
9mm Parabellum

Dimensions:
Length, stock extended: 780mm
Length, stock folded: 550mm
Barrel: 200mm
Weight, empty: 3.15kg
Rifling: 4 grooves, rh
Magazine capacity: 32 rounds
Rate of fire: 500 rds/min

In production: 1945-53

Markings:
`MADSEN' on right side of receiver. Serial number on top of receiver.

Safety:
Manual safety catch on the left side of receiver, a sliding button. Push forward for safe, rearward for fire. In addition there is a grip safety device behind the magazine housing which must be gripped and squeezed towards the housing to permit the bolt to close.

Unloading:
Magazine catch at rear of magazine housing. Remove magazine, pull back cocking handle to eject any round in the chamber. Inspect chamber via ejection port. Grip magazine housing and squeeze the grip safety, pull trigger.

on top of the receiver which has `wings' on the sides and can be grasped and pulled back. The Model 1946 was used by the Danish Army and also sold to some South American countries and to Thailand. The Model 1951 is similar but has the cocking handle in the form of a round knob on top of the receiver.

MAS 38 FRANCE

An odd-looking weapon because the body of the weapon is at an angle to the barrel; this is because the bolt moves in a tube which runs into the butt-stock. However this arrangement does mean that the recoil is straight back and thus the gun is well under control in automatic fire. The low-powered 7.65mm cartridge also helps in this; it also keeps this weapon restricted to countries with former ties with France, since this

cartridge was only ever used by and manufactured in France.

Specification & Operation

Cartridge:
7.65mm French Long

Dimensions:
Length o/a: 623mm
Barrel: 224mm
Weight, empty: 2.87kg
Rifling: 4 grooves, rh
Magazine capacity: 32 rounds
Rate of fire: 600 rds/min

In production: 1938-46

Markings:

'CAL 7.65 L MAS 1938 serial number' stamped on the left side of the receiver.

Safety:
The trigger acts as the safety catch; push the trigger forward and the bolt is locked. Pulling the trigger releases the safety before firing.

Unloading:
Pull the dust cover forward and up to release the magazine. Pull back the cocking handle to eject any round in the chamber, inspect the chamber via the ejection port, release the cocking handle, pull the trigger.

MAT 49 FRANCE

This replaced the MAS 38 submachine gun and fires a far more practical cartridge. It is a very compact design and the magazine housing, complete with magazine, can be folded forward to lie under to barrel and make it more convenient for carrying. It was more or less replaced in the French Army by the adoption of the 5.56mm FA-MAS rifle, but is still widely used by reserve forces

Specification & Operation

Cartridge:
9mm Parabellum

Dimensions:
Length, stock extended: 660mm
Length, stock retracted: 404mm**Barrel:** 230mm
Weight, empty: 3.63kg
Rifling: 4 grooves, lh
Magazine capacity: 32 rounds
Rate of fire: 600 rds/min

In production: 1949-

Markings:
`M.A.T. Mle 49 9m/m serial number' on left side of receiver.

Safety:
A grip safety in the rear edge of the pistol grip must be squeezed in to allow the bolt to move. There is no other form of safety device.

Unloading:
Magazine catch behind the magazine housing. Remove magazine, pull back cocking handle to eject any round in the chamber. Inspect chamber via ejection port. Release cocking handle, press trigger.

and by police and other para-military forces. It will also be encountered in former French colonies.

MEMS 52/58 ARGENTINA

Specification & Operation

Cartridge:
9mm Parabellum

Dimensions:
Length, stock extended: 800mm
Length, stock folded. 640mm
Barrel: 180mm
Weight, empty: 3.30kg
Rifling: 12 grooves, rh
Magazine capacity: 40 rounds
Rate of fire: 850 rds/min
In production: 1958-60

Markings:
'OTME SA CORDOBA MEMS 1958' and serial
number on right side of receiver.

Safety:
Pull cocking handle back and turn up into a
cut-away in the receiver slot.

Unloading:
Magazine catch behind magazine housing.
Remove magazine, pull back cocking handle to
eject any round in the chamber. Inspect
chamber via ejection port. Release cocking
handle, pull trigger.

Adopted by the Argentine air force,
gendarmerie and various other para-
military forces. It was a fairly simply design
with maximum tolerances. The exception
was the barrel, carefully rifled with 12 fine
grooves, this being a particular theory of
the inventor, that such rifling relieved wear
and aided accuracy. Various later models
may be encountered but they were never
made in quantity.

Mendoza HM-3 SPAIN

The construction of this weapon is somewhat unusual; the bolt is exposed in a gap at the top of the receiver, and is cocked by pulling back on the foresight guards. As a result, the firer needs to be careful where he is putting his supporting hand, or he might accidentally place it on the bolt. The folded stock provides a useful handgrip

Specification & Operation

Cartridge:
9mm Parabellum

Dimensions:
Length, stock extended: 635mm
Length, stock folded: 395mm
Barrel: 255mm
Weight, empty: 2.98kg
Rifling: 6 grooves, rh
Magazine capacity: 32 rounds
Rate of fire: 600 rds/min

In production: 1975–

Markings:
'PRODUCTOS MENDOZA HM-3' and serial number on right side of receiver.

Safety:
Manual safety catch/ fire selector on left side of receiver above pistol grip. When pointing DOWN, the weapon is safe. Turned horizontal, it permits full automatic fire, and turned to point UP it gives single shots. There is also a grip safety in the rear of the pistol grip which locks the bolt forward.

Unloading:
Magazine release in the heel of the pistol grip. Remove magazine. Grip the grip safety and pull the cocking lever to the rear to eject any round in the chamber. Inspect the chamber via the ejection port. Release the bolt, press the trigger.

for firing from the hip, but firing from the shoulder demands some care. The exact number of these weapons produced is not known, but is believed to be small.

MGP-15 PERU

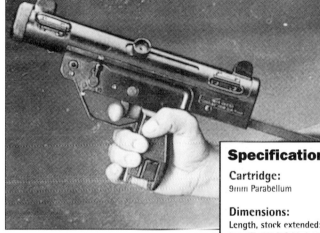

is based upon that of the Uzi submachine gun and Uzi magazines are interchangeable.

An exceptionally small weapon made in Peru and designed for use by special forces and security guards; it is well-balanced and can be fired one-handed if necessary. A screwed cap around the muzzle can be removed, leaving a screwed section available for the attachment of a suppressor, which is provided as an accessory. The magazine

Specification & Operation

Cartridge:
9mm Parabellum

Dimensions:
Length, stock extended: 490mm
Length, stock folded: 271mm
Barrel: 152mm
Weight, empty: 2.31kg
Rifling: 12 grooves, rh
Magazine capacity: 20 or 32 rounds
Rate of fire: 700 rds/min

In production: 1990-

Markings:
'SIMA-CEFAR 9mm MGP-15' and serial number on left side of receiver.

Safety:
Manual safety catch/selector lever on left side of receiver, above trigger guard. UP for safe, to the rear for automatic fire, forward for single shots.

Unloading:
Magazine catch at left bottom of pistol grip. Remove magazine, pull back cocking handle to eject any round in the chamber. Inspect chamber via ejection port, release cocking handle, press trigger.

MGP-79A PERU

This is the service submachine gun of the Peruvian armed forces, a simple and robust blowback design. The butt folds alongside the receiver so that the butt-plate can be grasped by the hand holding the magazine for extra grip. A threaded portion in the front end of the receiver is to allow a perforated barrel jacket to be fitted, allowing a better grip

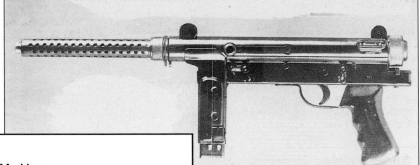

Specification & Operation

Cartridge:
9mm Parabellum

Dimensions:
Length, stock extended: 809mm
Length, stock folded: 544mm
Barrel: 237mm
Weight, empty: 3.08kg
Rifling: 12 grooves, rh
Magazine capacity: 20 or 32 rounds
Rate of fire: 850 rds/min

In production: 1979-85

Markings:
`SIMA-CEFAR 9mm MGP-79A' and serial number on left side of receiver.

Safety:
Manual safety catch on left side of receiver, above trigger. Rearward for safe, DOWN for fire. A manual fire selector switch is on the left side of the receiver just behind the magazine housing.

Unloading:
Magazine catch at left bottom of magazine housing. Remove magazine, pull back cocking handle to eject any round from the chamber. Inspect chamber via the ejection port, release cocking handle, pull trigger.

to be taken when talking deliberate aim, and the barrel can be removed and replaced by a combined barrel/silencer assembly.

MGP-87 PERU

This is more or less the same mechanism as the MGP-79A weapon, but slightly smaller by having a shorter barrel and shorter butt. The barrel can be removed by unscrewing the knurled retaining cap at the front of the receiver, and a combined barrel and suppressor can be screwed on to the receiver as a complete replacement unit. It has been adopted by the Peruvian armed forces

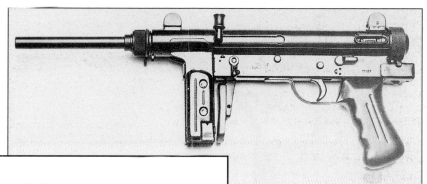

and will gradually replace the MGP-79A as the standard service weapon.

Specification & Operation

Cartridge:
9mm Parabellum

Dimensions:
Length, stock extended: 766mm
Length, stock folded: 500mm
Barrel: 194mm
Weight, empty: 2.90kg
Rifling: 12 grooves, rh
Magazine capacity: 20 or 32 rounds
Rate of fire: 800 rds/min

In production: 1987-

Markings:
'SIMA-CEFAR 9mm MGP-07' and serial number on left side of receiver.

Safety:
A combined safety catch and fire selector on the left side of the receiver. Back for safe, down to the first stop for automatic, forward to the second notch for single shots.

Unloading:
Magazine catch at left bottom of magazine housing. Remove magazine, pull back cocking handle to eject any round from the chamber. Inspect chamber via the ejection port, release cocking handle, pull trigger.

MP38 GERMANY

on a hole in the receiver, so as to lock the bolt in the forward position. When so modified, the weapon became the MP38/40.

This is the familiar German army weapon generally, and wrongly, called the 'Schmeisser'. It was made by the Erma company and designed by Vollmer, and like all his designs has the characteristic telescoping casing around the recoil spring and bolt assembly. It was later replaced in production by the MP40 (below) which simplified some features and made manufacture easier and quicker. The MP38 is distinguished by the corrugated surface of the machined steel receiver, the hole in the magazine housing and the machined aluminium grip frame. Numbers of these weapons were converted by modifying the cocking handle so that it could be pushed in, through the bolt, to engage

Specification & Operation

Cartridge:
9mm Parabellum

Dimensions:
Length, stock extended: 833mm
Length, stock folded: 630mm
Barrel: 251mm
Rifling: 6 grooves, rh
Weight, empty: 4.08kg
Magazine capacity: 32 rounds
Rate of fire: 500 rds/min

In production: 1938-40

Markings:
'MP38 (Year)' on rear receiver cap. Serial number on left side of rear cap. May have the factory code '27' stamped on the top of the receiver.

Safety:
Pull back the cocking handle and turn it up into a notch in the receiver slot. There is no selector device; the MP38 fires only in the automatic mode.

Unloading:
Magazine catch on rear of magazine housing. Remove magazine, pull back cocking handle to eject any round in the chamber. Inspect chamber via ejection port, release cocking handle, press trigger.

MP40 GERMANY

This replaced the MP38 (above), being easier and quicker to manufacture, and can be distinguished by the plain pressed steel receiver, corrugated magazine housing, and pressed steel grip frame. Well over a million of these weapons were turned out by three factories, and they have spread all over the world.

Specification & Operation

Cartridge:
9mm Parabellum

Dimensions:
Length, stock extended: 833mm
Length, stock folded: 630mm
Barrel: 251mm
Rifling: 6 grooves, rh
Weight, empty: 4.03kg
Magazine capacity: 32 rounds
Rate of fire: 500 rds/min

In production: 1940-45

Markings:
'MP40 (year)' on rear receiver cap, serial number on side of cap. Factory identifying code ('ayf' or '27' for Erma, 'bnz' or '660' for Steyr, 'fxo' for Haenel) on rear top of receiver.

Safety:
Pull back cocking handle and turn up into a notch in the receiver slot. Post April 1940 manufacture has a two-piece cocking handle which could be pushed into the bolt, in its forward position, and into a hole in the receiver to lock the bolt. Most pre-April weapons were later converted.

Unloading:
Magazine catch on rear of magazine housing. Remove magazine, pull back cocking handle to eject any round in the chamber. Inspect chamber via ejection port, release cocking handle, press trigger.

MP41 GERMANY

The MP41 is a rare example of wartime German private enterprise; it was an attempt by Schmeisser to produce a submachine gun to compete with the MP40, and he did it by simply taking the MP40 receiver and barrel and grafting it on to a wooden stock similar to that of the Schmeisser-designed Bergmann MP28. He also added a fire selector so that single shots could be fired. However,

Specification & Operation

Cartridge:
9mm Parabellum

Dimensions:
Length o/a: 864mm
Barrel: 251mm
Weight, empty: 3.70kg
Rifling: 6 grooves, rh
Magazine capacity: 32 rounds
Rate of fire: 600 rds/min

In production: 1941-42

Markings:
`MP41 Patent Schmeisser C.G.Haenel Suhl' on top of receiver. Serial number on rear of receiver, left side of barrel and left side of receiver.

Safety:
Pull back cocking handle and turn up into a notch in the receiver slot. The cocking handle can be pushed into the bolt, in its forward position, and into a hole in the receiver to lock the bolt.

Unloading:
Magazine catch on rear of magazine housing. Remove magazine, pull back cocking handle to eject any round in the chamber. Inspect chamber via ejection port, release cocking handle, press trigger.

the German Army was not interested and never adopted it. A small quantity was made and found their way into various military units as substitute standard weapons, but they are now relatively uncommon.

Orita ROMANIA

A blowback weapon, this was built in the Romanian arsenal of Cugir, commencing shortly before the Romanian army assisted the German Army in the invasion of Russia. A large number are said to have been made, and there is also a variant model with a folding stock similar to that used on the German MP38 and MP40 models. Most of these weapons vanished into Russia during the course of the war and are not very common in the West, but they can still turn up occasionally.

Specification & Operation

Cartridge:
9mm Parabellum

Dimensions:
Length o/a: 894mm
Barrel: 278mm
Weight, empty: 3.45kg
Rifling: 6 grooves, rh
Magazine capacity: 25 rounds
Rate of fire: 600 rds/min

In production: 1941-44

Markings:
CA monogram and serial on top of receiver

Safety:
A cross bolt safety catch is in the forward end of the trigger guard. When pushed from left to right the weapon is made safe. There is a fire selector lever on the left side of the receiver which is pushed DOWN for automatic fire, UP for single shots.

Unloading:
Magazine catch on rear of magazine housing. Remove magazine, pull back cocking handle to eject any round in the chamber. Inspect chamber via ejection port, release cocking handle, press trigger.

Owen AUSTRALIA

cooling fins around the rear of the barrel; from early 1943 a skeleton frame and plain barrel were used. These models were also issued painted in green/ochre camouflage colours.

An unusual weapon, firstly because of the top-mounted magazine and secondly for the quick-release barrel attachment. This is not in order to change barrels, but to allow the weapon to be dismantled quickly, since the bolt and spring have to be removed from the front of the receiver. Although heavy it was utterly reliable and much preferred to the Austen by Australian troops. It was retained in use well into the 1960s. Early models had a solid frame and

Specification & Operation

Cartridge:
9mm Parabellum

Dimensions:
Length o/a: 813mm
Barrel: 250mm
Weight, empty: 4.21kg
Rifling: 7 grooves, rh
Magazine capacity: 33 rounds
Rate of fire: 700 rds/min

In production: 1941-44

Markings:
`OWEN 9mm Mk I LYSAGHT PK AUSTRALIA

Patented 22/7/41 serial number' all on right side of frame.

Safety:
A combined safety catch and selector lever on the right side of the frame. Rotate backwards to set safe, when the bolt is locked. In the central position the weapon gives single shots, and in the forward position automatic fire.

Unloading:
Magazine catch on rear of magazine housing. Remove magazine, pull back cocking handle to eject any round in the chamber. Inspect chamber via ejection port, release cocking handle, press trigger.

Poland pz-63 POLAND

muzzle gases upwards to counteract the natural rise of the weapon when firing automatic. It is almost impossible to make accurate aimed automatic fire since the slide and sights are constantly moving during firing.

This is a peculiar weapon which resembles an over-grown automatic pistol. Instead of a bolt moving inside the receiver, it uses a moving slide, just like a pistol. The lower portion of the slide is extended beneath the muzzle to act as a compensator, deflecting the

Specification & Operation

Cartridge:
9mm Parabellum

Dimensions:
Length, stock extended: 503mm
Length, stock folded: 333mm
Barrel: 152mm
Weight, empty: 1.80kg
Rifling: 6 grooves, rh
Magazine capacity: 25 or 40 rounds
Rate of fire: 600 rds/min

In production: 1963-80

Markings:
Serial number right side of side and frame, Factory number (11) in oval.

Safety:
Manual safety catch on left side top of pistol grip; turn UP to make safe, turn DOWN to fire. Fire selection is performed by the trigger; a short pull gives single shots, a longer pull gives automatic fire.

Unloading:
Magazine catch at heel of butt. Remove magazine, grasp the serrated rear section of the slide and pull it to the rear, so ejecting any round in the chamber. Inspect the chamber through the ejection port, release the slide and pull the trigger.

261

PPD-1940 RUSSIA

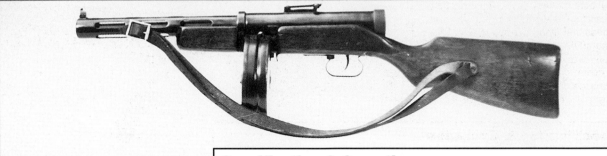

This is an improved version of an earlier model, the PPD-34/38; the principal difference lies in the improved magazine; the earlier version (which is unlikely to be met) was originally made for a box magazine; when a drum was adopted, it had to have a vulnerable extension piece to fit the box magazine housing. The 1940 version changed the magazine housing and method of attachment and made the drum magazine simpler and more robust. This weapon was distributed all over the Communist world after 1948 and might be encountered anywhere.

Specification & Operation

Cartridge:
7.62mm Soviet Pistol

Dimensions:
Length o/a: 790mm
Barrel: 260mm
Weight, empty: 3.63kg
Rifling: 4 grooves, rh
Magazine capacity: 71 rounds
Rate of fire: 800 rds/min

In production: 1940-41

Markings:
Serial number and factory identifying code on rear top of receiver.

Safety:
A latch on the cocking handle can be pushed into a recess in the receiver casing when the bolt is either fully to the rear or fully to the front.

Unloading:
Magazine release is behind the magazine housing. Press release and slide magazine out of the housing. Pull back cocking handle to eject any round in the chamber, inspect chamber via the ejection port, release cocking handle, press trigger.

PPS-43 RUSSIA

Probably the best of the three wartime Soviet submachine guns, the PPD was designed and manufactured inside Leningrad during the 900-day siege; the weapon was designed so as to be made on existing machinery using existing materials, since nothing could be brought in from outside. After the war

Specification & Operation

Cartridge:
7.62mm Soviet Pistol

Dimensions:
Length, stock extended: 808mm
Length, stock folded: 606mm
Barrel: 254mm
Weight, empty: 3.33kg
Rifling: 4 grooves, rh
Magazine capacity: 35 rounds
Rate of fire: 700 rds/min

In production: 1943-45

Markings:
Serial number and factory identifying mark on top or side of receiver.

Safety:
Manual safety catch in front edge of trigger guard. Push forward to make safe; this locks the bolt in either the fully forward or fully rearward position. There is no fire selector lever; the weapon fires only at full-automatic.

Unloading:
Magazine catch is around the rear of the magazine housing. Remove magazine, pull back cocking handle to eject any round in the chamber. Inspect chamber via ejection port, release cocking handle, pull trigger.

the Soviets got rid of them to fellow-travelling nations, largely because of political ill-feeling between Moscow and Leningrad. They were extensively used by the North Korean and Chinese armies during the Korean War and they are particularly common in the Far East.

have an adjustable tangent backsight; later models, the majority of production, have a simple two-position flip-over notch backsight.

The third wartime Soviet submachine gun and the most common, some five million having been made. They were widely distributed to Communist countries after 1947 and can be found all over the world. Conversions to 9mm Parabellum chambering have been done, though they are unlikely to be encountered in any number. This superseded the PPS-40 to provide a weapon capable of using box or drum magazines and which was simpler and quicker to manufacture. Early models

Specification & Operation

Cartridge:
7.62mm Soviet Pistol

Dimensions:
Length o/a: 828mm
Barrel: 265mm
Weight, empty: 3.56 kg
Rifling: 4 grooves, rh
Magazine capacity: 71 round drum or 35 round box
Rate of fire: 900 rds/min

In production: 1941-47

Markings:
Serial number and factory identifying code on receiver.

Safety:
Manual safety latch on the cocking handle; this can be pushed into notches cut into the receiver wall when the bolt is either fully forward or fully back, and locks the bolt in that position. There is a fire selector switch inside the trigger guard, in front of the trigger; push forward for automatic fire, back for single shots.

Unloading:
Magazine release is behind the magazine housing and folds up under the stock. Fold down, press forward and slide the magazine out. Pull back cocking handle to eject any round in the chamber, inspect the chamber via the ejection port, release the cocking handle, press trigger,

Reising 50 USA

An unusual weapon which used delayed blowback operation and fired from a closed bolt. Theoretically a sound enough design, it fell down in real life because it proved too susceptible to jamming from dirt and dust of combat. Issued to the US Marines in the Pacific it was rapidly abandoned, and most were used to arm police, factory guards and security staffs in the USA where its defects were less likely to appear. There was also a Model 55 which was the same weapon but with a folding wire butt-stock and a rear pistol grip.

Specification & Operation

Cartridge:
.45 ACP

Dimensions:
Length o/a: 959mm
Barrel: 279mm
Weight, empty: 3.06 kg
Rifling: 6 grooves, rh
Magazine capacity: 12 or 20 rounds
Rate of fire: 550 rds/min

In production: 1941-45

Markings:
'HARRINGTON & RICHARDSON WORCESTER MASS USA' on top of receiver. Serial number on left side of receiver.

Safety:
Sliding safety catch/fire selector switch on right side of receiver. In the rearward position the weapon is safe; move one notch forward for single shots, fully forward for automatic fire. The positions are marked 'SAFE', 'SA' and 'FA'.

Unloading:
Magazine catch is at rear of magazine housing. Remove magazine, pull back cocking handle to eject any round in the chamber. Inspect chamber through the ejection port, release cocking handle,

Rexim-Favor TURKEY

This weapon has an odd history; it is reputed to have been a French design, stolen by a glamorous female spy, which then passed to a Swiss company, who had the weapons made in Spain in the 1950s. The Swiss went bankrupt in 1957, the Spanish factory took over the guns, and where they went to after that is

Specification & Operation

Cartridge:
9mm Parabellum

Dimensions:
Length o/a: 870mm
Barrel: 340mm
Weight, empty: 3.79kg
Rifling: 6 grooves, rh
Magazine capacity: 32 rounds
Rate of fire: 600 rds/min

In production: 1953-70

Markings:
No markings have been seen on any Rexim-Favor weapon apart from those produced in Turkey, which carry Turkish markings and a serial number on the left side of the receiver; `XXXX A2 MOD 1968 ANKARA CAP 9MM'.

Safety:
A combined safety catch/fire selector is on the left side of the receiver, above the pistol grip. To the rear for safe, DOWN and central for single shots, forward for automatic.

Unloading:
The magazine catch is a thumb switch on the left side of the receiver, behind the magazine housing. Remove the magazine; pull back the cocking handle to eject any round in the chamber; inspect chamber via the ejection port, release the cocking handle, pull the trigger.

anybody's guess. A number were either made, modified or refurbished in Turkey in the late 1960s and used by the Turkish Army for some years. It has a somewhat complicated mechanism, which was one reason for the lack of military interest in the original design, but seems to be well made and accurate. It can be found with a wooden butt or with a folding butt.

SAF CHILE

a folding butt; there is also a fixed butt model, a version with an integral silencer, and the 'Mini-SAF', a shortened version with no butt and a fixed forward grip. The 30-round magazine is of translucent plastic, enabling the ammunition to be visually checked, and there are studs and slots allowing two or more magazines to be connected together.

This is the Chilean Army issue weapon and is also exported. The weapon is based upon the SIG 550 rifle design, which is made under licence in Chile, and the designer's object was to utilise as many parts of the rifle as possible to save production costs. The standard model has

Specification & Operation

Cartridge:
9mm Parabellum

Dimensions:
Length, stock extended: 640mm
Length, stock folded: 410mm
Barrel: 200mm
Weight, empty:2.90kg
Rifling: 6 grooves, rh
Magazine capacity: 20 or 30 rounds
Rate of fire: 1200 rds/min

In production: 1990-

Markings:
'FAMAE Mod SAF Cal 9mm serial number' on left side of receiver.

Safety:
Combined safety catch and fire selector on left side of receiver, above pistol grip. UP for safe; DOWN one notch for single shots, two notches for three-round burst.

Unloading:
Magazine catch on front edge of trigger guard, behind magazine housing. Remove magazine. Pull back cocking handle to eject any round in the chamber, inspect chamber via ejection port, release cocking handle., pull trigger.

Sanna 77 SOUTH AFRICA

This weapon appeared in South Africa in the 1970s and is based upon the Czech CZ25, though whether it was actually made in South Africa or whether the guns were refurbished CZ 75s bought from Czechoslovakia and modified so as to fire only in the semi-automatic mode is not certain. It was not a military weapon, but was sold for self-defence by farmers and others who felt the need for it, and it can be

Specification & Operation

Cartridge:
9mm Parabellum

Dimensions:
Length, stock extended: 650mm
Length, stock retracted: 450mm
Barrel: 290mm
Weight, empty: 2.80kg
Rifling: 6 grooves, rh
Magazine capacity: 40 rounds
Rate of fire: single shots

In production: 1977-80

Markings:
Serial number on left side of receiver.

Safety:
A manual safety catch is inside the trigger guard, behind the trigger. Pushed from left to right it locks the bolt rendering the weapon safe.

Unloading:
Magazine catch at the heel of the pistol grip. Remove magazine. Pull back cocking handle to eject any round in the chamber. Inspect chamber via the ejection port. Release cocking handle, press trigger.

assumed that several of them have passed into other hands by this time and are liable to appear anywhere in Africa.

SIG MP310 SWITZERLAND

This is based upon an earlier design which proved too expensive to make, and became the Swiss police submachine gun in the early 1960s. However it was still too expensive to become a popular military weapon and only a small quantity were sold in various parts of the world before the production line was

Specification & Operation

Cartridge:
9mm Parabellum

Dimensions:
Length, stock extended: 735mm
Length, stock retracted: 610mm
Barrel: 200mm
Weight, empty: 3.15kg
Rifling: 6 grooves, rh
Magazine capacity: 40 rounds
Rate of fire: 900 rds/min

In production: 1958-72

Markings:
'SIG NEUHAUSEN MOD 310 9mm' and serial number on top of receiver.

Safety:
There is no applied safety device on this weapon; the only safety measure that can be taken is to press in the catch on the left side of the magazine housing and pivot the entire magazine forward to lie underneath the barrel. This permits the weapon to be carried safely, provided there is no round in the chamber, and it can be brought into action simply by swinging the magazine back into position. Fire selection is done by trigger pressure; the first pressure gives single shots, harder pressure automatic fire.

Unloading:
Remove magazine. Pull back cocking handle to eject any round in the chamber. Inspect chamber via the ejection port, release cocking handle, press trigger.

dismantled in 1978. An extremely well-made gun, like all SIG products, it was a pioneer in the use of precision castings rather than machined forgings.

Skorpion CZECHOSLOVAKIA/YUGOSLAVIA

This was originally developed as a replacement for the pistol for the crews of armoured vehicles, though the choice of cartridge is peculiar. Reports say that other models in 9mm Short (.380 Auto) and 9mm Parabellum were made, but none have been seen in the west. The Yugoslav Zastava company manufacture the 7.65mm model for

Specification & Operation

Cartridge:
7.65mm Browning (.32 ACP)

Dimensions:
Length, stock extended: 513mm
Length, stock folded: 269mm
Barrel: 112mm
Rifling: 6 grooves, rh
Weight, empty: 1.59kg
Magazine capacity: 10 or 20 rounds
Rate of fire: 850 rds/min

In production: ca 1960-75

Markings:
Serial number on left side of receiver.

Safety:
There is a manual safety catch and fire selector on the left side, above the pistol grip. Back, to the notch marked `1', gives single shots. Central, the notch marked `0' is safe; forward to the notch marked `20' gives automatic fire.

Unloading:
Magazine catch is a button on the left side of the frame just behind the magazine housing. Remover the magazine. Grasp the cocking knobs on each side of the upper receiver and pull back to eject any round in the chamber. Inspect the chamber via the ejection port. Release the cocking knobs, press the trigger.

export as their M84. It has been widely distributed to various Communist countries and in central Africa, and is a popular weapon with terrorists. It can be expected to appear anywhere in the world.

Socimi Type 821 ITALY

This appears to be based upon the CZ25 pattern though with modern precision castings rather than sheet metal for the receiver and a generally more angular shape. The Socimi company promoted it for some years and claimed sales in various parts of the world, but they eventually went into liquidation and the design was then

Specification & Operation

Cartridge:
9mm Parabellum

Dimensions:
Length, stock extended: 600mm
Length, stock folded: 400mm
Barrel: 200mm
Weight, empty: 2.45kg
Rifling: 6 grooves, rh
Magazine capacity: 32 rounds
Rate of fire: 600 rds/min

In production: ca 1984-89

Markings:
'SOCIMI SpA Mod 821 9mm' and serial number on top of receiver.

Safety:
There is a combined safety catch and fire selector on the left side, above the pistol grip. In its rearmost position the weapon is safe; central, single shots; forward automatic fire.

Unloading:
Magazine catch is at the bottom left side of the pistol grip. Remove magazine; pull back cocking handle to eject any round in the chamber. Inspect chamber via the ejection port, release cocking handle, press trigger.

taken over by Franchi, who marketed it as the LF821. What success they have had with it is not currently known.

Sola Super LUXEMBOURG

This is a simple but well-made weapon which seems to have some affinity with an earlier, Belgian, design known as the RAN. The Sola was made in Luxembourg and was reputedly sold to some African and South American countries, so it could turn up anywhere. It failed to attract any major military

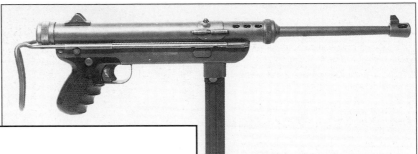

Specification & Operation

Cartridge:
9mm Parabellum

Dimensions:
Length, stock extended: 875mm
Length, stock retracted: 600mm
Barrel: 300mm
Weight, empty: 2.90kg
Rifling: 6 grooves, rh
Magazine capacity: 32 rounds
Rate of fire: 550 rds/min

In production: 1954-57

Markings:
'SOLA LUXEMBOURG [Year] serial number' all on left side of receiver.

Safety:
A combined safety catch/fire selector is on the left side of the receiver, above the pistol grip. UP and forward for safe, DOWN one notch for single shots, fully down for automatic fire. The hinged ejection port cover also acts as a safety device, preventing bolt movement when closed.

Unloading:
The magazine catch is a large button let into the left side of the receiver behind the magazine housing. Press in and remove the magazine. Pull back the cocking handle to eject any round in the chamber. Inspect the chamber via the ejection port, release the cocking handle, pull the trigger.

contracts, since it appeared at a time when there was a glut of surplus submachine guns on the world markets. The makers developed a simplified version - the Sola Light - but this found no takers either, and they then abandoned the weapons business for something more profitable.

Spectre ITALY

This unusual weapon is the only double-action submachine gun in existence and it has been widely adopted by European police forces since, like many modern pistols, it can be de-cocked, carried loaded but safely, and the fired in then double-action mode by

Specification & Operation

Cartridge:
9mm Parabellum

Dimensions:
Length, stock extended: 580mm
length, stock folded: 350mm
Barrel: 130mm
Weight, empty: 2.90kg
Rifling: 6 grooves, rh
Magazine capacity: 30 or 50 rounds
Rate of fire: 850 rds/min

In production: ca 1984-

Markings:
'SITES Mod SPECTRE Cal 9mm made in Italy patented' on right side of receiver.

Safety:
There is no conventional safety catch. There is a de-cocking lever on each side at the top of the pistol grip, and a fire selector lever on each side above the trigger. The weapon can be loaded and cocked and the de-cocking lever is then pressed to release the bolt without firing. To fire, all that is necessary is to pull the trigger which then cocks and releases the firing pin. The fire selector gives single shots in the UP position, automatic fire in the DOWN position.

Unloading:
Magazine catch is in the front edge of the trigger guard. Remove magazine. Pull back cocking handle to remove any round in the chamber, inspect chamber via the ejection port. Release the cocking handle. Press trigger.

simply pressing the trigger. The magazines are also unusual, having four columns of cartridges and thus compressing 50 rounds into less vertical space than is usually taken by a 30 rounds magazine. Semi-automatic long-barrelled versions can also be found.

Star Si35 SPAIN

Developed during the Spanish Civil War, this was one of three weapons which were similar except for their firing arrangements; the others were the RU35 which fired only at 300 rds/min, and the TN 35 which fired at 700 rds/min. As seen above the SI 35 fired at either rate, but the process of setting the speed was far too involved for practical use in battle and although the weapon was reliable and accurate, it never achieved much popularity. It was offered in the USA and Britain during the 1939-45 war and both countries tested it before turning it down in favour of something more simple.

Specification & Operation

Cartridge:
9 x 23mm Largo (Bergmann-Bayard)

Dimensions:
Length o/a: 900mm
Barrel: 270mm
Weight, empty: 3.80kg
Rifling: 6 grooves, rh
Magazine capacity: 30 or 40 rounds
Rate of fire: 300 or 700 rds/min

In production: 1936-44

Markings:
`STAR - SUB-FUSIL AMETRALLADORA MODELO SI 1935 CAL 9MM' on left side of receiver. Serial number on right side of receiver.

Safety:
There are two switches on the left side of the receiver, a three-position switch above the trigger and a two-position switch in front of it. To set the weapon safe, the forward switch is pushed forward and the rear switch pushed all the way to the rear. To fire single shots, the forward switch remains forward, and the rear switch is pushed fully forward. To fire automatic at 300 rds/min, the forward switch is pulled back and the rear switch left all the way forward. To fire automatic at 700 rds/min the forward switch is back and the rear switch in its central position.

Unloading:
Magazine catch behind the magazine housing. Remove magazine, pull back cocking handle to eject any round in the chamber, and inspect the chamber via the ejection port. Release the cocking handle, press the trigger.

Star Z-62 SPAIN

Specification & Operation

Cartridge:
9 x 23mm Largo (Bergmann-Bayard)

Dimensions:
Length, stock extended: 701mm
Length, stock folded: 480mm
Barrel: 201mm
Weight, empty: 2.87kg
Rifling: 6 grooves, rh
Magazine capacity: 20 or 30 rounds
Rate of fire: 550 rds/min

In production: 1963-70

Markings:
'STAR EIBAR ESPANA MODEL Z-62' and serial number on left side of magazine housing.

Safety:
A manual cross-bolt safety in the upper part of the pistol grip. When pushed from right to left it blocks the sear and the weapon is safe. Fire selection is performed by the trigger; pulling the upper part of the trigger produces single shots, pulling on the lower part produces automatic fire.

Unloading:
Magazine catch at the rear of the magazine housing. Remove magazine, pull back cocking handle to eject any round in the chamber. Inspect chamber via the ejection port, release cocking handle, pull trigger.

This was developed for the Spanish Army, replaced the Z-45 in 1953 and remained in service until 1971, when it was replaced by the Z-70B; this looks the same but has a conventional trigger and a selector lever above it to give single shots or automatic fire. Both weapons were offered on the export market and were also offered in 9mm Parabellum chambering, but whether any were adopted by other countries is not known.

Star Z-84 SPAIN

The Z-84 replaced the earlier Z-70B in Spanish service in the middle 1980s and is a thoroughly modern and compact design using pressed metal for lightness. The centre of balance is above the pistol grip, so that it can be easily fired one-handed if necessary. As well as being used by Spain, numbers have been

Specification & Operation

Cartridge:
9mm Parabellum

Dimensions:
Length, stock extended: 615mm
Length, stock folded: 410mm
Barrel: 215mm
Weight, empty: 3.00kg
Rifling: 6 grooves, rh
Magazine capacity: 25 or 30 rounds
Rate of fire: 600 rds/min

In production: 1985-

Markings:
`STAR EIBAR ESPANA MOD Z-84' and serial number on right of receiver.

Safety:
A cross-bolt safety button is set inside the trigger-guard. Pushed from right to left, the weapon is safe. Pushed from left to right it exposes a red mark and indicates the weapon is ready to fire. A sliding fire selector on the left side of the receiver which is pushed forward for single shots, rearward for automatic fire.

Unloading:
The magazine release is in the heel of the pistol grip. Remove the magazine. Pull back the cocking handle to eject any round in the chamber. Inspect the chamber via the ejection port, release the cocking handle, pull the trigger.

sold to security forces in several countries, though no details are forthcoming from the manufacturers.

Sten Mark I UK

This was the original Sten, designed at the Royal Small Arms Factory, Enfield, and made by BSA and various ordnance factories. It is recognisable by the spoon-like muzzle compensator and the wooden cover to the trigger mechanism, and also the folding forward grip. A Mark I* version appeared late in 1941 using a metal cover for the trigger mechanism and without the grip or muzzle compensator. About 100,000 of these models were made and most went to the regular forces. Various patterns of metal stock can be found

Specification & Operation

Cartridge:
9mm Parabellum

Dimensions:
Length o/a: 896mm
Barrel: 108mm
Weight, empty: 3.26kg
Rifling: 6 grooves, rh
Magazine capacity: 32 rounds
Rate of fire: 550 rds/min

In production: 1941-42

Markings:
`STEN Mk I' on top of magazine housing.

Safety:
Pull back cocking handle and turn down into a notch in the operating slot. Fire selection is done by a cross-bolt passing through the trigger mechanism housing; pushed in from left to right it gives single shots, pushed from right to left gives automatic fire.

Unloading:
Magazine catch on top of magazine housing. Press down and remove magazine, pull back cocking handle to eject any round in the chamber, and inspect the chamber via the ejection port. Release the cocking handle, press the trigger.

Sten Mk II UK

Specification & Operation

Cartridge:
9mm Parabellum

Dimensions:
Length o/a: 952mm
Barrel: 197mm
Weight, empty: 3.0 kg
Rifling: 2 or 6 grooves, rh
Magazine capacity: 32 rounds
Rate of Fire: 550 rds/min

In production: 1942-44

Markings:
`STEN MK II' on top of magazine housing.
Weapons made in Canada may also have `LONG
BRANCH' and year.

Safety:
Pull back cocking handle and turn up into a
notch in the operating slot. Fire selection is done
by a cross-bolt passing through the trigger
mechanism housing; pushed in from left to right
it gives single shots, pushed from right to left
gives automatic fire.

Unloading:
Magazine catch on top of magazine housing.
Press down and remove magazine, pull back
cocking handle to eject any round in the
chamber, and inspect the chamber via the
ejection port. Release the cocking handle, press
the trigger.

This was the most common version of
the Sten, over two million being made
in the UK, Canada and New Zealand. The
mechanism is the same as the Mark I but
the barrel and stock are removable for
easier packing and storage. The magazine
housing can also be rotated to close the
ejection port. Used by British forces, it
was also dropped to resistance
movements all over Europe and the Far
East, so that it can be encountered
anywhere in the world. It was also copied
by the resistance (notably in Denmark)
and by the Germans.

Sten Mk IIS UK

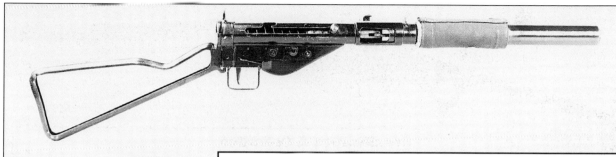

This is the 'Silent Sten', originally produced for clandestine forces but then taken into use by the British Army for use by patrols and raiding parties. The mechanism is that of the Mark II weapon, though using a lighter bolt, and the barrel and silencer are a special integral unit which screws into the receiver in place of the normal barrel and retaining sleeve. The canvas sleeve around the silencer is to protect the hand from heat, and it was not recommended to fire this weapon at full automatic except in the gravest emergencies.

Specification & Operation

Cartridge:
9mm Parabellum

Dimensions:
Length o/a: 900mm
Barrel: 90mm
Weight, empty: 3.48kg
Rifling: 6 grooves, rh
Magazine capacity: 32 rounds
Rate of fire: 450 rds/min

In production: 1943-45

Markings:
'STEN M.C. Mk IIS' on top of magazine housing.

Safety:
Pull back cocking handle and turn up into a notch in the operating slot. Fire selection is done by a cross-bolt passing through the trigger mechanism housing; pushed in from left to right it gives single shots, pushed from right to left gives automatic fire.

Unloading:
Magazine catch on top of magazine housing. Press down and remove magazine, pull back cocking handle to eject any round in the chamber, and inspect the chamber via the ejection port. Release the cocking handle, press the trigger.

Sten Mk III UK

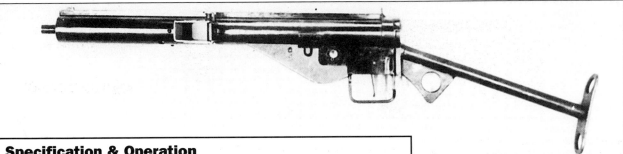

Specification & Operation

Cartridge:
9mm Parabellum

Dimensions:
Length o/a: 762mm
Barrel: 197mm
Weight, empty: 3.1kg
Rifling: 6 grooves, rh
Magazine capacity: 32 rounds
Rate of fire: 550 rds/min

In production: 1943-44

Markings:
'STEN M.C. Mk III' and year on top of magazine housing.

Safety:
Pull back cocking handle and turn up into a notch in the operating slot. Fire selection is done by a cross-bolt passing through the trigger mechanism housing; pushed in from left to right it gives single shots, pushed from right to left gives automatic fire.

Unloading:
Magazine catch on top of magazine housing. Press down and remove magazine, pull back cocking handle to eject any round in the chamber, and inspect the chamber via the ejection port. Release the cocking handle, press the trigger.

This is still the same mechanism as the Marks I and II but simply an alternative construction for factories which found it more convenient. The whole thing is welded, riveted and stamped, and the barrel is no longer detachable, nor is the magazine housing capable of being used as a dust cover. In general, this pattern was for use in Home Defence units - airfield guards and so forth - where the dismantling possible in the Mark II was not necessary. Nevertheless, a few found their way into resistance forces in Europe and like every Sten, can turn up anywhere in the world.

Sten Mk V UK

The Mark V Sten was an attempt to improve the quality of the weapon and produce something which looked less cheap and nasty than the Mark II. The mechanism remained unchanged, but the gun now had a wooden stock, a wooden pistol grip and had the muzzle formed in the same manner as the service No 4 rifle, so that the standard bayonet could be fitted. The gun was finished in stove enamel and the butt on early models had a brass butt-plate with a trap for carrying cleaning equipment; later models have a steel butt-plate without the trap. However, the greatest design defect of the Sten - the magazine - remained the same, so that the Mark V was little more reliable than the patterns which had gone before.

Specification & Operation

Cartridge:
9mm Parabellum

Dimensions:
Length o/a: 762mm
Barrel: 198mm
Weight, empty: 3.90kg
Rifling: 6 grooves, rh
Magazine capacity: 32 rounds
Rate of fire: 600 rds/min

In production: 1944-46

Markings:
'STEN M.C. Mk V' on top of magazine housing.

Safety:
Pull back cocking handle and turn up into a notch in the operating slot to lock the bolt in the cocked position. Press in the cocking handle when the bolt is forward to lock it to the receiver. Fire selection is done by a cross-bolt passing through the trigger mechanism housing; pushed in from left to right it gives single shots, pushed from right to left gives automatic fire.

Unloading:
Magazine catch on top of magazine housing. Press down and remove magazine, pull back cocking handle to eject any round in the chamber, and inspect the chamber via the ejection port. Release the cocking handle, press the trigger.

Sten Mk VI UK

This is a silenced weapon based on the Mark V design and is little more than the barrel/silencer assembly of the Mark IIS assembled to the receiver of the Mark V. The number made is believed to have been much less than the Mark IIS, since it was never intended for broadcast distribution to resistance groups, but simply for use by regular Commando and similar forces. The mechanical principles are the same, and thus there is the same embargo on automatic fire in anything other than grave emergencies. This is principally because automatic fire tends to vibrate the silencer and the bullets then clip the edges of the internal baffles.

Specification & Operation

Cartridge:
9mm Parabellum

Dimensions:
Length o/a: 900mm
Barrel: 90mm
Weight, empty: 5.01kg
Rifling: 6 grooves, rh
Magazine capacity: 32 rounds
Rate of fire: 450 rds/min

In production: 1944-46

Markings:
'STEN M.C. Mk VI' on top of magazine housing.

Safety:
Pull back cocking handle and turn up into a notch in the operating slot to lock the bolt in the cocked position. Press in the cocking handle when the bolt is forward to lock it to the receiver. Fire selection is done by a cross-bolt passing through the trigger mechanism housing; pushed in from left to right it gives single shots, pushed from right to left gives automatic fire.

Unloading:
Magazine catch on top of magazine housing. Press down and remove magazine, pull back cocking handle to eject any round in the chamber, and inspect the chamber via the ejection port. Release the cocking handle, press the trigger.

Sterling UK

Specification & Operation

Cartridge:
9mm Parabellum

Dimensions:
Length, stock extended: 710mm
Length, stock folded: 480mm
Barrel: 198mm
Weight, empty: 2.70kg
Rifling: 6 grooves, rh
Magazine capacity: 34 rounds
Rate of fire: 550 rds/min

In production: 1953-88

Markings:
'STERLING SMG 9mm' and serial number on top
of magazine housing on standard production.
'Gun Submachine 9mm L2A3', serial number,
NATO Stock Number, on top of magazine housing
on weapons produced for the British Army.

Safety:
Combined safety catch and fire selector lever on
left side of frame, above the pistol grip. To the
rear for safe; central for single shots; forward for
automatic fire.

Unloading:
Magazine catch at rear of magazine housing.
Press down and remove magazine, pull back
cocking handle to eject any round in the
chamber, and inspect the chamber via the
ejection port. Release the cocking handle, press
the trigger.

The Sterling has been used by some 50
or more countries; it is the Canadian
C1, and forms the basis of the Australian
F1 submachine gun, and although
Sterling collapsed in 1988 the gun is still
made under license in India; there must
be tens of thousands of them in existence
and they could appear anywhere. There is
a silenced version, known as the L34 in
British service, which bears the same
relationship to the L2A3 as did the Sten
IIS to the Mark II. There are also
innumerable semi-automatic versions of
the L2 pattern used by police and security
forces around the world.

Steyr MPi69 AUSTRIA

increased to about 700 rds/min. There is also a special long-barrel version of the MPi81, designed for firing out of the ports of an armoured personnel carrier and known as the 'Loop-Hole' model.

The MPi69 was adopted by the Austrian Army in 1969 and remains in wide use by several other armies and security forces. An excellent weapon, its only peculiarity is the attachment of the sling to the cocking system; some people do not like this, and for them the Steyr company makes the MPi81, which is the same weapon but with a conventional cocking handle and with the rate of fire

Specification & Operation

Cartridge:
9mm Parabellum

Dimensions:
Length, stock extended: 670mm
Length, stock folded: 465mm
Barrel: 260mm
Rifling: 6 grooves, rh
Weight, empty: 3.13kg
Magazine capacity: 25 or 32 rounds
Rate of fire: 550 rds/min

In production: 1969-90

Markings:
STEYR-DAIMLER-PUCH AG MADE IN AUSTRIA and serial pressed into plastic stock.

Safety:
Cross-bolt passing through the receiver; one end is marked 'S' in white and protrudes when the weapon is safe, the other is marked 'F' in red and protrudes when the weapon is set to fire. If the button is pushed only half-way in either direction, the gun will fire single shots only.

Unloading:
Magazine release in the heel of the butt. Withdraw the magazine. Cock the weapon by holding the pistol grip in one hand and grasping the sling with the other. Hold the sling out sideways, disengage the cocking slide catch from the front sight, then pull back the bolt by pulling back on the sling. Examine the chamber via the ejection port, ensuring it is empty, then press the trigger and allow the sling and bolt to go forward.

Steyr AUG Para AUSTRIA

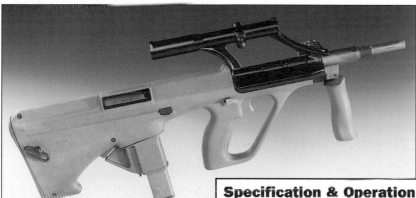

existing assault rifle design to the 9mm cartridge, so producing a submachine gun with the minimum requirement for new parts manufacture, and to date it is the most successful. For some time the company also sold a kit of parts from which any AUG rifle could be converted into the submachine gun version.

This is simply the Steyr AUG assault rifle, described elsewhere, converted to 9mm Parabellum calibre by fitting a new barrel, new bolt and a magazine adapter to take the MPi69 magazines. The gas operating system of the rifle is disabled and the AUG Para is a blowback weapon. The long barrel gives it excellent accuracy and a higher velocity than is usual from this cartridge. Steyr were one of the first to adapt an

Specification & Operation

Cartridge:
9mm Parabellum

Dimensions:
Length o/a: 665mm
Barrel: 420mm
Weight, empty: 3.30kg
Rifling: 6 grooves, rh
Magazine capacity: 25 or 32 rounds
Rate of fire: 700 rds/min
In production: 1988-

Markings:

STEYR-DAIMLER-PUCH AG MADE IN AUSTRIA and serial pressed into plastic stock.

Safety:
A cross-bolt safety catch above the trigger. Press in from left to right to make safe; press from right to left to fire. Fire selection is performed by the trigger; the first pressure gives single shots, further pressure gives automatic fire.

Unloading:
Remove magazine. Pull back cocking handle, inspect chamber, release it and pull trigger.

Steyr TMP AUSTRIA

There is a folding forward handgrip, and a sound suppressor can be fitted. There are plans to adopt a modular system of construction, similar to that of the AUG rifle, which will permit changing a few parts to convert the TMP to other calibres such as 10mm Auto. The same weapon, without the forward hand grip, and firing single shots only, is marketed as the SPP (Special Purpose Pistol).

The TMP (Tactical Machine Pistol) has replaced the MPi69 and MPi 81 as the standard Steyr production submachine gun. The receiver is almost entirely of synthetic material, and so tough that steel inserts to guide the bolt are not required.

Specification & Operation

Cartridge:
9mm Parabellum

Dimensions:
Length o/a: 270mm
Barrel: 150mm
Weight, empty: 1.30kg
Rifling: 6 grooves, rh
Magazine capacity: 15, 20 or 25 rounds
Rate of fire:

In production: 1993-

Markings:
'Steyr-Mannlicher' and serial number on left side of receiver.

Safety:
A cross-bolt safety catch lies in the top of the grip, behind the trigger. Pushed from left to right, the weapon is safe. Pushed from right to left, the weapon is set for automatic fire. Pushed half-way the weapon is set for single shots.

Unloading:
Magazine catch is a button in the left front edge of the butt, just behind the trigger. Remove magazine. Grasp cocking handle, a pair of wings beneath the rear sight, and pull back to eject any round in the chamber. Inspect chamber via the ejection port, pull trigger and allow cocking handle and bolt to run forward.

Steyr-Solothurn MP34 AUSTRIA

A solid and extremely well-made weapon, designed in Germany, perfected by a German-owned company in Switzerland and manufactured in Austria. It was used by the Austrian Army, was also taken into limited use by the German Army, and bought by the Portuguese in 1942, where it remained in use by their Fiscal Guards until the late 1970s. A number were also made in 9mm Parabellum calibre for the Germany Army in 1938-39. An unusual feature is a magazine loading device built into the magazine housing.

Specification & Operation

Cartridge:
9 x 23mm Steyr

Dimensions:
Length o/a: 808mm
Barrel: 200mm
Weight, empty: 4.36kg
Rifling: 6 grooves, rh
Magazine capacity: 32 rounds
Rate of fire: 500 rds/min

In production: 1934-39

Markings:
Serial number & year over chamber. Steyr monogram (SSW) may also be above the chamber.

Safety:
A sliding safety catch is on top of the receiver in front of the rear sight. Slide forward to make the weapon safe by locking the bolt whether in the open or closed position.

Unloading:
Magazine catch on magazine housing. Remove magazine, pull back cocking handle to eject any round in the chamber. Inspect chamber via ejection port, release cocking handle, press trigger.

Suomi M1931 FINLAND

One of the earliest non-German submachine guns, the Suomi was developed in Finland and saw use in Scandinavian armies, the Swiss Army, South America and Poland, and was built under license in Denmark and Switzerland. It was generally considered to be among the best designs available in 1939 when the British Army tried to

acquire some (without luck - the Russians attacked Finland and the Finns had no guns to spare). It remained in Finn service until well after 1945, most of their guns being modified to accept the Carl Gustav magazine, upon which the other Scandinavian countries had standardised.

Specification & Operation

Cartridge:
9mm Parabellum

Dimensions:
Length o/a: 870mm
Barrel: 314mm
Weight, empty: 4.60kg
Rifling: 6 grooves, rh
Magazine capacity: 71 round drum , or 20 or 50 round box
Rate of fire: 900 rds/min

In production: 1931-44

Markings:
Serial number on end cap and on left side of receiver.

Safety:
Manual safety lever in the front edge of the trigger guard. Push backwards, into the guard, to make safe; this locks the bolt in either the forward or rearward position.

Unloading:
Magazine release behind the magazine housing. Remove magazine. Pull back cocking lever to eject any round in the chamber. Examine chamber via the ejection port, release cocking lever, press trigger.

Suomi M1944 FINLAND

This is obviously based upon the Soviet PPS-43 design, numbers of which were acquired by the Finns in 1943-44. The principal difference is that the Suomi fires the 9mm Parabellum cartridge and is designed to accept the two standard magazines (box and drum) of the Suomi M1931 submachine gun, so that there was no need to complicate the supply lines with a new type of magazine. The designer of this adapted

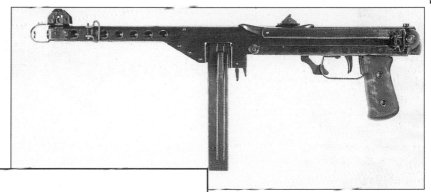

Specification & Operation

Cartridge:
9mm Parabellum

Dimensions:
Length, stock extended: 830mm
Length, stock folded: 620mm
Barrel: 248mm
Weight, empty: 2.90kg
Rifling: 4 or 6 grooves, rh
Magazine capacity: 36 round box or 71 round drum
Rate of fire: 650 rds/min

In production: 1944-45

Markings:
Serial number on left side of receiver.

Safety:
Manual safety catch in front edge of trigger guard; push forward, out of the guard, for safe.

Unloading:
Magazine release behind the magazine housing. Remove magazine. Pull back cocking lever to eject any round in the chamber. Examine chamber via the ejection port, release cocking lever, press trigger.

weapon later escaped to Spain and re-invented it as the `Dux', after which he hawked it round for several years but the only takers were the West German Border Police and the Dux vanished in the early 1960s. So far as the Finns go, the M44 is still held in their war reserve stocks.

Thompson M1928 USA

This can claim to be the first submachine gun insofar as Thompson was the man who invented the word, though it was not the first such weapon to see service. It did not appear until 1921, well after the Bergmann and Beretta designs, and the 1928 version

Specification & Operation

Cartridge:
.45 ACP

Dimensions:
Length o/a: 857mm with compensator
Barrel: 267mm
Weight, empty: 4.88kg
Rifling: 6 grooves, rh
Magazine capacity: 20 or 30 rounds box, 50 or 100 round drum
Rate of fire: 700 rds/min

In production: 1919-42

Markings:
'THOMPSON SUBMACHINE GUN/CALIBER .45 COLT AUTOMATIC CARTRIDGE/MANUFACTURED BY/ COLT'S PATENT FIREARMS MFG CO/HARTFORD,

CONN, USA/MODEL OF 1928\serial number' all on left side of receiver.

Safety:
Manual safety catch above the pistol grip on the left side of the receiver. Back for safe, forward for fire. The weapon can only be set to safe when the bolt is drawn back. A fire selector switch is further forward on the left side of the receiver; move forward for automatic fire, back for single shots.

Unloading:
Magazine catch is a thumb-operated latch just behind the trigger on the left grip. Release the magazine. Pull back the cocking handle to eject any round in the chamber, inspect the chamber via the ejection port. Release the cocking handle, pull the trigger.

was much the same as the 1921 except for some minor changes to the bolt to reduce the rate of fire. But it was this model which was adopted by the US Marines and initiated the submachine gun in American service, and its association with Chicago and the gangster era was also responsible for much of the distaste with which many armies viewed this class of weapon. But for reliability and solid construction, very few guns have ever come close to the Thompson.

Thompson M1 USA

M1 and M1A1. The M1 series also abandoned the drum magazine; it was too noisy on night patrols as the contents slid back and forth.

The great selling (and arguing) point about the Thompson was its method of locking the breech - or at least of delaying its opening. Whatever else it did, it made the weapon slower and more expensive to manufacture, and so in 1942 a simplified version, using pure blowback operation, appeared as the M1; a later model had the firing pin integral with the bolt, instead of separate, and became the M1A1. The visible identifying mark between the 'old' M1928 and the 'new' M1 series is the position of the cocking handle - on top for the M1928, on the right side of the receiver for the

Specification & Operation

Cartridge:
.45 ACP

Dimensions:
Length o/a: 013mm
Barrel: 268mm
Weight, empty: 4.74kg
Rifling: 6 grooves, rh
Magazine capacity: 20 or 30 round box
Rate of fire: 700 rds/min

In production: 1942-44

Markings:
'AUTO ORDNANCE CORPORATION/ BRIDGEPORT, CONNECTICUT, USA' or 'SAVAGE ARMS CO/ UTICA N.Y., USA' on right side of receiver. 'US Model M1 [M1A1]/serial number' on left side of receiver.

Safety:
Manual safety catch above the pistol grip on the left side of the receiver. Back for safe, forward for fire. The weapon can only be set to safe when the bolt is drawn back. A fire selector switch is further forward on the left side of the receiver; move forward for automatic fire, back for single shots.

Unloading:
Magazine catch is a thumb-operated latch just behind the trigger on the left grip. Release the magazine. Pull back the cocking handle to eject any round in the chamber, inspect the chamber via the ejection port. Release the cocking handle, pull the trigger.

This was designed in Italy and several thousand were made in 1944-45 for use by Italian troops. After the war it was offered for sale, and the Burmese government bought the production machinery and set up a factory which produced it as the 'BA-52' for the Burmese Army; the BA-52 was slightly shorter than the TZ-45 and there were one or two very small detail changes, but the two are essentially the same. As a result of this the TZ/BA can be expected to turn up anywhere in the Middle or Far East.

Specification & Operation

Cartridge:
9mm Parabellum

Dimensions:
Length, stock extended: 851mm
Length, stock folded: 546mm
Barrel: 229mm
Weight, empty: 3.26kg
Rifling: 6 grooves, rh
Magazine capacity: 20 or 40 rounds
Rate of fire: 550 rds/min

In production: 1944-45 (Italy); 1952-55 (Burma)

Markings:
Serial number stamped on left of receiver.

Safety:
A combined safety catch and fire selector lever is on the right side of the receiver above the trigger. When drawn back, the bolt is locked and the weapon safe. Pushed to the central position, single shot fire is operable; pushed completely forward for automatic fire. There is also a grip safety behind the magazine housing which must be squeezed in to release the bolt.

Unloading:
Magazine catch at bottom rear of magazine housing. Remove magazine. Squeeze the grip safety and pull back the cocking handle to eject any round in the chamber. Inspect chamber via the ejection port. Release cocking handle, pull trigger.

United Defense M42 USA

Developed in 1938-40, this was produced by Marlin in the USA for the US Government, though the destination of the 15,000 guns has never been clearly identified. They appear to have been distributed to clandestine organisations in Europe and the Far East. A large number went to the Netherlands

Specification & Operation

Cartridge:
9mm Parabellum

Dimensions:
Length o/a: 820mm
Barrel: 279mm
Weight, empty: 4.13kg
Rifling: 6 grooves, rh
Magazine capacity: 20 rounds
Rate of fire: 700 rds/min

In production: 1942-43

Markings:
`UNITED DEFENSE SUPPLY CORP/ US MODEL 42/ MARLIN FA CO NEW HAVEN' and serial number on left side of receiver.

Safety:
Manual safety catch and fire selector lever on right side of receiver above the trigger. Turn UP to the vertical position for Safe. Turn forward for automatic fire, rearward for single shots. Note that if the safety catch is applied, pulling back the cocking handle will automatically remove the safety and set the weapon for single shot fire.

Unloading:
Magazine catch at rear of magazine housing. Remove magazine, pull back cocking handle to eject any round in the chamber. Inspect chamber via ejection port, release cocking handle, press trigger.

government forces in the Dutch East Indies, so these weapons are probably more common in the Pacific area than elsewhere in the world. An excellent weapon made of good materials, the UD M42 will last for a very long time.

principal defects were its rudimentary safety mechanism and the unnecessarily complicated bolt retraction and cocking handle on the right-hand side, which soon gave problems due to breakages in action.

This could be called America's answer to the Sten gun, since it was their examination of the Sten which prompted the demand for a cheap and simple weapon to replace the Thompson. Designed by George Hyde assisted by a metal-pressing expert from General Motors, the M3 was designed so as to be capable of being changed to 9mm calibre by changing the bolt, barrel and magazine, though it seems very few such changes were ever made in the field. Its

Specification & Operation

Cartridge:
.45 ACP or 9mm Parabellum

Dimensions:
Length, stock extended: 745mm
Length, stock retracted: 570mm
Barrel: 203mm
Weight, empty: 3.67kg
Rifling: 4 grooves, rh
Magazine capacity: 30 rounds
Rate of fire: 400 rds/min

In production: 1942-44

Markings:
'GUIDE LAMP DIV OF GENERAL MOTORS/ US MODEL M3/ serial number' on top of receiver.

Safety:
A hinged cover over the ejection port carries a lug which, when the cover is closed, engages with a recess in the bolt if the bolt is forward, or with the front edge of the bolt when the bolt is to the rear, locking the bolt in either position.

Unloading:
Magazine catch is on the left side of the magazine housing. Open ejection port cover; remove magazine. Pull back bolt retracting lever on right side of receiver to cock the bolt. Inspect the chamber through the ejection port, press the trigger, close the ejection port cover.

Uzi ISRAEL

One of the most famous of submachine guns and one which is likely to appear anywhere in the world. The Uzi has been made under license in Belgium and Germany, and the general layout and principles of its mechanism have been copied in several countries. It is still in production in Israel, and has

Specification & Operation

Cartridge:
9mm Parabellum

Dimensions:
Length, fixed stock: 640mm
Length, stock extended: 640mm
Length, stock folded: 440mm
Barrel: 260mm
Weight, empty: 3.50kg
Rifling: 4 grooves, rh
Magazine capacity: 25, 32 or 40 rounds
Rate of fire: 600 rds/min

In production: 1953-

Markings:
Serial number left rear side of receiver on Israeli models; may also have Hebrew markings.

'M.P. UZI Kal 9mm serial number' on left rear side of receiver on German models.

Safety:
A combined safety catch and fire selector is fitted into the top of the pistol grip on the left side. Pulled back, the weapon is safe with the bolt locked; in the central position single shots are possible, and in the forward position automatic fire is possible. There is also a grip safety on the pistol grip which must be squeezed in so as to release the bolt.

Unloading:
The magazine catch is at the bottom left side of the pistol grip. Remove the magazine. Pull back the cocking handle so as to eject any round in the chamber, inspect the chamber via the ejection port, release the cocking handle and pull the trigger.

been joined in the past decade by two smaller models, the Mini-Uzi and the Micro-Uzi; these resemble the Uzi but are simply smaller in all dimensions except the calibre. They are easily identifiable by their similarity with the basic Uzi and by their names, which are marked on the left side of the receiver.

Vietcong K-50M VIETNAM

pattern. The result is quite a distinctive weapon, unlikely to be mistaken for anything else. So far as mechanism goes, though, it is still a Soviet PPSh.

In 1950 the Chinese produced a copy of the Soviet PPSh-41 submachine gun, calling it the Type 50. Numbers of these were supplied to North Vietnam, who then redesigned it and produced it as this K-50M. The major changes were the removal of the original fold-over butt, replacing it with a telescoping wire butt, shortening the barrel jacket and removing the muzzle compensator, and adding a pistol grip. The curved magazine is similar to the Chinese

Specification & Operation

Cartridge:
7.62mm Soviet Pistol (or 7.63mm Mauser)

Dimensions:
Length, stock extended: 756mm
Length, stock retracted: 571mm
Barrel: 269mm
Weight, empty: 3.40kg
Rifling: 4 grooves, rh
Magazine capacity: 25, 32 or 40 rounds
Rate of fire: 600 rds/min

In production: 1958-65

Markings:
Serial number on top of receiver.

Safety:
Manual safety latch on the cocking handle; this can be pushed into notches cut into the receiver wall when the bolt is either fully forward or fully back, and locks the bolt in that position. There is a fire selector switch inside the trigger guard, in front of the trigger; push forward for automatic fire, back for single shots.

Unloading:
Magazine release is behind the magazine housing and folds up under the stock. Fold down, press forward and slide the magazine out. Pull back cocking handle to eject any round in the chamber, inspect the chamber via the ejection port, release the cocking handle, press trigger.

Vigneron BELGIUM

Specification & Operation

Cartridge:
9mm Parabellum

Dimensions:
Length, stock extended: 872mm
Length, stock retracted: 695mm
Barrel: 300mm
Weight, empty: 3.28kg
Rifling: 6 grooves, rh
Magazine capacity: 32 rounds
Rate of fire: 600 rds/min

In production: 1952-62

Markings:
`ABL52 VIG M1' and serial number on right side of magazine housing.

`Licence Vigneron' cast into right side of receiver.

Safety:
A combined safety catch and fire selector lever is on the left side of the receiver. Turned to the rear makes the weapon safe; forward one notch for single shots, forward and DOWN for automatic fire. There is also a grip safety on the pistol grip which must be squeezed in to unlock the bolt.

Unloading:
Magazine catch on right side of magazine housing. Remove magazine. Pull back cocking handle to eject any round in the chamber, inspect chamber via the ejection port. Release cocking handle, pull trigger.

A Belgian design, this was issued to the Belgian Army in 1953 and then to the Belgian forces in the Belgian Congo. After the Congo became independent these weapons were taken over by Congo troops, after which they were undoubtedly dispersed all over Central Africa. Numbers also appear to have been acquired by the Portuguese, who took it into service as the M/961, and these were probably left in Angola. As a result, the Vigneron can be expected to turn up anywhere in Africa for some years to come.

Walther MPK and MPL GERMAN

Left: Long version. Right: Short version

The MPK and MPL are simply the same weapon with either long (L) or short (K) barrels. The long model has a 260mm barrel., which increases the overall length to 749mm. In spite of its excellent quality and performance it was never adopted by any army, but some German naval units and various European police forces took it into use in the 1960s. A silencer-equipped model was later developed but this apparently attracted few customers.

Specification & Operation

Cartridge:
9mm Parabellum

Dimensions: (MPK)
Length, stock extended: 659mm
Length, stock folded: 373mm
Barrel: 173mm
Weight, empty: 2.80kg
Rifling: 6 grooves, rh
Magazine capacity: 32 rounds
Rate of fire: 550 rds/min

In production: 1963-85

Markings:
Serial number on left side of receiver.

Safety:
There is a manual safety catch on both sides of the receiver, behind the trigger. When turned UP and to the rear, the weapon is safe; then turned forward and DOWN, the weapon is ready to fire. The original design had no provision for single shots; as an option, a different mechanism with a third position on the safety catch could be fitted to give single shots, but how many of these were actually made is not known.

Unloading:
Magazine release is behind the magazine housing, below the trigger guard. Remove the magazine, pull back the cocking handle to eject any round in the chamber. Inspect the chamber via the ejection port, release the cocking handle, pull the trigger.

Zastava M85 YUGOSLAVIA

This is obviously a Yugoslavian copy of the Soviet AKSU-74 submachine gun, differing in being chambered for the Western 5.56mm cartridge rather than the Soviet 5.45mm round, probably in order to attract the export market. Due to the current political situation in ex-Yugoslavia we have no idea of how many of these weapons have been made, or where they may have been distributed, but the possibility of their appearance should be borne in mind, and a weapon of this shape should not be automatically identified as the AKSU.

Specification & Operation

Cartridge:
5.56 x 45mm

Dimensions:
Length, stock extended: 790mm
Length, stock folded: 570mm
Barrel: 315mm
Weight, empty: 3.20kg
Rifling: 6 grooves, rh
Magazine capacity: 20 or 30 rounds
Rate of fire: 700 rds/min

In production: 1987-

Markings:
`CRVENA ZASTAVA M/85; [year]; serial number' on right side of receiver.

Safety:
This uses the standard Kalashnikov type of safety lever/fire selector on the right side of the receiver; in the top position it locks the trigger and blocks movement of the cocking handle and the weapon is safe; the first position DOWN gives automatic fire and the fully DOWN position gives single shots.

Unloading:
Magazine release is behind the magazine housing. Remove magazine, set the fire selector to one of the fire positions, pull back the cocking handle to eject any round in the chamber. Inspect the chamber via the ejection port, release the cocking handle, pull the trigger.

ZK-383 YUGOSLAVIA

Designed in Czechoslovakia in the early 1930s, the designer seems undecided whether he was making a submachine gun or a light infantry support gun, providing his design with a long barrel, a solid butt and a bipod. It also has a quick-change barrel, another adjunct more usual in support machine

Specification & Operation

Cartridge:
9mm Parabellum

Dimensions:
Length o/a: 875mm
Barrel: 325mm
Weight, empty: 4.25kg
Rifling: 6 grooves, rh
Magazine capacity: 30 rounds
Rate of fire: 500 and 700 rds/min

In production: 1936-48

Safety:
A manual cross-bolt safety above the trigger; pushed in from left to right, it locks the trigger and puts the weapon in the safe condition. Just in front of this is a fire selector switch; turned to the rear, to the figure `1', it gives single shots; turned forward to the figure `30' it gives automatic fire. Normal rate is 500 rds/min, but by removing a weight from the bolt this can be increased to 700 rds/min.

Unloading:
The magazine release is at the rear of the magazine housing on the left side of the receiver. Remove magazine. Pull back cocking handle to eject any round in the chamber. Inspect chamber via the ejection port, release the cocking handle, pull the trigger.

guns. It was used by the German and Bulgarian armies during 1939-1945, and remained in service in Bulgaria until the middle 1960s. It was also sold to South America and used as a heavy support weapon by some central European police forces, who generally dispensed with the bipod.

BOLT ACTION RIFLES

Bolt Action Rifles

There have only been a handful of successful bolt actions; there have been a number of unsuccessful ones , and there are some which appear to be different simply to avoid patent litigation, but knowledge of the principal systems will probably be a sufficient guide to anything which may be encountered. Bolt systems are divided into two - turn-bolts and straight-pull bolts:

Turn-bolts

so-called because to open them it is necessary to lift the handle and so rotate the body of the bolt in order to unlock it from the chamber or action:-

Mauser

The most widely used, because it is undoubtedly the strongest and generally considered to be the most reliable and accurate. The bolt carries lugs with which it locks firmly into the chamber so that there can be no movement of the bolt during firing. The drawback is that the bolt must revolve sufficiently to disengage these lugs before it can move backwards, and on loading it must close completely before it can be rotated to lock. Together with this bolt came the charger-loading system, adopted by many other bolt actions, in which the ammunition is held in some form of spring clip. This clip is positioned above the magazine and the cartridges are pushed from the clip, into the magazine, after which the clip is discarded. In order to avoid confusion between this system and the system developed by Mannlicher, the Mauser (and Lee, and others,) system is called 'charger loading', while the Mannlicher system is called 'clip loading'

Lee

The Lee turnbolt is theoretically weaker and less accurate than the Mauser, but it is undoubtedly the fastest and smoothest of all bolt actions; a trained soldier with a Lee-Enfield rifle can deliver aimed fire twice as fast as one with a Mauser. The fundamental difference is that the bolt lugs lock into recesses in the action body; these have curved surfaces so that as soon as the bolt begins to turn, it also begins to open and move backwards, and on closing it can begin rotation before it is completely closed. The theoretical disadvantage is that since the bolt is not locked into the chamber it can compress slightly under the pressure of the explosion and so affect the chamber pressure and ballistics. In practice this is scarcely noticeable.

Krag-Jorgensen

The Krag system, from Norway, is less a bolt system than a magazine system, since the bolt is of no great interest but the magazine lies laterally beneath the bolt and feeds up and around the left side to deliver the cartridge to the boltway on the left-hand side of the action. Loading is done by opening a hinged trap-door and pushing loose rounds in; on closing the door a magazine spring bears on the rounds and forces them up to the feedway. It is a reliable enough system, particularly with rimmed ammunition, but, as with so many other systems, one wonders whether avoiding existing patents was the major reason for its development.

Lebel

The French Lebel bolt system uses two forward locking lugs plus a large rectangular lug on the outside of the bolt body which locks into a recess in the action. A screw passes through this lug

Bolt Action Rifles

to retain the bolt head; the screw must be removed and the head detached in order to remove the bolt, since the head will not pass through the boltway and out of the back of the action. It also has a unique magazine, tubular in form, lying beneath the barrel, from which rounds are lifted up to the breech by a linkage operated by the movement of the bolt.

Mannlicher
The essence of the Mannlicher system is not so much the bolt, which is comparable to that of the Mauser, but the magazine, since Mannlicher invented the clip-loading system. In this system the cartridges are held in a clip, and clip and cartridges are dropped into the magazine as a unit. The clip is locked in place and a spring-loaded arm pushes the cartridges up as they are loaded. When the last shot is fired the clip can be expelled; in some later designs it expels itself.

Mosin-Nagant
Developed by Captain Mosin of the Russian Army, this bolt is a complex three-piece device which appears to have been designed primarily to avoid patent litigation.

Straight-pull bolts
so-called because to open them it is only necessary to grasp the handle and pull it straight back without lifting.

Mannlicher
The founder of the straight-pull system, Mannlicher developed two kinds. His first used a wedge beneath the bolt which was pushed down and lifted up by a sleeve attached to the bolt handle. The second also used a sleeve with helical grooves

inside which connected with lugs on the bolt body, carried inside the sleeve, so that as the handle was pulled back the sleeve rode over and forced the lugs to turn the bolt and unlock it.

Schmidt
This resembles the Mannlicher second type, but uses a bolt sleeve which carries the bolt body. A rod is driven back and forth by the handle and engages in a cam track in the bolt sleeve to rotate the sleeve. The locking lugs are actually on the sleeve, and the bolt body does not rotate. It was later modified to become much shorter but the principle remained the same. It has only ever been used on Swiss Army rifles and carbines.

Lee
The Lee straight pull is similar to the first Mannlicher system, using a wedge beneath the bolt which is controlled by the bolt handle; as the handle is pulled back it first lifts the wedge and then pulls on the bolt. It is unlikely to be encountered; almost all Lee straight-pull rifles are museum pieces.

Ross
The Ross resembles the second Mannlicher but uses a screw-thread in the bolt sleeve which engaged with a helical screw-thread on the bolt body, so that reciprocal movement of the sleeve rotates the bolt and its locking lugs. Unfortunately it proved susceptible to dirt on active service, and the bolt can be assembled wrongly, still close and fire, but is then blown open violently. Not to be recommended.

303

Accuracy International L96A1 UK

The standard sniping rifle of the British Army, this features an aluminium chassis to support the action and barrel, clothed in a plastic outer casing. It is also sold commercially in various models, the `Long Range' chambered for 7mm Remington Magnum or .300 Winchester Magnum; the `Counter-Terrorist' in 7.62mm, the `Moderated' with an integral silencer, and the `Infantry' with a non-zoom telescope sight. The Long Range model is a single shot, the rest are magazine rifles.

Specification & Operation

Cartridge:
7.62 x 51mm NATO

Dimensions:
Length o/a: 1.124m
Weight: 6.50kg
Barrel: 654mm
Rifling: 4 grooves, rh
Magazine capacity: 10 rounds

In production: 1985 -

Markings: CR 156 GA ACCURACY INTERNATIONAL ENGLAND NATO stock number; serial number (all on left side of action).

Safety:
Manual safety catch on the left rear of the action. Forward for fire, back for safe. The safety catch locks the bolt, trigger and firing pin; the bolt cannot be closed when the safety is applied, and the safety cannot be applied unless the striker is cocked.

Unloading:
Magazine catch behind magazine. Remove magazine, empty out any ammunition. Set the safety catch to `fire'. Open bolt to extract any round remaining in the chamber. Examine chamber and feedway, close bolt, press trigger, replace empty magazine.

Arisaka 38th Year rifle JAPAN

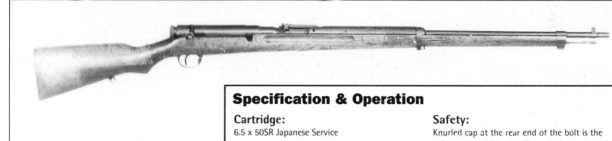

Japanese service rifle, based on the Mauser system, also supplied to Britain, Mexico, Russia, Indonesia and Thailand at various times. Can be found converted to fire the US .30-06 cartridge, done in the 1950s to provide weapons for South Korea, or for the 7.92mm Mauser, a conversion done by the Chinese. Something like three million were made and they can be found almost anywhere. Japanese nomenclature can confuse; `38th Year' refers to the reign of the Emperor at the time of introduction; it equates to 1905. The system changed in the 1930s (see p306).

Specification & Operation

Cartridge:
6.5 x 50SR Japanese Service

Dimensions:
Length o/a: 1.275m
Weight: 4.12kg
Barrel: 799mm
Rifling: 4 or 6 grooves, rh
Magazine capacity: 5 rounds

In production: 1907 44

Markings:
Japanese ideographs for `38 Year' above chamber; serial number and arsenal mark left side of frame.

Safety:
Knurled cap at the rear end of the bolt is the safety catch. With the rifle cocked, press in this cap with the palm of the hand and twist it to the right to make safe, to the left to fire. It only works with the rifle cocked.

Unloading:
Set safety catch to `fire'. Open bolt to extract any round left in the chamber. Examine the magazine aperture; if there is ammunition in the magazine, place one hand underneath the magazine plate under the stock, and with the other hand press forward the magazine catch in the front edge of the trigger guard. This will release the magazine floor plate and the contents of the magazine. Replace the magazine spring and plate (front edge first), check there is no ammunition in magazine or chamber, close bolt, press trigger.

Arisaka Type 99 short rifle JAPAN

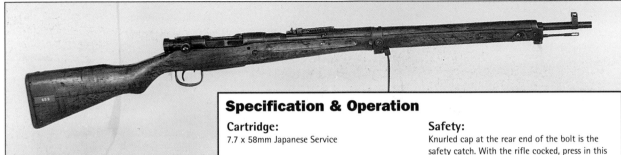

This began as a conversion of the 38th Year rifle to a 7.7mm cartridge. That proved unwieldy and the design was changed to a short rifle which did away with the need for carbines. Early models were excellent but those made in the last year of the war were crude; few have survived. The `Paratroop' version is similar but has either an interrupted thread or wedge joint between barrel and action, allowing it to be dismantled into two pieces. `Type 99' now refers to the year in the Japanese calendar and equates to 1939 in western chronology.

Specification & Operation

Cartridge:
7.7 x 58mm Japanese Service

Dimensions:
Length o/a: 1.15m
Weight: 3.80kg
Barrel: 657mm
Rifling: 4 grooves, rh
Magazine capacity: 5 rounds

In production: 1940-45

Markings:
Japanese ideographs for `Type 99' above chamber; serial number and arsenal mark left side of frame.

Safety:
Knurled cap at the rear end of the bolt is the safety catch. With the rifle cocked, press in this cap with the palm of the hand and twist it to the right to make safe, to the left to fire. It only works with the rifle cocked.

Unloading:
Set safety catch to `fire'. Open bolt to extract any round left in the chamber. Examine the magazine aperture; if there is ammunition in the magazine, place one hand underneath the magazine plate under the stock, and with the other hand press forward the magazine catch in the front edge of the trigger guard. This will release the magazine floor plate and the contents of the magazine. Replace the magazine spring and plate (front edge first), check there is no ammunition in magazine or chamber, close bolt, press trigger.

Boys anti-tank rifle UK

This is introduced as an example of the heavy anti-tank rifles which several nations developed and employed in the 1935-45 period. This class of weapon expired during the 1939-45 war as it became obvious they were ineffective against the improved tanks, but the principle was revived in the 1980s for heavy sniping, and several of the Boys and other rifles have been observed re-barrelled to take the .50 Browning cartridge. Original ammunition is now so scarce as to be collector's items.

Specification & Operation

Cartridge:
.55in Boys

Dimensions:
Length o/a: 1.613m
Weight: 16.33kg
Barrel: 914mm
Rifling: 7 grooves, rh
Magazine capacity: 5 rounds

In production: 1937-42

Markings:
`BOYS Mk I' and serial number on receiver.

Safety:
Manual safety catch on the left side of the receiver, at the rear of the magazine housing. Forward for fire, rearward for safe.

Unloading:
Magazine release behind the top-mounted magazine. Press release, remove magazine. Open bolt to extract any round in the chamber. Inspect chamber, close bolt, press trigger. Note that the bolt cannot be closed if an empty magazine is in place.

Beretta Sniper ITALY

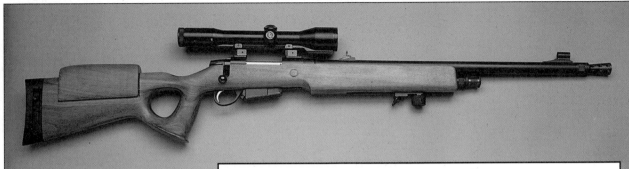

This is a conventional Mauser-type bolt action, with a heavy free-floating barrel and an harmonic balancer contained within a tube concealed by the wooden fore-end. This is vibrated by the shot being fired and is so designed as to damp out vibrations in the barrel, ensuring the maximum accuracy. There is a flash hider on the muzzle, and the tube of the balanced forms a point of attachment for a bipod. Fully adjustable iron sights are provided but it also carries a NATO-standard mount for telescope and electro-optical sights.

Specification & Operation

Cartridge:
7.62 x 51mm NATO

Dimensions:
Length o/a: 1.165m
Weight: 5.55kg
Barrel: 586mm
Rifling: 4 grooves, rh
Magazine capacity: 5 rounds

In production: 1985-

Markings:
`P.BERETTA` above chamber. Serial number right side of receiver.

Safety:
Thumb-catch behind bolt handle

Unloading:
Magazine catch behind magazine. Push safety catch to `fire`, remove magazine, open bolt to eject any round in the chamber. Inspect chamber, close bolt, press trigger.

De Lisle silent carbine UK

This unusual weapon was designed around the standard Lee-Enfield bolt action but barrelled for the US .45 pistol cartridge, and with an integral silencer. Since this cartridge is subsonic, the De Lisle is probably the most silent of all silenced weapons. Two versions were made, with a fixed butt and with a metal folding butt; and the resemblance between the folding butt of the De Lisle and that of the Sterling submachine gun is because both weapons were made by Sterling. A similar weapon, but based on the action of the Remington 700 rifle and chambered for the 7.62 x 51mm NATO round is currently manufactured in England and called the 'De Lisle Mark 4'.

Specification & Operation

Cartridge:
.45 ACP

Dimensions:
Length o/a: 960mm
Weight: 3.70kg
Barrel: 210mm
Rifling: 4 grooves, lh
Magazine capacity: 8 rounds

In production: 1942-45

Markings:
Serial number on right side of receiver.

Safety:
Manual safety catch on left side of receiver; forward for fire, back for safe.

Unloading:
Magazine catch inside trigger guard. Remover magazine. Place safety catch to 'fire', open bolt to extract any round in the breech. Close bolt, press trigger.

Enfield Rifle No 2 (Pattern '14) UK

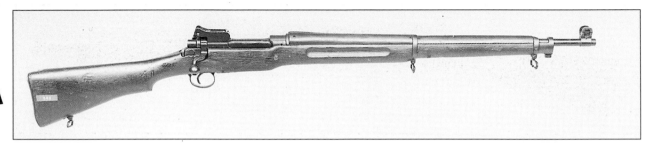

This was developed in 1912-14 as a potential replacement for the Lee-Enfield and uses a Mauser-type action. The design was in .276 calibre, firing a very powerful cartridge, and proved to be a ballistic disaster. On the outbreak of war in 1914 the project was abandoned, but to satisfy the enormous demand for rifles it was re-designed to fire the .303 cartridge and manufactured in the USA under contract by Remington and Winchester. The rifles remained in store during 1919-40 and were then brought out again and issued to the Home Guard and to some home defence units. Thousands were sold after 1945 for target rifles.

Specification & Operation

Cartridge:
.303 British

Dimensions:
Length o/a: 1.176m
Weight: 4.14kg
Barrel: 660mm
Rifling: 5 grooves, lh
Magazine capacity: 5 rounds

In production: 1915-17

Markings:
Maker's mark and serial number on top of chamber.

Safety:
Manual safety catch on right side of action, behind the bolt handle. Forward for fire, rearward for safe.

Unloading:
Place safety catch in the 'fire' position. Open bolt to extract any round in the chamber. Inspect magazine; if it contains ammunition continue working the bolt until all rounds have been loaded and ejected. Depress the magazine platform to allow the bolt to go forward, close the bolt, pull the trigger.

Enfield US service rifle M1917 (Pattern '17) UK

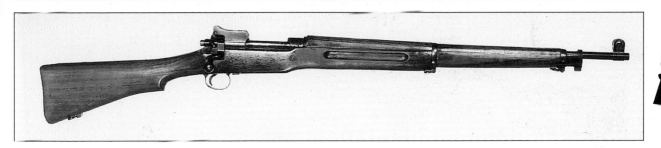

This is the same rifle as the British Pattern '14. When the USA entered the war in 1917 it, too, needed rifles, the British contract had just ended, so the Americans re-designed it to take the standard US .30 rimless cartridge and went on to make almost two million before the end of the war. They were extensively used by US troops and after the war went into store. About 119,000 were sent to Britain in 1940 and issued to the Home Guard where they had to be marked with a red band on stock and fore-end to distinguish them from the .303 Pattern 14 rifles. After 1946 most were sold off to target shooters and as hunting rifles.

Specification & Operation

Cartridge:
.30-06 US Service

Dimensions:
Length o/a: 1.175m
Weight: 4.08kg
Barrel: 660mm
Rifling: 5 grooves, rh
Magazine capacity: 5 rounds

In production: 1917-18

Markings:
`U.S.RIFLE M1917` over chamber. Serial number on right side of action.

Safety:
Manual safety catch on right side of action, behind the bolt handle. Forward to fire, rearward for safe.

Unloading:
Place safety catch in the `fire' position. Open bolt to extract any round in the chamber. Inspect magazine; if it contains ammunition continue working the bolt until all rounds have been loaded and ejected. Depress the magazine platform to allow the bolt to go forward, close the bolt, pull the trigger.

Enfield Enforcer UK

This was developed by the Royal Small Arms Factory as a result of requests from British police forces for a sniping rifle. It uses the basic Lee-Enfield action, allied to a heavy barrel and a shortened 'sporter' fore-end. It is, in fact, the same rifle as the British Army's L42A1 sniping rifle; the difference is that when issued to the British Army it had a plain sighting telescope, but when sold to the police it was given a more modern zoom telescope sight. A very similar weapon was also sold, without optical sight, in the civil market as the 'Envoy' target rifle.

Specification & Operation

Cartridge:
7.62 x 51mm NATO

Dimensions:
Length o/a: 1.180m
Weight: 4.42kg
Barrel: 700mm
Rifling: 4 grooves, rh
Magazine capacity: 10 rounds.

In production: 1970-85

Markings:
'ENFIELD' and year of manufacture on the stock band beneath the bolt. Serial number on right side of chamber.

Safety:
Manual safety catch on left side of action. Forward for fire, back for safe.

Unloading:
Magazine catch behind the magazine. Remove magazine. Place safety catch to 'fire', open bolt to eject any round in the chamber. Inspect chamber, close bolt, press trigger.

FN 30-11 Sniping rifle BELGIUM

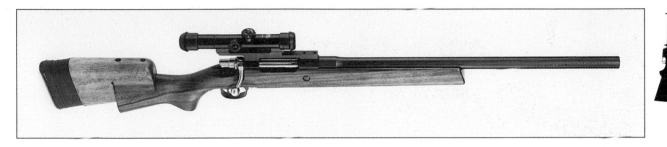

Developed as a sniping rifle for police and military use, this used a standard Mauser bolt action and integral magazine in a heavy receiver and barrel. Aperture sights were fitted but a telescope was the more usual sighting method. Accessories such as a firing sling and bipod were usually supplied with the rifle.

Specification & Operation

Cartridge:
7.62 x 51mm NATO

Dimensions:
Length o/a: 1.117m
Weight: 4.85kg
Barrel: 502mm
Rifling: 4 grooves, rh
Magazine capacity: 10 rounds

In production: 1978-86

Markings:
'FABRIQUE NATIONALE HERSTAL' on left side of barrel. Serial number on right side of action.

Safety:
Manual safety catch on the end of the bolt. To the left for fire, to the right for safe.

Unloading:
Place safety catch to 'fire'. Open the bolt to eject any round in the chamber. Inspect the magazine aperture; if ammunition is in the magazine, work the bolt to load and unload cartridges until the magazine is empty. Check both chamber and magazine, then depress the magazine platform and close the bolt. Press the trigger.

GIAT FR-F1 & FR-F2 FRANCE

Specification & Operation

Cartridge:
7.5 x 54mm or 7.62 x 51mm

Dimensions:
Length o/a: 1.138m
Weight: 5.20kg
Barrel: 552mm
Rifling: 4 grooves. rh
Magazine capacity: 10 rounds

In production: 1966-80 (F1); 1984- (F2).

Markings:
'FR-F1 7.62 N M.A.S.' and serial number on left
side of receiver.

Safety:
Manual safety catch inside the trigger guard,
behind the trigger. Press down to make safe;
press up and to the left to fire.

Unloading:
Magazine catch on the right side of the receiver
above the front end of the magazine. Remove
magazine. Place safety catch to 'fire' and open
the bolt to eject any round in the chamber.
Inspect the chamber, close the bolt, pull the
trigger.

This is a precision sniping rifle based
on the action of the MAS36 service
rifle; it was actually designed first as a
target rifle, and then modified for the
sniping role. The F1 was issued first in
7.5mm calibre, and then changed to
7.62mm calibre in the late 1970s. The
FR-F2 model is an improved version; the
fire-end is of plastic-covered metal
instead of wood, the bipod is stronger,
and there is a thermal insulating sleeve
over the barrel to prevent warping due
to heat and reduce the infra-red
signature.

Krag-Jorgensen rifles NORWAY

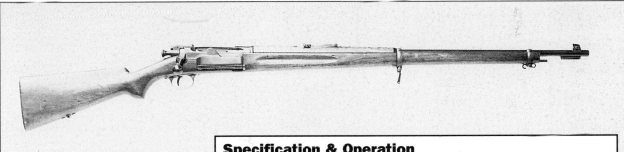

The Krag-Jorgensen was developed in Norway and is unusual because of its side-loading magazine. The door flap is opened, loose rounds placed inside, and the door closed, which puts pressure on the rounds and feeds them under and around the bolt to appear on the left side of the boltway. It was adopted by Denmark then Norway and then the USA, but only Norway stayed with it, developing their last version as late as 1930. Many thousands of these rifles and carbines were sold off for hunting purposes in Scandinavia and the USA and are still in use in both areas.

Specification & Operation

Cartridge:
6.5 x 55mm (Norway; .30 Krag (USA); 8 x 56R (Denmark)

Dimensions: (Norway, M1930)
Length o/a: 1.219m
Weight: 5,19kg
Barrel: 750mm
Rifling: 4 grooves, lh
Magazine capacity: 5 rounds

In production: 1888-1935

Markings:
`(USA): MODEL 1894 SPRINGFIELD ARMORY' and serial number on left side of receiver.

Safety:
Manual safety catch on the end of the bolt. Turn to the left for fire, to the right for safe.

Unloading:
Open the magazine by hinging the door forward (Danish weapons) or down (US and Norwegian), tipping the rifle to the right and allowing the cartridges to fall out on to some convenient surface. Close the magazine, set the safety catch to `fire' and open the bolt to eject any round in the chamber. Inspect the chamber and the magazine aperture to the left of the boltway to ensure no ammunition remains in the weapon. Close the bolt, press the trigger.

Lebel M1886 FRANCE

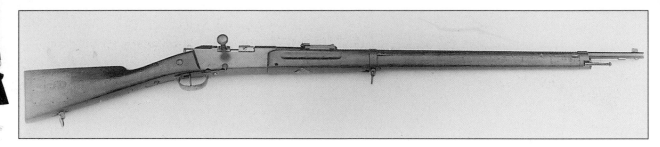

The first rifle designed to use a small-calibre bullet and smokeless powder, the Lebel was a technical advance but a clumsy piece of machinery. There were some small improvements in 1893 (the Mle 86/93) and numbers were converted into a short rifle in 1935 (Mle 86/93/R35) and it continued in limited use until 1945. Some four million were made, and there are still a lot of them about in Europe and ammunition is still manufactured.

Specification & Operation

Cartridge:
8 x 51R Lebel

Dimensions:
Length o/a: 1.307m
Weight: 4.18kg
Barrel: 815mm
Rifling: 4 grooves, lh
Magazine capacity: 8 rounds

In production: 1886-1919

Markings:
Factory mark, year and serial number on right side of receiver.

Safety:
There is no manual safety device on this weapon other than by grasping the cocking-piece at the rear of the bolt and pulling it to the half-cock position.

Unloading:
Open the bolt to extract any cartridge in the chamber. Close the bolt and DO NOT press the trigger. Open the bolt again. If another round is extracted, then the bolt must be worked back and forwards until the magazine has been emptied. The magazine is tubular, beneath the barrel, and there is no quick and easy way to empty it.

Lebel-Berthier 1907/15 rifle FRANCE

The tubular magazine of the Lebel rifle was an abomination, slow to load, slower to unload. The Berthier modification to the Lebel design gave it a box magazine with a Mannlicher-type clip, which considerably improved its combat abilities. The choice of a three-round clip came from a desire to avoid major surgery to the stock, but eventually a five-round clip was adopted, leading to a sheet-metal extension to the magazine below the stock in later models. These Berthier designs remained in service until the 1950s, many being converted to the 7.5mm French Service calibre.

Specification & Operation

Cartridge:
8 x 51R Lebel

Dimensions:
Length o/a: 1.306m
Weight: 3.81kg
Barrel: 803mm
Rifling: 4 grooves, lh
Magazine capacity: 3 rounds

In production: 1915-18

Markings:
Factory and model number - e.g. `CHATELLERAULT M1907/15' - on left side of action.

Safety:
There is no manual safety device other than the ability to draw the cocking piece (rear of the bolt) back to the half-cock position.

Unloading:
Open the bolt, extracting any round which may be in the chamber. Examine the magazine aperture. If ammunition can be seen, press the clip release catch in the front edge of the trigger guard. This will release the clip, which will be ejected upwards together with any ammunition which may be in it. Examine the magazine again to ensure that it is empty of cartridges, examine the chamber, close the bolt, press the trigger.

Lee-Enfield Carbine, Magazine, Mk 1 UK

A modification of the earlier Lee-Metford rifle by re-barrelling to the Enfield system and shortening. A well-balanced and handy little weapon, many were sold off and converted into sporting rifles by shortening the wooden fore-end. They can still be recognised by the flattened bolt knob, intended to make then easier to fit into saddle buckets. There are some variant models, for cavalry, artillery and engineer use, with or without sling bars and bayonet fittings, but all were basically the same. Carbines were superseded by the issue of the Short Lee-Enfield Rifle in 1904, though numbers remained in service for some years.

Specification & Operation

Cartridge:
.303 British Service

Dimensions:
Length o/a: 998mm
Weight: 3.37kg
Barrel: 527mm
Rifling: 5 grooves, lh
Magazine capacity: 6 rounds

In production: 1896-1905

Markings:
'ENFIELD', Crown and year on right side of the stock band beneath the bolt handle. Serial number on right side of chamber.

Safety:
Manual safety catch on the right side of the cocking-piece at the rear of the bolt. Press DOWN to fire, lift UP for safe.

Unloading:
Press up on magazine catch inside the trigger guard to release the magazine, which should be removed, with its contents, and emptied. Open the bolt to extract any cartridge in the chamber. Pull out the magazine cut-off by pressing down the round catch on the right side of the action and pulling it out. Examine the chamber and feedway, close the bolt, pull the trigger, replace the empty magazine and push the cut-off back in..

Lee-Enfield, Rifle, Short, Magazine, MkIII UK

The SMLE comes in one or two sub-varieties, with minor differences, but the Mark III is the one which matters; over three million were made in Britain, India and Australia and it served in both world wars. Indeed, many British soldiers in 1939-1945 went to great lengths to acquire one instead of the wartime replacement, the Rifle No 4 (below); there was nothing wrong with the No 4 but the SMLE was a legend in its own time. Utterly reliable and with the smoothest bolt-action ever made, the SMLE was sneered at by the purists for not being a Mauser, but it silenced all its critics in 1914: German units on the receiving end thought they were under machine-gun fire.

Specification & Operation

Cartridge:
.303 British Service

Dimensions:
Length o/a: 1.132m
Weight: 3.96kg
Barrel: 640mm
Rifling: 5 grooves, lh
Magazine capacity: 10 rounds

In production: 1907-43.

Markings:
Maker, date and `SHT L.E.' on right side of the stock band beneath the bolt. Serial number on right side of chamber.

Safety:
Manual safety catch on left side of action. Press forward to fire, rearward for safe.

Unloading:
Press up on magazine catch inside the trigger guard to release the magazine, which should be removed, with its contents, and emptied. Open the bolt to extract any cartridge in the chamber. Pull out the magazine cut-off by pressing down the round catch on the right side of the action and pulling it out. Examine the chamber and feedway, close the bolt, pull the trigger, replace the empty magazine and push the cut-off back in.

Lee-Enfield, Rifle No 4 UK

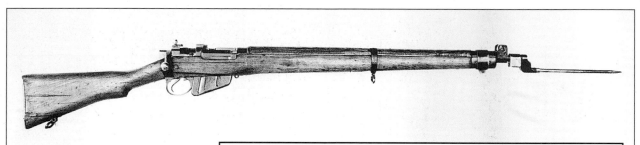

This was the replacement for the SMLE Mark III; it was virtually the same rifle but simplified in order to make wartime mass-production easier. The nosecap was changed and a spike bayonet replaced the old sword, and the sights changed to a tangent aperture pattern on the rear of the receiver instead of a U-notch tangent halfway along the rifle. It made teaching recruits easier but expert shots felt they had better control with the older pattern. About four million were made in Britain, the USA, Canada, India and Australia, and about 40,000 American-made rifles were also supplied to China.

Specification & Operation

Cartridge:
.303 British Service

Dimensions:
Length o/a:1.128m
Weight: 4.11kg
Barrel: 640mm
Rifling: 5 grooves, lh
Magazine capacity: 10 rounds

In production: 1940-45

Markings:
Maker and year on right of stock band beneath bolt handle. Serial number on right side of chamber. Rifles manufactured in the USA may have 'UNITED STATES PROPERTY' on the left side of the receiver; those made in Canada may have 'LONG BRANCH' in the same place.

Safety:
Manual safety catch on left side of action. Press forward to fire, rearward for safe.

Unloading:
Press up on magazine catch inside the trigger guard to release the magazine, which should be removed, with its contents, and emptied. Open the bolt to extract any cartridge in the chamber. Examine the chamber and feedway, close the bolt, pull the trigger, replace the empty magazine.

Lee-Enfield, Rifle No 5 UK

This is the familiar Lee-Enfield action attached to a short-barrelled compact rifle intended for jungle warfare. A handsome weapon, it never lived up to its appearance; blast and recoil were unpleasant due to the short barrel and powerful cartridge, and the rifle suffered from a 'wandering zero': zero it today and it would shoot beautifully, but tomorrow it would miss by miles and need re-zeroing. Much time and energy was spent on trying to solve this but in the end the authorities gave up and the rifle was declared obsolete in 1947.

Specification & Operation

Cartridge:
.303 British

Dimensions:
Length o/a: 1.000m
Weight: 3.24kg
Barrel: 478mm
Rifling: 5 grooves, lh
Magazine capacity: 10 rounds

In production: 1943-47

Markings:
No 5 Mk I on left side of action. Serial number, year and manufacturer's mark on left side of butt strap behind trigger.

Safety:
Manual safety catch on left side of action. Press forward to fire, rearward for safe.

Unloading:
Magazine catch at rear of magazine. Remove magazine. Place safety catch to 'fire', open bolt to eject any round in the chamber. Inspect chamber, close bolt, press trigger.

McMillan M87R USA

This was the start of a series of very similar heavy sniping rifles; the M87 was a single-shot; the 87R a magazine rifle. Some changes in minor details brought the M88 in 1988, then the M89 with a glass-fibre stock as standard, and, most recently, the M93 with a hinged butt and the ability to fit 10 or 20 round magazines. These, and similar, heavy sniping rifles are not for anti-personnel use but for anti-materiel use; a .50 bullet can do a great deal of damage to delicate equipment at small cost.

Specification & Operation

Cartridge:
12.7 x 99mm (.50 Browning)

Dimensions:
Length o/a: 1.346m
Weight: 9.52kg
Barrel: 736mm
Rifling: 8 grooves, rh
Magazine capacity: 5 rounds

In production: 1987-

Markings:
McMillan Gun Works and serial number on right side of action.

Safety:
Thumb-catch on right side behind bolt handle.

Unloading:
Magazine catch behind magazine. Remove magazine, empty out contents. Open bolt to extract any round in the chamber. Examine chamber and feedway, close bolt, pull trigger, replace magazine.

Mannlicher turnbolt rifles AUSTRIA

Specification & Operation

Cartridge:
6.5 x 53R (Dutch);   6.5 x 53mm (Romanian)

Dimensions: (Dutch M1895 rifle)
Length o/a: 1.295m
Weight: 4.30kg
Barrel: 790mm
Rifling. 4 grooves, rh
Magazine capacity: 5 rounds

In production: 1896 1940

Markings:
Manufacturer (`STEYR' or `HEMBRUG'), year and serial number above chamber.

Safety:
A thumb-switch at the top rear of the bolt. Turned to the right, the rifle is safe. Turned to the left, the rifle is ready to fire. Note that on the Romanian M1893 rifle the safety can only be applied when the striker is cocked, on the Dutch M1895 it can be applied in any condition of the bolt.

Unloading:
Open bolt to extract any cartridge in the chamber. Examine the magazine aperture; if there are cartridges in the magazine, press forward the clip release button in the front edge of the trigger guard. This will allow the clip, with any remaining ammunition, to be ejected upwards through the action. Check the chamber and magazine are both empty, close the bolt, press the trigger.

The essential difference between the Mannlicher and other turn-bolt systems lay in his pioneering of the clip loading system. The bolt is opened and a complete clip of ammunition is dropped into the magazine. An arm forces the cartridges up in the clip to be collected by the bolt, and when the last round is loaded, the clip drops out of the magazine through a hole in the bottom, or, in some designs, was ejected upwards when the bolt was opened after the last round was fired. Note that the clip is an essential part of the magazine system; without a clip the rifle is a single-shot weapon, since the magazine is unusable.

Mannlicher straight-pull bolt rifles AUSTRIA

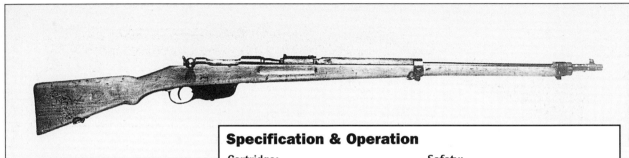

There are two varieties of straight-pull bolt used in Mannlicher rifles; the first has a wedge beneath the bolt which is forced down by movement of the handle, and is found on the M1886 Austrian rifle. The second uses a bolt sleeve with helical grooves, inside which is a bolt body with lugs; as the bolt handle, attached to the sleeve, is pulled back, the grooves in the sleeve force the bolt body to turn and unlock. This was used on the Austrian M1895 service rifle. Both are designed so that if the bolt is not securely locked, the firing pin cannot go forward.

Specification & Operation

Cartridge:
8 X 50R Austrian Service

Dimensions: (Austrian M1895 rifle)
Length o/a: 1.272m
Weight: 3.78kg
Barrel: 765mm
Rifling: 4 grooves, rh
Magazine capacity: 5 rounds

In production: 1895-1918

Markings:
`STEYR M.95' over chamber. Serial number on left of chamber.

Safety:
Manual safety catch on the left rear side of the action. When turned up it engages with the bolt, locking it in place, and also partly withdraws the striker. Turned down, to the left, the rifle is made ready to fire.

Unloading:
Place safety catch to the `fire' position. Open the bolt to extract any round in the chamber. Examine the magazine aperture; if there is ammunition in the magazine, press the clip release button in the front edge of the trigger guard. This will eject the clip and any ammunition upwards through the action. Check the chamber and magazine are both empty, close the bolt, pull the trigger.

Mannlicher-Carcano TS Carbine M1891 ITALY

The Mannlicher-Carcano family formed the Italian service weapons from 1891 to 1945. The TS (Truppo Special) carbine is one of the more common examples of the system; the other weapons - rifle M1891, cavalry carbine M1891, carbine M91/24 and rifle M91/38 - are identical in their mechanism. The bolt is basically Mauser, the magazine Mannlicher, with its associated clip, and the Carcano part of the title comes from the Italian who designed the bolt safety system. They were mostly sold off after 1945 and spread throughout the world; President Kennedy was shot with a Mannlicher-Carcano carbine.

Specification & Operation

Cartridge:
6.5 x 52mm Mannlicher

Dimensions:
Length o/a: 920mm
Weight: 3.13kg
Barrel: 450mm
Rifling: 4 grooves, rh
Magazine capacity: 6 rounds

In production: 1891-1918

Markings:
Year of manufacture and 'TERNI'and serial number on side of breech.

Safety:
Manual safety catch in the form of a collar with a knurled 'flag' around the end of the bolt. Turned DOWN to the right, the rifle is ready to fire. Turned UP so that it is visible in the line of sight, the rifle is set to safe.

Unloading:
Place safety catch to 'fire' and open the bolt, thus ejecting any round which may be in the chamber. Inspect the chamber and magazine. If there is ammunition in the magazine, press the clip latch in the front edge of the trigger guard; this will release the ammunition clip and it, together with any cartridges it contains, will be ejected upwards through the top of the action. Check again, close the bolt and press the trigger.

Mannlicher-Carcano M1938 ITALY

The 1914–18 war suggested that the Italian 6.5mm cartridge was insufficiently powerful, and experience in North Africa and Abyssinia reinforced this view, and the Model 1938 rifle and carbine were built around a new 7.5mm cartridge. However, they left it too late, and when Italy entered the war in 1940 it was decided to withdraw these new weapons and give them to the militia so as to simplify ammunition supply in the field. A handful of the carbines were modified in 1944 to fire German 7.92mm Mauser ammunition. These can be recognised by 7.92 S stamped into the top of the chamber; it is unwise to fire these converted weapons.

Specification & Operation

Cartridge:
7.35 x 51mm Italian M38

Dimensions:
Length o/a: 1.021m
Weight: 3.40kg
Barrel: 530mm
Rifling: 4 grooves, rh
Magazine capacity: 6

In production: 1937-40

Markings:
Year of manufacture, 'TERNI', and serial number on right side of chamber.

Safety:
Manual safety catch in the form of a collar with a knurled `flag' around the end of the bolt. Turned DOWN to the right, the rifle is ready to fire. Turned UP so that it is visible in the line of sight, the rifle is set to safe.

Unloading:
Place safety catch to 'fire' and open the bolt, thus ejecting any round which may be in the chamber. Inspect the chamber and magazine. If there is ammunition in the magazine, press the clip latch in the front edge of the trigger guard; this will release the ammunition clip and it, together with any cartridges it contains, will be ejected upwards through the top of the action. Check again, close the bolt and press the trigger.

Mannlicher-Schoenauer Greek M1903 AUSTRIA

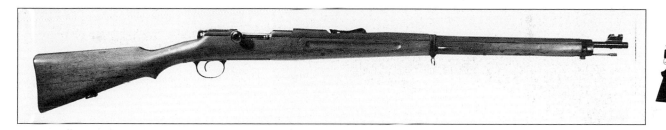

This was a combination of the Mannlicher turn-bolt breech with a rotary spool magazine developed by Otto Schoenauer. The magazine consists of a spindle with five grooves for cartridges around its circumference, held under tension by a spring. As the cartridges are fed into the magazine from a charger they slot into the grooves and turn the spindle, placing more tension on the spring. As the bolt is operated, so the spring turns the spindle to present each cartridge to the bolt in turn. The Greek 1903 rifle was the only service weapon to use this magazine, but it was widely used on sporting rifles and carbines and is still used today on the Steyr-Mannlicher SSG69 (below).

Specification & Operation

Cartridge:
6.5 x 54mm Greek Service

Dimensions:
Length o/a: 1.226m
Weight: 3.77kg
Barrel: 725mm
Rifling: 4 grooves, rh
Magazine capacity: 5 rounds

In production: 1903-30

Markings:
Year and place of manufacture ('BREDA' or 'STEYR') above breech. Serial number on right side of action.

Safety:
Manual safety catch at the rear of the bolt. Turn to the left to fire, to the right for safe.

Unloading:
Place the safety catch to 'fire'. Open the bolt to extract and eject any round in the chamber. Examine the chamber and magazine aperture; if there is ammunition remaining in the magazine, press down the knurled catch on the right-hand side of the action. This will release the cartridges remaining in the magazine and cause them to be ejected through the action. Check chamber and magazine again, close the bolt, pull the trigger.

MAS Mle 1936 FRANCE

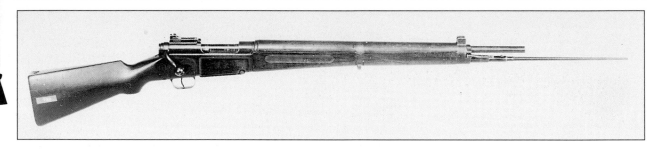

Ugly, roughly made, but immensely strong and reliable, this was the French Army's rifle to match the 7.5mm cartridge introduced in 1929. A folding-butt model was also made for paratroops and Alpine troops, though this is rarely encountered. Late models (converted in the 1950s) have an extended barrel with concentric rings to permit launching rifle grenades. The finish varies from phosphated, to browned to enamelled, according to when it was made and for which arm of the service.

Specification & Operation

Cartridge:
7.5 x 54mm French Service

Dimensions:
Length o/a: 1.022m
Weight: 3.75kg
Barrel: 575mm
Rifling: 4 grooves, rh
Magazine capacity: 5 rounds

In production: 1936-55

Markings:
`ST ETIENNE' and year of manufacture on left side of action. Serial number on right side of action.

Safety:
There is no manual safety device on this weapon. BE CAREFUL.

Unloading:
Open the bolt to extract any cartridge in the chamber. Then press in the magazine floor plate release button on the right side of the action body, at the front edge of the magazine, and allow the magazine contents to fall into the hand. Check that the magazine space and chamber are empty, close the bolt, press the trigger. Replace the magazine follower, spring and floor-plate.

Mauser Gewehr 98 GERMANY

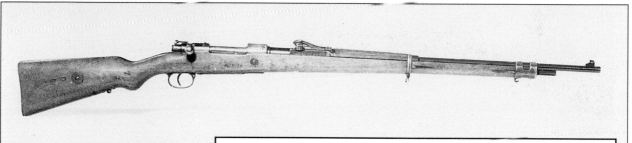

Mauser made many military rifles for various nations, but most of them were variations of this, the perfected Mauser rifle which armed the German Army for half a century; understand this and you understand them all. Robust, well-made, accurate and reliable, these rifles will last for years to come and still be serviceable. The Gew 98 improved on the basic Mauser design by having a third locking lug beneath the bolt, locking into a recess in the left action sidewall. The bolt sticks out at right-angles; a variation with a turned-down bolt was provided for cyclist troops in 1904 but is unlikely to be met.

Specification & Operation

Cartridge:
7.92 x 57mm Mauser

Dimensions:
Length o/a: 1.250m
Weight: 4.09kg
Barrel: 740mm
Rifling: 4 grooves, rh
Magazine capacity: 5 rounds

In production: 1898-1918

Markings:
'Mod 98', manufacturer's name and serial number on top of chamber.

Safety:
A manual safety catch on the rear of the bolt. Turned to the left, the rifle is ready to fire. Turned to the right the rifle is safe.

Unloading:
Place the safety catch to `fire' and open the bolt to extract any round in the chamber. Examine the magazine aperture. If there is ammunition in the magazine, press the magazine floor-plate catch in the front edge of the trigger guard. This allows the magazine floor plate to hinge at its front end, open, and dump the contents of the magazine. Examine the chamber and magazine aperture again, close the bolt, press the trigger, and then close the magazine floor plate.

Mauser Karabiner 98k GERMANY

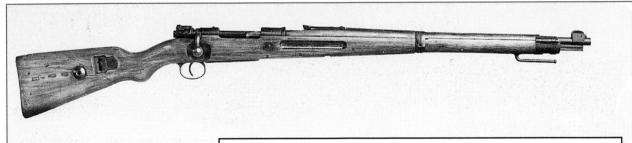

Specification & Operation

This is the 'short rifle' version of the Gewehr 98, developed in time for World War Two and is immediately recognisable by its shorter length, turned-down bolt, and recess in the woodwork to allow the bolt to be grasped. Rifles made from 1942 to 1945 are often of lesser quality - using stamped metal for the barrel bands and trigger-guard, for example, and laminated plywood for the furniture. They shot just as well, since there was no diminution in the quality of the bolt, barrel and action. About 11.5 million were made in ten years, so there will be Kar 98k's around for a long time yet.

Cartridge:
7.92 x 57mm Mauser

Dimensions:
Length o/a: 1.110kg
Weight: 3.92kg
Barrel: 600mm
Rifling: 4 grooves, rh
Magazine capacity: 5 rounds

In production: 1935-45

Markings:
'Kar 98k', manufacturer's code and serial number on sides of chamber.

Safety:
A manual safety catch on the rear of the bolt. Turned to the left, the rifle is ready to fire. Turned to the right the rifle is safe.

Unloading:
Place the safety catch to 'fire' and open the bolt to extract any round in the chamber. Examine the magazine aperture. If there is ammunition in the magazine, press the magazine floor-plate catch in the front edge of the trigger guard. This allows the magazine floor plate to hinge at its front end, open, and dump the contents of the magazine. Examine the chamber and magazine aperture again, close the bolt, press the trigger, and then close the magazine floor plate.

Mauser SP66

This is a heavy-barrelled rifle using the `short-throw` Mauser bolt so as to reduce the amount of movement required of the firer; it is purely a sniper rifle and thus various refinements can be accommodated which would not be found on hunting or military weapons. The stock is adjustable in several directions, the `lock time` between pulling the trigger and the bullet leaving the muzzle is extremely short, and there is a combined muzzle brake and flash hider. Optical sights are obligatory - there are no iron sights - and night sights can be very easily fitted.

Specification & Operation

Cartridge:
7.62 x 51mm NATO or .300 Winchester Magnum

Dimensions:
Length o/a: 1.120m
Weight: 6.25kg
Barrel: 730mm with muzzle brake
Rifling: 4 grooves, rh
Magazine capacity: 3 rounds

In production: 1976-

Markings:
`MAUSER-WERKE OBERNDORF GmbH' and serial number on left side of receiver.

Safety:
A manual safety catch on the rear of the bolt. Turned to the left, the rifle is ready to fire. Turned to the right the rifle is safe.

Unloading:
Place the safety catch to `fire' and open the bolt to extract any round in the chamber. Examine the magazine aperture. If there is ammunition in the magazine, press the magazine floor-plate catch in the front edge of the trigger guard. This allows the magazine floor plate to hinge at its front end, open, and dump the contents of the magazine. Examine the chamber and magazine aperture again, close the bolt, press the trigger, and then close the magazine floor plate.

Mauser 86 GERMANY

Specification & Operation

Cartridge:
7.62 x 51mm NATO

Dimensions:
Length o/a: 1.210m
Weight: 4.90kg
Barrel: 730mm with muzzle brake
Rifling: 4 grooves, rh
Magazine capacity: 9 rounds

In production: 1990-

Markings:
`MAUSER-WERKE OBERNDORF GmbH' and Serial Number on left of receiver.

Safety:
A manual safety catch on the rear of the bolt. Turned to the left, the rifle is ready to fire. Turned to the right the rifle is safe.

Unloading:
Withdraw the magazine from the bottom of the stock by pressing in the bottom catch. Empty the magazine of ammunition. Open the bolt, extracting any round remaining in the chamber. Examine the magazine aperture and the chamber to ensure both are empty, close the bolt, pull the trigger.

This was developed by Mauser as a somewhat less expensive sniping rifle than the SP66 described above, principally for police use. The bolt design is new, though it adheres to the well-tried Mauser double front lug system, and the barrel is cold forged and provided with a muzzle brake and flash hider. The stock is of laminated wood and ventilated so as to avoid warping of the barrel due to heat concentration. No iron sights are fitted, optical sights being the rule.

Mosin-Nagant rifles RUSSIA

This design originated in 1891 with a long rifle which remained in service until World War Two. It was generally superseded by the short 1938 carbine and the 1944, carbine which had an attached bayonet. Copies of the 1944 model were also made in China, Hungary and Poland, and Mosin-Nagant rifles were converted to 8mm in Austria and 7.92mm in Germany and Poland during and after World War One. Large numbers of 1891 rifles were made in France and the USA on contract.

Specification & Operation

Cartridge:
7.62 x 54R Russian Service

Dimensions: (Model 1938 Carbine)
Length o/a: 1.020m
Weight: 3.45kg
Barrel: 510mm
Rifling: 4 grooves, rh
Magazine capacity: 5 rounds

In production: 1892-1950

Markings:
Arsenal mark, year and serial number on top of chamber. Serial number on bolt.

Safety:
Manual safely by pulling back the cocking-piece at the rear of the bolt and rotating it to the left as far as it will go, then releasing it. This turns part of the cocking-piece so that it rests on a solid part of the receiver. The trigger still functions but the striker cannot go forward.

Unloading:
Open bolt to extract any round remaining in the chamber. Examine the magazine aperture; if there is ammunition in the magazine, release the magazine floor plate by pressing the catch behind the plate, in front of the trigger guard, and allowing the plate to hinge forward. This will allow the contents of the magazine to fall out. Close the magazine floor plate, check that the chamber and magazine are empty, close the bolt, pull the trigger.

Parker-Hale M82 UK

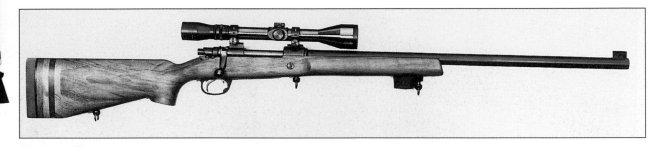

This is a sniping rifle which employs a commercial Mauser 98 bolt action allied to a heavy cold-forged barrel. It was adopted as the military sniping rifle of the Australian, New Zealand and Canadian armies. A version using a shorter butt and a shortened wooden fore-end was adopted by the British Army as the L81A1 Cadet Training Rifle in 1983. These rifles are still in service with the various forces, though Parker-Hale have given up rifle manufacture.

Specification & Operation

Cartridge:
7.62 x 51mm NATO

Dimensions:
Length o/a: 1.162m
Weight: 4.80kg
Barrel: 660mm
Rifling: 4 groove, rh
Magazine capacity: 4 rounds

In production: 1982-84

Markings:
PARKER-HALE LTD BIRMINGHAM ENGLAND 7.62 NATO on top of barrel. Serial on left of chamber.

Safety:
A manual safety catch on the rear of the bolt. Turned to the left, the rifle is ready to fire. Turned to the right the rifle is safe.

Unloading:
Press in the magazine floor plate catch in the front of the trigger guard; the floor plate will hinge forward and the contents of the magazine will fall out. Open the bolt to extract any round remaining in the chamber. Examine the chamber and the magazine space, close the bolt, pull the trigger, close the magazine floor plate.

Parker-Hale M83 UK

This stemmed from the Cadet Training rifle mentioned above under the M82; by restoring the butt to full length, it became the M83 NATO Target Rifle and was offered commercially, as well as being bought by various military units as a target rifle. In 1990 Parker-Hale sold the rights and designs of their rifles to the Gibbs Rifle Co in the USA and the M83 is still offered commercially, still using the Parker-Hale name.

Specification & Operation

Cartridge:
7.62 x 51mm NATO

Dimensions:
Length o/a: 1.187m
Weight: 4.98kg
Barrel: 660mm
Rifling: 4 grooves, rh
Magazine capacity: single shot

In production: 1983-90

Markings:
PARKER-HALE LTD BIRMINGHAM ENGLAND 7.62 NATO on top of barrel. M83 and serial number on left of chamber.

Safety:
A manual safety catch on the rear of the bolt.. Turned to the right the rifle is safe.

Unloading:
Open the bolt to extract any cartridge in the chamber. Inspect the chamber, close the bolt, pull the trigger.

Parker-Hale 85 UK

Specification & Operation

Cartridge:
7.62 x 51mm NATO

Dimensions:
Length o/a: 1.150m
Weight: 5.7kg with sight
Barrel: 700mm
Rifling: 4 grooves, rh
Magazine capacity: 10 rounds

In production: 1986-

Markings:
'PARKER HALE M85 GIBBS RIFLE CO MARTINSBURG WV USA' and serial number on right of receiver.

Safety:
A manual safety catch on the rear of the bolt. Turned to the left, the rifle is ready to fire. Turned to the right the rifle is safe.

Unloading:
Magazine catch behind magazine. Remover magazine and empty out any ammunition. Open bolt to extract any cartridge remaining in the chamber. Examine chamber and feedway. Close bolt, press trigger, replace empty magazine.

Parker-Hale designed this weapon as a potential sniping rifle for the British Army, but the Accuracy International L96A1 design was selected. Parker-Hale then gave up the rifle business and sold their designs to the Gibbs Rifle Co in the USA in 1990, and this company now manufactures the M85 under the Parkler-Hale title. The butt is adjustable for length and there is an easily detached bipod under the fore-end. A camouflage-pattern synthetic stock is also available.

Ross rifles CANADA

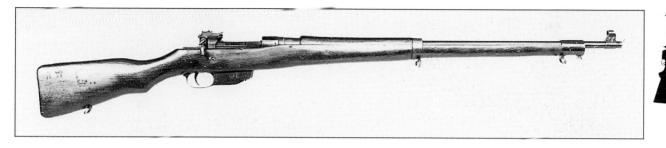

The Ross uses a straight-pull bolt; the handle draws on a sleeve, inside which is the actual bolt head unit, and the movement of the sleeve first rotates the bolt to unlock and then draws it back. It is a potentially dangerous weapon, since if the bolt is stripped and then reassembled wrongly it closes without locking, and firing the weapon can be fatal. If the bolt appears to close easily, it is probably wrong. The Ross was employed by the Canadian Army until 1915, when the mud of Flanders defeated the bolt by causing difficult extraction, but the rifles were put in reserve and many were sent to Britain in 1940 for use by the Home Guard.

Specification & Operation

Cartridge:
.303 British Service

Dimensions: (Mark III)
Length o/a: 1.284m
Weight: 4.47kg
Barrel: 768mm
Rifling: 4 grooves, lh
Magazine capacity: 5 rounds

In production: 1905-17

Markings:
Various: some have ROSS RIFLE CO QUEBEC CANADA 1905 PATENTED on left side of action.

Serial number always on left side of chamber.

Safety:
A flap on the bolt handle: when turned forward so the word SAFE is visible, the weapon is safe. When turned back so the word REAR is visible, it is ready to fire.

Unloading:
Extract any round in the chamber. Examine the magazine aperture; if there is ammunition in the magazine, continue working the bolt back and forth until the last round is ejected. Check that the chamber and magazine are both empty, close the bolt, pull the trigger.

Ruger M77 USA

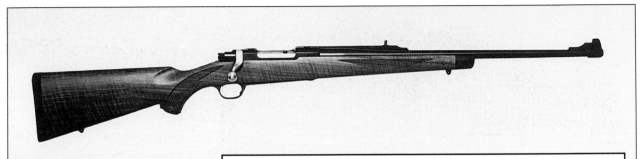

The Model 77 has been manufactured in a wide range of styles and calibres over the years and is widely distributed. The bolt action is adapted from the Mauser 98 pattern. The Model 77V, described here, is a `varmint' rifle, intended for small game, and has a heavy barrel and no iron sights, being invariably used with a telescope sight. As such it has been used by some police forces as a sniping rifle.

Specification & Operation

Cartridge:
7.62 x 51mm NATO and others

Dimensions: (M77V)
Length o/a: 1.118m
Weight: 4.08kg
Barrel: 610mm
Rifling: 4 grooves, rh
Magazine capacity: 5 rounds

In production: 1968-

Markings:
`STURM, RUGER INC SOUTHPORT CONN USA' and serial number on receiver

Safety:
A manual safety catch on the rear of the bolt. Turned to the left, the rifle is ready to fire. Turned to the right the rifle is safe.

Unloading:
Press in the magazine floor plate release catch in the front edge of the trigger guard to allow the floor plate to hinge forward and dump the contents of the magazine. Open the bolt to remove any cartridge remaining in the chamber. Examine the chamber and feedway. Close the bolt, press the trigger and close the magazine floor plate.

Sako TRG FINLAND

The TRG is a specialised sniping rifle. The receiver is of forged steel and the heavy barrel is also cold-forged and fitted with a combined flash hider and muzzle brake. The action and barrel are mounted to an aluminium skeleton frame, to which is attached the synthetic stock and fore-end. The muzzle brake can be removed and replaced with a silencer. The stock is fully adjustable in every direction and is also capable of adaptation to right- or left-handed firers. The TRG21 is the 7.62mm model; there is also a TRG41 which fires .308 Lapua Magnu; it has a 690mm barrel and a 5 round magazine.

Specification & Operation

Cartridge:
7.62 x 51mm NATO or .338 Lapua Magnum

Dimensions: (TRG21)
Length o/a: 1.150m
Weight: 4.70kg
Barrel: 660mm
Rifling: 4 grooves, rh
Magazine capacity: 10 rounds

In production: 1992-

Markings:
SAKO TRG21' and serial number on left side of receiver.

Safety:
Manual safety catch inside the trigger guard. Press forward to fire, pull back to make safe, which locks the bolt, trigger and firing pin.

Unloading:
Magazine release at rear of magazine. Remove magazine, empty out any ammunition. Open bolt to extract any cartridge left in the chamber. Examine chamber and feedway, close bolt, press trigger, replace empty magazine.

Schmidt-Rubin M1889 SWITZERLAND

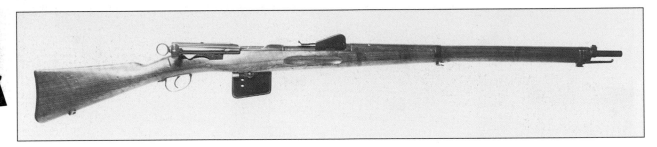

This is the first Schmidt straight-pull bolt design and is recognisable by the abnormally long receiver, due to the design of the bolt which has lugs locking into the action above the trigger. The bolt handle is connected to a rod which, when drawn back, drives a lug through a curved cam path on the bolt sleeve to rotate and unlock the bolt. Pulling further then opens the bolt. Although militarily obsolete, quite a number of these rifles survive for target shooting.

Specification & Operation

Cartridge:
7.5 x 53mm Swiss Service M1890

Dimensions:
Length o/a: 1.302m
Weight: 4.85kg
Barrel: 780mm
Rifling: 3 grooves, rh
Magazine capacity: 12 rounds

In production: 1889-1920

Markings:
Serial number at base of sight block.

Safety:
Pull back on the ring at the rear of the bolt, turn it to the left and release it. This withdraws the firing pin and locks it, making the rifle safe.

Unloading:
Magazine release at the left rear edge of the box magazine. Remove magazine. Open bolt to extract any round in the chamber. Examine chamber. Remove any ammunition from the magazine by pushing the rounds out forward. Close the bolt, pull the trigger, replace the magazine.

Schmidt-Rubin M1911 SWITZERLAND

The adoption of a new and more powerful cartridge demanded a stronger rifle; the existing Schmidt action was modified by placing the locking lugs at the front of the bolt sleeve, instead of the rear, so allowing the locking to take place closer to the breech. The action was thus slightly shorter than the M1889 weapons. A carbine was also produced using the 1911 action and cartridge, and some 1889 rifles and carbines were altered to take the new action and cartridge.

Specification & Operation

Cartridge:
7.5 x 54mm Swiss Service M1911

Dimensions:
Length o/a: 1.308m
Weight: 4.55kg
Barrel: 700mm
Rifling: 4 grooves, rh
Magazine capacity: 6 rounds

In production: 1911-25

Markings:
None - not even a serial number.

Safety:
Pull back on the ring at the rear of the bolt, turn it to the left and release it. This withdraws the firing pin and locks it, making the rifle safe.

Unloading:
Magazine release at the left rear edge of the box magazine. Remove magazine. Open bolt (by pulling straight back on the bolt handle) to extract any round in the chamber. Examine chamber. Remove any ammunition from the magazine by pushing the rounds out forward. Close the bolt, pull the trigger, replace the magazine.

Schmidt-Rubin M1931 carbine SWITZERLAND

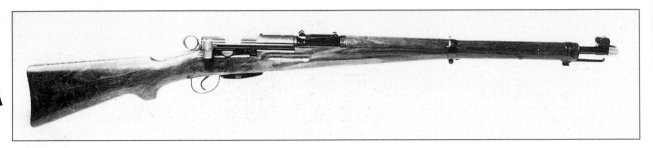

Although called a carbine, this was really a short rifle for use by the entire Swiss Army, and numbers are still in use today. The Schmidt action was completely revised; what had been the bolt sleeve became the bolt, with lugs at the front end locking into the chamber, so that the action body was shortened by almost half from the 1889 pattern. Numbers of these carbines were adapted as sniper rifles in 1942-43, and in the 1930s 100 were supplied to the Papal Guard in the Vatican City.

Specification & Operation

Cartridge:
7.5 x 54mm Swiss Service M1911

Dimensions:
Length o/a: 1.105m
Weight: 4.00kg
Barrel: 652mm
Rifling: 4 grooves, rh
Magazine capacity: 6 rounds

In production: 1933-58

Markings:
Serial number on left side of the action body and on bolt; Swiss cross on top of the chamber.

Safety:
Pull back on the ring at the rear of the bolt, turn it to the right and release it. This withdraws the firing pin and locks it, making the rifle safe.

Unloading:
Magazine catch on right side at top of magazine. Press in and remove magazine. Open bolt, examine chamber and feedway, close bolt. Press trigger.

SIG SSG-2000 SWITZERLAND

The SIG 2000 uses an unusual bolt system; hinged wedges just in front of the bolt handle are forced outwards by cam action when the handle is turned down. These lock into recesses in the receiver; the bolt body does not revolve. Once cocked the trigger is pulled to a distinct check to 'set' it; thereafter a slight touch is sufficient to fire. This weapon has been designed as a target

Specification & Operation

Cartridge:
7.62 x 51mm NATO and others

Dimensions:
Length o/a: 1.210m
Weight: 6.6kg with sight
Barrel: 610mm without flash hider
Rifling: 4 grooves, rh
Magazine capacity: 4 rounds

In production: 1989-

Markings:
SIG-SAUER SSG 2000 on left side of action. Serial number alongside chamber on right side.

Safety:
A sliding manual safety catch behind the bolt. When pushed forward, to reveal a red dot, the weapon is ready to fire. Pulled back, the weapon is safe.

Unloading:
Magazine catch behind the magazine. Remove magazine and empty it of ammunition. Open the bolt to extract any round in the chamber. Examine the chamber and feedway, close the bolt, pull the trigger, replace the empty magazine.

rifle and as a law enforcement sniper. There are no iron sights; a telescope is mandatory. In addition to the 7.62mm calibre it is also chambered for the 5.56 x 45mm and 7.5 x 55mm military calibres and the .300 Weatherby Magnum calibre.

SIG SSG-3000 SWITZERLAND

This is a military and police sniping rifle derived from a successful target rifle. It is modular in form; the barrel and receiver are joined by screw clamps, and the trigger and magazine systems form a single unit which fits into the receiver. The stock is of laminated wood and ventilated to counter possible heat warping the heavy barrel. The bolt has six lugs and locks into the barrel. There is

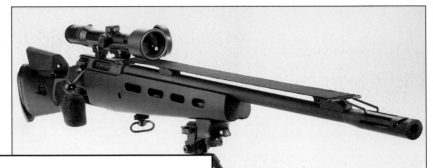

Specification & Operation

Cartridge:
7.62 x 51mm NATO

Dimensions:
Length o/a: 1.180m
Weight: 5.4kg without sight
Barrel: 610mm without flash suppressor
Rifling: 4 grooves, rh
Magazine capacity: 5 rounds

In production: 1991-

Markings:
SIG-SAUER SSG 3000 on left side of action. Serial number alongside chamber on right side.

Safety:
A sliding manual safety catch above the trigger, inside the trigger guard. When pushed forward the weapon is ready to fire. Pulled back, the weapon is safe.

Unloading:
Magazine catch behind the magazine. Remove magazine and empty it of ammunition. Open the bolt to extract any round in the chamber. Examine the chamber and feedway, close the bolt, pull the trigger, replace the empty magazine.

a rail under the fore-end to take a bipod or a firing sling. There are no iron sights; a mount for the standard Hensoldt telescope sight is normal, but a NATO STANAG sight mount can also be found.

Springfield US M1903 USA

Specification & Operation

Cartridge:
.30-06 (7.62 x 63mm)

Dimensions:
Length o/a: 1097mm
Weight: 3.94kg
Barrel: 610mm
Rifling: 4 grooves RH; WWII make may have 2 grooves
Magazine capacity: 5 rounds

In production: 1903-65

Markings:
'SPRINGFIELD ARSENAL' above the chamber.
'UNITED STATES PROPERTY' on left side of receiver. Serial number on right side of receiver, bolt handle and magazine cover.

Safety:
Manual safety catch on the rear end of the bolt: Turn to the RIGHT for safe, when the word 'Safe' will be seen. Turn LEFT for fire, when the word 'Fire' can be seen.

Unloading:
There is a magazine cut-off which prevents rounds feeding from the magazine to the breech; the control for this is on the left side of the receiver. Press down and the word 'OFF' can be seen, meaning that the magazine contents will NOT load. Lift up until the word 'ON' is visible and the magazine can be loaded and the contents can be fed to the breech. Now lift and pull back bolt handle to eject cartridge in the breech. Close bolt and repeat opening until the magazine is empty. When the cut-off is set 'OFF' the bolt cannot move back far enough to collect a cartridge from the magazine but the rifle can be used as a single-shot weapon, loading each round individually.

Standard US service rifle from 1903 to the mid-1940s, though it remained in service until the early 1960s as a sniping rifle. The M1903 had a straight stock; the 1903A1 a pistol-grip stock; both had the rear sight ahead of the chamber. The 1903A3 had a straight stock and the sight was just in front of the bolt handle; the 1903A4 is the sniper version of the A3, has no iron sights and has the bolt handle cut away to avoid striking the sighting telescope when opening.

Steyr-Mannlicher SSG-69 AUSTRIA

Developed as a sniping rifle for the Austrian Army in 1969, this was later put on the commercial market and was also adopted by numerous military and police forces. Minor changes have been such as a heavier and larger bolt knob, a short-barrelled version, a special `Police Version' which will accept a silencer, but they all use the same basic mechanism, a turnbolt locking by lugs on the bolt turning into recesses in the receiver behind the magazine. The magazine is now the Schoenauer type, though for some years a ten-round detachable box was offered as an alternative.

Specification & Operation

Cartridge:
7.62 x 51mm NATO

Dimensions:
Length o/a: 1.140m
Weight: 3.90kg
Barrel: 650mm
Rifling: 4 grooves, rh
Magazine capacity: 5 rounds

In production: 1969-

Markings:
`STEYR-MANNLICHER SSG69' and serial number on left side of receiver.

Safety:
Manual safety catch on right rear of receiver. Push forward to fire, back for safe

Unloading:
Squeeze in the two sides of the magazine release catch at the bottom edge of the stock and withdraw the rotary magazine; the rear end is transparent and reveals the contents; empty out any ammunition by pushing the top round out and allowing the spool to turn and present the next round. Open the bolt to extract any round in the chamber. Examine the chamber and feedway, close the bolt, press the trigger, replace the empty magazine.

US M40A1 Sniper USA

This is a militarised version of the commercial Remington 700 sporting rifle. The bolt is a Remington design, using two lugs locking into the receiver behind the chamber. There is a catch inset into the front of the trigger guard which, when pressed, allows the bolt to be removed from the receiver. The barrel is particularly heavy and rigid, and no iron sights are fitted, the rifle being issued with a 10x telescope sight. It is currently in service with the US Marine Corps, and the commercial original (the Model 700) has sold in large numbers.

Specification & Operation

Cartridge:
7.62 x 51mm NATO

Dimensions:
Length o/a: 1.117m
Weight: 6.57kg
Barrel: 610mm
Rifling: 4 grooves, rh
Magazine capacity: 5 rounds

In production: 1962-

Markings:
'US RIFLE M40A1' and serial number over chamber.

Safety:
Manual safety catch at right rear of receiver. Forward to fire, back for safe.

Unloading:
Press the release catch at the front edge of the magazine floor plate, so allowing the plate, spring and magazine contents to be removed. Open the bolt to eject any round in the chamber. Examine chamber and feedway, close bolt, press trigger, replace magazine spring and floor plate.

Vapensmia NM149S NORWAY

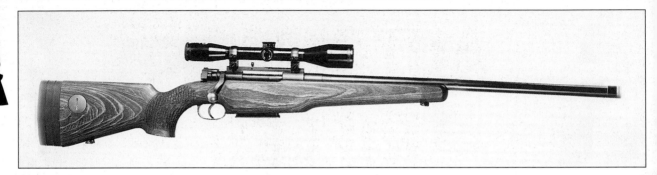

This was developed as a sniper rifle for the Norwegian Army and police forces and is also available commercially as a target or hunting rifle. The action is that of the Mauser Gew. 98, using the standard Mauser three-lug bolt. The barrel is exceptionally heavy, and it is normally issued with a 6 x 42 telescope sight; there are emergency iron sights fitted, but optical sights are virtually mandatory. The stock is of laminated beech and the butt is adjustable for length and may be fitted with a cheek-piece. A bipod and a sound suppressor are also available for this rifle.

Specification & Operation

Cartridge:
7.62 x 51mm NATO

Dimensions:
Length o/a: 1.120m
Weight: 5.6kg
Barrel: 600mm
Rifling: 4 grooves, rh
Magazine capacity: 5 rounds

In production: 1990-

Markings:
NM149 on left side of action. Serial on right side.

Safety:
Manual safety catch on rear end of bolt. Turn to the right for safe, to the left to fire.

Unloading:
Magazine catch behind the magazine. Remove magazine and empty it of ammunition. Open the bolt to extract any round in the chamber. Examine the chamber and feedway, close the bolt, pull the trigger, replace the empty magazine.

AUTOMATIC RIFLES

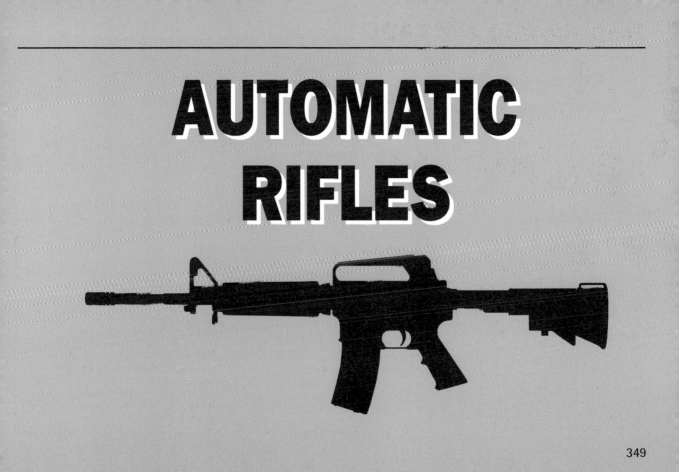

Armalite AR-18 USA/UK

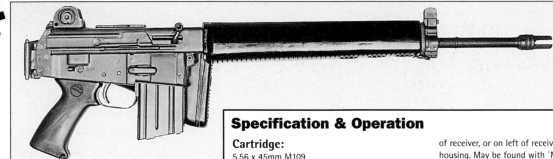

The AR-18 was intended to be the poor man's M16, a simplified weapon capable of being made in countries with limited manufacturing capability. But it was still cheaper to buy M16s than to set up a factory to make AR-18s. ArmaLite sold the rights to Howa Machinery of Japan in the early 1960s, but the Japanese government forbade them to make war weapons. Then Sterling Armaments of England bought the rights in 1974 and began manufacturing, but they found few takers before they went out of business in the 1980s.

Specification & Operation

Cartridge:
5.56 x 45mm M109

Dimensions:
Length, stock extended: 940mm
Length, stock folded: 738mm
Weight: 3.17kg
Barrel: 464mm
Rifling: 6 grooves, rh
Magazine capacity: 20, 30 or 40 rounds
Rate of fire: 800 rds/min

In production: ca 1966-79

Markings:
'AR 18 ARMALITE' moulded into the pistol grips.
'ARMALITE AR-18 PATENTS PENDING' on left side of magazine housing. Serial number on top rear of receiver, or on left of receiver or on magazine housing. May be found with 'MADE BY STERLING ARMAMENTS' on left side of receiver.

Safety:
A combined manual safety catch and fire selector switch is on the left side, above the pistol grip. The switch is turned to the rear, so that the pointer points forward, to make the rifle safe. With the switch vertical the weapon is set for single shots, and with the switch forward and the pointer to the rear, the weapon fires full-automatic.

Unloading:
Magazine catch on right side of magazine housing. Remove magazine. Pull back cocking handle on right side, inspect chamber through the ejection port. Release cocking handle, pull trigger.

Barrett 'Light Fifty' M82A1 USA

One of the first heavy sniping rifles to achieve success, the Barrett has been adopted by several military and police forces as an anti-material sniping weapon and also for detonating explosive devices at a safe distance. Originally there was little danger of confusing it with anything else, but in the late 1980s a number of competing designs appeared and the Barrett is no longer quite so individual.

Specification & Operation

Cartridge:
12.7 x 99 (.50 Browning)

Dimensions:
Length o/a: 1.549m
Weight: 13.40kg
Barrel: 737mm
Rifling: 12 grooves, rh
Magazine capacity: 11 rounds
Rate of fire: semi-automatic only

In production: 1983-92

Markings:
'BARRETT FIREARMS MANUFACTURING INC MURFREESBORO, TN, USA . CAL .50' and serial number on left side of receiver.

Safety:
Thumb-operated manual safety on left side of receiver, above the pistol grip. Turned to the horizontal position, the weapon is safe; to the vertical position for fire.

Unloading:
Magazine catch behind magazine. Remove magazine and empty out any ammunition. Pull back cocking handle, examine chamber via the ejection slot. Release cocking handle, press trigger, replace empty magazine.

Barrett M82A2 USA

This was developed in order to make the heavy sniping rifle a little less cumbersome. The change is simply to a `bullpup' layout, in which the action and barrel are placed further back in the stock so as to retain the same length of barrel but in a lesser overall length. This places the receiver and action alongside the firer's face and the magazine now lies behind the pistol grip and trigger.

Specification & Operation

Cartridge:
12.7 x 99mm (.50 Browning)

Dimensions:
Length o/a: 1.409m
Weight: 12.24kg
Barrel: 736mm
Rifling: 12 grooves, rh
Magazine capacity: 11 rounds
Rate of fire: semi-automatic only

In production: 1990 -

Markings:
`BARRETT FIREARMS MANUFACTURING INC

MURFREESBORO, TN, USA . CAL .50' and serial number on left side of receiver.

Safety:
Thumb-operated manual safety on left side of receiver, above the pistol grip. Turned to the horizontal position, the weapon is safe; to the vertical position for fire.

Unloading:
Magazine catch behind magazine. Remove magazine and empty out any ammunition. Pull back cocking handle, examine chamber via the ejection slot. Release cocking handle, press trigger, replace empty magazine.

Beretta BM59 ITALY

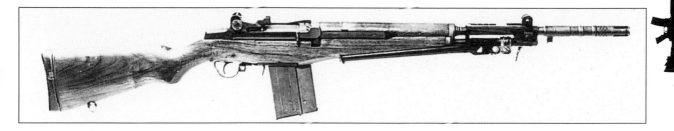

In the late 1940s the Beretta company began making the US Rifle M1 under license for the Italian Army, and they later made more for Denmark and Indonesia. In 1959 they set about redesigning the Garand, giving it the capability for automatic fire, fitting it with a larger magazine and adapting the barrel to grenade launching. Apart from these points it is much the same as any US M1 Garand. Various models were produced, with bipods, folding butts, folding bayonets, removable grenade launching adapters, or shorter barrels, but the mechanism remains the same. If it looks like a Garand but has a removable magazine it is either a US M14 or an Italian BM59.

Specification & Operation

Cartridge:
7.62 x 51mm NATO

Dimensions:
Length o/a: 1.095m
Weight: 4.60kg
Barrel: 490mm
Rifling: 4 grooves, rh
Magazine capacity: 20 rounds
Rate of fire: 750 rds/min

In production: 1961-66

Markings:
`P BERETTA BM59 serial number'; on top rear end of receiver.

Safety:
Manual safety catch in the front edge of the trigger guard; push forward to fire, rearward for safe. A fire selector is mounted on the left side of the receiver alongside the chamber, marked 'A' for automatic fire and 'S' for single shots. It may be permanently locked in the single-shot position in some rifles.

Unloading:
Magazine catch is behind the magazine. Remove magazine. Pull back cocking handle to open bolt and extract any round left in the chamber. Examine the chamber and feedway, release the bolt, press the trigger.

Beretta AR 70/.223 ITALY

This was Beretta's first 5.56mm rifle, using gas actuation and a two-lug bolt. It was adopted by Italian Special forces and sold to some other countries but it failed to attract much of a market and experience showed it to have a few minor defects, notably a lack of rigidity in the receiver. It appeared with some variations; a solid butt model was standard but there was also a folding butt model with long

and short barrels. The muzzle is adapted for grenade firing, and a hinged tap on the gas block has to be raised to allow a grenade to be loaded; this also shuts off the gas supply to the cylinder, ensuring that all the gas from the launching cartridge goes to propel the grenade.

Specification & Operation

Cartridge:
5.56 x 45mm (M109)

Dimensions:
Length o/a: 955mm
Weight: 3.80kg
Barrel: 450mm
Rifling: 4 grooves, rh
Magazine capacity: 30 rounds
Rate of fire: 650 rds/min

In production: 1972-80

Markings:
`P BERETTA AR 70/223 MADE IN ITALY serial number', on left side of receiver.

Safety:
Manual safety catch and fire selector on left side of receiver above pistol grip. Turned DOWN for safe, UP for automatic fire, midway for single shots.

Unloading:
Magazine catch is behind the magazine. Remove the magazine. Pull back the cocking handle to eject any round left in the chamber. Inspect the chamber via the ejection port. Release the cocking handle, pull the trigger.

Beretta AR 70/90 ITALY

In the early 1980s the Italian Army announced a requirement for a new 5.56mm rifle; the AR 70/90 was the Beretta entrant, which was eventually selected and issues began in the early 1990s. It can be easily distinguished from the earlier 70/223 by the fixed carrying handle/sight mount above the receiver. There are a number of variant models; the standard model uses a fixed butt, there are long and short-barrelled models with folding butts, and any model may or may not have a bipod fitted beneath the fore-end.

Specification & Operation

Cartridge:
5.56 x 45mm SS109 (NATO)

Dimensions:
Length o/a: 998mm
Weight: 3.99kg
Barrel: 450mm
Rifling: 6 grooves, rh
Magazine capacity: 30 rounds
Rate of fire: ca 650 rds/min

In production: 1990-

Markings:
'FUCILE AUT BERETTA AR70/90 CAL 5.56' and serial number, on left side of receiver.

Safety:
A manual combined safety catch and fire selector on both sides of the receiver. With the white 'S' opposite the white index mark, the weapon is safe. With the red '1' opposite the index, it fires single shots, with the red '3' opposite the index, it fires three-round bursts; and with the red '30' against the index it fires full automatic.

Unloading:
Magazine catch on both sides of receiver, above magazine. Remove magazine. Pull back cocking handle to eject any round in the chamber. Inspect chamber via the ejection port, release cocking handle and press trigger.

Bofors AK5 SWEDEN

Specification & Operation

Cartridge:
5.56 x 45mm NATO

Dimensions:
Length, stock extended: 1008mm
Length, stock folded: 753mm
Weight: 3.90kg
Barrel: 450mm
Rifling: 6 grooves, rh
Magazine capacity: 30 rounds
Rate of fire: 650 rds/min

In production: 1984-

Markings:
Month/year of manufacture at bottom right of receiver. Serial number and month/year of manufacture on left side.

Safety:
Manual safety catch and selector lever on left side of receiver, above the trigger. Turn to the letter `S` for safe, `1` for single shots, `30` for full automatic fire.

Unloading:
Remove magazine. Pull back cocking handle. Inspect the chamber via the ejection port. Release cocking handle, press trigger.

This is actually a variant of the Belgian FN-FNC rifle, extensively modified to meet Swedish requirements after a comprehensive series of trials in the mid-1980s. Changes were made to the butt, sights, cocking handle, bolt, selector switch, trigger guard and sling swivels, largely in order to better withstand extreme cold conditions and be more easily operated by gloved hands. The three-round burst option was removed. The metal is finished in a deep green enamel, making the rifle very easily recognisable.

Calico M-900 USA

This is basically the same weapon as the Calico submachine gun, differing principally in having a longer barrel. This length of barrel in a 9mm weapon is unusual and should result in reasonable accuracy to upwards of 200 metres, though the bullet is not really designed for that sort of range. This rifle variant fires only in the single-shot mode and uses a roller-locked delayed blowback system similar to that of the German G3 rifle.

Specification & Operation

Cartridge:
9 x 19mm

Dimensions:
Length, stock extended: 804mm
Length, stock retracted: 724mm
Weight: 1.68kg
Barrel: 406mm
Rifling: 6 grooves, rh
Magazine capacity: 50 or 100 rounds

In production: 1988-

Markings:
'CALICO M-900' on left side of magazine mounting. Serial number on left side of frame.

Safety:
Manual safety catch/fire selector in the front edge of the trigger guard, with levers on both sides of the weapon. When to the rear, and projecting into the trigger guard, the system is safe. Pushed forward one notch permits single shots, all the way for automatic fire. Safety can be set by using the outside levers, removed by pressing forward with the trigger finger.

Unloading:
Magazine catch on top of receiver. Squeeze in, then remove magazine by withdrawing back and up. Pull back cocking lever to remove any round in the chamber, inspect chamber via the ejection slot, release cocking handle, pull trigger.

Chinese Type 56 carbine CHINA

The Type 56 is simply a Chinese copy of the Soviet Simonov SKS rifle; any differences between this weapon and its Soviet ancestor are minimal matters of manufacturing convenience. Later versions have a folding spike bayonet in place of the normal folding sword bayonet. It has been retired from military service, except for occasional appearances in ceremonials, for some years, but is still widely sold commercially as a hunting rifle. Without the bayonet, of course.

Specification & Operation

Cartridge:
7.62 x 39mm Soviet M1943

Dimensions:
Length o/a: 1025mm
Weight: 3.85kg
Barrel: 521mm
Rifling: 4 grooves, rh
Magazine capacity: 10 rounds

In production: 1956-

Markings:
Chinese factory mark and serial number on left front of receiver.

Safety:
Manual safety catch on the rear of the trigger guard is pushed forward and UP to make the weapon safe, when it obstructs the trigger finger and movement of the trigger.

Unloading:
Magazine catch at the rear of the magazine, under the receiver. Press in and the magazine swings open, allowing the contents to be removed. Pull back the cocking handle, inspect the chamber and feedway, release the cocking handle, press the trigger. Close the empty magazine.

Chinese Type 56 assault rifle CHINA

The Type 56 is, quite obviously, the Chinese copy of the Kalashnikov, and it well illustrates the dangers of terminology; this is the Type 56 rifle, it is 874mm long; the Type 56 carbine (above) is 1025mm long; yet carbines are always supposed to be shorter than

Specification & Operation

Cartridge:
7.62 x 39mm Soviet M1943

Dimensions:
Length o/a: 874mm
Weight: 3.80kg
Barrel: 414mm
Rifling: 4 grooves, rh
Magazine capacity: 30 rounds
Rate of fire: 600 rds/min

In production: 1958-

Markings:
Chinese markings for factory, year and serial number on left side of receiver. There may also be Chinese symbols on the safety lever on early production models.

Safety:
Combined safety catch and fire selector lever on the right rear side of the receiver. When pressed all the way UP it is in the safe position and obstructs the movement of the cocking handle and bolt; moved DOWN one notch to the first mark or the letter 'L' gives full automatic fire, and moved to the bottom position, or the letter 'D', produces single shots.

Unloading:
Magazine catch at rear of magazine housing. Remove the magazine. Pull back the cocking handle to extract any round which may be in the chamber. Inspect the chamber via the ejection port. Release the cocking handle, pull the trigger.

rifles. There are three variants; the Type 56 has a fixed butt and folding bayonet; the 56-1 has a folding stock which passes over the receiver, and the 56-2 has a folding stock which folds sideways to lie along the right side of the receiver. Neither the 56-1 or 56-2 have folding bayonets. All these models are commercially available in semi-automatic form.

Chinese Type 68 rifle CHINA

This is a purely Chinese design which has adapted the best features of various rifles of which the Chinese have had experience. Although it resembles the Type 58 carbine the mechanism is based upon that of the AK47 Kalashnikov rifles. It has the usual type of folding bayonet beneath the fore-end. The standard magazine is a 15-round box, but it is possible to use the 30-round AK47 magazine if the hold-open stop for the bolt is removed or ground down; so that it may be found with either type. In current use with the Chinese forces, it is also available for export.

Specification & Operation

Cartridge:
7.62 x 39mm Soviet M1943

Dimensions:
Length o/a: 1029mm
Weight: 3.49kg
Barrel: 521mm
Rifling: 4 groove, rh
Magazine capacity: 15 or 30 rounds
Rate of fire: 750 rds/min

In production: 1970-

Markings:
Chinese symbols for factory identification and year, and serial number on left side of receiver.

Safety:
Combined safety catch and selector lever in front of the trigger on the right side. Pulled to the rear, to the mark `0', the weapon is safe; the trigger is locked but the bolt can be opened. Moved to the vertical position, to the mark `1', gives single shots, and moved fully forward to the mark `2' gives automatic fire.

Unloading:
Magazine catch beneath the receiver, behind the magazine. Remove the magazine. Pull back the cocking handle to eject any round left in the chamber. Inspect the chamber and feedway via the ejection port. Release the cocking handle, pull the trigger.

Colt Commando USA

The 'Commando' began as a private venture by Colt to develop a short barrelled compact version of the standard M16 rifle. It was received with some approbation by the US Special Forces and was thereafter given various minor improvements to become the XM177 submachine gun. Further small improvements followed and it is now commercially available as the Model 733. It has been adopted by various US Federal and security agencies and other armed forces worldwide, since it is an attractive short and concealable weapon.

Specification & Operation

Cartridge:
5.56 x 45mm NATO

Dimensions:
Length, stock extended: 760mm
Length, stock retracted: 680mm
Weight: 2.44kg
Barrel: 290mm
Rifling: 6 grooves, rh
Magazine capacity: 20 or 30 rounds
Rate of fire: 700 to 1000 rds/min

In production:

Markings:
'MOD 733 CAL 5.56MM' or 'COMMANDO CAL 5.56MM' and 'PROPERTY OF US GOVT COLT 'S FIREARMS DIVISION COLT INDUSTRIES HARTFORD CONN U.S.A.' and serial number; all on left side of magazine housing and receiver.

Safety:
Combined safety catch and fire selector on left side of receiver above the trigger. With the catch pulled back so that the pointer is directed to 'SAFE' the weapon is safe. With the catch pressed DOWN and forward to the vertical, the weapon fired single shots. And with the catch pressed forward so that the pointer is to the rear against 'AUTO' automatic fire is available.

Unloading:
Magazine catch is a push-button on the right side of the receiver above the trigger. Remove magazine. Pull back cocking handle (T-shaped 'wings' behind the carrying handle) to eject any round remaining in the chamber. Inspect chamber and feedway via the ejection port. Release cocking handle, pull trigger.

CZ52 CZECHOSLOVAKIA

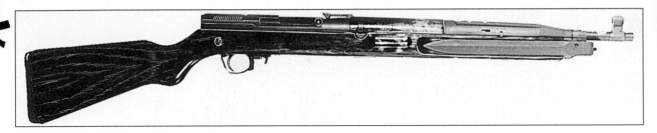

The CZ52 was developed in Czecho-slovakia in the short time between the end of WWII and the country's absorption into the Communist Bloc. It was an unusual design, gas-operated with a gas piston in the form of a sleeve surrounding part of the barrel and acting on the bolt carrier, and it fired a unique cartridge. When the country came under Soviet domination, it was required to conform to Soviet standards and the rifle was therefore redesigned to fire the 7.62 x 39 Soviet cartridge. Such models are known as the `vz.52/57' and are so marked. They are not as accurate or reliable as the original 7.62 x 45mm models. Note that there is a permanently-attached folding sword bayonet on both models of this rifle.

Specification & Operation

Cartridge:
7.62 x 45mm M52 or 7.62 x 39mm Soviet M1943

Dimensions:
Length o/a: 1003mm
Weight: 4.10kg
Barrel: 523mm
Rifling: 4 grooves, rh
Magazine capacity: 10 rounds

In production: 1952-59

Markings:
Factory identifier and serial number on right side of receiver. The later model 52/57 will be so marked at the right front of the receiver.

Safety:
A manual safety catch is fitted in the forward edge of the trigger guard. Pulled back, so that it protrudes into the trigger-guard space, the weapon is safe. Push forward to fire.

Unloading:
Magazine catch behind magazine. Remove magazine. Pull back cocking handle to extract any round remaining in the chamber. Examine chamber and feedway via the ejection port. Release cocking handle, pull trigger.

CZ58 CZECHOSLOVAKIA

Although this may resemble the Kalashnikov, it is an entirely different weapon, of Czech design although, due to Warsaw Pact standardisation, chambered for the standard Soviet cartridge. It is gas operated and the bolt is locked to the receiver by a vertically-moving block similar to that of the Walther P38 pistol. Gas pressure on a

Specification & Operation

Cartridge:
7.62 x 39mm Soviet M1943

Dimensions:
Length, stock extended: 820mm
Length, stock folded: 635mm
Weight: 3.14kg
Barrel: 401mm
Rifling: 4 grooves, rh
Magazine capacity: 30 rounds
Rate of fire: 800 rds/min

In production: 1959-80

Markings:
Factory identifier and serial number on rear top of receiver.

Safety:
Combined manual safety catch and fire selector on right side of receiver above trigger. Rotate to the vertical position for safe; this locks the trigger but permits the bolt to be opened. Turn the selector forward for automatic fire, rearward for single shots.

Unloading:
Magazine catch between magazine and trigger guard. Remove magazine. Pull back the cocking handle to extract any round remaining in the chamber. Inspect chamber and feedway via the ejection port. Release cocking handle, press trigger.

piston drives a bolt carrier back, this lifts the lock and the bolt then opens. The original design used a fixed stock of plastic material; later versions used a folding metal stock. Either may be fitted with a flash hider on the muzzle and a bipod attached to the barrel.

Daewoo K2 SOUTH KOREA

Developed for the South Korean Army after the manufacturer had gained experience by building M16 rifles under license, this rifle uses a long-stroke gas piston with a rotating bolt, generally similar to the mechanism of the Soviet Kalashnikov rifles. The receiver is made of aluminium forgings and the butt folds sideways. The magazine interface is standardised on the M16 and will therefore accept most NATO magazines.

Specification & Operation

Cartridge:
5.56 x 45mm NATO

Dimensions:
Length, stock extended: 980mm
Length, stock folded: 730mm
Weight: 3.26kg
Barrel: 465mm
Rifling: 6 grooves, rh
Magazine capacity: 30 rounds
Rate of fire: ca 750 rds/min

In production: 1990-

Markings:
DAEWOO PRECISION INDUSTRIES LTD on right of receiver; 5.56mm K2 and serial number on the left, above magazine housing.

Safety:
Manual safety catch and fire selector lever on left side of receiver above trigger. Move the catch to the rear for safe.

Unloading:
Remove magazine. Pull back the cocking handle to eject any round remaining in the chamber. Inspect chamber and feedway via the ejection port. Release cocking handle, press trigger.

Gepard M3 HUNGARY

This is the heaviest of a series of anti-materiel rifles developed in Hungary in the middle 1980s. The others fire the 12.7mm Soviet round; this one fires the much more powerful 14.5mm armour-piercing round originally developed for an anti-tank weapon, and it is quite capable of penetrating one inch of steel at 650 metres range. The highly efficient muzzle brake and a hydraulic recoil system allowing the barrel and breech to recoil inside the receiver, do much to cut down the recoil to the level of a heavy sporting rifle, but even so, this is not a weapon to be handled carelessly.

Specification & Operation

Cartridge:
14.5 x 114mm Soviet

Dimensions:
Length o/a: 1880mm
Weight: 20.0kg
Barrel: 1400mm
Rifling: 8 grooves, rh
Magazine capacity: 5 or 10 rounds

In production: 1988-

Markings:
CAL 14.5mm GEPARD M3 and serial on top of receiver.

Safety:
Manual safety catch on the right side of the receiver. Forward to fire, back for safe.

Unloading:
The magazine is on the left side of the receiver, alongside the pistol grip, and the release is in front of it. Remove the magazine. Pull back the cocking handle to eject any round remaining in the chamber. Inspect the chamber and feedway via the ejection port. Release the cocking handle, press the trigger.

Dragunov RUSSIA

Although similar to the Kalashnikov in principle, this rifle differs in using a short-stroke piston to operate the bolt carrier; the AK series uses a long-stroke piston, which would be inappropriate in this case, since this is a sniping rifle and the shift of balance during a long-stroke piston's movement can degrade the accuracy. The rifle is normally provided with the PSO-1 telescope sight, though the image-intensifying night sight NSPU-3 is also a item of issue with this rifle. It is claimed to have an effective range of 1000 metres and is now on open sale.

Specification & Operation

Cartridge:
7.62 x 54R Soviet

Dimensions:
Length o/a: 1225mm
Weight: 4.31kg
Barrel: 610mm
Rifling: 4 grooves, rh
Magazine capacity: 10 rounds

In production: 1963-

Markings:
Factory identification, year and serial number on left side of receiver.

Safety:
This uses a similar safety lever to the Kalashnikov rifles, mounted on the left rear of the receiver. Pressed UP it makes the weapon safe; pressed DOWN it permits single shots.

Unloading:
Magazine catch behind the magazine. Remove magazine. Pull back the cocking handle to extract any cartridge remaining in the chamber. Inspect chamber and feedway via the ejection port. Release cocking handle, press trigger.

Enfield L85A1 UK

eventually the various defects were eliminated. It may be found fitted with the optical SUSAT sight, or with iron sights, the latter being standard issue for non-infantry troops. There is also a carbine version, which is not yet adopted by the British Army, and a single-shot cadet training version.

The Enfield L85A1 (also called the SA80) was developed by the Royal Small Arms Factory, originally in 4.85mm calibre. The designers were astute enough to realise that this calibre had little chance of being adopted as NATO standard, and thus when the standard was eventually defined as 5.56mm, the re-design was relatively easy. Unfortunately, the transition from hand-built prototypes to mass-produced service weapons was less easy and the initial issues had many serious defects. After the privatisation of the RSAF, an entirely new factory was erected in Nottingham, contractor's standards were tightened and

Specification & Operation

Cartridge:
5.56 x 45mm NATO

Dimensions:
Length o/a: 785mm
Weight: 3.80kg
Barrel: 518mm
Rifling: 6 grooves, rh
Magazine capacity: 30 rounds
Rate of fire: 700 rds/min

In production: 1985-94

Markings:
RIFLE 5.56MM L85A1 and NATO stock number

Impressed into right side of handguard.

Safety:
A push-through bolt above the trigger, pushed from the left to the right for safe. On the left side of the stock is a fire selector: up for single shots and down for fully automatic.

Unloading:
Magazine catch on left side of receiver above magazine housing. Remove magazine. Pull back cocking handle to eject any round remaining in the chamber. Inspect chamber and feedway via the ejection port. Release cocking handle, pull trigger.

FAMAS FRANCE

handguard instead of a small trigger guard and a NATO-standard magazine housing to accept M16 type magazines. Note that all 5.56mm ammunition will chamber in this weapon but optimum performance is only achieved with the French service ammunition.

This odd-looking weapon is the standard French Army rifle and was the first 'bullpup' design to enter military service. It uses a two-part bolt in a delayed blowback system and has the chamber fluted to avoid difficult extraction, so that cartridges from this weapon are easily recognised by their longitudinal marks. It handles well and shoots accurately, and can also launch grenades. There is also a .22 rimfire training version which looks exactly like the service weapon. In 1994 a new model, the F2, appeared with a full-sized

Specification & Operation

Cartridge:
5.56 x 45mm Type France

Dimensions:
Length o/a: 757mm
Weight: 3.61kg
Barrel: 488mm
Rifling: 6 grooves, rh
Magazine capacity: 25 rounds
Rate of fire: 950 rds/min

In production: 1975-

Markings:
FA MAS 5.56 F1 and serial on right side of magazine housing. Serial repeated on bolt..

Safety:
A rotary switch inside the front of the trigger guard acts as safety catch and fire selector When parallel with the bore it is set safe; when switched to the right it gives single shots, and when to the left, automatic fire. With the switch in the automatic position, operation of a burst-limiting button, beneath the buttstock and behind the magazine, brings in a three-round burst limiter.

Unloading:
Magazine catch in front of magazine. Remove magazine. Pull back cocking handle (between the receiver and the carrying handle) to eject any round left in the chamber. Inspect chamber via the ejection port. Release cocking handle, pull trigger.

FARA 83 ARGENTINA

This was developed in the early 1980s for the Argentine Army but financial problems led to slow production and it is probable that only a part of the army received this weapon. It is of local design and uses the usual gas piston, bolt carrier and rotating bolt method of operation. Note that the cocking handle lies on top of the gas cylinder, well

Specification & Operation

Cartridge:
5.56 x 45mm

Dimensions:
Length, stock extended: 1000mm
Length, stock folded: 745mm
Weight: 3.95kg
Barrel: 452mm
Rifling: 6 grooves, rh
Magazine capacity: 30 rounds
Rate of fire: 750 rds/min

In production: 1984-90

Markings:
'FMAP DOMINGO MATHEU', year and serial number on top of receiver.

Safety:
Manual safety catch inside the trigger guard. Push to the rear for safe, forward to fire. There is a fire selector for either single shots or automatic fire on the right side of the receiver above the trigger.

Unloading:
Magazine catch behind magazine housing. Remove magazine. Pull back cocking handle to eject any round remaining in the chamber. Inspect chamber and feedway via the ejection slot. Release cocking handle, press trigger.

forward of the receiver and actually operates on the gas piston, which has the bolt carrier machined as an integral part. The rifle may be encountered with a bipod attached below the gas block, in which case it has a special fore-end with a recess to accept the folded bipod legs. Note also that the twist of rifling allows M193 or NATO ammunition to be fired with equal facility.

FG 42 GERMANY

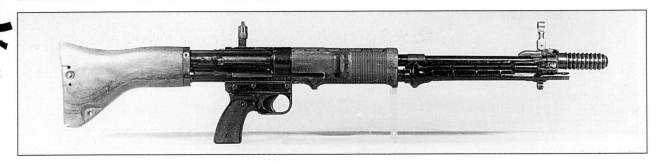

This rifle was developed by Rheinmetall for the German Luftwaffe Parachute regiments; the German Army were against it, since they considered a full automatic rifle firing 7.92mm Mauser cartridges was impractical. A remarkable weapon, it functioned as both a rifle and the section light machine gun, but was really too light for the latter task. The magazine fits into the left side. There are two versions; the first has a straight pistol grip sloped back very severely and a steel butt-stock. The second has a curved pistol grip and wooden or plastic butt-stock. Magazines are similar but not interchangeable between the two versions.

Specification & Operation

Cartridge:
7.92 x 57mm Mauser

Dimensions:
Length o/a: 940mm
Weight: 4.50kg
Barrel: 508mm
Rifling: 4 grooves, rh
Magazine capacity: 20 rounds
Rate of fire: 750 rds/min

In production: 1943-45

Markings:
`FG 42 fzs (Manufacturer - H Krieghoff)', year and serial number on top of receiver.

Safety:
Safety catch above pistol grip on left; up for safe, down for fire. It can only be used when rifle is cocked. Fire selector is a large switch with spring-loaded knob above trigger. Pull out and swing the lever forward to E for single shots.

Unloading:
Inspect chamber and feedway via ejection port. Release cocking handle, pull trigger.

FN 1949 BELGIUM

Development of this rifle actually started in the 1930s but the war caused a halt in the proceedings and it was not until 1949 that it was completed. It was adopted in various calibres by Belgium, Egypt, Argentine, Luxembourg, Venezuela, Brazil and Colombia and was reliable, if somewhat expensive. The locking system used a tilting bolt, gas-operated, and generally formed the prototype for the later and better-known FAL model. The magazine was loaded by chargers, through the top of the open action. The designer, M.Saive, worked with the British in Enfield during the Second World War and the earliest version of this rifle was tested by the British in 7.92mm calibre in 1946/47.

Specification & Operation

Cartridge:
7.92 x 57mm Mauser and others

Dimensions:
Length o/a: 1116mm
Weight: 4.31kg
Barrel: 590mm
Rifling: 4 grooves, rh
Magazine capacity: 10 rounds

In production: 1950-58

Markings:
FABRIQUE NATIONALE D'ARMES DE GUERRE HERSTAL BELGIQUE on right of action. Serial number on side of chamber and on bolt.

Safety:
Manual safety catch on the right side of the trigger guard. Press DOWN for safe, which also places the catch in a position to interfere with the finger if an attempt it made to press the trigger. There is no fire selector - this rifle fires only single shots.

Unloading:
Magazine catch is in front of the magazine and needs to be pressed in by a bullet or some similar pointed tool. Remove the magazine and pull back the cocking handle to eject any round remaining in the chamber. Inspect chamber and feedway through the ejection port. Release the cocking handle, press the trigger.

FN FAL BELGIUM

The FN-FAL is probably the most widely-used rifle in history, adopted by over 90 countries. Many of these have demanded their own minor modifications; many countries have manufactured under license and, again, have incorporated their own

Specification & Operation

Cartridge:
7.62 x 51mm NATO

Dimensions:
Length o/a: 1090mm
Weight: 4.45kg
Barrel: 533mm
Rifling: 4 grooves, rh
Magazine capacity: 20 rounds
Rate of fire: 650 rds/min

In production: 1953-

Markings:
'FABRIQUE NATIONALE HERSTAL' on Belgian-made weapons. Since this rifle has appeared in numerous variations, has been employed by 90 countries and made under license or copied in many of them, the variety of possible markings is infinite and a full list cannot be given. The origin of the weapon will usually be evident from the markings.

Safety:
Manual safety catch and fire selector lever on left side of receiver over the trigger. In semi-automatics the weapon is safe with the catch pressed UP, ready to fire when pressed DOWN. The same applies to weapons capable of automatic fire but they also have a third position, pushed down and forward past the single-shot position, which gives full automatic fire.

Unloading:
Magazine catch is behind the magazine housing. Remove magazine. Pull back cocking handle to eject any round left in the chamber. Examine chamber and feedway through the ejection port. Release cocking handle, press trigger.

modifications. The FN factory recognises four standard models; the fixed-butt rifle 50-00; the folding butt rifle 50-64; a folding-butt carbine 50-63; and a fixed-butt heavy-barrel model with bipod 50-41. Moreover most models were available in either semi-automatic-only or selective-fire form. Permutate all these and there are a huge number of minor variant models possible. Add to that the commercial semi-automatic models and it becomes obvious that a complete book would scarcely scratch the surface of absolute identification of some models. All one can do is identify it as an FN-FAL, decide the nationality from its markings, and leave it at that.

FN CAL BELGIUM

The CAL (Carabine, Automatic, Legère) was broadly a scaled-down FAL, using the same sort of gas action but with a rotating bolt instead of a tilting breech-block. It was a reasonable enough weapon, but it was somewhat in advance of its time, since most countries were happy with their 7.62mm weapons and did not regard the 5.56mm cartridge with much enthusiasm, so sales of the CAL were poor. Experience also showed that its reliability was not up to the usual FN standards, and FN realised that a better rifle could be made more cheaply, so the design was closed down and work began on the FNC.

Specification & Operation

Cartridge:
5.56 x 45mm M193

Dimensions:
Length o/a: 978mm
Weight: 3.35kg
Barrel: 467mm
Rifling: 6 grooves, rh
Magazine capacity: 20, 25 or 30 rounds
Rate of fire: 650 rds/min

In production: 1966-75

Markings:
'FABRIQUE NATIONALE HERSTAL Mod CAL 5.56mm serial number' on left side of receiver.

Safety:
A combined safety catch and fire selector lever is on the left side of the receiver above the trigger. Rotated to the rear for safe; DOWN one notch for single shots; forward to the next notch for three-round bursts; fully forward for automatic fire.

Unloading:
Magazine catch at left rear of magazine housing. Remove magazine. Pull back cocking handle to eject any round remaining in the chamber. Examine chamber and feedway through the ejection slot. Release cocking handle, press trigger.

FN FNC BELGIUM

This succeeded the CAL at a time when the potential customers were taking note of the NATO adoption of a 5.56mm cartridge, and consequently it met with a better reception; it was also cheaper and more reliable than the CAL. Steel, alloy and plastic have been used in the construction and much use has been made of pressings and stampings. The mechanism is similar to that of the CAL, gas operated with a rotating bolt, and the magazine interface is NATO standard and will thus accept M16 and similar types of magazine. A variant model is used by Sweden as the AK5, and it is also made under license in Indonesia.

Specification & Operation

Cartridge:
5.56 x 45mm NATO

Dimensions:
Length, stock extended: 997mm
Length, stock folded: 766mm
Weight: 3.80kg
Barrel: 450mm
Rifling: 6 grooves, rh
Magazine capacity: 30 rounds
Rate of fire: 700 rds/min

In production: 1979-

Markings:
`FN' monogram; `FNC 5.56 serial number'; all on left side of receiver.

Safety:
A combined safety catch and fire selector lever is on the left side of the receiver above the trigger. Rotated to the rear for safe; DOWN one notch for single shots; forward to the next notch for three-round bursts; fully forward for automatic fire.

Unloading:
Magazine catch at left rear of magazine housing. Remove magazine. Pull back cocking handle to eject any round remaining in the chamber. Examine chamber and feedway through the ejection slot. Release cocking handle, press trigger.

Galil ISRAEL

Specification & Operation

Cartridge:
5.56 x 45mm M193

Dimensions:
Length, stock extended: 979mm
Length, stock folded: 742mm
Weight: 3.95kg
Barrel: 460mm
Rifling: 6 grooves, rh
Magazine capacity: 35 or 50 rounds
Rate of fire: 550 rds/min

In production: 1971-

Markings:
Hebrew markings on left side of receiver,
including serial number.

Safety:
A combined safety catch and fire selector is on
the left side, at the top of the pistol grip. Forward
is safe; fully rearward gives single shots, the
central position gives automatic fire.

Unloading:
Magazine catch at rear of magazine housing.
Remove magazine. Pull back cocking handle to
eject any round remaining in the chamber.
Examine chamber and feedway through the
ejection slot. Release cocking handle, press
trigger.

The Galil was the result of careful
Israeli examination of practically
every rifle they could find, and in the
end they settled for a modified version
of the Kalashnikov rotating bolt system;
indeed, the first rifles were built up from
Finnish M62 rifle bodies. It was originally
developed in 5.56mm calibre, but later a
7.62 x 51mm model was also produced,
though this was never as popular as the
5.56mm version. It is, of course, used by
the Israeli Defence Force and has also
been adopted by several Central and
South American and African armies.

Heckler & Koch G3 GERMANY

The heart of the G3, as with almost every other Heckler & Koch weapon, is the roller-delayed blowback breech system, which has a long and curious history. It was designed by Mauser in 1944-45; taken to Spain and developed further by CETME, taken to Holland to manufacture, then given to Heckler & Koch to perfect. Which they did to very

Specification & Operation

Cartridge:
7.62 x 51mm NATO

Dimensions:
Length o/a: 1025mm (fixed butt)
Weight: 4.40kg
Barrel: 450mm
Rifling: 4 grooves, rh
Magazine capacity: 20 rounds
Rate of fire: 550 rds/min

In production: 1964-

Markings:
`G3 HK serial number month/year of manufacture' on left side of magazine housing. Weapons which have been refurbished will have `HK' and the

month/year stamped into the right side of the magazine housing.

Safety:
A combined safety catch and fire selector is on the left side, above the trigger. In the topmost position (marked `0' or `S') the weapon is safe; fully down (`F' or `20') gives full automatic fire, while the mid-position (`E' or `1') gives single shots.

Unloading:
Magazine catch at rear of magazine housing. Remove magazine. Pull back cocking handle to eject any round remaining in the chamber. Examine chamber and feedway through the ejection slot. Release cocking handle, press trigger.

good effect. The G3 has armed the German Army for many years and is made under license in Mexico, Portugal, Greece, Turkey, Pakistan, Norway, Greece and Saudi Arabia as well as being employed by some 60 armies. There are variant models with short barrels, fixed or folding butts, and there are also variations in the licence-produced models of some countries, but these are generally minor.

Heckler & Koch PSG1 GERMANY

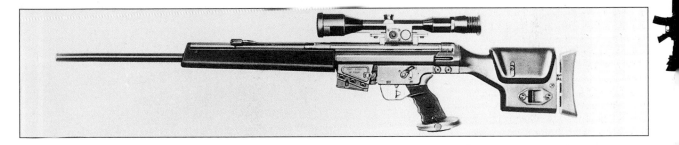

The PSG1 is a high-precision sniping rifle using the standard H&K roller-locked delayed blowback breech system with a special long and heavy barrel. The trigger unit can be removed from the pistol grip, and can be adjusted for pull. The stock is fully adjustable in all directions so that every individual can fit the weapon to his own stance. No iron sights are fitted; a NATO-standard mounting is built into the receiver top and the rifle is always issued with a 6 x 42 telescope with illuminated graticule. The accuracy is outstanding; it will put 50 rounds of match ammunition inside an 80mm circle at 300 metres range.

Specification & Operation

Cartridge:
7.62 x 51mm NATO

Dimensions:
Length o/a: 1208mm
Weight: 8.1kg
Barrel: 650mm
Rifling: 4 grooves, rh
Magazine capacity: 5 or 20 rounds

In production: 1975 -

Markings:
'PSG1 HK Kal 7.62x51 serial number'; all on left side of magazine housing.

Safety:
Manual safety catch on left side of receiver, above trigger. UP for safe, DOWN to fire.

Unloading:
Magazine catch on right side behind magazine housing. Remove magazine. Pull back cocking handle to eject any round remaining in the chamber. Examine chamber and feedway through the ejection slot. Holding the cocking handle, press the trigger and allow the cocking handle to go forward under control. Push on the bolt-closing catch on the right side of the receiver to firmly close the bolt.

Heckler & Koch MSG90 GERMANY

This is intended as a military sniping rifle and is really a lighter and less expensive version of the PSG1. The barrel is lighter, cold-forged and tempered; the trigger mechanism is pre-adjusted to a 1.5kg pull and the trigger has an adjustable shoe which gives better control. There is usually a bipod fitted to a rail in the fore-end, and the standard sight is a 10x telescope with range settings to 1200 metres. The sight mount

Specification & Operation

Cartridge:
7.62 x 51mm NATO

Dimensions:
Length o/a: 1165mm
Weight: 6.4kg
Barrel: 600mm
Rifling: 4 grooves, rh
Magazine capacity: 5 or 20 rounds

In production: 1987-

Markings:
`HK MSG90 7.62 x 51 serial number'; all on left side of magazine housing.

Safety:
Manual safety catch on left side of receiver, above trigger. UP for safe, DOWN to fire.

Unloading:
Magazine catch at rear of magazine housing. Remove magazine. Pull back cocking handle to eject any round remaining in the chamber. Examine chamber and feedway through the ejection slot. Release cocking handle, press trigger.

is to NATO standard and thus any compatible day or night sight can be fitted. The butt can be adjusted in most directions to obtain an individual fit.

Heckler & Koch HK33E GERMANY

This is more or less the standard G3 reduced to 5.56mm calibre; its mechanical operation is exactly the same, as is its outline; several parts are common, but interchanging parts is not to be recommended; some are not common, though they may look and fit in apparently the same way in both

Specification & Operation

Cartridge:
5.56 x 45mm NATO or M193

Dimensions:
Length, stock extended: 940mm
Length, stock retracted: 735mm
Weight: 3.65kg
Barrel: 390mm
Rifling: 6 grooves, rh
Magazine capacity: 25 rounds
Rate of fire: 750 rds/min

In production: 1968-

Markings:
'HK 33E 5.56mm serial number'; all on left side of magazine housing.

Safety:
A combined safety catch and fire selector is on the left side, above the trigger. In the topmost position (marked '0' or 'S') the weapon is safe; fully down ('F' or '20') gives full automatic fire, while the mid-position ('E' or '1') gives single shots.

Unloading:
Magazine catch at rear of magazine housing. Remove magazine. Pull back cocking handle to eject any round remaining in the chamber. Examine chamber and feedway through the ejection slot. Release cocking handle, press trigger.

weapons. There is a fixed butt model and also a short-barrelled carbine version known as the HK33K E. There was also an HK33SG1 sniper version, with special sight mount and telescope sight, and the fixed butt model can be found with a bipod. It has been used by Chile, Brazil, Malaysia and Thailand and various other forces in SE Asia and South America.

Heckler & Koch G41 GERMANY

This was designed as an improved HK33 specifically for the NATO-standard 5.56mm cartridge. It incorporates the low-noise bolt closing device first used on the PSG1 sniping rifle, has a dust-cover on the ejection port, has a hold-open device that keeps the bolt open when the magazine is emptied, uses the NATO-standard

Specification & Operation

Cartridge:
5.56 x 45mm NATO

Dimensions:
Length o/a: 997mm
Weight: 4.1kg
Barrel: 450mm
Rifling: 6 grooves, rh
Magazine capacity: 30 rounds
Rate of fire: 850 rds/min

In production: 1983-

Markings:
`HK G41 5.56mm serial number', all on left side of magazine housing.

Safety:
A combined safety catch and fire selector is on the left side, above the trigger. In the topmost position (marked by a white bullet and cross) the weapon is safe; one notch down (single red bullet) gives single shots; two notches down (three red bullets) gives a three-round burst, and fully down (7 red bullets) gives full automatic fire.

Unloading:
Magazine catch at rear of magazine housing. Remove magazine. Pull back cocking handle to eject any round remaining in the chamber. Examine chamber and feedway through the ejection slot. Release cocking handle, press trigger.

magazine interface, accepting M16 and similar magazines, has a NATO-standard sight mount for day or night optical sights, and may be fitted with a bipod. There is also a folding-butt model.

Heckler & Koch G11 GERMANY

This revolutionary weapon was destined to become the German Army's standard in 1990 but politics got in the way and only a limited number were issued to Special Forces. A similar weapon was tested in the USA as the `Advanced Combat Rifle'. It uses entirely different principles to any other firearm and fires a special caseless cartridge which is simply a block of explosive with

Specification & Operation

Cartridge:
4.7 x 33mm caseless

Dimensions:
Length o/a: 750mm
Weight: 3.65kg
Barrel: 540mm
Rifling: 6 grooves rh
Magazine capacity: 50 rounds
Rate of fire: 600 rds/min

In production: 1989 -1990

Markings:
`HK G11K3 4.7 x 33 serial number'. On left of body.

Safety:
Manual safety catch on left side, above trigger. Rear (`S') position is safe; forward one notch (`1') single shots; forward two notches (`3') three-round burst; fully forward (`50') full automatic.

Unloading:
Magazine catch beneath the front end of the carrying handle/sight. Remove magazine by sliding it out forwards. Unfold the rotary key on the left side of the body and turn it counterclockwise until it stops. Point the gun in a safe direction and pull the trigger. Repeat. The weapon is now empty.

a bullet buried inside it. The mechanism moves back and forth in recoil inside the outer plastic casing, the amount of recoil varying with the type of fire selected. Although of peculiar appearance it is comfortable to use and shoots well; it delivers its three-round burst at a rate of 2000 rds/min and puts them all into the target.

IMBEL MD2 BRAZIL

IMBEL (Industrias de Materiel Belico), the government arms manufacturer for Brazil, began making FN FAL rifles under licence in the early 1950s. Using this design as a basis, they have developed their own 5.56mm rifle for supply to the Brazilian Army and also for export. Except for being slightly shorter it is virtually identical with the 7.62mm FAL

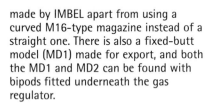

Specification & Operation

Cartridge:
5.56 x 45mm NATO or M193

Dimensions:
Length, stock extended: 1010mm
Length, stock folded: 764mm
Weight: 4.40kg
Barrel: 453mm
Rifling: 6 grooves, rh
Magazine capacity: 20 or 30 rounds
Rate of fire: 700 rds/min

In production: 1990 -

Markings:
`FABRICA DE ITAJUBA - BRASIL MD2 5.56mm' and serial number left side of receiver.

Safety:
Manual safety catch and fire selector lever on left side of receiver above the trigger. Back for safe, central for single shots, forward for automatic fire.

Unloading:
Magazine release behind magazine housing, beneath the receiver. Remove magazine. Pull back cocking handle to eject any round in the chamber. Inspect chamber and feedway via the ejection slot. Release cocking handle, pull trigger.

made by IMBEL apart from using a curved M16-type magazine instead of a straight one. There is also a fixed-butt model (MD1) made for export, and both the MD1 and MD2 can be found with bipods fitted underneath the gas regulator.

Japan Type 64 JAPAN

Specification & Operation

This rifle was developed in Japan and made by the Howa Machinery Company. It uses a gas-piston operating system driving a tilting bolt. The principal concern was to provide a rifle suited to the smaller stature of the Japanese soldier, and this weapon fires a special reduced-load cartridge as standard and uses a muzzle brake to further reduce the recoil force. The gas regulator is adjustable and can be set to a position permitting the use of full-power NATO cartridges if required. The rifle can also launch grenades.

Cartridge:
7.62 x 51mm Japanese Service

Dimensions:
Length o/a: 990mm
Weight: 4.40kg
Barrel: 450mm
Rifling: 4 grooves, rh
Magazine capacity: 20 rounds
Rate of fire: 500 rds/min

In production: 1964-90

Markings:
Ideographs 64 and 7.62mm with serial number and year in western form and arsenal mark all on left side of receiver.

Safety:
Manual safety catch and fire selector on right side of receiver, above trigger. Rearward for safe, forward for single shots, fully upward for automatic.

Unloading:
Magazine catch behind magazine housing. Remove magazine. Pull back cocking handle to remove any round in the chamber. Examine chamber and feedway through the ejection port. Release cocking handle, press trigger.

Japan Type 89 JAPAN

mechanism, so that if anything should go wrong with it, the single-shot and automatic functions are not impaired.

This rifle was designed by the Japanese Defence Agency and is replacing the Type 64 as the standard Japanese service rifle. Gas-operated, with a rotating bolt, it uses a somewhat unusual gas system which ensures a lower initial impulse on the gas piston, so giving a lower felt recoil and prolonging the life of the weapon. There is a fixed-butt version as well as the folding butt type, and both models are equipped with a bipod. Another unusual feature is the fitting of an entirely separate three-round burst

Specification & Operation

Cartridge:
5.56 x 45mm NATO

Dimensions:
Length, stock extended: 916mm
Length, stock folded: 670mm
Weight: 3.50kg
Barrel: 420mm
Rifling: 6 grooves, rh
Magazine capacity: 20 or 30 rounds
Rate of fire: 750 rds/min

In production: 1990-

Markings:
Ideographs 89 and 5.56mm with serial number and year in western form and arsenal mark all on left side of receiver.

Safety:
Manual safety catch and fire selector on right side of receiver above trigger. UP for safe, DOWN one notch for single shots, DOWN and fully forward for automatic fire. Set at automatic, operate the other catch behind trigger for 3-round burst.

Unloading:
Magazine catch is in the right side of the magazine housing. Remove magazine. Pull back cocking handle to eject any round remaining in the chamber. Inspect chamber and feedway. Release cocking handle, pull trigger.

Johnson M1941 USA

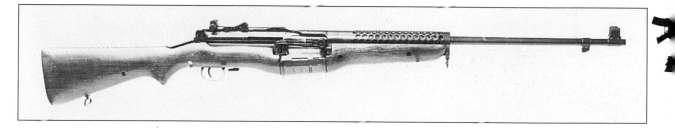

roduced by a US Marine Reserve officer to compete against the Garand for US service adoption, but by the time it arrived the Garand was in production. An estimated 70,000 were made; some were bought by the US Marines, who were low priority for the Garand issues, more by the Dutch for use in the Dutch East Indies, but most of these were undelivered because the Indies had fallen by the time they were ready. They were used by US troops and by 1945 they were fairly well distributed around the world. Another thousand were made in 7mm Mauser calibre for Chile. The rifle was recoil operated and had a rotary magazine which could be loaded from Springfield chargers.

Specification & Operation

Cartridge:
7.62 x 63mm (US .30-06)

Dimensions:
Length o/a: 1156mm
Weight: 4.31kg
Barrel: 558mm
Rifling: 4 grooves, rh
Magazine capacity: 11 rounds

In production: 1940-44

Markings:
'Cal 30-06 Semi-Auto/ JOHNSON AUTOMATICS/Made in Providence RI USA/ serial Number/ Model of 1941'. All above chamber.

Safety:
A manual safety catch in front of the trigger. Switch to the left for safe, to the right to fire.

Unloading:
The magazine is closed by a hinged cover on the loading port on the right side of the receiver. Press this cover firmly in as far as possible; this releases a catch which allows the magazine spring to force the rounds out of the magazine and into the hand.

Kalashnikov AK47 and variants RUSSIA

The various Kalashnikov models, variants, clones and copies would fill a book on their own; indeed have done. But no matter how they vary, the basic structure remains the same and is always recognisable. The basic AK47 turned into the AKM by virtue of improved production design and into the AK74 by

Specification & Operation

Cartridge:
7.62 x 39mm Soviet M1943

Dimensions:
Length, stock extended: 869mm
Length, stock folded: 699mm
Weight: 4.30kg
Barrel: 414mm
Rifling: 4 grooves, rh
Magazine capacity: 30 rounds
Rate of fire: 600 rds/min

In production: 1947-

Markings:
Model number, factory identifier and serial number on top of rear end of receiver.

Safety:
Combined safety catch and fire selector lever on the right rear side of the receiver. When pressed all the way UP it is in the safe position and obstructs the movement of the cocking handle and bolt; moved DOWN one notch to the first mark or the letters 'AB' gives full automatic fire, and moved to the bottom position, or the letter 'O', produces single shots.

Unloading:
Magazine catch at rear of magazine housing. Remove the magazine. Pull back the cocking handle to extract any round which may be in the chamber. Inspect the chamber via the ejection port. Release the cocking handle, pull the trigger.

Above: The AKM can be distinguished from the original AK47 by the small indentation above the magazine. On the AK47 this is longer, running the full width of the magazine housing.

changing calibre to 5.45mm. The various versions turned out by other countries are usually distinguished by personal preference - handgrips, different styles of butt, grenade launching attachments and so forth, but the basic Kalashnikov can always be seen in the receiver and

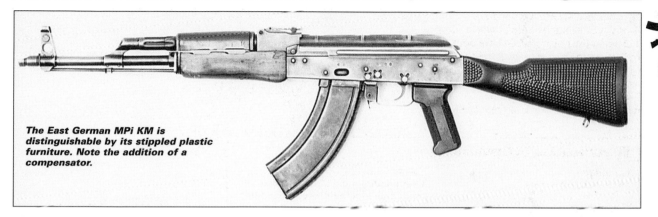

The East German MPi KM is distinguishable by its stippled plastic furniture. Note the addition of a compensator.

Right: Ugliest and least successful of the many Kalashnikov variants, the Hungarian AMD has a flimsy folding stock. Like Rumanian AKs, it has a forward pistol grip.

the safety lever. Larger differences may appear when the principle is applied to a 'new' design, e.g. the Galil, R4 and Finnish models. Once seen as being a Kalashnikov in origin, the nationality can then be determined by the markings.

La France M16K USA

suppressor, necessary with such a short barrel since otherwise there would be considerable flash and blast.

This is a much-modified M16 rifle which has been designed to provide a very compact rifle for special forces, aircrews and others who require automatic firepower in a small and convenient package. The gas system has been slightly modified to reduce the rate of fire to a figure more controllable in a weapon of this size, and the carrying handle contains a unique aperture foresight which is intended to make quick aiming easier and more accurate. There is also a `vortex' flash

Specification & Operation

Cartridge:
5.56 x 45mm NATO

Dimensions:
Length, stock extended: 686mm
Length, stock retracted: 610mm
Weight: 2.50kg
Barrel: 213mm
Rifling: 6 grooves, rh
Magazine capacity: 20, 30 or 90 rounds
Rate of fire: 600 rds/min

In production: 1992-

Markings:
`LA FRANCE SPECIALTIES SAN DIEGO CA USA MODEL M16K 5.56mm' and serial number on right side of magazine housing.

Safety:
Combined safety catch and fire selector on left side of receiver above the trigger. With the catch pulled back so that the pointer is directed to `SAFE' the weapon is safe. With the catch pressed DOWN and forward to the vertical, the weapon fires single shots. And with the catch pressed forward so that the pointer is to the rear against `AUTO' automatic fire is available.

Unloading:
Magazine catch is a push-button on the right side of the receiver above the trigger. Remove magazine. Pull back cocking handle (T-shaped `wings' behind the carrying handle) to eject any round remaining in the chamber. Inspect chamber and feedway via the ejection port. Release cocking handle, pull trigger.

Ljungman AG42 SWEDEN

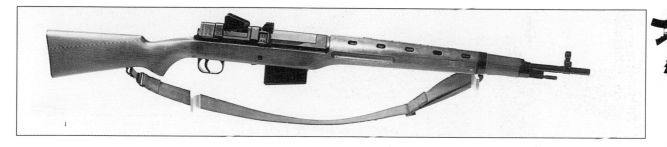

This appeared in Sweden in 1942 and uses a direct gas impingement system acting on the bolt carrier. Used by the Swedish Army until the 1970s, it was also used by the Danish Army in 7.92mm Mauser calibre from 1945 to the 1960s. In 1954 the Swedish tooling was bought by Egypt and the rifle produced there as the 'Hakim', also in 7.92mm Mauser calibre In 1959-60 a somewhat modified design, chambered for the 7.62 x 39mm Soviet cartridge was produced in Egypt as the 'Rashid' in small numbers.

Specification & Operation

Cartridge:
6.5 x 55mm Swedish service

Dimensions:
Length o/a: 1214mm
Weight: 4.71kg
Barrel: 622mm
Rifling: 6 grooves, rh
Magazine capacity: 10 rounds

In production: 1942-62

Markings:
MADSEN and serial number on left side of chamber.

Safety:
Lever at end of receiver: move right for safe.

Unloading:
There are two types of rifle, one with the magazine fixed and the other removable. In the case of the fixed model the only way to unload is to operate the cocking handle back and forth until the magazine is empty. Then check the chamber and feedway, release the cocking handle and pull the trigger. Where there is a magazine catch behind the magazine, remove the magazine, pull back the cocking handle to eject any round in the chamber, inspect chamber and feedway, release the cocking handle and pull the trigger.

MAS-49 FRANCE

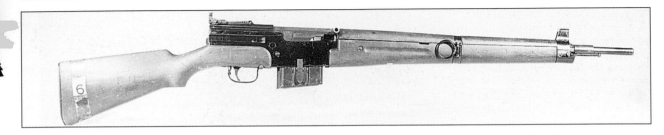

This was adopted somewhat hurriedly in 1949 when the French Army was anxious to equip with a modern rifle instead of the collection of oddments which had survived the war.

Gas-operated, it uses direct gas blast to blow the bolt carrier backwards, instead of the more usual piston. . It remained the standard French rifle until the arrival of the FAMAS in 1980, and large numbers were handed over to former colonies, who later disposed of them. A very small number were converted to 7.62 x 51mm calibre for use by French Gendarmeries, which suggests that such conversions could also be done by others, since the French 7.5mm ammunition is not now in common supply.

Specification & Operation

Cartridge:
7.5 x 54mm French Service

Dimensions:
Length o/a: 1100mm
Weight: 4.70kg
Barrel: 580mm
Rifling: 4 grooves, lh
Magazine capacity: 10 rounds

In production: 1951-65

Markings:
`MAS 49`, year and serial number on left side of receiver. May have script `St Etienne` marking in the same area.

Safety:
Manual safety catch is on the right side of the receiver, above the front end of the trigger guard. Turn DOWN to make safe, UP to fire.

Unloading:
Magazine catch is on the right side of the magazine housing; press in the lower end with the thumb to remove the magazine. Pull back the cocking handle to eject any round remaining in the chamber. Examine the chamber and feedway, release the cocking handle, pull the trigger.

MP 44 GERMANY

This is the father of all assault rifles, developed in Germany in 1941-42 and using a new short cartridge. Originally known as the MP (Machine Pistol) 44 for Nazi political reasons, it was renamed the 'Sturmgewehr 44' after its successful introduction into battle on the Eastern Front. It introduced the

Specification & Operation

Cartridge:
7.92 x 33mm 'Kurz'

Dimensions:
Length o/a: 940mm
Weight: 5.22kg
Barrel: 419mm
Rifling: 4 grooves, rh
Magazine capacity: 30 rounds
Rate of fire: 500 rds/min

In production: 1943-45

Markings:
'MP44'; factory mark - 'fxo' (Haenel & Co) or 'ayf' (Ermawerke); year; serial number. All on top of receiver, and serial number often repeated on the left side of the magazine housing.

Safety:
Manual safety catch on the left of the receiver, above the pistol grip. Press UP for safe, DOWN to fire. There is also a push-button, just behind and above the safety catch, which selects single shots or automatic fire.

Unloading:
The magazine release is a push-button on the left side of the magazine housing. Remove the magazine. Pull back the cocking handle to eject any round left in the chamber. Inspect the chamber and feedway via the ejection port. Release the cocking handle, pull the trigger.

concept of using a short cartridge with limited range in order to permit controllable automatic fire and a compact weapon, and because experience showed that most rifle fire was conducted at ranges under 400 metres. After the war it was examined and dissected by almost every major gunmaking nation and led, in one way and another, to the present-day 5.56mm assault rifles. In postwar years it was used by East German Border Guards and many found their way into central Africa.

Ruger Mini-Thirty USA

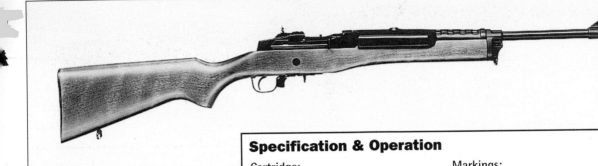

This came about as a variation of the Mini-14 Ranch Rifle, being chambered for the Soviet 7.62 x 39mm cartridge since this allowed a compact rifle with a cartridge superior to the .223 Remington for medium game shooting. However, it also offers an excellent para-military semi-automatic weapon in a calibre which is widely used throughout the world. It is a robust weapon and uses Ruger's patented optical sight mount, with which, it is claimed, accuracy superior to any other rifle in this calibre can be achieved.

Specification & Operation

Cartridge:
7.62 x 39mm Soviet M1943

Dimensions:
Length o/a: 948mm
Weight: 3.26kg
Barrel: 470mm
Rifling: 6 grooves, rh
Magazine capacity: 5 rounds

In production: 1987-

Markings:
'STURM, RUGER & Co Inc SOUTHPORT CONN USA' on left rear of receiver. Serial number on left of receiver alongside chamber. 'RUGER MINI-30 Cal 7.62' on rear top of receiver.

Safety:
Manual safety catch in front edge of trigger-guard. Push back into the guard for safe, forward for fire.

Unloading:
Magazine catch beneath receiver. Remove magazine. Pull back cocking handle to eject any round left in the chamber. Inspect chamber and feedway. Release cocking handle, pull trigger.

Ruger Mini-14 USA

The Mini-14 is based on the same gas piston and rotating bolt mechanism as used by the US M1 and M14 rifles, but the use of modern high tensile alloy steels has allowed considerable weight and bulk to be saved, making this a light and handy weapon firing a now-common cartridge. Although intended as a hunting rifle it was gladly adopted by many para-military and police forces throughout the world. A militarised version, the K Mini/14-20GB has a bayonet lug, flash suppressor and heat resistant glass-fibre handguard and is also available with a folding stock. The AC-556 is also militarised and provided with selective fire, giving automatic fire at about 750 rds/min.

Specification & Operation

Cartridge:
5.56 x 45mm M193 or NATO

Dimensions:
Length o/a: 946mm
Weight: 2.90kg
Barrel: 470mm
Rifling: 6 grooves, rh
Magazine capacity: 5, 20 or 30 rounds

In production: 1973-

Markings:
'STURM, RUGER & Co Inc SOUTHPORT CONN USA' on left rear of receiver. Serial number on left of receiver alongside chamber. 'RUGER MINI-14 Cal .223' on rear top of receiver.

Safety:
Manual safety catch in front edge of trigger-guard. Push back into the guard for safe, forward for fire.

Unloading:
Magazine catch beneath receiver. Remove magazine. Pull back cocking handle to eject any round left in the chamber. Inspect chamber and feedway. Release cocking handle, pull trigger.

Sako M90 FINLAND

The Sako M90 is the successor to the Valmet M62/M76 series of Finnish service rifles, Sako having absorbed Valmet in the late 1980s. The original Valmet designs were based upon Kalashnikov AK 47s obtained from Russia in the 1950s; they followed the Kalashnikov pattern but had a few small changes due to Finnish preferences.

Specification & Operation

Cartridge:
7.62 x 39mm Soviet M1943 or 5.56 x 45mm NATO

Dimensions: (7.62mm version)
Length, stock extended: 930mm
Length, stock folded: 675mm
Weight: 3.85kg
Barrel: 416mm
Rifling: 4 grooves, rh
Magazine capacity: 30 rounds
Rate of fire: 700 rds/min

In production: 1991-

Markings:
'M90' and serial number on left side of receiver.

Safety:
Combined safety catch and fire selector lever on the right rear side of the receiver. When pressed all the way UP it is in the safe position and obstructs the movement of the cocking handle and bolt; moved DOWN one notch to the first mark gives full automatic fire, and moved to the bottom position produces single shots.

Unloading:
Magazine catch at rear of magazine housing. Remove the magazine. Pull back the cocking handle to extract any round which may be in the chamber. Inspect the chamber via the ejection port. Release the cocking handle, pull the trigger.

There was no wood, the fore-end and pistol grip both being steel with a plastic coating; the butt was a large-diameter tube with a cross-member welded on at the end, and there was a prominent pronged flash hider. The M90 merely streamlined and improved the design, adopting a new side-folding butt, new sights with night-firing aids, and a new flash hider which also functions as a grenade launcher. It is probably the best Kalashnikov clone ever made.

Santa Barbara CETME Model L SPAIN

CETME (Centre for Technical Studies of Military Equipment) is a Spanish design agency; the weapons are actually made by the Empresa Nacional Santa Barbara at Oviedo arsenal. CETME began designing rifles shortly after WWII and were responsible for the design which eventually became the German G3. The

Specification & Operation

Cartridge:
5.56 x 45mm NATO

Dimensions:
Length o/a: 925mm
Weight: 3.40kg
Barrel: 400mm
Rifling: 6 grooves, rh
Magazine capacity: 10 or 30 rounds
Rate of fire: 650 rds/min

In production: 1984-

Markings:
'CETME 5.56 (.223)' on left side of magazine housing. Serial number on left side of receiver above trigger.

Safety:
Manual safety catch and fire selector lever on left side of receiver above the pistol grip. With the catch pushed UP to the letter 'S' the rifle is safe; one notch DOWN to 'T' gives single shots; two notches DOWN to 'R' for automatic fire. Some weapons will have a fourth notch, though the lever will not move into it; this is because the design originally had a three-round burst setting but this was not adopted by the Spanish Army. However the receivers are made with the notch since the three-round burst mechanism can be fitted as an option for other customers.

Unloading:
Magazine catch behind magazine housing on the right side. Press in and remove magazine. Pull back

CETME rifles all use the same roller-locked delayed blowback system that is used by the G3; they began with a 7.92mm weapon, then 7.62mm NATO and with the Model L moved into the 5.56mm field. There is also a short-barrel carbine with folding butt known as the Model LC.

SIG SG510-4 (Stgw 57) SWITZERLAND

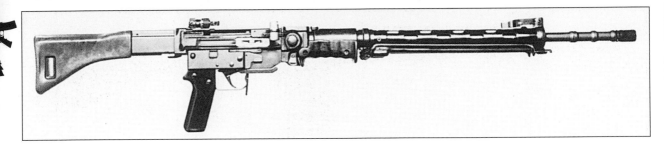

This Swiss service rifle is related to the German G3 and Spanish CETME Model L rifles insofar as they are all based on the roller-locked delayed-blowback system first designed by Mauser in Germany for the abortive Sturmgewehr 45. Somewhat heavy, it is a superbly accurate and comfortable-to-shoot rifle and is noted for its reliability in harsh climatic conditions. The commercial version, semi-automatic only, is the SIG 510-4, chambered for the 7.62mm cartridge; the two can be best told apart by the Stgw 57 having a rubber-covered butt which is virtually straight behind the receiver, while the 510-4 has a wooden butt with a distinct drop.

Specification & Operation

Cartridge:
7.5 x 55mm Swiss Service or 7.62 x 51mm NATO

Dimensions:
Length o/a: 1016mm
Weight: 4.25kg
Barrel: 505mm
Rifling: 4 grooves, rh
Magazine capacity: 20 rounds
Rate of fire: 600 rds/min

In production: 1957-83

Markings:
Serial number on left rear of receiver.

Safety:
A combined safety catch and fire selector is on the left side of the receiver, above the trigger. Vertical for safe, slanting forward for single shots, horizontal for automatic fire.

Unloading:
Magazine catch in rear of magazine housing. Remove magazine. Pull back cocking handle to eject any round left in the chamber. Inspect chamber and feedway via the ejection port. Release cocking handle, press trigger.

SIG SG540 (SG542) series SWITZERLAND

This family - the SG540 in 5.56mm with long barrel, SG542 in 7.62mm with long barrel, and SG543 in 5.56mm with short barrel - was designed by SIG of Switzerland and forthwith licensed to Manurhin of France for manufacture; Swiss arms export laws making it impossible for SIG to supply weapons to most countries. Manurhin made about 20,000 for the French Army who used them while FAMAS rifle production got up to speed, and they were supplied to Chile, Bolivia, Paraguay, Ecuador and Nicaragua. In 1988 the license was relinquished and passed to INDEP of Portugal,. who re-assigned it to Chile, who currently make the 540 and 542.

Specification & Operation

Cartridge:
5.56 x 45mm or 7.62 x 51mm

Dimensions: (SG542)
Length o/a: 1000m
Weight: 3.55kg
Barrel: 465mm
Rifling: 4 grooves, rh
Magazine capacity: 20 or 30 rounds
Rate of fire: 800 rds/min

In production: 1977-

Markings:
`MANURHIN FRANCE SG54X' and serial number on right side of receiver. May also have national army markings, e.g. `EJÉRCITO DE CHILE'.

Safety:
A four-position safety catch and fire selector on the left side of the receiver, above the pistol grip. The upper position is safe; rotated DOWN and forward there are positions for single shots, three-round burst, and full automatic fire.

Unloading:
Magazine catch in rear of magazine housing. Remove magazine. Pull back cocking handle to eject any round left in the chamber. Inspect chamber and feedway via the ejection port.

SIG SG 550/551 (Stgw 90) SWITZERLAND

This is an improved SG540 developed in competition to meet a Swiss Army requirement in 1984. The SIG design was selected and became the Sturmgewehr 90 and will eventually replace the Stgw 57 as the official Swiss rifle. It is also made in a civilian version, without automatic fire. An interesting feature of this rifle is the provision of studs and slots on the plastic magazines so that two or three magazines can be clipped together side-by-side; one can then be inserted into the magazine housing, and when the last shot is fired, changing to a full magazine can be done by pulling the assembly out, shifting it sideways and pushing in one of the loaded magazines.

Specification & Operation

Cartridge:
5.56 x 45mm NATO

Dimensions: (SG550)
Length, stock extended: 998mm
Length, stock folded:772mm
Weight: 4.10kg
Barrel: 528mm
Rifling: 6 grooves, rh
Magazine capacity: 20 or 30 rounds
Rate of fire: 700 rds/min

In production: 1986-

Markings:
'SG 550' and serial number on left side of receiver.

Safety:
A four-position safety catch and fire selector on the left side of the receiver, above the pistol grip. The rear position is safe; rotated UP and forward there are positions for single shots, three-round burst, and full automatic fire.

Unloading:
Magazine catch in rear of magazine housing. Remove magazine. Pull back cocking handle to eject any round left in the chamber. Inspect chamber and feedway via the ejection port. Release cocking

Simonov SKS RUSSIA

Simonov survived the SVT fiasco and set about designing a new carbine, but this was abandoned when the German invasion took place in 1941. He returned to it when the Soviets captured their first MP44s from the Germans and developed their own 7.62 short cartridge. Changing the design to suit this new cartridge , experimental models were in the hands of troops in combat in 1944, modifications were made, and in1946 mass-production of the first Soviet weapon to fire the 7.62 x 39mm cartridge began. It was thereafter widely issued, and also supplied to several Communist bloc countries, being copied in China, North Korea, East Germany and Yugoslavia. It is estimated that perhaps 15 million have been made.

Specification & Operation

Cartridge:
7.62 x 39mm Soviet M1943

Dimensions:
Length o/a: 1122mm
Weight: 3.86kg
Barrel: 520mm
Rifling: 4 grooves, rh
Magazine capacity: 10 rounds

In production: 1946-

Markings:
Serial number on left side receiver and on bolt.

Safety:
Manual safety catch on the rear of the trigger guard is pushed forward and UP to make the weapon safe, when it obstructs the trigger finger and movement of the trigger.

Unloading:
Magazine catch at the rear of the magazine, under the receiver. Press in and the magazine swings open, allowing the contents to be removed. Pull back the cocking handle, inspect the chamber and feedway, release the cocking handle, press the trigger. Close the empty magazine.

Simonov AVS-36 RUSSIA

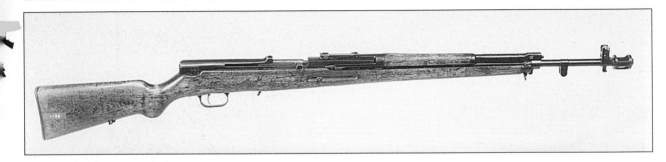

Under development from 1931, this was put into production before trials were completed, with the intention of providing the Soviet Army with an automatic rifle. It proved to be far too light a weapon to fire the heavy 7.62 x 54R cartridge at full automatic, the gas operating system was unreliable, and the design allowed dirt and dust to enter the action so that jams were frequent. Manufacture was halted and its place taken by the Tokarev SVT (qv), though those rifles which had been issued - some 32,000 or so - remained in use. Many were captured by the Finns in 1939 and thereafter used by them.

Specification & Operation

Cartridge:
7.62 x 54R Soviet Service

Dimensions:
Length o/a: 1259mm
Weight: 4.40kg
Barrel: 627mm
Rifling: 4 grooves, rh
Magazine capacity: 20 rounds
Rate of fire: 600 rds/min

In production: 1936-38

Markings:
Factory identifier and serial number on right side of receiver.

Safety:
Thumb-operated safety catch at the right rear of the receiver. Forward to fire, back for safe.

Unloading:
Magazine catch behind magazine, beneath receiver. Remove magazine. Pull back cocking handle to eject any round remaining in the chamber. Inspect chamber and feedway. Release cocking handle, pull trigger

Singapore SR88 SINGAPORE

Chartered Industries of Singapore began by making the M16 under license from Colt. They then had Sterling of Britain design an automatic rifle for them which they produced as the SAR-80. The SR88 is an improved version and became the standard rifle of the Singapore armed forces. It has also been

Specification & Operation

Cartridge:
5.56 x 45mm M198

Dimensions:
Length o/a: 972mm
Weight: 3.66kg
Barrel: 460mm
Rifling: 6 grooves, rh
Magazine capacity: 20 or 30 rounds
Rate of fire: 750 rds/min

In production: 1988-

Markings:
Serial Number; 'CAL 5.56 SR 88' on right side of magazine housing.

Safety:
Manual safety catch and fire selector on left side of receiver, over the trigger. Rearward position for safe, forward in two steps, first for single shots, second for automatic fire.

Unloading:
Magazine catch is a push-button on the right rear side of the magazine housing. Remove magazine. Pull back cocking handle to eject any round left in the chamber. Inspect chamber and feedway via the ejection port, release the cocking handle, pull trigger.

sold elsewhere in the Far East. The mechanism is different to that of the M16, using a gas piston to drive the bolt carrier back and operate a rotating bolt. The gas cylinder is chromed to reduce fouling and corrosion, the butt, fore-end and pistol grip are of glass-reinforced nylon, and the US M203 grenade launcher can be fitted beneath the barrel.

Singapore SR88A SINGAPORE

An improved version of the SR88; mechanically it is the same but there are significant differences in construction. The lower receiver is now an aluminium alloy casting, and the upper receiver a steel pressing. Stock, fore-end and pistol grip are of fibre-glass reinforced nylon, and the fixed stock model has part of the

Specification & Operation

Cartridge:
5.56 x 45mm NATO

Dimensions:
Length, fixed or extended stock: 960mm
Length, stock retracted: 810mm
Weight: 3.68kg
Barrel: 460mm
Rifling: 6 grooves, rh
Magazine capacity: 30 rounds
Rate of fire: 800 rds/min

In production: 1990-

Markings:
Serial Number 'SR88A CAL 5.56' on right side of magazine housing.

Safety:
Manual safety catch and fire selector on left side of receiver, over the trigger. Rearward position for safe, forward in two steps, first for single shots, second for automatic fire.

Unloading:
Magazine catch is a push-button on the right rear side of the magazine housing. Remove magazine. Pull back cocking handle to eject any round left in the chamber. Inspect chamber and feedway via the ejection port, release the cocking handle, pull trigger.

stock cut away for lightness and strength. The barrel is fitted to the receiver by a locknut and locating lug system which considerably simplifies barrel replacement in the field. The barrel is hammer-forged and has a chromed chamber. There is also a carbine version with shorter barrel, intended for use by paratroops or others requiring a compact rifle.

Steyr-Mannlicher AUG AUSTRIA

This was designed to an Austrian Army specification and was adopted by them in 1979. It has since been adopted by Ireland, Australia, several Middle Eastern countries, the US Customs service, the Falkland Islands Defence Force, and recently the Netherlands. It is made under licence in Australia as the F88. Modular in

Specification & Operation

Cartridge:
5.56 x 45mm M198 or NATO

Dimensions:
Length o/a: 790mm
Weight: 3.05kg
Barrel: 500mm
Rifling: 6 grooves, rh
Magazine capacity: 30 or 42 rounds
Rate of fire: 650 rds/min

In production: 1978-

Markings:
'STEYR-DAIMLER-PUCH AG AUSTRIA' or 'STEYR-MANNLICHER GmbH AUSTRIA', and 'AUG/A1' moulded into the stock on the right side. Serial number on right side of barrel.

Safety:
A push-through safety is fitted into the stock behind the trigger. When pushed from left to right, the rifle is safe. Pushed from right to left, the rifle is ready to fire. Selection of fire is performed by the trigger; a light pull gives single shots, a heavier pull gives automatic fire.

Unloading:
Magazine catch is behind the magazine. Remove magazine. Pull back cocking handle to eject any round remaining in the chamber, inspect chamber and feedway via the ejection slot. Release the cocking handle, pull the trigger.

design, the barrel can be quickly removed and changed for a longer or shorter one, the firing mechanism can be removed and changed for one giving three-round bursts or semi-automatic fire only or any other combination of possibilities; the receiver can be changed to replace the built-in telescope by a mounting platform to which other types of sight can be fitted. It was the first rifle to make extensive use of plastics, not only for the furniture but also for the firing mechanism.

Stoner SR-25 USA

This remarkable weapon is actually an M16 modified to fire the 7.62mm NATO cartridge. It s purpose in life is suggested as a support weapon for sniper teams, the second man using it for local defence but having sufficient accuracy to stand in for the sniper should some accident befall him or his weapon. It is certainly designed for accuracy, with a very heavy free-floating

Specification & Operation

Cartridge:
7.62 x 51mm NATO

Dimensions:
Length o/a: 1117mm
Weight: 4.88kg
Barrel:
Rifling: 4 grooves, rh
Magazine capacity: 10 or 20 rounds

In production: 1992-

Markings:
`KNIGHT'S ARMAMENT CO SR25 serial number' on left side of magazine housing.

Safety:
Manual safety catch on the left side of the receiver, above the trigger. Rear for safe, forward for fire.

Unloading:
Magazine catch in rear of magazine housing. Remove magazine. Pull back cocking handle (`wings' above the rear of the receiver) to eject any round in the chamber. Release the cocking handle, pull the trigger.

barrel and with the bipod attached to the fore-end and the fore-end attached only to the receiver so as not to place any strain on the barrel. The receiver is a flat top design to which the user can apply various options, from a carrying handle to the most sophisticated night vision sights. Tests show that this rifle can consistently put all the shots of a group into a 19mm circle at 100m range.

Taiwan Type 65 TAIWAN

This rifle was developed and manufactured by the Taiwanese Hsing Hua arsenal and is broadly based upon the M16. The general shape of the receiver is similar to that of the M16, though only prototypes were made with the carrying handle, the production rifle having a flat top. The fore-end is longer than that used with the M16, and a bipod may be fitted, though it is not a standard fitment. A later model of this rifle has a three-round burst facility in addition to full automatic fire.

Specification & Operation

Cartridge:
5.56 x 45mm M193 or NATO

Dimensions:
Length o/a: 990mm
Weight: 3.17kg
Barrel: 508mm
Rifling: 4 grooves, rh
Magazine capacity: 20 or 30 rounds
Rate of fire: 750 rds/min

In production: 1976-

Markings:
5.56m Type 65 on left of magazine housing.

Safety:
Combined safety catch and fire selector on left side of receiver above the trigger. With the catch pulled back so that the pointer is directed to 'SAFE' the weapon is safe. With the catch pressed DOWN and forward to the vertical, the weapon fires single shots. With the catch pressed forward so that the pointer is to the rear against 'AUTO' automatic fire is available.

Unloading:
Magazine catch is a push-button on the right side of the receiver above the trigger. Remove magazine. Pull back cocking handle (T-shaped 'wings' behind the carrying handle) to eject any round remaining in the chamber. Inspect chamber and feedway via the ejection port. Release cocking handle, pull trigger.

Tokarev SVT38 RUSSIA

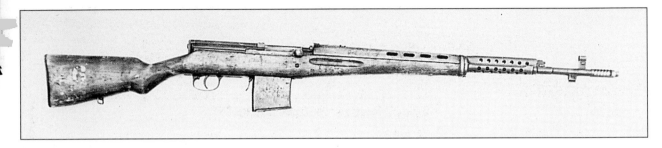

There are two models of this rifle, the SVT1938 and the SVT1940, the latter having full automatic fire facility. Otherwise similar, they are gas operated weapons. The 1938 model was plagued by poor manufacture, and various minor design changes made the weapon more reliable, to the extend that about 2 million of the 1940 version were eventually made. The principal visual difference between the 1938 and the 1940 is that in the 1938 the cleaning rod lies in a slot in the side of the wooden fore-end and stock, while in the 1940 it is concealed underneath the barrel. The 1938 is fitted with a six-baffle muzzle brake, the 1940 has a two or three-baffle brake.

Specification & Operation

Cartridge:
7.62 x 54R Soviet Service

Dimensions:
Length o/a: 1220mm
Weight: 3.95kg
Barrel: 635mm
Rifling: 4 grooves, rh
Magazine capacity: 20 rounds

In production: 1939-45

Markings:
Factory identifier and serial number on right side of receiver.

Safety:
A manual safety catch inside the rear of the trigger-guard. When pressed DOWN it blocks movement of the trigger and the weapon is allegedly safe. In the 1940 model, swinging this lever to the right sets the trigger for automatic fire.

Unloading:
Magazine catch behind magazine housing. Remove magazine. Pull back cocking handle to eject any round remaining in the chamber. Inspect chamber and feedway through the ejection port. Release the cocking handle, press the trigger.

US M1 Rifle (Garand) USA

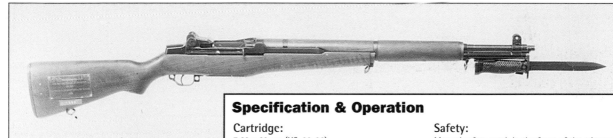

The first automatic rifle to achieve the status of being the regulation sidearm for a major army, the Garand served well and was popular for its reliability and power. If it had a defect, it was the clip loading system which prevented 'topping up' the magazine during a lull in the firing; it was a full clip or nothing. There was also the embarrassment of the empty clip being ejected after the last round and advertising the fact if it fell on a hard surface. But these were minor faults, and with over six million rifles made and distributed to many countries after 1945, they will continue to appear for many years to come.

Specification & Operation

Cartridge:
7.62 x 63mm (US .30-06)

Dimensions:
Length o/a:1106mm
Weight: 4.30kg
Barrel: 610mm
Rifling: 4 grooves, rh
Magazine capacity: 8 rounds

In production: 1936-59

Markings:
'U.S RIFLE .30 M1 SPRINGFIELD ARSENAL' and serial number on upper rear of receiver. Other manufacturer's names are: 'WINCHESTER'; 'INTERNATIONAL HARVESTER'; 'HARRINGTON & RICHARDSON'. May also be found with 'BERETTA' and with Indonesian markings.

Safety:
Manual safety catch in the front of the trigger guard. Pulled back toward the trigger, the rifle is safe; push forward to fire.

Unloading:
Ensure the safety catch is forward. Pull back the cocking handle to eject any round in the chamber, and hold it to the rear. Inspect the chamber and magazine. If there is ammunition in the magazine, grasp the rifle with the left hand in front of the trigger guard and, without releasing the cocking handle, reach across the action with the right thumb and press the clip latch on the left side of the receiver. The clip, with any remaining ammunition will be ejected from the magazine into the right hand. Remove the clip and ammunition, check chamber and magazine area again, release the cocking handle, press the trigger.

US M1/M2 Carbine USA

One of the most appealing of weapons, light, handy, easy to shoot and totally useless at ranges over 200 yards, since it fired a pistol bullet. It was intended simply to replace the pistol with something having more range, but it found itself being used as a light rifle more often than not. Over six million were made in various forms; the M1 was the original semi-automatic; the M1A1 had a folding steel butt, for use by paratroops; the M2 added automatic fire; and the M3 was an M2 with special fittings for mounting infra-red sights. After the war several companies began making them for the commercial market and still do.

Specification & Operation

Cartridge:
7.62 x 33mm (.30 Carbine)

Dimensions: (M1)
Length o/a: 904mm
Weight: 2.36kg
Barrel: 458mm
Rifling: 4 grooves, rh
Magazine capacity: 15 or 30 rounds
Rate of fire: (M2/M3) 750 rds/min

In production: 1942-

Markings:
'U.S.CARBINE CAL .30 M1' across the top of the chamber. Serial number and maker's mark on the rear of the receiver. Various maker's marks and initials may be found on the receiver and barrel.

Safety:
Manual safety catch on the right front edge of the trigger guard. Push DOWN for fire, UP for safe. Original models had a push-through cross-bolt but this was later changed and almost all were modified. The M2 and M3 models have a selector switch on the front left side of the receiver, alongside the chamber; push forward for automatic fire, rearward for single shots.

Unloading:
Magazine release is a push-button on the right side of the receiver, behind the magazine. Remove magazine. Pull back cocking handle to eject any round remaining in the chamber. Inspect chamber and feedway, release cocking handle, pull trigger.

US M4 Carbine USA

This is a true carbine, being simply a short-barrelled version of the M16A2 rifle and with a collapsible stock; it can be thought of as an intermediate between the full sized rifle and the ultra-short Commando. All mechanical components are interchangeable with those of the M16A2, and it will accept any M16 or NATO STANAG 4179 magazines. As well as being used by US forces it is in service with the Canadian Army as their C8 rifle and with a number of Central and South American forces.

Specification & Operation

Cartridge:
5.56 x 45mm NATO

Dimensions:
Length, stock extended: 840mm
Length, stock retracted: 760mm
Weight: 2.54kg
Barrel: 368mm
Rifling: 6 grooves, rh
Magazine capacity: 20 or 30 rounds
Rate of fire: 700 - 1000 rds/min

In production: 1984-

Markings:
'COLT FIREARMS DIVISION COLT INDUSTRIES HARTFORD CONN USA' on left side of receiver. 'COLT M4 CAL 5.56mm serial number' on left side of magazine housing.

Safety:
Combined safety catch and fire selector on left side of receiver above the trigger. With the catch pulled back so that the pointer is directed to 'SAFE' the weapon is safe. With the catch pressed DOWN and forward to the vertical, the weapon fired single shots. And with the catch pressed forward so that the pointer is to the rear against 'AUTO' automatic fire is available.

Unloading:
Magazine catch is a push-button on the right side of the receiver above the trigger. Remove magazine. Pull back cocking handle (T-shaped 'wings' behind the carrying handle) to eject any round remaining in the chamber. Inspect chamber and feedway via the ejection port. Release cocking handle, pull trigger.

M14 Rifle USA

When the US needed a new 7.62mm rifle to meet NATO standardisation requirements, it seemed good sense to give the Garand a few tweaks; give it a detachable magazine instead of the clip feed and rebarrel it. Job done. Or it would have been, if somebody hadn't said `Let's make it automatic'. Provision of automatic fire with a cartridge as heavy as the 7.62 meant strengthening everything, and the result was a clumsy weapon. Most were converted by locking the system at semi-automatic, and with some modifications the weapon was reasonably serviceable. Early models had wooden furniture, then with a glass-fibre handguard, finally with all-synthetic furniture.

Specification & Operation

Cartridge:
7.62 x 51mm NATO

Dimensions:
Length o/a: 1120mm
Weight: 5.1kg loaded
Barrel: 559mm
Rifling: 4 grooves, rh
Magazine capacity: 20 rounds
Rate of fire: 750 rds/min

In production: 1957-63

Markings:
`US RIFLE 7.62MM M14'; Maker's name (e.g. `WINCHESTER'; `SPRINGFIELD ARMORY') and serial number on top rear of receiver.

Safety:
Manual safety catch in the front of the trigger guard. Pulled back toward the trigger, the rifle is safe; push forward to fire. Fire selection is by a rotary catch in the right side of the receiver above the trigger. Press in and turn to point DOWN for single shots, UP for automatic fire.

Unloading:
Magazine catch behind the magazine housing beneath the receiver. Remove magazine. Pull back cocking handle to eject any round remaining in the chamber. Inspect chamber and feedway, release cocking handle, pull the trigger.

US M16 rifle USA

sights. The M16A3 is an A2 with a removable carrying handle which, when removed, leaves a telescope mounting rail.

The M16 and its derivatives have been adopted all over the world, either distributed by the USA or manufactured locally under licence; there are also a goodly number of rifles bearing other names which are M16s under the skin. The M16A1 differs from the original M16 by having a manual bolt closing device on the right side of the receiver, allowing some extra pressure to counter a dirty chamber or sticky cartridge case. The M16A2 has a slower twist of rifling, to suit it to NATO ammunition, a heavier barrel and a case deflector on the right side to prevent left-handed firers from being assaulted by ejected cases. It also has improvements in the furniture and

Specification & Operation

Cartridge:
5.56 x 45mm M193 or NATO

Dimensions: (M16A1)
Length o/a: 990mm
Weight: 3.18kg
Barrel: 533mm with flash hider
Rifling: 6 grooves, rh
Magazine capacity: 20 or 30 rounds
Rate of fire: 700 - 950 rds/min

In production: M16, M16A1:-1964-80; M16A2:-1982- ; M16A3:- 1994-

Markings:
'COLT AR-15 PROPERTY OF U.S.GOVT. M16A1 CAL 5.56MM serial number' on left side of magazine housing. 'COLTS PATENT FIRE ARMS MFG CO HARTFORD CONN U.S.A.' or 'COLT'S FIREARMS DIVISION COLT INDUSTRIES HARTFORD CONN U.S.A.' on left side of receiver. Similar markings but with different maker include 'HARRINGTON & RICHARDSON WORCESTER MASS U.S.A.' with the company monogram at the top of the magazine housing; or 'HYDRAMATIC DIV G.M.CORP USA' at the top of the magazine housing. Other markings will be found on license-made models, which will have 'MADE IN XXX UNDER LICENSE FROM COLT'S HARTFORD CT U.S.A.' on right of mag. housing.

Safety:
Combined safety catch and fire selector on left side of receiver above the trigger. With the catch pulled back so that the pointer is directed to 'SAFE' the weapon is safe.

Unloading:
Remove magazine. Pull back cocking handle (T-shaped 'wings' behind the carrying handle) to eject any round remaining in the chamber. Inspect chamber and feedway via the ejection port. Release cocking handle, pull trigger.

VAL Silent Sniper RUSSIA

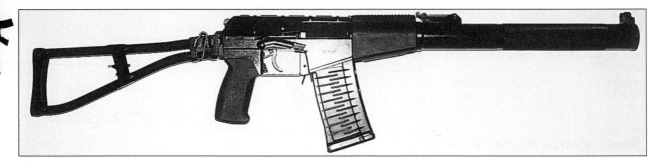

This weapon was only revealed in 1994 and full examination has not yet been possible. It is a silent semi-automatic rifle firing a heavy 9mm bullet at subsonic velocity, and, in view of the current accessibility of Russian small arms, it is likely to attract attention from various quarters, eventually turning up in the wrong hands. It is claimed that the special cartridge will defeat all levels of body armour protection out to ranges of 400 metres or more; as with all Russian weapons, such claims should be treated with reserve until confirmed independently.

Specification & Operation

Cartridge:
9 x 39mm special

Dimensions:
Length, stock extended: 875mm
Length, stock folded: 615mm
Weight: 2.5kg
Barrel: not known
Rifling: not known
Magazine capacity: 20 rounds
Rate of fire: not known

In production: 1993-

Markings:
Factory identifier and serial number on right side of receiver.

Safety:
Manual safety catch behind trigger, press upper portion in for safe, press lower portion in for fire.

Unloading:
Magazine catch behind magazine on front end of trigger guard. Remove magazine, pull back cocking handle to eject any round in the chamber. Inspect chamber and feedway via the ejection slot. Release cocking handle, press trigger.

Valmet M76 FINLAND

This is simply the Finnish version of the Kalashnikov AK rifle and the differences are largely those which the Finns regard as being necessary to withstand their permanently Arctic conditions. The first model was the M60, which had a plastic fore-end and tubular steel butt; some were without trigger-

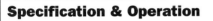

Specification & Operation

Cartridge:
7.62 x 39mm Soviet M1943

Dimensions:
Length, stock extended. 950mm
Length, stock folded: 710mm
Weight: 3.60kg
Barrel: 418mm
Rifling: 4 grooves, rh
Magazine capacity: 15, 20 or 30 rounds
Rate of fire: 700 rds/min

In production: 1976-86

Markings:
'VALMET Jyvaskyla' and serial number on right side of receiver.

Safety:
Combined safety catch and fire selector lever on the right rear side of the receiver. When pressed all the way UP it is in the safe position and obstructs the movement of the cocking handle and bolt; moved DOWN one notch to the first mark (three dots) gives full automatic fire, and moved to the bottom position, a single dot, produces single shots.

Unloading:
Magazine catch at rear of magazine housing. Remove the magazine. Pull back the cocking handle to extract any round which may be in the chamber. Inspect the chamber via the ejection port. Release the cocking handle, pull the trigger.

guards for use with Arctic mittens. Then came the M62, with a machined steel receiver and some changes to the sights and furniture. Then came the M71 which adopted a stamped steel receiver, but this proved less strong and was dropped for a return to the M62 but with a new folding butt. Finally came the M76 with a stronger sheet steel receiver and a variety of fixed or folding steel, plastic or wooden butts. As well as being used by the Finns, these rifles have also been bought by Qatar and Indonesia and have also been sold in semi-automatic form on the commercial market.

Valmet M78 FINLAND

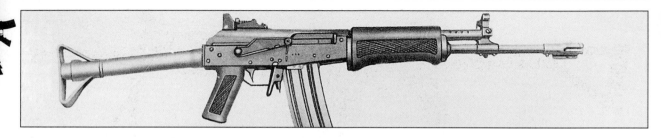

The M78 is essentially a heavy-barrelled model of the M76 intended as a light squad support weapon. The longer and heavier barrel extends the effective range from the 400m or so of the rifle to 600/700 metres. It appears to have been taken into service in small numbers by the Finnish Army, but other sales are not known. It was also offered in 5.56 x 45mm calibre with selective fire and in 7.62 x 51mm in semi-automatic form as a long range rifle.

Specification & Operation

Cartridge:
7.62 x 39mm Soviet M1943 and others

Dimensions:
Length o/a: 1060mm
Weight: 4.70kg
Barrel: 480mm
Rifling: 4 grooves, rh
Magazine capacity: 15 or 30 rounds
Rate of fire: 650 rds/min

In production: 1978-86

Markings:
`VALMET Jyvaskyla M78' and serial number on right side of receiver.

Safety:
Combined safety catch and fire selector lever on the right rear side of the receiver. When pressed all the way UP it is in the safe position and obstructs the movement of the cocking handle and bolt; moved DOWN one notch to the first mark (three dots) gives full automatic fire, and moved to the bottom position (single dot), produces single shots.

Unloading:
Magazine catch at rear of magazine housing. Remove the magazine. Pull back the cocking handle to extract any round which may be in the chamber. Inspect the chamber via the ejection port. Release the cocking handle, pull the trigger.

Vektor R4 SOUTH AFRICA

Specification & Operation

Cartridge:
5.56 x 45mm M193

Dimensions:
Length, stock extended: 1005mm
Length, stock folded: 740mm
Weight: 4.30kg
Barrel: 460mm
Rifling: 6 grooves, rh
Magazine capacity: 35 rounds
Rate of fire: 700 rds/min
In production: 1982-

Markings:
Vektor badge (V in circle) on right of receiver in front of ejection port. Serial number on left.

Safety:
Combined safety catch and fire selector lever on the right rear side of the receiver. When pressed all the way UP it is in the safe position (letter 'S') and obstructs the movement of the cocking handle and bolt; moved DOWN one notch to the first mark or the letter 'A' gives full automatic fire, and moved to the bottom position, or the letter 'R', produces single shots.

Unloading:
Remove the magazine. Pull back the cocking handle to extract any round which may be in the chamber. Inspect the chamber via the ejection port. Release the cocking handle, pull the trigger.

This is the South African standard rifle and is a slightly modified Israeli Galil; the modifications consisted of changing the butt and fore-end to synthetic materials rather than steel, in consideration of the bush temperatures common in Africa, and lengthening the butt since the average South African was rather larger than the average Israeli. Other components were strengthened, a bipod with wire-cutting ability was provided. There is also a carbine version, the R5, with a 332mm barrel, and a compact version, the R6, with a 280mm barrel. Semi-automatic versions of all three weapons are produced for use by police and para-military forces and for export.

415

Zastava M59/66 YUGOSLAVIA

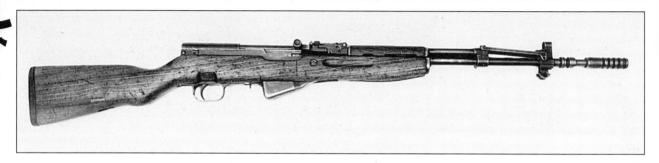

Yugoslavia adopted the Simonov SVS in the 1950s as their M59, but after some experience decided to modify it better to suit their requirements. The barrel was lengthened and provided with a 22mm grenade-launching sleeve, the gas cylinder connection to the barrel was altered and a new foresight unit, which includes a night sight and a grenade sight, was attached to the extended barrel. The fore-end was shortened, but the hinged sword bayonet was retained, making several generations of Yugoslav conscripts very wary about where they put their fingers. They were widely exported before the end of Yugoslavia.

Specification & Operation

Cartridge:
7.62 x 39mm Soviet M1943

Dimensions:
Length o/a: 1120mm
Weight: 4.10kg
Barrel: 620mm
Rifling: 4 grooves, rh
Magazine capacity: 10 rounds

In production: 1966-72

Markings:
Factory identifier and serial number on right side of receiver.

Safety:
Thumb-operated safety catch at the right rear of the receiver. Forward to fire, back for safe.

Unloading:
Magazine catch behind magazine, beneath receiver. Remove magazine. Pull back cocking handle to eject any round remaining in the chamber. Inspect chamber and feedway. Release cocking handle, pull trigger.

Zastava M70B1 YUGOSLAVIA

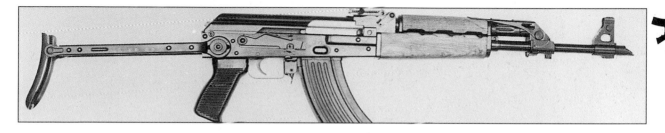

This is generally based on the AK47 Kalashnikov which the Yugoslavs obtained from the USSR and adopted as their M60. As with the Simonov, they felt that there were a few alterations that needed doing, and the M70 is the result. While the general layout remains the same, there is a folding grenade sight behind the foresight which, when raised, shuts off the gas supply to the gas actuating cylinder. There is no grenade launching fitment on the rifle but one can be quickly fitted, a groove around the muzzle acting as anchor for a snap ring. Both fixed and folding stock models were made and it remains the standard Yugoslavian service rifle.

Specification & Operation

Cartridge:
7.62 x 39mm Soviet M1943

Dimensions:
Length o/a: 900mm
Weight: 3.70kg
Barrel: 415mm
Rifling: 4 grooves, rh
Magazine capacity: 30 rounds
Rate of fire: 650 rds/min

In production: 1974-

Markings:
Model number, factory identifier and serial number on top of rear end of receiver.

Safety:
Combined safety catch and fire selector lever on the right rear side of the receiver. When pressed all the way UP it is in the safe position and obstructs the movement of the cocking handle and bolt; moved DOWN one notch to the first mark or the letter 'R' gives full automatic fire, and moved to the bottom position, or the letter 'J', produces single shots.

Unloading:
Magazine catch at rear of magazine housing. Remove the magazine. Pull back the cocking handle to extract any round which may be in the chamber. Inspect the chamber via the ejection port. Release the cocking handle, pull the trigger.

Zastava M76 YUGOSLAVIA

This is based on the action of the M70 rifle but chambered for a much more powerful cartridge and with a longer and heavier barrel as befits a sniping rifle. The sight bracket can be adapted to almost any type of optical or electro-optical sight. The rifle was taken into service by Yugoslavian forces and was also offered for export chambered for the 7.62 x 51mm NATO and the 7.62 x 54R Soviet cartridges, but details of any sales have never been made public.

Specification & Operation

Cartridge:
7.92 x 57mm Mauser and others

Dimensions:
Length o/a: 1135mm
Weight: 4.20kg
Barrel: 550mm
Rifling: 4 grooves, rh
Magazine capacity: 10 rounds

In production: 1975-

Markings:
Model number, factory identifier and serial number on top of rear end of receiver.

Safety:
Manual safety catch on the right rear side of the receiver. When pressed all the way UP it is in the safe position and obstructs the movement of the cocking handle and bolt; moved DOWN to the lower notch, the rifle is ready to fire.

Unloading:
Magazine catch at rear of magazine housing. Remove the magazine. Pull back the cocking handle to extract any round which may be in the chamber. Inspect the chamber via the ejection port. Release the cocking handle, pull the trigger.

Zastava M80 YUGOSLAVIA

This rifle, and its folding-stock companion the M80A, was designed in order to provide the export market with a Kalashnikov pattern rifle in 5.56mm calibre. The gas regulator has been redesigned in order to cope with the different energy levels possible with various makes of 5.56mm ammunition, and there is a grenade launching spigot and sight provided with every rifle which can be attached when required. How far this particular export venture had got when the present war broke out is not known, but the possibility of these rifles appearing anywhere in the world cannot be overlooked.

Specification & Operation

Cartridge:
5.56 x 45mm M193 or NATO

Dimensions:
Length o/a: 990mm
Weight: 3.5kg
Barrel: 460mm
Rifling: 6 grooves, rh
Magazine capacity: 30 rounds
Rate of fire: 750 rds/min

In production: 1985-

Markings:
Model number, factory identifier and serial number on top of rear end of receiver.

Safety:
Combined safety catch and fire selector lever on the right rear side of the receiver. When pressed all the way UP it is in the safe position and obstructs the movement of the cocking handle and bolt; moved DOWN one notch to the first mark gives full automatic fire, and moved to the bottom position produces single shots.

Unloading:
Magazine catch at rear of magazine housing. Remove the magazine. Pull back the cocking handle to extract any round which may be in the chamber. Inspect the chamber via the ejection port. Release the cocking handle, pull the trigger.

ZH-29 CZECHOSLOVAKIA

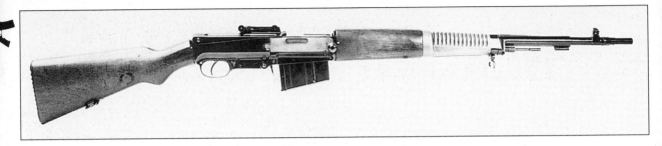

This was designed by the Czechs as a partner to the ZB26 light machine gun, with some commonality of parts and design features. It used a long-stroke gas piston and cams the bolt sideways to lock into the receiver. It is generally recognisable by the aluminium fore-end. It also had an unusual feature; after the last round is fired the bolt remains open. The magazine is then recharged from two five-round chargers, after which a pressure on the trigger will release the bolt to close, and a second pressure then fires the rifle. Numbers were bought by China, Ethiopia and Siam during the 1930s, and in theory they could turn up anywhere in Africa and the Far East.

Specification & Operation

Cartridge:
7.92 x 57mm Mauser

Dimensions:
Length o/a: 1150mm
Weight: 4.48kg
Barrel: 545mm
Rifling: 4 grooves, rh
Magazine capacity: 5, 10 or 25 rounds

In production: 1929-38

Markings:
Unknown

Safety:
Safety lever on the front right of the trigger guard. Turn DOWN for fire, UP for safe.

Unloading:
Magazine catch at rear of magazine housing, beneath the receiver. Remove the magazine. Pull back the cocking handle to eject any round remaining in the chamber. Inspect the chamber and feedway via the ejection port. Release the cocking handle, press the trigger

MACHINE GUNS

AAT-F1 FRANCE

absolute safety, and the extraction is violent. Nevertheless, the gun is reliable and efficient and has been put into service by several former French colonies.

Known variously as the AAT-52, MAS-52 or F1, this is the standard French Army general purpose machine gun. Operation is by delayed blowback, using a two-piece bolt similar to that of the FA-MAS rifle, in which the light forward part of the bolt has to overcome the inertia of the heavy rear section before the breech can be opened. The chamber is fluted so as to float the case on a layer of gas to ease extraction, but the result is somewhat on the borders of

Specification & Operation

Cartridge:
7.5 x 54 French Service; 7.62 x 51mm NATO

Dimensions:
Length o/a: 990mm
Weight: 9.88kg
Barrel: 488mm
Rifling: 4 grooves, rh
Feed system: 50-round belt
Rate of fire: 700 rds/min

In production: 1952-

Markings:
'AA F1 MAT' and serial number on left side of receiver (or AA 52 as applicable).

Safety:
A cross-bolt safety catch in the top of the pistol grip. Push through from right to left to make safe, from left to right to fire.

Unloading:
Pull the cocking handle back and then push it fully forward and press the safety catch to the left. Press the cover latch (on top of the receiver) and open the feed cover. Lift out the belt if present. Inspect the feedway, close the cover. Push the safety catch to the right, pull the cocking handle back and, while holding it, press the trigger and ease the handle forward.

Alfa SPAIN

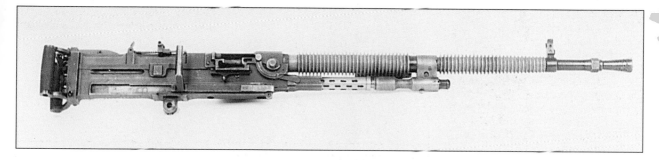

Specification & Operation

Cartridge:
7.92 x 57mm Mauser

Dimensions:
Length o/a: 1447mm
Weight: 12.92kg
Barrel: 750mm
Rifling: 6 grooves, rh
Feed system: belt
Rate of fire: 800 rds/min

In production: 1944-62

Markings:
'ALFA 7.92', serial number, 'OVIEDO' (year) on top of receiver.

Safety:
A safety catch is fitted between the spade grips and rests in a notch on the firing button. To fire it is necessary to raise this catch with one thumb and press the firing button with the other.

Unloading:
Press in the pawl latch under the belt feedway and remove belt. Pull back cocking handle and, holding it back, examine the feedway and chamber. Release handle, press trigger.

The Alfa is a gas-operated weapon designed in Spain during WWII when their stock of machine guns required replacement and no outside source was available. It was originally chambered for the 7.92mm Mauser cartridge, but in 1955 a new model was put into service using the 7.62mm NATO cartridge. The weapons were replaced by other types in the late 1960s and disposed of in various ways; many turned up in Central African armies and since then have found their way into various hands.

Ameli SPAIN

Although this looks like a scaled-down MG42 it is entirely different in its operation, using the same roller-locked delayed blowback mechanism as the CETME Model L rifle or the Heckler & Koch rifles and machine guns. Several of the parts are interchangeable with the Model L rifle. It can be used on its bipod for squad support or on a tripod for sustained fire, having a quick-change

Specification & Operation

Cartridge:
5.56 x 45mm NATO

Dimensions:
Length o/a: 970mm
Weight: 6.35kg
Barrel: 400mm
Rifling: 6 grooves, rh
Feed system: belt
Rate of fire: 850 or 1200 rds/min

In production: 1982-

Markings:
'CETME AMELI 5.56' and serial number; or 'AMELI 5.56 9.223' and Santa Barbara monogram and serial number. All on left side of receiver.

Safety:
A manual safety catch on the right side of the pistol grip. Turn forward for safe, back for fire.

Unloading:
Slide forward the cover catch at the front edge of the butt and open the cover. Lift the cartridge belt from the feedway and lift the belt box from its attachment to the side of the gun. Pull back the cocking handle. Inspect the feedway and chamber. Close the cover, press the trigger.

barrel. It has been adopted by the Spanish Army and it will probably find acceptance elsewhere, as it is certainly one of the best 5.56mm light machine guns currently on offer.

Armalite AR-10 USA/HOLLAND

Developed by the ArmaLite Division of the Fairchild Aircraft Company, manufacture of this weapon was licensed to Artillerie Inrichtingen of Holland since ArmaLite had no production facilities. Small numbers were sold to Nicaragua, Burma and the Sudan, and others were purchased by various countries for trial, but large orders eluded the company and production

Specification & Operation

Cartridge:
7.62 x 51mm NATO

Dimensions:
Length o/a: 1029mm
Weight: 4.10kg
Barrel: 508mm
Rifling: 4 grooves, rh
Feed system: 20 round magazine
Rate of fire: 700 rds/min

In production: 1958-61

Markings:
'ArmaLite AR10 Manufactured by AI Nederland'
on left side of magazine housing. 'CAL 7.62 NATO' and serial number on left side of receiver.

Safety:
Combined safety catch and selector switch on left side, above trigger. Vertical for safe; forward for single shots, rearward for automatic fire.

Unloading:
Magazine catch is a serrated plate on the left side of the receiver behind the magazine. Remove magazine. Pull back cocking handle (inside carrying handle) to eject any round in the chamber, inspect chamber through the ejection slot, release cocking handle, pull trigger.

stopped in 1961. Shortly after that ArmaLite began the development which was to result in the AR15/M16 rifle, and it is not hard to see the family resemblance between the AR10 and the M16.

Beretta M70/78 ITALY

The AR 70/84 was designed in company with the 70/.223 rifle and many of the parts are the same. The principal difference is that this machine gun version has a heavy interchangeable barrel and a bipod which is adjustable for height. The internal mechanism is still the same gas-actuated rotating bolt, and all the controls are similar to those of the rifle, making training a little

Specification & Operation

Cartridge:
5.56 x 45mm M198

Dimensions:
Length o/a: 946mm
Weight: 5.31kg
Barrel: 450mm
Rifling: 6 grooves, rh
Feed system: 30 or 40 round magazine
Rate of fire: 700 rds/min

In production: 1979-83

Markings:
`P BERETTA FM 70/78 MADE IN ITALY' serial number, on left side of receiver.

Safety:
Manual safety catch and fire selector on left side of receiver above pistol grip. Turned DOWN for safe, UP for automatic fire, midway for single shots.

Unloading:
Magazine catch is behind the magazine. Remove the magazine. Pull back the cocking handle to eject any round left in the chamber. Inspect the chamber via the ejection port. Release the cocking handle, pull the trigger.

easier. However, when this appeared much of the world was waiting to see the result of a long NATO trial to select a new round of ammunition, and sales were sluggish. A few eastern countries bought the rifle/machine gun combination before production ended.

Besa CZECHOSLOVAKIA

The Besa, like the Bren, was originally a Czech design and was adopted by Britain for use in armoured vehicles. It can also be tripod mounted. The name came from being made by the BSA company. There are several variants; the Marks 1 and 2 had two rates of fire; the Mark 3 was fixed at the high rate, the Mark 3* fixed at the low rate. Other marks were based on these but with various changes to fit into different

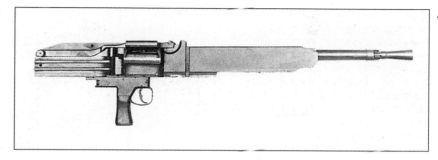

Specification & Operation

Cartridge:
7.92 x 57mm Mauser

Dimensions:
Length o/a: 1105mm
Weight: 21.46kg
Barrel: 736mm
Rifling: 4 grooves, rh
Feed system: belt
Rate of fire: 500 or 800 rds/min

In production: 1939-46

Markings:
'BESA Mk I BSA Ltd', year and serial number on top of receiver.

Safety:
A manual safety on the left side of the pistol grip. Forward to fire, back for safe.

Unloading:
Remove belt. Pull back cocking handle and inspect chamber and feedway. Release handle and pull trigger.

tanks. The Besa's operation was unusual; the barrel and bolt unit recoiled inside the receiver, reloaded, and then fired while the parts were still moving forwards. This made the cartridge explosion first brake the forward movement before starting the next recoil movement, so reducing the recoil force. In a mounting as substantial as a tank, one wonders why they bothered.

there is from sheet-steel magazines which get knocked about. On the debit side, if anything goes wrong with the one magazine, the gun is useless, and the slow method of loading reduces the effective rate of fire to a very low figure. Another oddity is that the barrel can be quickly changed but there is no handle, so getting the hot barrel off must have been an interesting exercise.

This was another of the idiosyncratic machine guns which the Italians were so expert at in the 1930s. In this case, the oddity lay in the feed system; the magazine is a box on the right side of the receiver which can be unlatched and hinged forward. In this position the gunner's mate loaded it from rifle chargers; he then swung the box back and latched it, whereupon the moving bolt could feed the rounds one by one. The advantage is that the whole magazine can be very well made, and the lips carefully machined, so that there is less likelihood of a stoppage than

Specification & Operation

Cartridge:
6.5 x 52mm Carcano

Dimensions:
Length o/a: 1230mm
Weight: 10.20kg
Barrel: 520mm
Rifling: 4 grooves, rh
Feed system: 20-round box magazine
Rate of fire: 475 rds/min

In production: 1930-37

Markings:
'Mtr Legg Mod 30, serial number, BREDA ROMA' on top of receiver.

Safety:
Spring-loaded catch alongside cocking handle. Having pulled cocking handle to rear, press catch to lock in cocked position. To release: pull back slightly on cocking handle.

Unloading:
Press magazine release catch behind magazine and hinge magazine forward. Pull back cocking handle, inspect chamber and feedway. Release handle and pull trigger.

Breda Model 37 ITALY

Standard heavy machine gun of the Italian Army from 1937 to 1945, this had some peculiarities. The ammunition had to be oiled before it was loaded, to prevent the cases sticking in the chamber after firing, which was a feature of some other machine guns, but the Breda was fed by metallic strips into which cartridges were clipped. The gun took the cartridge from the strip, fired it,

Specification & Operation

Cartridge:
8 x 59mm Breda

Dimensions:
Length o/a: 1270mm
Weight: 19.50kg
Barrel: 679mm
Rifling: 4 grooves, rh
Feed system: 20-round strip
Rate of fire: 450 rds/min

In production: 1936-43

Markings:
MITRAGLIATRICE BREDA MOD 37, serial number, ROMA and year on left side of receiver.

Safety:
Manual safety between grips: push right to lock trigger.

Unloading:
Push in pawl depressor on left side under feedway and remove feed strip. Pull back cocking handle to eject any round in chamber. Release cocking handle, pull back a second time, examine feedway and chamber. Release cocking handle and pull trigger.

and then put the empty case neatly back into the strip before loading the next round. No reasonable explanation for this has ever appeared; it sounded good, but the fact remained that the overworked gunner had to remove all the empties from the strip before he could reload it. In spite of this it was well liked, principally for its reliability.

reliable, accurate, slow-firing, the Bren was probably the best light machine gun of the WWII period and, changed to 7.62mm NATO calibre, is still in use today. There are a number of variant models, differing in the sights, barrel length, bipod and general degree of refinement, but all operate in the same way.

Britain adopted this from Czechoslovakia, where it was known as the vz26, under which name it appears elsewhere. The Bren version differs because the British .303 cartridge was rimmed, whereas the vz26 was designed around the 7.92mm Mauser, a rimless round. This is the reason for the characteristic curved magazine and some less visible minor internal changes. Very

Specification & Operation

Cartridge:
.303 British Service; 7.62 x 51mm NATO

Dimensions:
Length o/a: 1150mm
Weight: 10.15kg
Barrel: 635mm
Rifling: 6 grooves, rh
Feed system: 30-round box magazine
Rate of fire: 500 rds/min

In production: 1936-

Markings:
'BREN Mk XX' on right side.

Safety:
A combined safety catch and selector lever is on the left side above the trigger. Forward position for automatic fire, central for safe, rearward for single shots.

Unloading:
Magazine catch behind magazine housing. Press in and remove magazine. Pull cocking handle to the rear, examine the chamber through the magazine opening. Hold the cocking handle and press the trigger, easing the cocking handle forward. Close the magazine cover by sliding it back, close the ejection port cover (beneath the gun) by sliding it back.

Browning M1917 USA

survived through WWII in the same form and well into the 1950s before it was finally ousted by the air-cooled models, largely because it was there and still worked well.

The M1917 was Browning's original recoil-operated military machine gun, upon which all the later models (except the BAR) were based. As was the accepted form in those days, it was a heavy water-cooled gun mounted on a tripod, reliable and long-wearing. It

Specification & Operation

Cartridge:
.30-06 US Service

Dimensions:
Length o/a: 978mm
Weight: 14.97kg
Barrel: 610mm
Rifling: 4 grooves, rh
Feed system: 250-round cloth belt
Rate of fire: 500 rds/min

In production: 1917-45

Markings:
US INSP BROWNING MACHINE GUN US CAL 30

MODEL OF 1917 MFD BY (manufacturer's name).

Safety:
There is no safety device on this machine gun.

Unloading:
Pull back the milled knob on the top cover (behind the rear sight) to release the cover; lift it open. Remove any belt. Pull back the operating handle and inspect the front face of the bolt, pushing out any cartridge which may have been extracted. Examine the chamber of the gun. Close the cover, release the cocking handle, pull the trigger.

Browning M1919 A4 USA

This is an air-cooled version of the M1917, developed in 1918-19 to arm American tanks. The barrel was shortened to 457mm and placed in a perforated jacket, and a small tripod was provided so that it could be used outside the tank. This proved that air-cooled guns could work as well as water-cooled and the gun was adopted by the US Cavalry in the early 1920s. Various

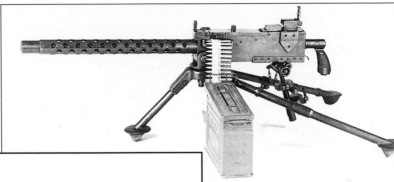

Specification & Operation

Cartridge:
.30-06 US Service

Dimensions:
Length o/a: 1041mm
Weight: 14.05kg
Barrel: 610mm
Rifling: 4 grooves, rh
Feed system: 250-round cloth belt
Rate of fire: 500 rds/min

In production: 1934-

Markings:
'BROWNING M1919A4 US Cal .30' (Maker's name) (year) (serial number) on left side of receiver.

Safety:
There is no safety device on this machine gun.

Unloading:
Pull back the milled knob on the top cover (in front of the rear sight) to release the cover; lift it open. Remove any belt. Pull back the operating handle and inspect the front face of the bolt, pushing out any cartridge which may have been extracted. Examine the chamber of the gun. Close the cover, release the cocking handle, pull the trigger.

modifications were made and eventually the M1919A4 appeared, having reverted to the same barrel length as the M1917. It was adopted as the standard ground gun for all arms in the late 1930s and remained so until replaced by the M60 in the 1960s. Many are still in use in various parts of the world, some modified to 7.62mm NATO and other calibres, and they will undoubtedly be around for many years to come.

Browning M1919 A6 USA

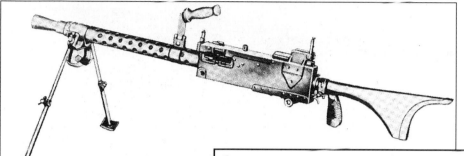

BAR being retained as long as possible as the squad automatic. The arrival of the M60 machine gun enabled the remaining A6's to be got rid of; some were unloaded on to other, unsuspecting, armies and may turn up from time to time, particularly in Central America.

The M1919A6 was developed during WWII and adopted in 1943 to be the squad light machine gun in place of the BAR. As the figures above show, it was far from light, since it was no more than the M1919A4 with the addition of a shoulder stock, muzzle flash hider and a bipod. It was heavy, cumbersome and heartily disliked by all who encountered it; most of them appear to have had the shoulder stock and bipod removed so as to bring them back to M1919A4 standard and then put on tripods, the

Specification & Operation

Cartridge:
.30-06 US Service

Dimensions:
Length o/a: 1346mm
Weight: 14.73kg
Barrel: 610mm
Rifling: 4 grooves, rh
Feed system: 250-round cloth belt
Rate of fire: 500 rds/min

In production: 1943-54

Markings:
US INSP BROWNING MACHINE GUN US CAL 30

MFD BY (manufacturer's name).

Safety:
There is no safety device on this machine gun.

Unloading:
Pull back the milled knob on the top cover (in front of the rear sight) to release the cover; lift it open. Remove any belt. Pull back the operating handle and inspect the front face of the bolt, pushing out any cartridge which may have been extracted. Examine the chamber of the gun. Close the cover, release the cocking handle, pull the trigger.

Browning M2HB .50 USA

In 1918 the Germans developed a 13mm anti-tank machine gun; the US Army in France demanded something similar. The Winchester company developed a .50 inch cartridge, and Browning scaled-up his M1917 machine gun to fire it. It originally appeared as a water-cooled anti-aircraft machine gun, but in the 1930s the M2 air-cooled

Specification & Operation

Cartridge:
12.7 x 99mm (.50 Browning)

Dimensions:
Length o/a: 1653mm
Weight: 38.22kg
Barrel: 1143mm
Rifling: 8 grooves, rh
Feed system: belt
Rate of fire: 500 rds/min

In production: 1933-

Markings:
US serial number BROWNING MACHINE GUN CAL 50 M2 MFD BY (manufacturer's name).

Safety:
There is no safety catch as such, but a bolt latch release, in the centre of the thumb trigger, will lock the bolt to the rear. This must be pressed DOWN before pressing the trigger.

Unloading:
Press down the bolt latch release. Turn the catch on the top cover and open the cover. Remove any belt in the gun. Pull back the operating handle on the right side of the gun until the bolt locks back. Examine the front of the bolt, knocking free any cartridge which may have been extracted from the chamber, and check that the chamber is empty. Press down the extractor at the front of the bolt, close the cover, press the bolt latch release and allow the bolt to go forward, press the trigger.

version was developed for use on tanks. Since it used a very thick barrel to dissipate the heat generated by firing, it became the `HB' for Heavy Barrel. Some three million have been made by different companies, they have been used by virtually every armed force outside the Communist bloc, they never wear out, and there are a lot of them about. In the 1980s quick-change barrel versions became common; these do away with the need for a ticklish adjustment when changing barrels or re-assembling the weapon after cleaning.

Browning Automatic Rifle (BAR) USA

This is a gas-operated, magazine-fed weapon, entirely different to the other Browning machine guns. Designed as a light machine gun for World War I, the BAR became the US Army's squad automatic weapon, remaining in service until the Korean war. It was finally replaced by the M249 Minimi in the 1980s. Numbers were also issued to the

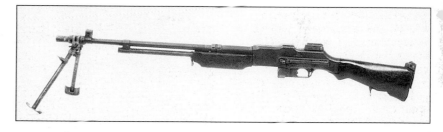

Specification & Operation

Cartridge:
.30-06 US Service

Dimensions:
Length o/a: 1219mm
Weight: 7.28kg
Barrel: 610mm
Rifling: 4 grooves, rh
Feed system: 20-round box magazine
Rate of fire. 500 rds/min

In production: 1917-45

Markings:
BROWNING BAR M1918 CAL 30 MFD BY
(manufacturer's name).

Safety:
There is a combined safety catch and fire selector lever above the trigger on the left side. In the rear position the rifle is safe; pushed forward to the central position the rifle fires at the slow automatic rate; pushed fully forward the rifle fires at the fast automatic rate.

Unloading:
Press in the magazine release button in the front of the trigger guard and remove the magazine. Pull back the cocking handle, on the left side of the receiver, to eject any round in the chamber. Inspect the chamber through the ejection port. Push the cocking handle back to its forward position, pull the trigger.

British Home Guard in 1940-45. With a fixed barrel and a limited-capacity magazine the BAR was never really a serious light machine gun; too much sustained fire and the fore-end burst into smoke and flames. It was too heavy to be a serious automatic rifle either, but since there was nothing better, it survived. It was also sold commercially by Colt as the 'Monitor' for police use, in semi-automatic form.

were handed over to the armies of former French colonies when they became independent, and when replaced they then found their way into all sorts of places.

Having had some unsatisfactory weapons during WWI the French considered a new machine gun to be imperative, and wisely began by developing a new rimless cartridge in 7.5mm calibre. After some modification the combination worked successfully and as the M1924/29 the light machine gun became standard in the French Army and remained in use until the 1950s. Numbers were also seized by the Germans in 1940 and used by them, so that specimens with German markings can appear from time to time. Numbers

Specification & Operation

Cartridge:
7.5 x 54mm French Service

Dimensions:
Length o/a: 1082mm
Weight: 9.24kg
Barrel: 500mm
Rifling: 4 grooves, rh
Feed system: 25-round box magazine
Rate of fire: 500 rds/min

In production: 1930-40

Markings:
`Mle 1924M29" and serial number on right side of receiver.

Safety:
Manual safety catch behind the rear trigger. Turn DOWN for safe, UP for fire.

Unloading:
Magazine catch behind the magazine housing. Push the safety catch DOWN, remove the magazine, pull the cocking handle to the rear. Inspect the feedway and chamber through the magazine opening. Push the safety catch UP and holding the cocking handle, press one of the triggers and ease the cocking handle forward. Close the magazine dust cover and ejection port dust cover. Press the safety catch down and pull back the magazine catch until it locks.

Chatellerault M1931 FRANCE

This is really the same gun as the M1924/29 discussed above, but modified for use in tanks and fortifications, such as the Maginot Line. The most obvious change was the adoption of a side-mounted drum magazine holding 150 rounds and a somewhat heavier barrel, both in order to provide sustained fire which was thought to be more likely in these roles

than in the basic infantry squad role. As with the M1924/29 the German Army took over most of the existing French stock in 1940 and applied it to their various fortifications on the coastline of Europe, so that with the end of the war these guns were spread far and wide. Although not so common as the 24/29, they can still turn up.

Specification & Operation

Cartridge:
7.5 x 54mm French Service

Dimensions:
Length o/a: 1030mm
Weight: 11.80kg
Barrel: 600mm
Rifling: 4 grooves, rh
Feed system: 150-round drum
Rate of fire: 600 rds/min

In production: 1931-40

Markings:
Mle 1931 C1 on left. Serial at rear end of barrel.

Safety:
There is no manual safety on this weapon.

Unloading:
Grasp the handle of the drum magazine and pull off the magazine. Pull back the cocking handle and inspect the feedway and chamber. If there is a round in the feedway, push it forward so it falls through and out of the bottom of the receiver. Release cocking handle and pull trigger.

06 rimless cartridge the magazine could be straight, but the mechanism was then over-stressed by the more powerful cartridge. As the 'Gladiator' it was supplied to the Greek, Polish and Belgian Armies in postwar years, though the Belgians soon got rid of it. It appeared once more in the Spanish Civil War and there were even reports of specimens showing up in central Africa in the 1950s and Vietnam in the 1960s.

This is without doubt the worst machine gun ever to reach service in any army. Designed by a committee (the initials CSRG being those of the principal members) it used the long recoil principle of operation and had to be designed round the rimmed 8mm Lebel cartridge which led to the unique semi-circular magazine on the French model. Crudely made of poor material, it was almost impossible to fire a complete magazine without a stoppage, which generally demanded complete disassembly to remedy. The US Army were talked into adopting it, and since they used the .30-

Specification & Operation

Cartridge:
8 x 50R Lebel; .30-06 US Service; and others

Dimensions:
Length o/a: 1143mm
Weight: 9.07kg
Barrel: 469mm
Rifling: 4 grooves, rh
Feed system: 20-round box magazine
Rate of fire: 250 rds/min

In production: 1915-24

Markings:
'C.S.R.G.' on left side receiver. Serial number on right side.

Safety:
The selector is above the pistol grip: S is for safe, M for automatic and C for single shots.

Unloading:
Magazine catch behind magazine. Press, remove magazine, pull back cocking handle, inspect chamber, release cocking handle and pull trigger.

CZ Model 52/57 CZECHOSLOVAKIA

Although classed as a light machine gun, this obviously leans toward the 'general purpose' concept, being capable of using magazines or belts without need for modification. It was originally designed to fire the Czech 7.62 x 45mm cartridge, as the CZ52, but was then modified to fire the 7.62 x 39mm Soviet round when Warsaw Pact countries standardised on Soviet calibres. Either model may be encountered, though the earlier version is less common. They were supplied to Communist bloc countries in some numbers and have turned up in central Africa and the Far East at various times.

Specification & Operation

Cartridge:
7.62 x 45mm Czech; 7.62 x 39mm Soviet M1943

Dimensions:
Length o/a: 1041mm
Weight: 7.96kg
Barrel: 686mm
Rifling: 4 grooves, rh
Feed system: 25 round box or 100-round belt
Rate of fire: 900 rds/min (magazine) or 1150 rds/min (belt)

In production: 1952-

Markings:
Serial number on top behind magazine housing, with 'egf' or 'tgf' factory mark.

Safety:
Manual safety catch above the pistol grip on the left side. Press UP for safe, DOWN for fire. Fire selection is done by the trigger; press the upper portion (marked 1) for single shots, and the lower portion (marked D) for automatic fire.

Unloading:
Magazine catch in rear of magazine housing. Press in and remove the magazine if the weapon is being magazine fed; if it is being belt fed, press in so that the magazine feed cover swings open, then lift the side feed cover lever (on the right slide, alongside the magazine housing) UP and forward until the side feed cover opens. Lift and remove the belt if one is present. Inspect to see that no ammunition remains in the feedways, close all covers. Grasp the pistol grip, press the pushbutton in the left side of the grip and allow the grip to run forward under control. Then push UP the safety catch to lock the weapon.

Darne FRANCE

The Darne company were shotgun makers for many years, but became interested in machine guns as a result of making Lewis guns under contract to the French Army during WWI. Unlike many makers they saw no sense in applying commercial standards of finish to military weapons and thus produced cheap, crude-looking weapons which were nevertheless efficient. Having designed them, Darne had them made in Spain for even less than they would have cost to make in France. Gas-operated

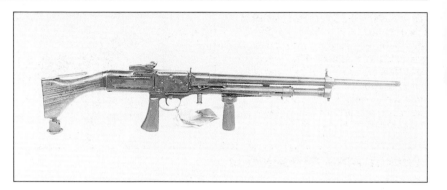

Specification & Operation

Cartridge:
7.5 x 54mm French Service and others

Dimensions:
Length o/a: 1120mm
Weight: 9.70kg
Barrel: 600mm
Rifling: 4 grooves, rh
Feed system: 100- or 250-round metal belt
Rate of fire: 650 rds/min

In production: 1922-39

Markings:
DARNE (year) and serial number above chamber.

Safety:
There is no manual safety on this weapon.

Unloading:
Press pawl depressing catch (behind feedway on left side) and remove belt. Pull back cocking handle, release, pull back a second time and inspect the chamber and feedway. Release cocking handle and pull trigger.

and with a high rate of fire, they were employed by many European air forces to equip fighter planes in the 1930s but their high rate of fire made them less popular in the ground role. Various models were made, using belt or magazine feed and after passing on from their original owners they tend to turn up in various parts of the world.

Degtyarev DP

Adopted by the Soviet Army in 1928 after two years of trials, the DP became the standard infantry squad machine gun. It remained in service until the 1950s in the Warsaw Pact and was widely distributed to sympathisers around the world. It fires only at automatic, and uses the old rimmed 7.62mm round. The thin flat pan

Specification & Operation

Cartridge:
7.62 x 54R Soviet

Dimensions:
Length o/a: 1290mm
Weight: 9.12kg
Barrel: 605mm
Rifling: 4 grooves, rh
Feed system: 47-round drum
Rate of fire: 550 rds/min

In production: 1928-41

Markings:
Factory identifier and serial number on top of receiver.

Safety:
This weapon has an automatic grip safety device behind the trigger guard; when the butt is gripped in order to position the hand on the trigger, the safety is pressed in and the weapon can be fired. As soon as the butt is released the weapon is made safe.

Unloading:
The magazine release is also the rear sight guard. Pull back, and lift the drum magazine upwards off the receiver. Pull back the cocking handle, inspect the feedway and chamber to ensure no cartridge is present, release the cocking handle, pull the trigger.

magazine is somewhat susceptible to damage, and the piston return spring, beneath the barrel, tends to lose its spring after being subjected to barrel heat for long periods. The bipod was too weak for its job and frequently bent. All these defects came to light during 1941, when the gun was first put to the test of war, which led to the development of the DPM (below).

441

Degtyarev DPM RUSSIA

The DPM appeared in 1942 and was a modification of the DP to get over the two principal defects. The return spring was removed from around the gas piston and put behind the bolt, necessitating a tubular extension behind the receiver; this meant that it could no longer be gripped around the butt and a pistol grip had to be added. The bipod was strengthened and attached to the barrel casing, raising the roll centre and making the weapon easier to hold upright. It almost completely replaced the DP and was widely distributed to various Communist-backed forces after the war.

Specification & Operation

Cartridge:
7.62 x 54R Soviet

Dimensions:
Length o/a: 1265mm
Weight: 12.20kg
Barrel: 605mm
Rifling: 4 grooves, rh
Feed system: 47-round drum
Rate of fire: 550 rds/min

In production: 1941-50

Markings:
Factory identifier and serial number on top of receiver.

Safety:
A manual safety catch above the right side of the trigger. Turn forward for safe, DOWN and to the rear to fire.

Unloading:
The magazine release is also the rear sight guard. Pull back, and lift the drum magazine upwards off the receiver. Pull back the cocking handle, inspect the feedway and chamber to ensure no cartridge is present, release the cocking handle, pull the trigger.

Degtyarev DT and DTM RUSSIA

The DT was more or less the same weapon as the DP, described above, but intended for fitting into tanks and other armoured vehicles. It had a heavier barrel and a two-layer magazine, and was fitted with a telescoping metal butt and pistol grip. To allow it to be used outside the vehicle a bipod and front sight were carried, to be fitted when required. Like the DP it suffered from the

return spring beneath the barrel weakening from heat, and like the DP it was modified into the DTM in 1942, the same solution being applied: the return spring was put into a tubular receiver extension behind the bolt. After being cast from tank employment many were given to other countries as infantry light machine guns.

Specification & Operation

Cartridge:
7.62 x 54R Soviet

Dimensions: (DTM)
Length o/a: 1181mm
Weight: 12.90kg
Barrel: 597mm
Rifling: 4 grooves, rh
Feed system: 60-round drum
Rate of fire: 600 rds/min

In production: 1929-45

Markings:
Factory identifier and serial number on top of receiver.

Safety:
A manual safety catch above the right side of the trigger. Turn forward for safe, DOWN and to the rear to fire.

Unloading:
Magazine release may be in front of, or behind, the rear sight. Press it to the side or to the rear and remove the drum magazine. Pull back the cocking handle, inspect the chamber and feedway, release the cocking handle and press the trigger.

Enfield L86 UK

held open, while when set for single shots it stops with the breech closed and a fresh round loaded. At single shot it is exceptionally accurate, a function of the longer and heavier barrel, and in 1995 a single-shot-only version was being promoted as a sniper weapon.

This should really be classed as a 'machine rifle', since it lacks that vital feature of a light machine gun, a quick-change barrel, and it also uses a low-capacity rifle magazine. It is, nevertheless, the British 5.56mm squad automatic weapon or 'Light Support Weapon' as the current phrase has it. It uses some 80 percent of the components of the L85 rifle, has a heavier and longer barrel, some changes in the trigger mechanism so that when set to automatic it stops firing with the breech

Specification & Operation

Cartridge:
5.56 x 45mm NATO

Dimensions:
Length o/a: 900mm
Weight: 5.40kg
Barrel: 646mm
Rifling: 6 grooves, rh
Feed system: 30-round box magazine
Rate of fire: 700 rds/min

In production: 1985-

Markings:
MG 5.56mm LIGHT SUPPORT L86 ENFIELD on right of receiver. Serial above magazine housing.

Safety:
Push-through bolt above trigger: push from left to right for safe. Selector on left UP for single shots, DOWN for automatic.

Unloading:
Remove magazine. Pull back cocking handle to eject any round in the chamber. Inspect chamber and feedway via ejection port. Release cocking handle and pull trigger.

Fiat-Revelli M1914 ITALY

The first Italian-designed machine gun to appear in any quantity, this is a peculiar weapon. It uses a delayed blowback system allied to a recoiling barrel; it fires the 6.5mm Italian cartridge yet is as heavy as the contemporary Maxim gun. It has an externally moving buffer rod which comes out of the receiver to strike a buffer pad in front of the handgrips, which is alarming when firing. And it has a most unusual feed system in which ten

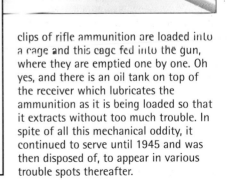

Specification & Operation

Cartridge:
6.5 x 52mm Carcano

Dimensions:
Length o/a: 1180mm
Weight: 17.00kg
Barrel: 654mm
Rifling: 4 grooves, rh
Feed system: 50 round strip-feed box
Rate of fire: 400 rds/min

In production: 1914–18

Markings:
Serial number on top of receiver.

Safety:
A latch above trigger in the spade grip turns up to lock the trigger.

Unloading:
Press latch under feed aperture and remove the ammunition 'cage'. Lift the spring-loaded cover plate over the feedway, pull back the cocking handle (two wings at rear of receiver) and check chamber and feedway. Release handle, pull trigger.

clips of rifle ammunition are loaded into a cage and this cage fed into the gun, where they are emptied one by one. Oh yes, and there is an oil tank on top of the receiver which lubricates the ammunition as it is being loaded so that it extracts without too much trouble. In spite of all this mechanical oddity, it continued to serve until 1945 and was then disposed of, to appear in various trouble spots thereafter.

Fiat-Revelli M1935 ITALY

Even the Italian Army, which was very tolerant of eccentricity, felt that the 1914 Fiat-Revelli could be improved, and the result was the M1935. The water cooled barrel was replaced by a simpler air-cooled pattern; the calibre was changed from 6.5mm to 8mm for better terminal effects; the chamber was fluted so as to 'float' the cartridge case on a layer of gas and thus avoid the need to lubricate the cases; and the peculiar ten-clip feed cage system was changed to a conventional belt feed. But the fluted chamber didn't work very well and the lubrication had to be reinstated; the gun stopped firing with the bolt closed and a fresh round loaded, which led to it 'cooking off' in a hot barrel; and one way and another the 1935 was worse than the 1914 it had set out to better. It survived with the Italian Army until 1945 and was then promptly disposed of.

Specification & Operation

Cartridge:
8 x 59mm Breda

Dimensions:
Length o/a: 1270mm
Weight: 18.10kg
Barrel: 653mm
Rifling: 4 grooves, rh
Feed system: 50-round belt
Rate of fire: 500 rds/min

In production: 1935-40

Markings:
Serial number on top of receiver.

Safety:
A latch above trigger in the spade grip turns up to lock the trigger.

Unloading:
Press latch under feed aperture and remove the ammunition 'cage'. Lift the spring-loaded cover plate over the feedway, pull back the cocking handle (two wings at rear of receiver) and check chamber and feedway. Release handle, pull trigger.

FN BAR Type D BELGIUM

This is the Browning Automatic Rifle as improved by Fabrique Nationale of Belgium. As with most of Browning's designs, they held a license to manufacture and to modify it as they saw fit, and in line with European thought of the 1920s they soon did so. By fitting it with a quick-change barrel, modifying it so as to fire from belt or magazine as required, giving it a pistol

Specification & Operation

Cartridge:
Various - see below

Dimensions:
Length o/a: 1145mm
Weight: 9.20kg
Barrel: 500mm
Rifling: 4 grooves, rh
Feed system: 20-round magazine
Rate of fire: 450 or 650 rds/min
In production: 1923-39

Markings:
FN monogram, BROWNING PATENTED (year) and serial number on top of receiver above magazine.

FABRIQUE NATIONALE D'ARMES DE GUERRE HERSTAL-BELGIQUE on left above magazine.

Safety:
Combined safety catch and rate regulator on the left side above the trigger. Set to 'S' for safe, to 'F' for slow rate automatic fire and to 'M' for fast rate automatic fire.

Unloading:
Magazine release is below the trigger guard. Remove magazine. Pull back cocking handle to eject any round remaining in the chamber. Inspect chamber and feedway. Release cocking handle, pull trigger

grip, changing the system of dismantling to make it easier, and redesigning the gas regulator. Belt-fed versions failed to appeal, but the magazine-fed version was adopted by Belgium, Poland, Egypt and various other countries in the pre-1939 period. Well-made, many have survived and can be encountered in Central Africa and the Middle East. Calibre may be 6.5mm Swedish Mauser, 7mm Spanish Mauser, 7.5mm Belgian Mauser or 7.92 x 57mm Mauser.

the top of the bolt to carry a lug which drives the feed system, which is adapted from that of the German MG42. There are a number of minor variations of the MAG to suit firing it from vehicles or helicopters.

This was the Belgian entry into the 'general purpose' machine gun stakes, and it became extremely popular, being adopted by at least 80 countries and license-made in the USA, UK, Argentina, Egypt, India and Singapore. Well-made and reliable, it uses a similar gas system to that of the Browning Automatic Rifle, but inverted so that the bolt locks into the bottom of the receiver. This allows

Specification & Operation

Cartridge:
7.62 x 51mm NATO

Dimensions:
Length o/a: 1250mm
Weight: 10.15kg
Barrel: 546mm
Rifling: 4 grooves, rh
Feed system: belt
Rate of fire: 850 rds/min

In production: 1955-

Markings:
'Fabrique Nationale d'Armes de Guerre Herstal Belgium' on right side receiver. Weapons produced by other countries will have their own markings; e.g. British 'L7A1'.

Safety:
The safety catch is a push-button above the trigger. Push from left side to right to make safe; from right side to left to fire.

Unloading:
Press the cover catch, in front of the rear sight, and open the cover. Lift out the belt if present, inspect the feedway, close the cover. Pull the cocking handle back to eject any round in the chamber, and while holding it back press the trigger and then ease the cocking handle forward.

FN Minimi BELGIUM

The Minimi was designed to extract the utmost performance from the 5.56mm cartridge and has acquired a reputation for reliability. It is gas operated, using a simple rotating bolt system, but is unusual in being able to fire from an M16-type magazine or a belt without any modification having to be made. A special cover plate closes the belt aperture when a magazine is loaded, or closes the magazine aperture when a belt is in place, so that there is no

danger of trying to double-feed. There is a light, short-barrelled paratroop version with a collapsible butt, and a slightly modified version of the standard model is produced for the US Army as the M249 machine gun.

Specification & Operation

Cartridge:
5.56 x 45mm NATO

Dimensions:
Length o/a: 1040mm
Weight: 6.85kg
Barrel: 466mm
Rifling: 6 grooves, rh
Feed system: 30-round magazine or 200-round belt
Rate of fire: 700-1000 rds/min

In production: 1982-

Markings:
'FN MINIMI 5.56' on left side receiver.

Safety:
Push-through safety catch on left of receiver: push from right to left to fire. Left to right for safe.

Unloading:
Press in the two spring catches at top rear of receiver and lift cover. Remove belt or magazine. Pull back cocking handle, examine chamber and feedway, release cocking handle, press trigger.

Furrer M25 SWITZERLAND

mounted sideways, together with a side-mounted magazine. It also uses the differential recoil method of absorbing recoil; the sear is released to fire the gun while the barrel and breech are still moving forward on their return stroke from the previous shot. All this adds up to a complex mechanical assembly which has to be very carefully and expensively made; which is why his designs never caught on outside Switzerland.

A very odd weapon which is unlikely to be found in the wrong hands, this was designed by Colonel Furrer, Superintendent of the Swiss Arsenal in the 1920s and 1930s. He had a passion for the toggle lock, probably because his arsenal made Parabellum pistols and therefore had machinery which could adapt to making toggles in various sizes. His machine gun uses a toggle similar to that of the Luger Parabellum pistol, but

Specification & Operation

Cartridge:
7.5 x 55mm Swiss Service

Dimensions:
Length o/a: 1163mm
Weight: 10.59kg
Barrel: 583mm
Rifling: 4 grooves, rh
Feed system: 30-round box
Rate of fire: 450 rds/min

In production: 1925-

Markings:
WAFFENFABRIK + BERN and serial number on top of magazine housing.

Safety:
Safety on top of magazine housing: move left to S for safe, M for automatic and F for single shots.

Unloading:
Remove magazine, pull back cocking handle, toggle opens left to allow inspection of chamber and feedway. Release handle and pull trigger.

Goryunov SG43 RUSSIA

The SG43 became the standard Soviet medium machine gun during World War II, replacing the Maxim 1910 as the latter were lost in action or wore out. Gas-operated, the mechanism is rather complex since the feed has to pull the cartridge out of the belt backwards, lower it into the feed way and then chamber it. The locking system is similar

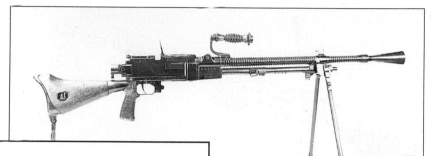

Specification & Operation

Cartridge:
7.62 x 54R Soviet

Dimensions:
Length o/a: 1120mm
Weight: 13.60kg
Barrel: 720mm
Rifling: 4 grooves, rh
Feed system: 250-round cloth belt
Rate of fire: 650 rds/min

In production: 1943-55

Markings:
Factory identifier and serial number on top of receiver.

Safety:
There is a safety device on the firing button between the spade grips which prevents the button being pushed in. The safety flap must be lifted with the thumb to permit the firing button to be pressed.

Unloading:
The cover latch is on the left rear side of the cover. Press forward and open the cover. Lift the belt off the feed pawls and remove it. Lift the lower feed cover and remove any cartridge which may be in the feed. Pull the cocking handle to the rear, examine the interior of the receiver, press the trigger and ease the cocking handle forward. Close both covers.

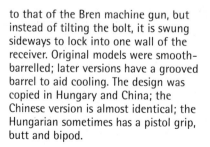

to that of the Bren machine gun, but instead of tilting the bolt, it is swung sideways to lock into one wall of the receiver. Original models were smooth-barrelled; later versions have a grooved barrel to aid cooling. The design was copied in Hungary and China; the Chinese version is almost identical; the Hungarian sometimes has a pistol grip, butt and bipod.

somewhat early in the 5.56mm era, and consequently its initial sales were largely to South-East Asian countries. It has since been improved into the HK33E mode, which incorporates a three-round burst setting in the selector lever and which can be changed to belt feed by replacing the magazine housing and bolt.

This was developed to accompany the HK33 5.56mm rifle and was among the earliest 5.56mm calibre machine guns; it is generally similar to the rifle but has a heavier barrel which can quickly be removed and exchanged during sustained fire. The action is that of the rifle, a delay blowback using a roller-locked delay system, and the magazines are interchangeable with those of the HK33 rifle. The HK13 was

Specification & Operation

Cartridge:
5.56 x 45mm M193 or NATO

Dimensions:
Length o/a: 980mm
Weight: 6.03kg
Barrel: 450mm
Rifling: 6 grooves, rh
Feed system: 20 or 40 round magazine
Rate of fire: 750 rds/min

In production: 1972-

Markings:
'HK 13 5.56 x 45' and serial number on left side of magazine housing.

Safety:
A combined safety catch and fire selector is on the left side of the receiver, above the pistol grip. UP for safe, midway for single shots (marked 'E') and fully DOWN for automatic fire (marked 'A').

Unloading:
Magazine catch behind magazine housing, beneath the receiver. Remove magazine. Pull back cocking handle to eject any round in the chamber. Inspect chamber and feedway via the ejection port. Release the cocking handle, press the trigger.

Heckler & Koch HK21 GERMANY

39mm calibres by changing the barrel, belt feed plate and bolt, making it a very versatile design. It was adopted by Portugal and some African and South-East Asian countries in the 1970s and many are still in use. It was replaced in production by the HK21A1, an improved model, and then by the present HK21E which has a three-round burst facility and various other improvements.

The HK21 was designed as a general-purpose machine gun, capable of being used on a bipod or tripod, to accompany the G3 rifle. It is much the same as the rifle but with a heavier barrel which can quickly be changed and is belt-fed. However, it is possible to remove the belt-feed mechanism and replace it with a magazine adapter, using the G3 rifle magazine. It could also be converted to 5.56 x 45mm or 7.62 x

Specification & Operation

Cartridge:
7.62 x 51mm NATO

Dimensions:
Length o/a: 1021mm
Weight: 7.92kg
Barrel: 450mm
Rifling: 4 grooves, rh
Feed system: belt
Rate of fire: 900 rds/min

In production: 1970-

Markings:
Serial number on rib of receiver top.

Safety:
A combined safety catch and fire selector is on the left side of the receiver, above the pistol grip. UP for safe, midway for single shots (marked 'E') and fully DOWN for automatic fire (marked 'A').

Unloading:
Press the serrated catch beneath the rear end of the belt slot and allow the belt feed to hinge down and forward. Pull back the cocking handle to eject any round in the chamber. Inspect the chamber and feedway via the ejection port. Release the cocking handle, press the trigger, close the belt feed assembly by hinging it up until the catch engages.

Hotchkiss M1909 FRANCE

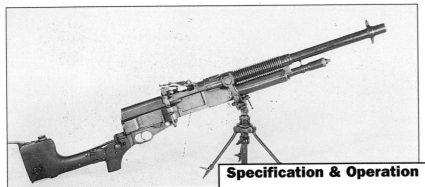

The Hotchkiss was the earliest practical gas-operated machine gun; it appeared in 1895 and was first used in the Russo-Japanese War in 1904 on the Japanese side. The design went through several modifications before it settled down, and the 1909 version was an attempt to provide a light automatic which fitted the French army 'walking fire' tactic. It uses an odd breech locking system; the chamber mouth is surrounded by a 'fermeture nut', a sleeve with lugs. This is revolved by the gas piston so that when the lugs are aligned the bolt can be pushed open by further movement of the piston; when the bolt returns the nut revolves again and the lugs now lock the bolt to the chamber. Like most early Hotchkiss guns it fed from a metal strip filled with cartridges. The French didn't take to it but it was adopted by the US Army as the 'Benet-Mercie Machine Rifle M1909' and by the British as the 'Hotchkiss Mark 1'.

Specification & Operation

Cartridge:
8 x 50R Lebel

Dimensions:
Length o/a: 1187mm
Weight: 12.25kg
Barrel: 596mm
Rifling: 4 grooves, rh
Feed system: 30-round metal strip
Rate of fire: 500 rds/min
In production: 1909-18

Markings:
HOTCHKISS MACHINE GUN Mk I CALIBER 303 and serial number on left hand side.

Safety:
The cocking handle, which looks like a rifle bolt is the safety/selector too. Its rear face has 3 lines labelled S, R and A. When S is opposite a line on the receiver and the weapon is safe. Turn up to R for single shots, A for automatic.

Unloading:
Press pawl latch on left to remove feed strip. Unlock and pull back cocking handle. Inspect chamber, releease cocking handle, turn to the first notch and pull trigger.

Hotchkiss M1914 FRANCE

By 1914 Hotchkiss had made some more changes and this gun was adopted as the standard medium machine gun of the French Army and was to remain in service until 1945. It was heavy but reliable, and there were various different tripod mounts available. The feed system relied upon the usual Hotchkiss metal strip, but these could be joined together to form a species of belt, each link of which held three cartridges. In 8mm Lebel calibre it

was used by France, Greece and other Balkan states and also by US troops in France in 1917-1918. In 7mm calibre it was exported to Mexico, Spain and Brazil in the 1920s.

Specification & Operation

Cartridge:
8 x 50R Lebel

Dimensions:
Length o/a: 1270mm
Weight: 23.58kg
Barrel: 775mm
Rifling: 4 grooves, lh
Feed system: 30-round metal strip
Rate of fire: 600 rds/min

In production: 1914-30

Markings:
MITRAILLEUSE AUTOMATIQUE HOTCHKISS M1914 SGDG CALIBRE 7mm92 (or other calibre) on left of receiver. Serial number on top.

Safety:
There is no safety catch.

Unloading:
Press in pawl latch on left side, withdraw the feed strip. Pull back cocking handle, examine chamber and feedway, release cocking handle and pull the trigger.

Hotchkiss M1922/26 FRANCE

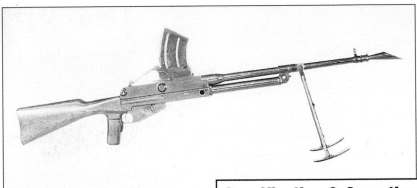

Czechoslovakia, and unknown quantities to the Dominican Republic and Brazil, which were supplied variously as the M1922, M1924 or M1926 model, there were scarcely sufficient sales to keep Hotchkiss in business.

This was Hotchkiss' post-WWI design, put on the market in 1922. It used gas operation, locking the breech by a tilting plate, and also had a rate of fire regulator in a housing in front of the trigger. Feed was either by a top-mounted magazine or by the usual type of side-feeding Hotchkiss trip, including the three-cartridge-per-link strip belt devised for the M1914 gun. Business was slow in the 1920s, however, and apart from some 5000 to Greece, 1000 to

Specification & Operation

Cartridge:
Various calibres

Dimensions:
Length o/a: 1215mm
Weight: 9.52kg
Barrel: 577mm
Rifling: 4 grooves, rh
Feed system: 25 or 30-round metal strip
Rate of fire: 500 rds/min

In production: 1922-39

Markings:
'HOTCHKISS 1922 Brevete' on right of receiver.
Serial number on top rear of receiver.

Safety:
Grip safety in front of pistol grip

Unloading:
Magazine catch is behind magazine. Remove magazine, pull back cocking handle, inspect chamber. Release cocking handle and pull trigger.

Japanese Type 11 JAPAN

This was the first light machine gun to be designed in Japan, and obviously had the pre-war Hotchkiss as one of its guiding lights. The unique part is the loading system, a hopper into which six clips of cartridge are dropped and which then feeds the rounds one at a time to the bolt. The idea was the if the machine-gunner ran short of ammunition, the riflemen could

Specification & Operation

Cartridge:
6.5 x 51SR Arisaka reduced charge

Dimensions:
Length o/a: 1104mm
Weight: 10.19kg
Barrel: 482mm
Rifling: 4 grooves, rh
Feed system: 30-round hopper
Rate of fire: 500 rds/min

In production: 1922-45

Markings:
Model and serial number on top of receiver.

Safety:
There is no safety device.

Unloading:
Ensure that no ammunition is in the hopper on the left side of the receiver. Pull back the cocking handle to extract any round in the chamber, release it and pull back a second time to ensure that no round was left in the feedway. Inspect the chamber via the ejection port, release the cocking handle and pull the trigger.

contribute. Like most Japanese machine guns the extraction system was abrupt and the cartridges were lubricated by an oiler; in addition, a special reduced-charge cartridge was issued for this weapon. Another oddity, making it easily recognisable, is that the butt and sights are offset to the right of the bore axis.

being loaded into the gun. An odd feature of this weapon is that it is usually fitted with a telescope sight, a refinement which is scarcely of value on a weapon so inherently inaccurate as a light machine gun.

This was introduced in 1936 to replace the Type 11, though the latter continued in service until 1945. The feed system was changed to a more conventional 30-round magazine and the cartridge oiler was removed; the reduced-charge cartridge still had to be oiled, but this was now done as they were loaded into the magazine, after which they probably had plenty of time to accumulate a coating of dirt before

Specification & Operation

Cartridge:
6.5 x 51SR Arisaka reduced charge

Dimensions:
Length o/a: 1054mm
Weight: 9.07kg
Barrel: 552mm
Rifling: 4 grooves, rh
Feed system: 30-round box magazine
Rate of fire: 550 rds/min

In production: 1936-45

Markings:
Model and serial number on top of the receiver.

Safety:
Safety catch in front of trigger guard: push down and forward to fire, up and back for safe.

Unloading:
Magazine catch behind magazine. Remove magazine and pull back cocking handle. Inspect chamber and feedway, release cocking handle and pull trigger.

Japanese Type 99 JAPAN

When the Japanese Army decided to adopt a 7.7mm rimless cartridge instead of the 6.5mm round, this gun was developed to fire it. To save development time the Type 96 was taken as the basis, but the 99 was a considerable improvement. The 7.7mm cartridge did not need to be oiled, the extraction system was designed so as to give a slow unseating movement before a more rapid extraction, so curing all the ruptured case problems, the quick-

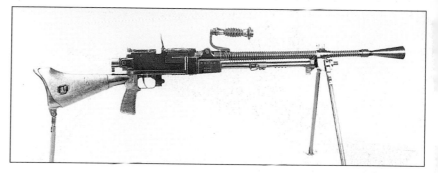

change barrel was far easier to use, and manufacturing tolerances were held to a fine limit. There was more than one item of the design which suggested that a good look had been taken at the Czech vz26 gun, several of which had been captured from the Chinese in the middle 1930s.

Specification & Operation

Cartridge:
7.7 x 58mm Arisaka

Dimensions:
Length o/a: 1181mm
Weight: 10.43kg
Barrel: 645mm
Rifling: 4 grooves, rh
Feed system: 30-round box magazine
Rate of fire: 850 rds/min

In production: 1939-45

Markings:
Model and serial number on top of the receiver

Safety:
Safety catch in front of trigger guard on right side; push down and forward to fire, up and back for safe.

Unloading:
Magazine catch behind magazine. Remove magazine and pull back cocking handle. Inspect chamber and feedway, release cocking handle and pull trigger.

Johnson M1941 and 1944 USA

prolonged use, it was nevertheless ordered in quantity for the Dutch East Indies in 1941, but the Japanese got there first, and the guns went to the US Marines and other special forces. The 1941 model had a wooden butt and a bipod; a later, 1944, version used a monopod and a tubular metal butt, though few of these were made. The design was later taken over by Israel and became their 'Dror' light machine gun in the early 1950s.

The Johnson machine gun was partner to the Johnson rifle of the same period, and like the rifle it had a few novelties. It fed from a side-mounted magazine which could be topped up through the action from the right side using clips, and was recoil operated, the barrel and action sliding back and forth in the receiver. It fired from an open bolt for automatic fire and from a closed bolt in single shots. The rate of fire could be changed by adjusting the buffer. Too flimsy and too prone to jamming in

Specification & Operation

Cartridge:
.30-06 US Service

Dimensions:
Length o/a: 1066mm
Weight: 6.48kg
Barrel: 558mm
Rifling: 4 grooves, rh
Feed system: 20-round box magazine
Rate of fire: 200 - 900 rds/min variable

In production: 1941-45

Markings:
'Light Machine Gun Johnson Automatics Model of 1941' and serial number above magazine housing.

Safety:
A 3 position selector on right of receiver: vertical for safe, forward for automatic, rearward for single shots.

Unloading:
Magazine catch on top of magazine housing. Remove magazine, pull back cocking handle, examine chamber. Release handle and pull trigger.

Knorr-Bremse GERMANY

This originated in Sweden as the LH33, but the Swedes were not interested; neither were the Norwegians, and the inventor sold the design to the Knorr-Bremse company of Berlin. They were in the motor-car brake business but in 1935 fancied their chance to make some money out of the German armament programme with a machine gun. The gun fed from a side-mounted magazine and was gas-operated in a conventional manner, but it was poorly manufactured

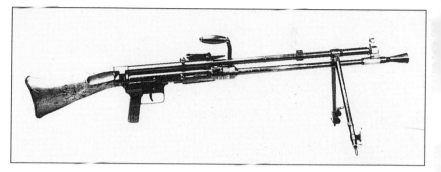

Specification & Operation

Cartridge:
7.92 x 57mm Mauser

Dimensions:
Length o/a: 1308mm
Weight: 10.0kg
Barrel: 691mm
Rifling: 4 grooves, rh
Feed system: 20-round box magazine
Rate of fire: 500 rds/min

In production: 1935-40

Markings:
Serial number over chamber.

Safety:
Safety catch above trigger on left side: forward for safe, rearward one notch for single shot and all the way back for automatic.

Unloading:
Magazine catch behind magazine housing on left. Remove magazine, pull back cocking handle, examine chamber and feedway. Release cocking handle and pull trigger.

and has some glaring defects. One was that the safety, if wrongly applied, could release the bolt and fire the gun; another was that the butt had a tendency to fall off during firing. The Waffen-SS bought a batch of guns but were not impressed and gave them to their various foreign 'legions' formed during the war, and most of them ended up in the Baltic states. Knorr-Bremse sold another batch to Sweden in 1940, when the Swedes were glad of anything they could get, after which they returned to the brake business.

Lewis Mark 1 (Ground) BELGIUM/UK

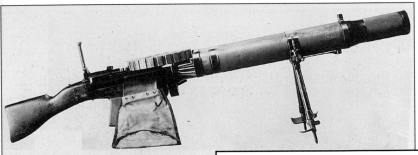

around the barrel conceals a series of longitudinal fins; the muzzle blast sets up a current which draws air in at the rear of the jacket and so cools the barrel. After WWI many countries bought the Lewis gun, which had demonstrated its reliability in combat, although the US Army were slow to accept it, took relatively few, and rapidly discarded it for the Browning rifle after 1920.

The Lewis gun derives from a design by a man named MacLean; it was then refined and perfected by Col Lewis, USA, who then found that the US Army didn't want to know. So, like Browning, he took his idea to Belgium where the gun was accepted by the Belgian Army and Lewis set up a manufacturing company. The British expressed interest and the BSA company obtained a licence, so that the British were receiving them soon after the outbreak of war in 1914. Gas operated, the gun has a rotating bolt driven by the gas piston and a curious clock-type return spring. The thick casing

Specification & Operation

Cartridge:
.303 British service and others

Dimensions:
Length o/a: 1283mm
Weight: 11.80kg
Barrel: 666mm
Rifling: 4 grooves, lh
Feed system: 47 or 97-round drum
Rate of fire: 550 rds/min

In production: 1912-25

Markings:
'Lewis Automatic Machine Gun/ Model 1914

Patented/' behind drum. 'Manufactured by the BSA Co Ltd England/for/Arme Automatique Lewis BELGIUM' on flat area behind drum, or 'LEWIS AUTO GUN Mod 1914 Patent' on same area.

Safety:
Vertically sliding latch on left of receiver above trigger: DOWN for SAFE; UP for FIRE.

Unloading:
Magazine catch is in the centre of the drum magazine. Press or slide according to type and lift drum off. Pull back cocking handle and examine chamber and feedway. Release cocking handle and pull the trigger.

Lewis Mark 2 (Air) BELGIUM/UK

The Lewis aircraft gun is precisely the same mechanism as the Lewis ground gun, but does away with the jacket-and-fins cooling system; the theory was that the airflow around an aircraft gun would cool it quite well, and this proved to be so, with the Lewis being one of the most-used aircraft machine guns in WWI and for many years afterwards. In 1940 the British bought a large quantity of

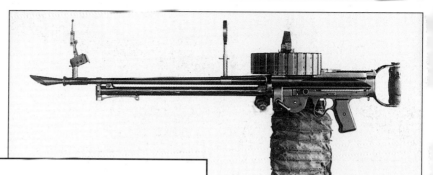

Specification & Operation

Cartridge:
.303 British and others

Dimensions:
Length o/a: 915mm
Weight: 10.43kg
Barrel: 666mm
Rifling: 4 grooves, lh
Feed system: 97-round drum
Rate of fire: 550 rds/min

In production: 1915-30

Markings:
'Lewis Automatic Machine Gun/ Model 1914

Patented/' behind drum. 'Manufactured by the BSA Co Ltd England/for/Arme Automatique Lewis BELGIUM' on flat area behind drum, or 'LEWIS AUTO GUN Mod 1914 Patent' on same area.

Safety:
Vertically sliding latch on left of receiver above trigger: DOWN for SAFE; UP for FIRE.

Unloading:
Magazine catch is in the centre of the drum magazine. Press or slide according to type and lift drum off. Pull back cocking handle and examine chamber and feedway. Release cocking handle and pull the trigger.

this type of gun from the USA, calling them the Savage-Lewis after the manufacturers. Intended for naval use, principally for the Merchant Navy as protection against dive-bombers, many were issued to the Home Guard as ground weapons, fitted with a bipod and butt, and it was discovered that they didn't overheat even without any cooling airstream. There were a number of minor variants in this group of aircraft weapons, but all look more or less the same and all function in the same way.

Madsen DENMARK

it was certainly the first practical light machine gun, pioneered the overhead magazine among other things, was adopted by the Danish Marines in the 1890s, and first saw action with Russia in the Russo-Japanese war in 1904. After that the same model, with very minor modifications, stayed in production for fifty years and was used all over the world in tanks and aircraft as well as on the ground, yet it never became the official weapon of any major army.

It has been said that the remarkable thing about the Madsen is not that it works well, but that it works at all. The mechanism is practically a mechanised version of the Martini breech-block, swinging up and down by the action of a cam driven by the barrel recoil. Since there is no bolt to push the cartridge into the chamber it has a separate rammer. The cartridge actually travels in a curve during loading, which is theoretically almost impossible. However

Specification & Operation

Cartridge:
Various, from 6.5 to 8mm

Dimensions:
Length o/a: 1143mm
Weight: 9.07kg
Barrel: 584mm
Rifling: 4 grooves, rh
Feed system: 25, 30 or 40-round box magazine
Rate of fire: 450 rds/min

In production: 1897-55

Markings:
'Madsen Model' (year) and serial number, right side receiver.

Safety:
Safety catch on left above trigger. Move UP for SAFE when gun is cocked.

Unloading:
Press in catch behind magazine and remove magazine. Pull back operating handle, inspect chamber and release. Pull trigger.

Madsen-Saetter DENMARK

This was the last Madsen military weapon before they left the arms business. It was designed as a general purpose machine gun, to be used on a tripod for sustained fire support or on a bipod as the squad light automatic weapon. It was designed so that by simply changing the barrel and bolt it could accommodate any calibre from 6.5mm to 8mm, and construction was largely of pressings and sheet metal. Gas operated, the bolt is locked by lugs

Specification & Operation

Cartridge:
7.62 × 51mm NATO

Dimensions:
Length o/a: 1165mm
Weight: 10.65kg
Barrel: 565mm
Rifling: 4 grooves, rh
Feed system: belt
Rate of fire: 650 to 1000 rds/min

In production: 1952-60

Markings:
MADSEN SAETTER and serial on front left of receiver beneath the sight.

Safety:
There is no safety on this weapon.

Unloading:
Open the feed cover by pressing the catch at its rear end. Remove the belt. Pull back the cocking handle, examine the feedway and chamber. Release the cocking handle, pull the trigger.

entering recesses in the receiver sides and the rate of fire was adjustable between wide limits. It was adopted by Indonesia, who built it under licence, but no other army was interested and Madsen decided they could find better things to do.

Marlin USA

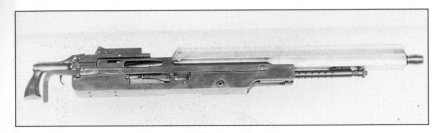

they were used to arm merchant ships against air attacks. These, and the remaining US stocks, were all disposed of after 1945, and there have been occasional reports of them turning up on improvised ground mounts in odd places.

In 1895 Colt produced a gas-operated machine gun which relied upon blast driving a swinging arm down beneath the barrel to operate the bolt; the action of this arm caused the gun to acquire the nickname 'Potato Digger'. In 1915 the US Army gave the Marlin company a contract to manufacture several thousand of these, but Marlin decided to redesign it to use a conventional gas piston under the barrel instead of the swinging arm. The resulting weapon was adopted as an aircraft gun and as a tank gun (using large cast aluminium cooling fins around the barrel), and in the former role it served the US Army Air Force until the early 1930s. Several thousand of these, taken from store, were sent to Britain in 1940 where

Specification & Operation

Cartridge:
.30-06 US Service

Dimensions:
Length o/a: 1016mm
Weight: 10.20kg
Barrel: 711mm
Rifling: 4 grooves, rh
Feed system: 250-round cloth belt
Rate of fire: 600 rds/min

In production: 1916-19

Markings:
'MARLIN-ROCKWELL Corp/NEW HAVEN CONN USA/INSP JAD' (year) serial number' all front top of receiver.

Safety:
There is no safety device on this weapon.

Unloading:
There is a pawl depressor on the right side of the belt feedway: depress this and remove belt. Operate cocking handle to eject any round in chamber, inspect chamber and feedway. Release cocking handle and pull the trigger.

Maxim MG'08 GERMANY

This is the classic Maxim recoil-operated machine gun and is essentially the same as every other Maxim of the period; heavy, water-cooled, and in the case of the '08 model, mounted on a unique four-legged 'sledge' mounting which folded up to allow the crew to drag the gun across the ground. Mounted on this, the total weight became 62kg. The gun uses a toggle system of breech-locking; barrel and toggle recoil together, until a spur

Specification & Operation

Cartridge:
7.92 x 57mm Mauser

Dimensions:
Length o/a: 1175mm
Weight: 26.44kg
Barrel: 719mm
Rifling: 4 grooves, rh
Feed system: 250-round cloth belt
Rate of fire: 450 rds/min
In production: 1908-18

Markings:
'Deutsche Waffen und Munitionsfabriken BERLIN'

(Year) on left receiver. '8mm MASCH GEWEHR 1908' and serial number top rear of receiver.

Safety:
Safety latch between spade grips. It has to be lifted by the fingers to allow trigger to be pressed.

Unloading:
Press pawl depressor on right of feedway to remove belt. Pull back and release cocking handle twice. With a pencil or similar tool, check ejection hole under barrel for possible live cartridge. Press trigger.

on the toggle strikes a lug on the receiver wall. This causes the toggle to fold and withdraw the breech-block. A spring then folds the toggle forward again to load a fresh cartridge and fire. A very reliable weapon, during World War I MG '08s proved able to fire for hours on end provided they had cooling water and ammunition. It remained in the postwar German Army and one or two were actually taken to war in 1939, though they were soon discarded in favour of more modern and lighter designs.

Maxim '08/15 GERMANY

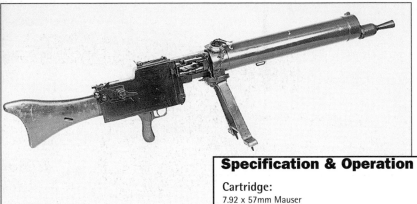

the standard 250-round belt could be used. There was also an aircraft version of this gun which has a perforated barrel jacket instead of the water jacket, relying upon the airstream to cool the barrel.

The '08/15 was an attempt to provide the German infantry with something rather more portable than the standard '08 on its sledge mount. It was given a small bipod, a shoulder stock and a pistol grip, and the receiver was re-designed in order to try and save weight. Feed was still by a cloth belt, but a special short belt was used which could be coiled on a reel and carried in a container clamped to the side of the gun. In fixed positions

Specification & Operation

Cartridge:
7.92 x 57mm Mauser

Dimensions:
Length o/a: 1448mm
Weight: 14.06kg
Barrel: 719mm
Rifling: 4 grooves, rh
Feed system: 50-round cloth belt
Rate of fire: 500 rds/min

In production: 1915-18

Markings:
'LMG 08/15 SPANDAU' (year) on top of receiver

or 'MG 08/15 SPANDAU (year) GEWEHRFABRIK' on lock spring cover at left rear side of receiver. Serial number on left side of receiver.

Safety:
Safety latch between spade grips. It has to be lifted by the fingers to allow trigger to be pressed.

Unloading:
Press pawl depressor on right of feedway to remove belt. Pull back and release cocking handle twice. With a pencil or similar tool, check ejection hole under barrel for possible live cartridge. Press trigger.

Maxim 1910 RUSSIA

This is much the same weapon as the German '08, since they were both built from the same licensee. The Russians adopted the Maxim in 1905, using a bronze water jacket; they changed this in 1910 to the cheaper and easier corrugated type of jacket as used by the British Vickers gun, after which no change was made until 1942, when the jacket was fitted with an over-sized water filler which allowed handfuls of snow to be dumped into it quickly when

Specification & Operation

Cartridge:
7.62 x 54R Soviet

Dimensions:
Length o/a: 1107mm
Weight: 23.80kg
Barrel: 721mm
Rifling: 4 grooves, rh
Feed system: 250-round cloth belt
Rate of fire: 550 rds/min

In production: 1910-50

Markings:
Factory identifier, year and serial number on spring cover, left or top of receiver.

Safety:
Latch above between spade grips. Lift to fire.

Unloading:
Press pawl depressor on right of feedway to remove belt. Pull back and release cocking handle twice. With a pencil or similar tool, check ejection hole under barrel for possible live cartridge. Press trigger.

necessary. The most usual mounting is the 'Sokolov' which is wheeled and had the gun on a small turntable. It weighs 45.22kg with its small steel shield, though this was usually removed since it was too small to be of much use. The gun remained in use until the 1960s, after which it was given away freely to various other countries and numbers can be expected to be available, particularly in the Far East, for some years to come.

simply removing a lock pin, the stock and rear of the receiver can be folded down to allow the bolt and piston to be withdrawn backwards.

Mendoza has been producing machine guns for the Mexican Army since 1933 and all have been noted for their lightness and cheap construction without sacrificing reliability. They use a gas cylinder system which delivers a short impulse to the piston, and the bolt is similar to that of the Lewis gun, rotating and driven by two cams engaged with the piston rod. The RM2 is the most recent model and adds a simplified method of stripping; by

Specification & Operation

Cartridge:
.30-06 US Service

Dimensions:
Length o/a: 1092mm
Weight: 6.30kg
Barrel: 609mm
Rifling: 4 grooves, rh
Feed system: 20-round box magazine
Rate of fire: 600 rds/min

In production: c. 1965 -

Markings:
'Fusil Ametrallador Mendoza/ Hecho en Mexico/ Caliber 30-06/ Modeleo RM2' (year) all on left side of receiver.

Safety:
Left side above trigger: forward for SAFE, up for single shot and to the rear for automatic fire.

Unloading:
Magazine catch behind magazine. Remove magazine, pull back cocking handle, inspect chamber, release cocking handle and pull trigger.

MG13 GERMANY

During WWI the Rheinmetall company had developed a recoil-operated machine gun, but the German Army were content with the Maxim and relatively few were made. In the early 1930s it was decided to convert these into a light machine gun by putting a perforated jacket around the barrel, adding a bipod and simple butt, and developing a saddle-type magazine. They went into service with the German Army in 1933-34, but as soon as supplies of the much better MG34 were available

Specification & Operation

Cartridge:
7.92 x 57mm Mauser

Dimensions:
Length o/a: 1466mm
Weight: 10.90kg
Barrel: 717mm
Rifling: 4 grooves, rh
Feed system: 75-round saddle drum
Rate of fire: 650 rds/min

In production: ca 1930-35

Markings:
Serial number on left of receiver.

Safety:
Latch in trigger must be pressed for the weapon to fire.

Unloading:
Pawl depressor on left behind feedway. Depress and remove belt, pull back cocking handle, examine feedway and chamber, release cocking handle and press trigger.

they were withdrawn, refurbished, and sold to Portugal. There they were used until the 1950s, even later in the colonies, and from there they found their way into various Central African countries.

MG 15Na Bergmann GERMANY

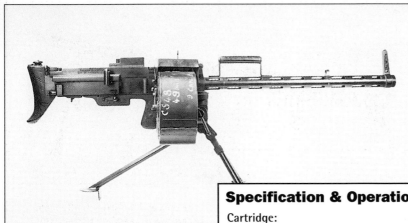

receiver and a pistol grip underneath it, and a light tripod fitted at the point of balance. It was fed by a short belt coiled up in a side-mounted box. This was issued to German troops on the Italian front in 1916 and remained in service until the early 1930s.

Bergmann began making machine guns in 1901 and produced a useful recoil-operated, water-cooled model which looked much like the Maxim. During WWI, when the German Army was demanding lighter weapons, it was modified by discarding the water jacket and replacing it with a thin, perforated jacket to allow air-cooling. A shoulder pad was added to the rear end of the

Specification & Operation

Cartridge:
7.92 x 57mm Mauser

Dimensions:
Length o/a: 1121mm
Weight: 12.92kg
Barrel: 726mm
Rifling: 4 grooves, rh
Feed system: 200-round belt
Rate of fire: 500 rds/min

In production: 1915-18

Markings:
L MG15 nA and serial on top of receiver.

Safety:
There is no safety device on this weapon.

Unloading:
Press pawl depressor on right of feedway to remove belt. Pull back and release cocking handle twice. With a pencil or similar tool, check ejection hole under barrel for possible live cartridge. Press trigger.

MG34 GERMANY

This began as the Solothurn Model 30, developed in Switzerland in the 1920s. The company was then bought by Rheinmetall, after which Solothurn became their development engineering and production plant, since this work was outlawed in Germany by the Versailles Treaty. Rheinmetall then went to work on the MG30 and modified it into the MG34 which was introduced

Specification & Operation

Cartridge:
7.92 x 57mm Mauser

Dimensions:
Length o/a: 1219mm
Weight: 12.10kg
Barrel: 627mm
Rifling: 4 grooves, rh
Feed system: 50-round belt or 75-round saddle drum
Rate of fire: 900 rds/min

In production: 1934 - 1945

Markings:
'MG34' serial number, top rear receiver.

Safety:
Manual safety catch on the left side above the trigger. Press in and UP for fire, press in and DOWN for safe.

Unloading:
Cover latch at rear of receiver. Press in and allow the cover to open. Remove the belt if one is present, check that no cartridge remains in the feed tray. Pull the cocking handle to the rear and inspect the chamber and feedway. Push the feed slide to the left and close the cover. Press the trigger.

into the German Army in 1936 and became their standard weapon until superseded by the MG42, although it continued in production until the end of the war. The notable features of this design include the method of stripping by simply twisting the butt; the straight-line layout which reduced the tendency to lift the muzzle in firing, and the ability to use it on a bipod as the rifle squad automatic weapon or on a tripod for sustained support fire; it was the original 'general purpose' machine gun.

MG42 GERMANY

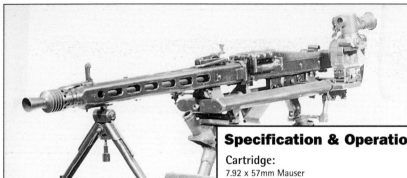

German Army was established, they simply put the MG42 back into production since they could see no other weapon which was as good, and as the MG1, and later MG3, it is still in use. As the MG42/59 it is used by the Austrian and Italian armies, and as the `Sarac' it was manufactured in Yugoslavia.

Good as the MG34 was, it suffered from being complex and expensive to make, and in 1941 the German Army asked for something which retained all the advantages of the MG34 but was easier to mass-produce. Experts in metal stamping were called in to assist the Mauser company in the redesign, and the result was the MG42. It used a new system of locking the breech, a highly efficient method of changing the barrel, and it was highly resistant to dust and dirt. In the 1950s, when the Federal

Specification & Operation

Cartridge:
7.92 x 57mm Mauser

Dimensions:
Length o/a: 1219mm
Weight: 11.50kg
Barrel: 533mm
Rifling: 4 grooves, rh
Feed system: 50-round belt
Rate of fire: 1200 rds/min

In production: 1938-45

Markings:
`MG42', serial number and factory identifier on left side of receiver.

Safety:
Push-button safety catch in the top of the pistol grip. Push through from right to left for safe, from left to right to fire.

Unloading:
Pull the cocking handle to the rear, push the safety catch to the left. Press the cover latch at the rear of the receiver and lift the cover. Lift the belt from the feed tray. Push forward the barrel cover lock (right side of receiver) until the barrel swings out and the chamber can be inspected. Pull back on the lock and replace the barrel, check that no cartridge is in the feed tray or receiver and close the cover. Press the safety catch to the right, grasp the cocking handle, press the trigger and ease the cocking handle forward.

Neuhausen KE7 SWITZERLAND

Designed by Kiraly and Ende (KE) this machine gun was made in Switzerland by the SIG company and sold in considerable numbers to China. Recoil-operated and air-cooled, it was an attempt to produce an inexpensive but reliable weapon; it succeeded in this but by the time it was perfected most European nations had made their choice and were busy manufacturing them. Surprisingly light, it could almost be called a machine rifle, since the barrel could not be changed and the magazine was of small capacity. It was generally issued with a small bipod and a monopod beneath the butt, but a tripod was also available for sustained fire tasks.

Specification & Operation

Cartridge:
7.5 x 55mm Swiss Service

Dimensions:
Length o/a: 1190mm
Weight: 7.80kg
Barrel: 600mm
Rifling: 4 grooves, rh
Feed system: 20-round box magazine
Rate of fire: 550 rds/min

In production: 1929-35

Markings:
Serial number on top rear surface of receiver

Safety:
Safety catch on the right side of the receiver, above the pistol grip. Push down and forward for safe; up and back for fire.

Unloading:
The magazine catch is behind the magazine. Remove magazine, pull back cocking handle on left side and examine chamber and feedway. Release cocking handle and pull trigger.

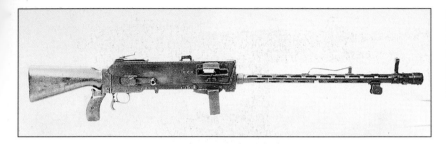

other parts. Two versions can be found; one, the original aircraft observer's gun, had a large perforated barrel jacket; the second version, produced as a ground gun in early 1918, has a much thinner perforated barrel jacket and a bipod or tripod fitting beneath the receiver.

The Parabellum is, in many respects, the German equivalent of the Vickers, since it was arrived at by the same process of lightening the inverting Maxim action that produced the Vickers. The German Army liked the Maxim but complained of its weight, more so when they came to the problem of aircraft. This question arose quite early, and a new gun was demanded in 1909. Deutsche Waffen & Munitionswerke produced their answer in 1911, arrived at by inverting the Maxim toggle lock so that it broke upwards and lightening the whole gun by reducing the safety factor to a more sensible figure and reducing the amount of metal in the receiver and

Specification & Operation

Cartridge:
7.92 x 57mm Mauser

Dimensions:
Length o/a: 1223mm
Weight: 9.80kg
Barrel: 705mm
Rifling: 4 grooves, rh
Feed system: 250-round cloth belt
Rate of fire: 700 rds/min

In production: 1916-18

Markings:
'DWM' in script on top of receiver. 'SM GEW MOD PARABELLUM (year) BERLIN' top of receiver. Serial number on base of rear sight.

Safety:
Spur under trigger blocks its movement when set.

Unloading:
Pawl depressor on right side under feedway. Press in and remove belt. Pull back cocking handle, examine feedway and chamber. Release cocking handle and press trigger.

St Etienne 07/16 FRANCE

The St Etienne machine gun is an object lesson in how not to design weapons. It was an attempt to improve an earlier design which itself was an attempt to improve the Hotchkiss. The designer began by reversing the action of the gas piston so that it blew forward; this then demanded a rack and pinion system to reverse the movement so that the bolt went backwards. The return spring was placed around the piston rod, beneath the barrel, so that

Specification & Operation

Cartridge:
8 x 50R Lebel

Dimensions:
Length o/a: 1180mm
Weight: 25.73kg
Barrel: 710mm
Rifling: 4 grooves, rh
Feed system: 24- or 30-round metal strips
Rate of fire: 500 rds/min

In production: 1907 - 1918

Markings:
MITRAILLEUSE Mo 1907 ST ETIENNE 1915 and serial number on top of receiver.

Safety:
Thumb catch on left of spade grip: when raised this prevents the trigger moving.

Unloading:
Pawl depressor in front of feedway. Press in and remove belt. Pull back cocking handle, examine feedway and chamber. Release cocking handle and press trigger.

barrel heat rapidly drew its tempering and weakened it. An adjustment on the gas cylinder allowed the rate of fire to be changed, but the overall effect was to so complicate the gun that when introduced into the trenches in 1916 it jammed frequently. To save face it was officially decided that it was best suited to dry climates, so the whole production was shipped off to the African colonies, from where they eventually scattered across the continent.

Schwarzlose AUSTRIA

Although sensitive to its ammunition, it was reliable and very simple to operate and maintain. After 1918 large numbers were acquired as war reparations by the Italian Army and it was still in use by them and by the Hungarian army in 1945.

The only unlocked-breech machine gun ever to see any serious use, the Schwarzlose relied on a massive breech-block and a toggle system which worked at a mechanical disadvantage to delay the opening of the block on firing. Adopted by the Austro-Hungarian army in 1905, some minor improvements were made and it was supplied also to the Dutch and German armies prior to 1918.

Specification & Operation

Cartridge:
8 x 50R Austrian Mannlicher; 7.92 x 57mm Mauser; 6.5 x 54R Dutch Mannlicher

Dimensions:
Length o/a: 1066mm
Weight: 19.90kg
Barrel: 621mm
Rifling: 4 grooves, rh
Feed system: 250-round cloth belt
Rate of fire: 400 rds/min

In production: 1912-18

Markings:
MG SCHWARZLOSE M7/12 on rear of receiver.

Safety:
Catch on back plate above trigger locks trigger when centred. Push to the right to fire.

Unloading:
Push cover locking catch left, lift cover and remove belt. Operate cocking handle and examine feedway and chamber. Release cocking handle and press trigger.

NSV RUSSIA

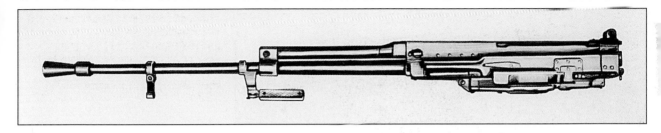

This weapon appeared in the late 1970s on tank turrets as a commander's machine gun; it was later seen on a tripod for heavy support use by infantry, and then on an air defence mounting. The gun is gas operated, using a piston to drive a bolt carrier, and can be set up during manufacture to feed from the left or from the right as required. In addition to being made in Russia, it has been licensed to Poland, Bulgaria and Yugoslavia, all of whom have offered it on the export market for some years. It appears to have been developed as a replacement for the DShK model, but there seems to be little advance in performance over the earlier weapon.

Specification & Operation

Cartridge:
12.7 x 107mm Soviet

Dimensions:
Length o/a: 1560mm
Weight: 25.00kg
Barrel: 1070mm
Rifling: 8 grooves, rh
Feed system: belt
Rate of fire: 750 rds/min

In production: ca 1980-

Markings:
Serial number on the top of the receiver.

Safety:
There is no safety device on this weapon

Unloading:
Press catch in front of the sight and lift cover. Remove the belt. Pull back the cocking handle, examine chamber and feedway. Release cocking handle, press trigger and close cover.

There are a number of variant models: the PK is the basic company gun; the PKS is the tripod-mounted battalion support weapon; the PKT is the version for use in tanks, with no pistol grip or butt. As with other Soviet designs, the PK family can be found in all the former Warsaw Pact countries.

The PK was the first general purpose machine gun to go into Soviet service; it replaced the RP46 but, surprisingly, retained the old rimmed cartridge, presumably because of its better long-range performance when compared to the M1943 rimless round. The design is a combination of Kalashnikov breech mechanism and a new feed system; it is light in weight and the quality of manufacture is high.

Specification & Operation

Cartridge:
7.62 x 54R Soviet

Dimensions:
Length o/a: 1193mm
Weight: 8.90kg
Barrel: 660mm
Rifling: 4 grooves, rh
Feed system: belt
Rate of fire: 650 rds/min

In production: 1964–

Markings:
Serial number and year on top of feed cover.

Safety:
Manual safety catch above the trigger. Turn forward to fire, rearward for safe.

Unloading:
Cover latch is at the rear of the receiver. Press in and allow the cover to open. Lift out the belt, if one is present, and check that no cartridge remains in the cartridge gripper. Pull back the cocking handle, inspect the chamber and feedway. Close the cover. Press the trigger.

RPK RUSSIA

The RPK replaced the RPD as the standard squad automatic for Soviet infantry and then went on to arm the Warsaw Pact armies and be distributed to sympathisers across the world. It is simply a heavy-barrelled version of the standard AK47 rifle and it will accept AK magazines, which makes resupply in the field relatively easy. Like the rifle, the

Specification & Operation

Cartridge:
7.62 x 39mm Soviet M1943

Dimensions:
Length o/a: 1035mm
Weight: 4.76kg
Barrel: 590mm
Rifling: 4 grooves, rh
Feed system: 3- or 40-round box or 75-round drum magazine
Rate of fire: 660 rds/min

In production: 1955-

Markings:
Serial and factory mark on left of receiver.

Safety:
Combined safety catch and fire selector on the left side of the receiver. Lifted to its upper position the weapon is safe; one notch DOWN gives single shots, all the way DOWN gives automatic fire.

Unloading:
Magazine catch behind magazine housing. Remove magazine. Pull back cocking handle to eject any round in the chamber, inspect chamber via the ejection slot, release the cocking handle and pull the trigger.

barrel is fixed, so that sustained fire is not entirely practical, though the bore and chamber are chromium-plated in an endeavour to keep the wear rate down as far as possible.

RP-46 RUSSIA

further modification of the original DP design, and almost all the RP46 were shipped off to sympathisers overseas; they turn up in Africa and the Middle East quite regularly.

The RP46 was a modernisation of the DPM, intended for use as a company support gun. The basic layout of the DPM was retained, the principal addition being that of a belt feed so that sustained fire could be delivered. However, the original 47 round DP drum can still be used if required, so the RP46 could still be used in the squad automatic role. The barrel has been made heavier, again something demanded by the sustained fire role. It was replaced in Soviet service by the RPD, which was a

Specification & Operation

Cartridge:
7.62 x 54R Soviet

Dimensions:
Length o/a: 1283mm
Weight: 13.00kg
Barrel: 607mm
Rifling: 4 grooves, rh
Feed system: 250-round cloth belt
Rate of fire: 600 rds/min

In production: 1946-54

Markings:
Factory identifier and serial number on top rear of receiver.

Safety:
A manual safety catch above the trigger on the right side. Turn forward for safe, rearward to fire.

Unloading:
Belt cover catch is behind the rear sight. Press the catch backwards and the cover will open. Lift out the belt if one is present. Pull the cocking handle to the rear and inspect the chamber and feedway. Press the trigger and ease the operating handle forward. Close the cover.

RPK-74 RUSSIA

The RPK-74 bears the same relationship to the AK-74 rifle as the RPK does to the AK-47 rifle; in other words it is the heavy-barrel squad automatic in 5.45mm calibre. Once the Soviets adopted the 5.45mm cartridge it was simply a matter of time before they produced the light automatic weapon to go with it, but it was not until 1980 that

Specification & Operation

Cartridge:
5.45 x 39mm Soviet

Dimensions:
Length o/a: 1060mm
Weight: 4.60kg
Barrel: 616mm
Rifling: 4 grooves, rh
Feed system: 30, 40 or 45-round magazines
Rate of fire: 650 rds/min

In production: 1977-

Markings:
Factory identifier and serial number on top rear of receiver.

Safety:
Combined safety catch and fire selector lever on the right rear side of the receiver. When pressed all the way UP it is in the safe position and obstructs the movement of the cocking handle and bolt; moved DOWN one notch to the first mark or the letters 'AB' gives full automatic fire, and moved to the bottom position, or the letter 'O', produces single shots.

Unloading:
Magazine catch at front end of trigger guard. Remove magazine. Pull back cocking handle, inspect chamber and feedway via the ejection port. Release cocking handle, pull trigger.

the first details reached the western world. It seems likely that the Soviets, too, had found problems in developing a small-calibre machine gun that didn't shoot the rifling out of its barrel within 5000 rounds. There are four variant models; the RPK-74 is the basic weapon; the RPKS-74 has a folding butt; the RPK-N3 is the standard weapon with a special mount on the left side of the receiver for an electronic night sight; and the RPKS-N3 is the folding stock model with night sight mount.

DShK RUSSIA

form of flat shuttle feed, so that the receiver cover became flat once more. Copies of these models have been made at various times in China, Pakistan and Romania and can be identified by their national markings.

This has been the premier heavy machine gun of the Soviet and Warsaw Pact armies since 1946 and is still in wide use, though now being replaced by the NSV (above). It has also been widely distributed to sympathisers around the world and will undoubtedly be used for many more years. It was originally produced in 1934 in limited numbers, revised in 1938 (the DShK-38), used during WWII and then revised once more in 1946 (the DShK38/46). The 1938 revision gave it a rotary feed, and thus a characteristic rounded cover to the receiver. The 1946 change reverted to a

Specification & Operation

Cartridge:
12.7 x 107mm Soviet

Dimensions:
Length o/a: 1588mm
Weight: 35.70kg
Barrel: 1070mm
Rifling: 4 grooves, rh
Feed system: 50 round belt
Rate of fire: 550 rds/min

In production: 1938-80

Markings:
Factory mark (arrow), year and serial number on

top rear of the receiver, above the grips.

Safety:
Manual safety catch on the lower left edge of the receiver. Turn forward for safe, backward to fire.

Unloading:
Cover latch in front of the rear sight. Press in and lift the cover. Remove any belt, lift the feed drum and check that no cartridges remain in it. Inspect to see that no rounds remain in the feedway or chamber. Close all covers, turn the safety catch to the rear, pull back the cocking handle, press the trigger.

Ultimax SINGAPORE

The Ultimax was developed by Chartered Industries of Singapore as the partner to their SAR-80 5.56mm rifle; unfortunately their timing was out, and it appeared some time after the FN Minimi, with the result that several armed forces which would probably have chosen the Ultimax had already committed themselves to the Minimi. The Ultimax is an excellent weapon and is particularly comfortable to fire, using

Specification & Operation

Cartridge:
5.56 x 45mm M193 or NATO

Dimensions:
Length o/a: 1030mm
Weight: 4.79kg
Barrel: 508mm
Rifling: 6 grooves, rh
Feed system: 30-round box or 100-round drum
Rate of fire: 550 rds/min

In production: 1982-

Markings:
'ULTIMAX Mk III Mfd by Singapore Chartered Industries 5.56' and serial number on left side of receiver.

Safety:
Manual safety catch on left side above trigger. Forward for automatic fire, rearward for safe.

Unloading:
Remove magazine. Pull back cocking handle to eject any round in the chamber. Inspect chamber and feedway via the ejection port. Release cocking handle, pull trigger.

a long-stroke bolt and buffer system which keeps the recoil impulse to a very low level. It can be fed from a drum or a box magazine and uses the now-common bolt carrier and rotating bolt driven by a gas piston. It is currently used by the Singapore armed forces and has been favourably evaluated by several armies. It has also been seen in the current civil war in Bosnia.

Vickers UK

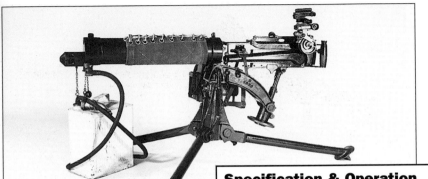

armed the earliest armoured cars and tanks and was, of course, also adopted by the various armies of the British Empire and Commonwealth, some of whom continued using it into the 1970s. It was also made in .50 calibre for aircraft and tank use, and a number were made by Colt in the USA in .30 calibre for the US Army in 1915. Vickers also sold the gun commercially in the 1920-38 period, principally to South American countries.

Like many others, the British started with the Maxim gun and then sought something lighter. Vickers developed their answer, reducing the weight by use of high quality steel and aluminium and better stress analysis, and inverting the Maxim toggle system for compactness. The resulting 'Mark 1' Vickers gun entered service in 1912 and stayed unchanged until made obsolete in 1968. Utterly reliable, it set up world records for non-stop firing during WWI, was adopted as the standard synchronised aircraft gun,

Specification & Operation

Cartridge:
.303 British and others

Dimensions:
Length o/a: 1155mm
Weight: 18.10kg
Barrel: 723mm
Rifling: 4 grooves, rh
Feed system: 250 round cloth belt
Rate of fire: 450 rds/min

In production: 1912-45

Markings:
Serial number on top rear of water jacket.

Safety:
Safety catch above trigger, between spade grips. Lift with the fingers to allow trigger to be pressed.

Unloading:
Pawl depressor on right side under feedway. Press in and remove belt. Pull back cocking handle, examine feedway and chamber. Release cocking handle and press trigger.

Vickers-Berthier UK

Adolphe Berthier was a French officer who devised a machine gun in the early 1920s; he sold the patents to Vickers, who developed the Vickers-Berthier machine gun and marketed it vigorously. The British Army took the Bren instead, but the Indian Army adopted the V-B, and numbers were sold to other countries. The gun can easily be confused, particularly at a distance, with the Bren, since they both used curved

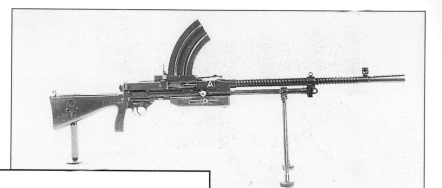

magazines and were generally similar in outline. The V-B is gas operated, had few working parts, and was notably smooth in its action, helped by a rather slow rate of fire. There were a number of Marks, each showing some small improvement, and most of the Indian Army weapons were Mark 3 or 3B and made at the Ishapore Rifle Factory.

Specification & Operation

Cartridge:
.303 British

Dimensions:
Length o/a: 1180mm
Weight: 9.40kg
Barrel: 607mm
Rifling: 5 grooves, rh
Feed system: 30-round box magazine
Rate of fire: 500 rds/min

In production: 1929-45

Markings:
'VICKERS-BERTHIER' serial number, top rear receiver.

Safety:
Safety catch above trigger on left. DOWN for SAFE, UP for FIRE.

Unloading:
Magazine catch behind magazine housing. Remove magazine. Pull back cocking handle to eject any round in the chamber. Inspect chamber and feedway through the magazine aperture. Release cocking handle, pull trigger.

VZ-26 CZECHOSLOVAKIA

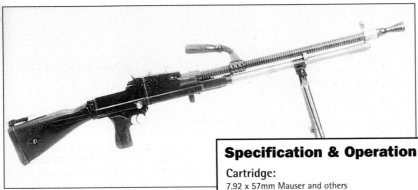

vz26, so that the same gun was being used on both sides in 1939-45. ZB continued to offer the gun in their catalogues after 1946, but none were ever made after the war. The vz26 can be distinguished from the Bren or Vickers-Berthier by the finned barrel and by the long gas cylinder beneath the barrel, extending almost to the muzzle.

The vz26 (vz = vzor = model) was designed by the Zbrojovka Brno (Brno Arms Factory) in Czechoslovakia in the early 1920s and was one of those rare occasions when everything came together first time. It was an immediate success and was adopted by over 25 countries around the world. A slightly modified version became the ZGB33, the modification being to suit it to the British .303 cartridge, and this, in turn, became the famous Bren light machine gun. The German Army used it as the

Specification & Operation

Cartridge:
7.92 x 57mm Mauser and others

Dimensions:
Length o/a: 1161mm
Weight: 9.60kg
Barrel: 672mm
Rifling: 4 grooves, rh
Feed system: 30-round box magazine
Rate of fire: 500 rds/min

In production: 1928-45

Markings:
'VZ 26' and serial number top rear receiver.
'BRNO' and factory marks on left side of receiver,

'LEHKY KULOMET ZB VZ 26' on right side of receiver.

Safety:
A combined safety catch and fire selector on the right side, above the trigger. Turn forward for automatic fire, midway for safe, rearward for single shots.

Unloading:
Magazine catch is behind magazine. Remove magazine. Pull back cocking handle, examine chamber and feedway through the magazine opening. Release the cocking handle, pull the trigger.

VZ-37 CZECHOSLOVAKIA

The vz37 was another Zbrojovka Brno product from Czechoslovakia, intended to accompany the vz26 as the heavy support weapon. It was belt fed and could be adjusted to two rates of fire. An odd feature, repeated in some other Czech designs, is the use of the pistol grip and trigger unit as the cocking handle. To cock the gun, push

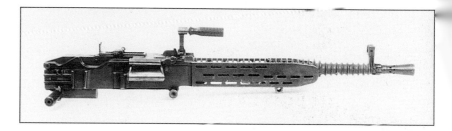

Specification & Operation

Cartridge:
7.92 x 57mm Mauser

Dimensions:
Length o/a: 1104mm
Weight: 18.60kg
Barrel: 635mm
Rifling. 4 grooves, rh
Feed system: 100-round belt
Rate of fire: 500 or 700 rds/min

In production: 1937-45

Markings:
'VZ37' and serial number on rear top of receiver.
'BRNO' on left side of receiver.

Safety:
A combined safety catch and fire selector is on the right side of the receiver, behind the grips. When in its central position the gun is safe. Turned left it provides single shots, turned right automatic fire. There is also a rate of fire selector on the left side of the receiver just in front of the grip. UP and forward gives slow rate, DOWN and back gives fast rate.

Unloading:
Set the safety catch to safe. Pull out the cover pin, at the right rear corner of the receiver, press and hold back the cover catch on the left side of the cover, and lift the cover open as far as it will go. Inspect to see that no rounds remain in the

the pistol grip forward until it engages with the bolt system, then pull back. Another oddity is that it is recoil operated and the cartridge is fired while the barrel and bolt are still moving forwards on the return stroke; this means that the recoil force must first stop the moving parts before driving them back, and this additional load soaks up quite a lot of the recoil energy. The gun was widely adopted in Europe in 1938/9 and was licensed by the British, who used it as the Besa gun on armoured vehicles.

BRAND NAMES

Explanatory Notes:

Scope: This covers as many brand names as can be discovered from the beginning of the metallic cartridge era. Percussion pistols and peculiar cartridge weapons are not considered here, since we are primarily concerned with weapons which are likely to be used today, and for which ammunition is available. Age does not come into this: a .22 pistol made in 1870 can be as effective a weapon as a .22 pistol made in 1995.

Name: Brand names given here are those actually marked on weapons; names identifying catalogue variations or purely for factory record purposes are not given. Weapons named for their maker will be identified from the List of Manufacturers

Type: Rev - revolver; Pistol - semi-automatic pistol; RP - repeating pistol or multi-barrelled pistol; MP - machine (automatic) pistol; MG - machine gun; SMG - submachine gun; SS - single shot pistol; Shotg - shotgun

Calibre: Most are obvious. Oblique strokes indicate alternative calibres. Suffixes:- RF rimfire; P Parabellum; S Short; B-B Bergmann-Bayard. `Various' indicates the full range of calibres usually to be found in that class, eg 10,12,16,20,28 bore for shotguns.

Maker: This is the 'short title'; the full name, location and other information will be found in the List of Manufacturers. Where the maker is not positively known, the country of origin or probable maker is shown in [square brackets]

Name	Type	Calibre	Maker
A			
AAA	Pistol	6.35/7.65	Aldazabal
ABILENE	Rev	357	Mossberg
ABILENE	Rev	357/44	US Arms (2)
ACE	Pistol	22	Colt
ACME ARMS	Rev	22/32	J. Stevens
ACME HAMMERLESS	Rev	32	Hopkins & Allen
ACRA	Rifle	Various	R. Fajen
ACTION	Pistol	6.35/7.65	Modesto Santos
ADLER	Pistol	7.65	Engelbrecht & Wolff
AETNA	Rev	22/32	Harrington & Richardson
AG	Pistol	7.65	Gavage
AJAX ARMY	Rev	44RF	Meacham
AKAH	Rifle`	Various	Kind
ALAMO	Rev	22	Stoeger
ALASKA	Rev	22	Hood
ALASKAN	Rifle	Various	Skinner's
ALASKAN MARK X	Rifle	Various	Zastava
ALERT	Rev	22	Hood
ALEXIA	Rev	32/38/41RF	Hopkins & Allen
ALEXIS	Rev	22	Hood
ALFA	Rev	38	Armero Especialistas
ALFA	All types	Various	Adolf Frank
ALKAR	Pistol	6.357.65	Alkartasuna
ALLEN	Rev	22	Hopkins & Allen

Name	Type	Calibre	Maker	Name	Type	Calibre	Maker
ALLEN	Shotgun	Various	McKeown	AUBREY	Rev	32/38	Meriden Arms/Sears
ALLIES	Pistol	6.35/7.65	Bersaluze				
ALPINE	Rifle	Various	Firearms	AUDAX	Pistol	6.35/7.65	Pyrenees
AMERICA	Rev	22	Bliss & Goodyear	AURORA	Pistol	6.35	[Spain]
AMERICA	Rev	32RF	Norwich Falls	AUTOGARDE	Rev	7.65	SFM
AMERICAN, THE	Rev	38	Hopkins & Allen	AUTO-MAG	Pistol	.44	Automag
AMERICAN BARLOCK				AUTOMASTER	Pistol	45	Sokolovsky
WONDER	Shotgun	Various	Crescent Firearms	AUTOMATIC	Rev	32/38	Hopkins & Allen
AMERICAN BOY	Rev	22	Bliss & Goodyear	AUTOMATIC			
AMERICAN BULLDOG	Rev	Various	Johnson, Bye	HAMMERLESS	Rev	32/38	Iver Johnson
AMERICAN CHAMPION	Shotgun	12	?	AUTOMATIC LESTON	Pistol	6.35	Unceta
AMERICAN EAGLE	Rev	22/32	Hopkins & Allen	AUTOMATIC POLICE	Rev	32	Forehand & Wadsworth
AMERICAN EAGLE 380	Pistol	9S	American Arms				
AMERICAN GUN Co	Rev/Shotgun	Various	Crescent Firearms	AUTOMATIQUE			
AMERICUS	Rev	22	Hopkins & Allen	FRANCAISE	Pistol	6.35	Soc. Franc. d'Armes
APACHE	Rev	38	Garantizada				
APACHL	Pistol	6.35	Ojanguren y Vidosa	AUTO-POINTER	Shotgun	12	Yamamoto
				AUTOSHOT	SS	.410	Stevens
ARICO	Pistol	6.35	Pieper	AUTOSTAND	SS	22	Manufrance
ARISTOCRAT	Rev	22/32RF	Hopkins & Allen	AVION	Pistol	6.35	Azpiri
ARISTOCRAT	Shotgun	Various	Stevens	AYA	Shotgun	Various	Aguirre y Aranzabal
ARMINIUS (pre-19450	Rev	Various	F Pickert				
ARMINIUS (Post-1945)	Rev	Various	Weirauch	AZUL	Pistol	Various	Arostegui
ARMSCOR 38	Rev	38	Squires, Bingham	**B**			
ARVA	Pistol	6.35	[Spain, pre 1914]	BABY	Pistol	6.35	FN
ASIATIC	Pistol	6.35/7.65	[Spain, 1920s]	BABY BULLDOG	Rev	22	[USA; ca 1885]
ASTRA	Pistols	Various	Astra-Unceta	BABY RUSSIAN	Rev	38	American Arms Co
ATLAS	Pistol	6.35	Domingo Acha				

Name	Type	Calibre	Maker	Name	Type	Calibre	Maker
BACKUP	Pistol	9S	AMT	BLACKHAWK	Rev	357	Ruger
BAIKAL	Shotg/Rifle	Various	Russian State	BLOODHOUND	Rev	22	Hopkins & Allen
BANG-UP	Rev	32RF	Bacon Arms	BLUE JACKET	Rev	22/32RF	Hopkins & Allen
BARRACUDA	Rev	9P	FN Herstal	BLUE WHISTLER	Rev	32RF	Hopkins & Allen
BASCULANT	Pistol	6.35	Aguirre Zamacolas	BOCK-FITZKOW	SS	22	Buchel [Spain}
				BOIX	Pistol	7.65	
BASQUE	Pistol	7.65	Echave & Arizmendi	BOLTUN	Pistol	7.65	Francisco Arizmendi
BATAVIA	Rifle/Shotg	22/Various	Baker	BONANZA	Rev	22	Bacon Arms
BANG-UP	Rev	22	Hopkins & Allen	BOOM	Rev	22	Shattuck
BANTAM	Pistol	6.35	Beretta	BORCHARDT	Pistol	7.65	Loewe/DWM
BAYARD	All types	Various	Pieper	BOSTON BULLDOG	Rev	Various	Iver Johnson
BEHOLLA	Pistol	7.65	Becker & Hollander	BOY'S CHOICE	Rev	22	Hood
				BREN TEN	Pistol	10mm	Dornaus & Dixon
BELLMORE	Shotgun	Various	Crescent Arms	BRIGADIER	Pistol	9P	Beretta
BENEMERITA	Pistol	6.35/7.65	Aldazabal	BRIGADIER	Pistol	.45	North American Arms
BENGAL NO 1	Rev	22	Iver Johnson				
BERSA	Pistol	22/38	Ange	BRISTOL	Pistol	7.65	Bolumburu
B.H.	Rev	38	Beistegui Hermanos	BRITISH BULLDOG	Rev	Various	Forehand & Wadsworth
BICYCLE	Rev	22/32	Harrington & Richardson	BRITISH BULLDOG	Rev	Various	Johnson, Bye
				BRNO	Rifle/shotgun	Various	Zbrojovka Brno
BIG BONANZA	Rev	22	Bacon Arms	BROMPETIER	Rev	6.35/7.65	Retolaza
BIG HORN	SS	22	Big Horn Arms Co	BRONCHO	Pistol	6.35/7.65	Errasti
BIJOU	Rev	Various	Debouxtay	BRONCO	Pistol	6.35/7.65	Echave y Arizmendi
BIJOU	Pistol	6.35	Menz				
BISLEY	Rev	Various	Colt	BRON-GRAND	Rev	6/6.35/7.65	Fernando Ormachea
BISLEY	Rev	357	Ruger				
BISON	Rev	22	Herbert Schmidt	BRONG-PETIT	Rev	6.35	Crucelegui

Name	Type	Calibre	Maker
DRON-SPORT	Rev	6.35/7.65/8	Crucelegui
BROW	Rev	6.35/7.65/38	Ojanguren & Marcaido
BROWNIE	RP	22	Mossberg
BROWREDUIT	Rev	6.35/7.65	Salvator Arostegui
BRUNSWIG	Pistol	7.65	Esperanza & Unceta
BRUTUS	Rev	22	Hood
BUCCANEER	Pistol	7.65	Pyrenees
BUCKHORN	Rev	357	Uberti
BUDISCHOWSKY	Pistol	22/25	Korriphila
BUFALO	Pistol	6.35/7.65	Gabilondo
BUFFALO STAND	SS	22	Manufrance
BULL DOZER	Rev	Various	Norwich Pistol
BULL DOZER	SS	22RF	Conn Mfg
BULLDOG	Rev	Various	Forehand & Wadsworth
BULLDOG	Rev	44	Charter Arms
BULLDOG TRACKER	Rev	357	Charter Arms
BULLFIGHTER	Rev	.300	[Belgium]
BULLSEYE	Rev	22	[USA; ca 1885]
BULWARK	Pistol	6.35/7.65	Beistegui
BURGHAM SUPERIOR	Pistol	7.65	Pyrenees
BURGO	Rev	22	Rohm
BUSHMASTER	Pistol/Rifle	223	Gwinn Arms

C

Name	Type	Calibre	Maker
CADET	Rev	22	Maltby, Curtis

Name	Type	Calibre	Maker
CADIX	Rev	22/32/38	Astra-Unceta
CAMINAL	Pistol	7.65	[Spain]
CAMPEON	Pistol	6.35/7.65	Hijos de C Arrizabalaga
CAMPER	Pistol	22/6.35	Astra-Unceta
CANTABRIA	Pistol/Rev	Various	Garate Hermanos
CAPITAN	Pistol	7.65	Pyrenees
CAPTAIN JACK	Rev	22	Hopkins & Allen
CAROLINE ARMS	Shotgun	Various	Crescent Firearms
CA-SI	Pistol	7.65	Grand Precision
CASULL	Rev	454	Freedom Arms
CATTLEMAN	Rev	357/44	Uberti
CAVALIER	Rifle	Various	Zastava
C.D.M.	Rev	22	[USA ca 1980]
CEBRA	Pistol	6.35	Arizmendi Zulaica
CELTA	Pistol	6.35	Urizar
CENTAUR	Pistol	6.35	Reunies
CENTENNIAL 1876	Rev	32/38RF	Derringer
CENTRAL	Shotgun	Various	Stevens
CENTRAL ARMS CO	Shotgun	Various	Crescent Firearms
CENTURION	Pistol	9P	Beretta
CENTURION MODEL 100	Rifle	Various	Golden State
CESAR	Pistol	7.65	Pyrenees
J.CESAR	Pistol	6.35	Tomas de Urizar
C.H.	Rev	38	Crucelegui Hermanos
CHALLENGE	Rev	32RF	Bliss & Goodyear
CHAMPION	Pistol	22	Manufrance

Name	Type	Calibre	Maker
CHANTECLER	Pistol	7.65	Pyrenees
CHANTICLER	Pistol	6.35	Isidor Charola
CHARLES LANCASTER	Rifle	Various	Atkin
CHAROLA Y ANITUA	Pistol	5/7mm	Garate Anitua
CHEROKEE ARMS CO	Shotgun	Various	Crescent Firearms
CHESAPEAKE GUN CO	Shotgun	Various	Crescent Firearms
CHEYENNE SCOUT	Rev	22	Herbert Schmidt
CHICAGO ARMS CO	Rev	32/38	Meriden
CHICAGO CUB	Rev	22	Reck
CHICAGO PROTECTOR	RP	32	Ames Sword Co
CHICHESTER	Rev	38RF	Hopkins & Allen
CHIEFTAIN	Rev	32RF	Norwich Pistol
CHIMERE RENOIR	Pistol	7.65	Pyrenees
CHORERT	Rev	8mm	[Belgium]
CHURCHILL	Rifles	Various	Kassnar
CHYLEWSKI	Pistol	6.35	SIG
CILINDRO LADEABLE	Rev	32	Ojanguren & Matiade
CLEMENT	Rev	38	Clement, Neumann
CLEMENT	Pistol	5/6.35	Charles Clement
CLEMENT-FULGOR	Pistol	7.65	Charles Clement
CLIMAS	Shotgun	12	Stevens
COBOLD	Rev	9.4mm	HDH
COBOLT	Rev	Various	Ancion Marx
COBRA	Pistol	7.65	[Spain]
COLON	Pistol	6.35	Azpiri
COLON	Rev	32-20	Orbea Hermanos
COLONIAL	Pistol	7.65	Pyrenees
COLONIAL	Pistol	6.35/7.65	Grand Precision
COLUMBIAN	Rev	38	Crescent Firearms
COLUMBIAN AUTOMATIC	Rev	32/38	Foehl & Weeks
COMANCHE	Rev	357	Gabilondo
COMMANDER	Pistol	45	Colt
COMMANDO ARMS	S/A Carbine	Various	Volunteer
COMBAT COMMANDER	Pistol	9P/45	Colt
COMPEER	Shotgun	Various	Crescent Firearms
CONSTABLE	Pistol	7.65	Astra-Unceta
CONSTABULARY	Rev	7.5mm	Ancion Marx
CONSTABULARY	Rev	32/38/45	Robar
CONQUEROR	Rev	22/32RF	Bacon Arms
CONTINENTAL	Pistol	6.35	Bertrand
CONTINENTAL	Pistol	6.35/7.65	RWS
CONTINENTAL	Rifle/Shotgun	Various	Stevens
CONTINENTAL	Rev	22/32RF	Great Western
CONTINENTAL	Rev	22/32RF	Hood
CONTINENTAL	Pistol	6.35	Tomas de Urizar
CORLA	Pistol	22	Zaragoza
CORRIENTES	Pistol	6.35	Modesto Santos
COSMI	Shotgun	Various	Abercrombie & Fitch
COSMOPOLITE OSCILLATORY	Rev	38	Garate Anitua
COUGAR	Pistol	7.65/9	Beretta
COW-BOY	Pistol	6.35	Fabrique Francaise
COWBOY RANGER	Rev	Various	Liege United Arms

Name	Type	Calibre	Maker	Name	Type	Calibre	Maker
CRESCENT	Rev	32RF	Norwich Falls	DEMON	Pistol	7.65	Pyrenees
CREEDMORE	Rev	22	Hopkins & Allen	DEMON	Pistol	7.65	[Spain]
CRIOLLA	Pistol	22	Hafdasa	DEMON MARINE	Pistol	7.65	Pyrenees
CROWN JEWEL	Rev	32RF	Norwich Falls	DEPREZ	Rev	11mm	[Belgium]
CRUCERO	Pistol/Rev	7.65/32	Ojanguren &	DEPUTY ADJUSTER	Rev	38	Herbert Schmidt
			Vidosa	DEPUTY MAGNUM	Rev	357	Herbert Schmidt
CRUSO	Rifle/Shotgun	Various	Stevens	DEPUTY MARSHAL	Rev	38	Herbert Schmidt
CUB	Pistol	22/6.35	Astra-Unceta	DESERT EAGLE	Pistol	Various	Taas Israel
CUMBERLAND ARMS CO	Shotgun	Various	Crescent Firearms				Industries
CZ	All	Various	Ceskoslovenska	DESPATCH	Rev	22	Hopkins & Allen
CZAR	Rev	22	Hood	DESTROYER	Pistol	6.35/7.65	Gaztanaga
CZAR	Rev	22/32RF	Hopkins & Allen	DESTRUCTOR	Pistol	6.35/7.65	Salaverria
				DETECTIVE	Rev	32	Garate Anitua
D				DETECTIVE SPECIAL	Rev	38	Colt
DAISY	Rev	22	Bacon Arms	DEWAF MODEL IV	Pistol	6.35	[Spain, 1920s]
DAKOTA	Rev	30/45	Uberti	DIAMOND	Shotgun	Various	Stevens
DANTON	Pistol	6.35/7.65	Gabilondo	DIAMONDBACK	Rev	22/38	Colt
DEAD SHOT	Rev	22	Pond	DIANA	Pistol	6.35	[Spain]
DEFENSE	Pistol	6.35	[Spain]	DIANE	Pistol	6.35	Wilkinson
DEFENDER	Rev	22/32RF	Johnson, Bye	DIANE	Pistol	6.35	Erquiaga,
DEFENDER	Pistol	6.35	Javier Echaniz				Muguruzu
DEFENDER 89	Rev	22	Iver Johnson	DICKSON BULLDOG	Rev	22	Weirauch
DEFENSE	Pistol	6.35	[Spain; 1920s]	DICKSON SPECIAL			
DEFIANCE	Rev	22	Norwich Falls	AGENT	Pistol	7.65	Echave &
DEK-DU	Rev	5.5/6.35	Tomas de Urizar				Arizmendi
DELPHIAN	Shotgun	Various	Stevens	DICTATOR	Pistol	6.35	Reunies
DELTA	Pistol	6.35	[Spain]	DICTATOR	Rev	22/32RF	Hopkins & Allen
DELTA ELITE	Pistol	10mm	Colt	DIPLOMAT	Pistol	9S	Bernadelli
DE LUXE	Pistol	6.35	Bolumburu	DOMINO	Pistol	22	Italguns

Name	Type	Calibre	Maker	Name	Type	Calibre	Maker
DOUBLE DEUCE	Pistol	22	Steel City	EASTERN ARMS CO	Rev	32/38	Meriden/Sears
DOUBLE NINE	Rev	22	High Standard	E.B.A.C.	Pistol	6.35	Pyrenees
DOUGLAS	Pistol	6.35	Lasagabaster	ECHASA	Pistol	22/6.35/7.65	Echave y
DREADNOUGHT	Rev	38	Errasti				Arizmendi
DREADNOUGHT	Rev	22/32RF	Hopkins & Allen	ECIA	Pistol	7.65	Esperanza y Cia
DREUX	Pistol	6.35	[France]	ECLIPSE	SS	22/25/32RF	Johnson, Bye
DREYSE	Pistol	Various	Rheinmetall	EICHEL	Rifle	Various	Kind
DRULOV	SS	22	Lidove Drusztvo	EIG	Rev	22	Rohm
DUAN	Pistol	6.35	Ormachea	EL BLANCO	Rev	22	Ojanguren &
DUC	Pistol	6.35	[France?]				Matiade
DUCO	Rev	7.5mm	Dumoulin	EL CANO	Rev	32	Arana y Cia
DUO	Pistol	6.35	Dusek	EL CID	Pistol	6.35	Casimir Santos
DUPLEX	Rev	22/32RF	Osgood Gun	ELECTOR	Rev	22/32RF	Hopkins & Allen
			Works	ELECTRIC	Rev	32RF	Forehand &
DURABEL	Pistol	6.35	Warnant				Wadsworth
DURA-MATIC	Pistol	22	High Standard	ELES	Pistol	6.35	[Spain]
DURANGO	Rev	22	High Standard	ELEY	Pistol	6.35	[Spain]
				ELGIN ARMS CO	Shotguns	Various	Crescent Firearms

E

Name	Type	Calibre	Maker	Name	Type	Calibre	Maker
				ELITE	Pistol	7.65	Pyrenees
E.A.	Pistol	6.35	Echave y	EL LUNAR LEBEL RAPIDE	Rev	8mm	Garate Anitua
			Arizmendi	EL PERRO	Pistol	6.35	Lascuraren &
E.A.	Pistol	6.35	Arostegui				Olasolo
EAGLE 1	Rev	45	Phelps	EM-GE	Rev	22	Gerstenberger
EAGLE 380	Pistol	9S	American	EMPIRE	Rev	22/38/41RF	Rupertus
			Arms (2)	EMPIRE	Rifle	22	Vickers
EAGLE ARMS CO	Rev	Various	Johnson, Bye	EMPIRE ARMS	Rev	32/38	Meriden
FARI HOOD	Rev	32RF	Dickinson	EMPIRE ARMS CO	Shotgun	Various	Crescent Firearms
EARTHQUAKE	Rev	32RF	Dickinson	EMPIRE STATE	Rev	32/38	Meriden
EASTERN	Shotgun	Various	Stevens	EMPRESS	Rev	32RF	Rupertus

Name	Type	Calibre	Maker
ENCORE	Rev	22/32/38RF	Johnson, Bye
ENDERS OAKLEAF	Shotgun	Various	Crescent Firearms
ENDERS ROYAL SERVICE	Shotgun	Various	Crescent Firearms
ENFORCER	Pistol	45	Safari Arms
ERIKA	Pistol	4.25	Pfannl
ERMA	All	Various	Ermawerke
ERMUA 1924	Pistol	6.35	Acha
ERMUA 1925	Pistol	6.35	Ormachea
E.S.A.	Pistol	6.35/7.65	[Spain; 1920s]
ESCORT	Pistol	22	Echeverria
ESPECIAL	Pistol	6.35	Arrizabalaga
ESPINGARDA	Rev	38	Machado
ESSEX	Shotgun	Various	Crescent Firearms
ESSEX	Rifle/Shotgun	Various	Stevens
ESTRELA	Pistol	6.35/7.65	Echeverria
ETAI	Pistol	6.35	[Spain]
ETNA	Pistol	6.35	Salaberrin
EUREKA	Rev	22	Johnson, Bye
EUSKARO	Rev	38/44	Esprin Hermanos
EUSIA	Pistol	7.65/9S	[West Germany]
EXCELSIOR	Rev	32RF	Norwich Pistol
EXCELSIOR	Rev	0.1mm	SJ & D
EXPRESS	Rev	22	Bacon Arms
EXPRESS	Pistol	6.35/7.65	Urizar
EXTRACTEUR	Rev	7.5mm	Ancion Marx

F

Name	Type	Calibre	Maker
F.A.	Rev	32	Francisco Arizmendi

Name	Type	Calibre	Maker
F.A.G.	Rev	7.62/8	Arizmendi & Goenaga
FALCON	Pistol	7.65	Astra-Unceta
FAST	Pistol	Various	Echave y Arizmendi
FAULTLESS	Shotguns	Various	Crescent
FAVORIT	Pistol	6.35	[Spain]
FAVORIT	Rifle	Various	Frankonia
FAVORIT SAFARI	Rifle	Various	Frankonia
FAVORITE	Rev	22/32/38/41RF	Johnson, Bye
FAVORITE NAVY	Rev	44RF	Johnson, Bye
FEDERAL ARMS	Rev	32/38	Meriden
F.E.G.	Pistol	Various	Femaru
FIEL	Pistol	6.35/7.65	Erquiaga, Muguruzu
FIELD KING	Pistol	22	High Standard
FINNISH LION	Rifle	22	Valmet
FIREBALL	SS	221	Remington
FIREBIRD	Pistol	9P	Femaru
FLITE-KING	Pistol	22	High Standard
FLORIA	Pistol	6.35	[Spain]
FME	Pistol	6.35	FAMAE
FORBES	Shotgun	Various	Crescent
FOREHAND 1901	Rev	32	Hopkins & Allen
FORTUNA	Pistol	7.65	Unceta
FORTY-NINER	Rev	22	Harrington & Richardson
FOUR ACES	Rev	22	Svendsen
FOUR ACES	RP	22	ESFAC

Name	Type	Calibre	Maker
FOX	Pistol	6.35	Tomiska
FRANCAISE	Pistol	6.35	Societe Francaise
FRANCO	Pistol	6.35	Manufrance
FREEHAND	Rev	38	[Germany?]
FRONTIER	Rev	32RF	Norwich Falls
FRONTIER ARMY	Rev	44	Ronge
FURIA	Pistol	7.65	Ojanguren & Vidosa
FUROR	Pistol	7.65	Pyrenees

G

Name	Type	Calibre	Maker
G.A.C. FIREARMS MFG CO	Rev	32-20	Garate Anitua
GALEF	Pistol	7.65	[Spain]
GALEF STALLION	Rev	22/357	[Italy]
GALLIA	Pistol	7.65	Pyrenees
GALLUS	Pistol	6.35	Retolaza
GAME GETTER	Rifle/Shotg	.22/410	Marble
GARRISON	Rev	22	Hopkins & Allen
GARRUCHA	DB Pistol	22	Amadeo Rossi
GAUCHO	Pistol	22	[Argentine]
GAULOIS	Rep Pist	8	Manufrance
G & E	Rev	22	Gerstenberger
GECADO	Pistol	6.35	Dornheim
GECO	Rev	6.35/7.65	Genschow
GECO	Shotgun	12	Genschow
GEM	Rev	22	Bacon Arms
GEM	SS	22/30RF	Stevens Tool
GERMAN BULLDOG	Rev	32/38	Genschow

Name	Type	Calibre	Maker
G.H.	Rev	38	Guisasola Hermanos
GIBRALTAR	Rrev	32/38	Meriden
GIRALDA	Pistol	7.65	Bolumburu
GLENFIELD	Rifle	30-30	Marlin
GLORIA	Pistol	6.35/7.65	Bolumburu
G.M.C.	Pistol	22	Garb, Moretti & Co
GOLDEN BISON	Rev	.45-70	Super Six
GOLDEN EAGLE	Rifle	Various	Nikko
GOLIAT	Rev	32	Antonio Errasti
GOOSE GUN	Shotgun	Various	Stevens
GOVERNOR	Rev	22	Bacon Arms
GP-100	Rev	357	Rugcr
GRAND	Rev	357/38	Zbrojovka Brno
GRIZZLY	Pistol	Various	LAR
GRUENEL	Rifle	Various	Gruenig & Elmiger
G.S.M.	Pistl	7.65	[Hungary]
GUARDIAN	Rev	22/32RF	Bacon Arms
GUEURE	Pistol	6.35	Arizmendi
GYROJET	Pistol	13mm	MBA

H

Name	Type	Calibre	Maker
HAKIM	Rifle	7.92	Maadi
HALF-BREED	Rev	32RF	Hopkins & Allen
HAMADA	Pistol	7.65	Japan Gun Co
HANDY MODEL 1917	Pistol	9S	[Spain]
HARDBALLER	Pistol	45	AMT

Name	Type	Calibre	Maker	Name	Type	Calibre	Maker
HARD PAN	Rev	22/32RF	Hood	HOPKINS, C.W.	Rev	32/38RF	Bacon Mfg Co
HARTFORD ARMS CO	Rev	32RF	Norwich Falls	HORSE DESTROYER	Rev	38	Gaztanaga
HARTFORD ARMS CO	Shotgun	Various	Crescent Firearms	HOWARD ARMS	Rev	32/38	Meriden
HARVARD	Shotgun	Various	Crescent Firearms	HOWARD ARMS	Shotgun	Various	Crescent Firearms
HAWES WESTERN MARSHAL	Rev	Various	Sauer	H.R.	SS	22	Haidurov
HAWES SILVER CITY	Rev	22	Sauer	H.S.	Rev	22	Herbert Schmidt
HAWES CHIEF MARSHAL	Rev	Various	Sauer	HUDSON	Pistol	6.35	[Spain]
H&D	Rev	Various	Henrion & Dassy	HUNTER	SS	Various	Wichita Arms
HEGE	Pistol/Combo	Various	Hebsacker	HUNTER'S PET	SS	22/25/32RF	Stevens
HEIM	Pistol	6.35	Heinzelmann	H.V.	Pistol	6.35	Hourat
HELFRICHT	Pistol	6.35	Krauser	HY HUNTER	Rev	22	Rohm
HELKRA	Pistol	6.35	Krauser	HY-SCORE	Rev	22	Rohm
HELVICE (or HELVECE)	Pistol	6.35	Grand Precision				
HE-MO	Pistol	7.65	Moritz	**I**			
HERCULES	Shotgun	Various	Stevens	I.A.G.	Pistol	7.65	Galesi
HERITAGE 1	Rev	45	Phelps	IDEAL	SS	22	Buchel
HERMAN	Pistol	6.35	[Belgium]	IDEAL	Pistol	6.35	Dusek
HERMETIC	Pistol	7.65	Bernadon-Martin	ILLINOIS ARMS CO	Rev	6.35	Pickert
HERMITAGE	Shotgun	Various	Stevens	IMPERATO	Pistol	6.35/7.65	Heckler & Koch
HERMITAGE ARMS CO	Shotgun	Various	Crescent Firearms	IMPERIAL	Pistol	6.35	Tomas de Urizar
HERMITAGE GUN CO	Shotgun	Various	Crescent Firearms	IMPERIAL	Rev	22/32RF	{USA}
HERO	Rev	22/32/38/41RF	Rupertus	IMPERIAL ARMS	Rev	32/38RF	Hopkins & Allen
HEROLD	Rifle	22	Jager	INDIAN	Pistol	7.65	Gaztanaga
HERTER	Rev	357	[Germany]	INDISPENSABLE	Rev	5.5mm	[Belgium]
HEYM	Rev	22	[Germany]	INFALLIBLE	Pistol	7.65	Davis-Warner
HIGHLANDER	Rifle	Various	Kassnar	INGRAM	SMG	9/45	MAC
HIGH SIERRA	Rev	22	High Standard	INSPECTOR	Rev	38	Uberti
HIJO	Pistol	6.35/7.65	Galesi	INTERNATIONAL	Rev	22/32Rf	Hood
HIJO QUICK-BREAK	Rev	22/32/38	Iver Johnson	INTERNATIONAL	SS	Various	Wichita Arms

Name	Type	Calibre	Maker
INTERSTATE ARMS CO	Shotgun	Various	Crescent Firearms
INVICTA	Pistol	7.65	Salaberrin
IRIQUOIS	Rev	22	Remington
IRIS	Rev	32-20	Ojanguren
ISARD	Pistol	9B-B	[Spain]
IXOR	Pistol	7.65	Pyrenees
IZARRA	Pistol	7.65	Echeverria

J

Name	Type	Calibre	Maker
JACKRABBIT	Rifle/Shotgun	Various	Continental Arms
JACKSON ARMS CO	Shotgun	Various	Crescent Firearms
JAGA	Pistol	6.35	Dusek
J.CESAR	Pistol	6.35	Urizar
JENKINS SPECIAL	Pistol	6.35	[Spain]
JERICHO	Pistol	9P	Ta'as
JETFIRE	Pistol	6.35	Beretta
JEWEL	Rev	22	Hood
J.G.A.	Rev	7.65	Anschutz
JIEFFECO	Pistol	6.35/7.65	Robar
JOHA	Pistol	6.35/7.65	[Spain]
JO-LO-AR	Pistol	7.65	Arrizabalaga
JUBALA	Pistol	6.35	Larranaga & Elartza
JUBILEE	Rifle	22	Vickers
JUNIOR	Pistol	6.35	Pretoria Arms Factory
JUNIOR	Pistl	22/6.35	Colt
JUPITER	Pistol	7.65	Grand Precision
JUPITER	Rev	5.5mm	Francotte

Name	Type	Calibre	Maker

K

Name	Type	Calibre	Maker
KABA SPEZIAL	Pistol	7.65	Menz
KABA SPECIAL	Pistol	6.35/7.65	Arizmendi
KAPITAIN	Pistol	7.65	Alkartasuna
KAPPORA	Pistol	6.35	[Spain]
KEBLER	Pistol	7.65	[Spain]
KING COBRA	Rev	357	Colt
KINGLAND SPECIAL	Shotgun	Various	Crescent Firearms
KINGLAND 10-STAR	Shotgun	Various	Crescent Firearms
KING NITRO	Rifle/Shotgun	Various	Stevens
KIRRIKALE	Pistol	9S	MKEK
KITTEMAUG	Rev	32RF	[USA}
KITU	Pistol	6.35	[Spain]
KLESZEZEWSKI	Pistol	6.35	[Spain]
KNICKERBOCKER	Shotgun	Various	Crescent Firearms
KNOCKABOUT	Shotgun	Various	Stevens
KNOCKABOUT	SS	22	Sheridan
KNOXALL	Shotgun	Various	Crescent Firearms
KOBOLD	Rev	Various	Raick Freres
KOBRA	Pistol	6.35	[Germany]
KOLIBRI	Pistol	3mm	Grabner
KOLIBRI	Pistol	6.35	Arizaga
KRAUSER	Pistol	22	Manurhin

L

Name	Type	Calibre	Maker
LA BASQUE	Pistol	6.35	[Spain]
LA's DEPUTY	Rev	22	Herbert Schmidt
LADYSMITH	Rev	32,38	Smith & Wesson

Name	Type	Calibre	Maker	Name	Type	Calibre	Maker
LA FURY	Pistol	6.35	Reck	LE RAPIDE	Pistol	6.35	Bertrand
LA INDUSTRIA	Pistol	7.65	Orbea Hermanos	LE SANS PARIEL	Pistol	6.35	Pyrenees
LA LIRA	Pistol	7.65	Garate Anitua	LE SECOURS	Pistol	6.35	Grand Precision
LAMPO	RP	8mm	Tribuzio	LE SECOURS	Pistol	7.65	Tomas de Urizar
LANCER	Pistol	22	Echeverria	LE STEPH	Pistol	6.35	Bergeron
LA SALLE	Shotgun	Various	Manufrance	LE TOUT ACIER	Pistol	6.35/7.65	Pyrenees
LAWMAN	Rev	357	Colt	LEADER	Rev	22/32RF	Hopkins & Allen
L.E.	Rev	32	Larranaga y Elartza	LEADER GUN CO	Shotgun	Various	Crescent Firearms
				LEE SPECIAL	Shotgun	Various	Crescent Firearms
LE AGENT	Rev	8mm	Manufrance	LEE'S MUNNER SPECIAL	Shotgun	Various	Crescent Firearms
LE BASQUE	Pistol	7.65	Urizar	LEFT WHEELER	Rev	32	HDH
LE BRONG	Rev	5/6.35/7.65	Crucelegui	LEGIA	Pistol	6.35	Pieper
LE CAVALIER	Pistol	7.65/9S	Bayonne	LEONHARDT	Pistol	7.65	Gering
LE CHASSEUR	Pistol	11	Bayonne	LEPCO	Pistol	6.35	[Spain]
L'ECLAIR	Rev	6mm	Garate Anitua	LES.	Pistol	9P	Steyr-Mannlicher
LE COLONIAL	Rev	8mm	Manufrance	LESTON	Pistol	6.35	Unceta
LL DRAGON	Pistol	6.35	Urizar	L.H.	Pistol	6.35	[Germany]
LE FRANCAIS	Pistol	Various	Manufrance	LIBERATOR	SS	.45	Guide Lamp
LE GENDARME	Pistol	9S	Bayonne	LIBERTI	Pistol	7.65	[Spain]
LEGITIMO TANQUE	Rev	38	Ojanguren & Vidosa	LIBERTY	Rev	22/32RF	Hood
				LIBERTY	Pistol	6.35/7.65	Retolaza
LE MAJESTIC	Pistol	7.65	Pyrenees	LIBERTY-11	Rev	22	Herbert Schmidt
LE MARTINY	Pistol	6.35	[Belgium]	LIBERTY RG-12	Rev	22	Rohm
LE METEORE	Pistol	6.35	[Belgium]	LIBERTY CHIEF	Rev	.38	Miroku
LE MILITAIRE	Pistol	9P	Bayonne	LIBIA	Pistol	6.35/7.65	Beistegui
LE MONOBLOC	Pistol	6.35	Jacquemart	LIEGOISE D'ARMES A FEU	Pistol	6.35/7.65	Robar
LE NOVO	Rev	6.35	Galand	LIGHTNING	Pistol	6.35	Echave y Arizmendi
LE PETIT FORMIDABLE	Rev	6.35	Manufrance				
LE PROTECTOR	RP	6mm	Turbiaux	LILIPUT	Pistol	4.25/6.35	Menz

Name	Type	Calibre	Maker
LILIPUT	Pistol	6.35	Fegyver
LINCOLN	Rev	32	Ancion Marx
LINCOLN	Rev	22/32RF	HDH
LINCOLN BOSSU	Rev	5.5/6.35	HDH
LINCOLN BULLDOG	Rev	32	Robar
LINCOLN HAMMERLESS	Rev	320	Robar
LINDA	Pistol	.22	Wilkinson Arms
LION	Rev	22/32/38/41RF	Johnson, Bye
LITTLE ALL RIGHT	Rev	22	All Right Firearms
LITTLE GIANT	Rev	22	Bacon Arms
LITTLE JOHN	Rev	22	Hood
LITTLE JOKER	Rev	22	Marlin, John
LITTLE PET	Shotgun	Various	Stevens
LITTLE TOM	Pistol	6.35/7.65	Tomiska
LITTLE TOM	Pistol	6.35	Wiener Waffenfabrik
LLAMA	Pistol	Various	Gabilondo
LLANERO	Rev	.22	[Argentina]
LOBO	Pistol	6.35	[Spain]
LONGHORN	Rev	22	High Standard
LONGINES	Pistol	7.65	Cooperativa Orbea
LONG RANGE WONDER	Shotgun	Various	Sears Roebuck
LONG TOM	Shotgun	Various	Stevens
LOOKING GLASS	Pistol	6.35/7.65	Acha
LOSADA	Pistol	7.65	[Germany]
LUGER	Pistol	7.65P/9P	Stoeger
LUNA	SS	22	Buchel
LUR-PANZER	Pistol	22	Echave y Arizmendi [Spain]
LUSITANIA	Pistoo	7.65	[Spain]
LUTETIA	Pistol	6.35	[Spain]
LYNX	Rev	357	[South Africa, ca 1979]

M

Name	Type	Calibre	Maker
M & H	Rev	.44-40	Hopkins & Allen
MAB	Pistol	Various	Bayonne
MAJESTIC	Pistol	6.35	[Spain]
MAGMATIC	Pistol	44Mag	Powers
MALTBY, HENLEY & Co	Rev	22/32/38	Columbia Armory
MAMBA	Pistul	9P	Relay Products
MAMBA	Pistol	9P	Navy Arms
MARINA	Pistol	6.35	Bolumburu
MARKE	Pistol	6.35	Bascaran
MARK X	Rifle	Various	Zastava
MARQUIS OF LORNE	Rev	22/32RF	Hood
MARS	Pistol	6.35/7.65	Kohout
MARS	Pistol	9/45	Webley
MARS	Pistol	9BB	Pieper
MARS	Pistol	7.65	Pyrenees
MARSHWOOD	Shotgun	Various	Stevens
MARTE	Pistol	6.35	Erquiaga, Muguruzu
MARTIAL	Rev	357	Gabilondo
MARTIAN	Pistol	6.35/7.65	Martin A Bascaran
MARTIGNY	Pistol	6.35	Jorge Bascaran

502

Name	Type	Calibre	Maker	Name	Type	Calibre	Maker
MASSACHUSETTS ARMS	Shotgun	Various	Stevens	MOHAWK	Shotgun	Various	Crescent Firearms
MAXIM	Pistol	6.35	Galesi	MOHEGAN	Rev	32RF	Hood
MAXIMUM	SS	Various	MOA Corp	MONARCH	Rev	22/32/38/41RF	Hopkins & Allen
MELIOR	Pistol	Various	Robar	MONDIAL	Pistol	6.35	Arrizaga
MENTA	Pistol	6.35/7.65	Menz	MONITOR	Shotgun	Various	Stevens
MERCURY	Pistol/Shotgun	Various	Robar	MONOBLOC	Pistol	6.35	Jacquemart
MERKE	Pistol	6.35	Ormachea	M.S.	Pistol	6.35/7.65	Modesto Santos
MERKUR	Rifle	Various	Kind	MOSSER	Pistol	6.35	[Spain]
MERVEILLEAUX	RP	6mm	[France]	MOUNTAIN EAGLE	Rev	32RF	Hopkins & Allen
METEOR	Rifle	22	Stevens	MUELLER SPECIAL	Rev	6.35	Decker
METROPOLITAN	Shotgun	Various	Crescent Firearms	MUGICA	Pistols	Various	Gabilondo
METROPOLITAN POLICE	Rev	32RF	Norwich Falls	MUNICIPAL	Rev	8mm	HDH
MIDLAND GUN CO	Rifle	Various	Parker-Hale	MUSEUM	Pistol	6.35	Echeverria
MIKROS	Pistol	Various	Pyrenees	MUSTANG	Pistol	9S	Colt
MILADY	Rev	7.65	Ancion-Marx	MUSTANG POCKETLITE	Pistol	9S	Colt
MILADY	Rev	8mm	Jannsen Fils	MUXI	Pistol	6.35	[Spain]
MILITARY	Pistol	6.35	Retolaza				

N

Name	Type	Calibre	Maker	Name	Type	Calibre	Maker
MILITARY MODEL 1914	Pistol	7.65	Retolaza	NALAVA	Pistol	6.35	Eiler
MILITAR Y POLICIA	Rev	38	Ojanguren & Vidosa	NAPOLEON	Rev	22/32RF	Ryan
MILITAR Y POLICIAS	Rev	38	Ojanguren & Matiade	NATIONAL	Rev	32/38RF	Norwich Falls
				NATIONAL	SS	41RF	Norwich Falls
MINERVA	Pistol	6.35	Grand Precision	NATIONAL ARMS CO	Shotgun	Various	Crescent Firearms
MINIMA	Pistol	6.35	Boyer	NERO	Rev	22/32RF	Rupertus
MINX	Pistol	6.35	Beretta	NERO	Rev	22/32RF	Hopkins & Allen
MISSISSIPPI VALLEY	Shotgun	Various	Crescent Firearms	NEVER MISS	Rev	22/32/41RF	Marlin
MITRAILLEUSE	RP	8mm	St Etienne	NEW ACE	Pistol	22	Colt
MITRAILLEUSE	Pistol	6.35	[Spain]	NEW BABY	Rev	22	Kolb
ML	Pistol	6.35/7.65	Robar	NEW CHIEFTAIN	Shotgun	Various	Stevens

Name	Type	Calibre	Maker	Name	Type	Calibre	Maker
NEW JAGUAR	Pistol	22/7.65	Beretta	OLYMPIA	Pistol	6.35/7.65	SEAM
NEW NAMBU	Rev/Pistol	Various	Shin Chuo Kogyo	OLYMPIC	Shotgun	Various	Stevens
NEW RIVAL	Shotgun	Various	Crescent Firearms	O.M.	Rev	Various	Ojanguren y
NEW YORK ARMS CO	Shotgun/Rev	Various	Crescent Firearms				Matiade
NEW YORK PISTOL CO	Rev	22	Hood	OMEGA	Pistol	6.35/7.65	Armero
NEWPORT	Shotgun	Various	Stevens				Especialistas
NIGHTHAWK	Pistol	9P	Weaver	OMEGA	Pistol	10mm	Springfield
NITRO PROOF	Shotgun	Various	Stevens	OMEGA	Rev	22	Gerstenberger
NIVA	Pistol	6.35	Kohout	OMEGA	Rev	32	Weirauch
NOMAD	Pistol	22	Browning Arms	OMEGA III	Rifle	Various	Hi-Shear
NONPARIEL	Rev	32RF	Norwich Falls	OMNI	Pistol	45/9P	Gabilondo
NORTHWESTERNER	Rifle/Shotgun	22/Various	Stevens	ONANDIA	Rev	32	Onandia
NORWICH ARMS CO	Shotgun	Various	Crescent Firearms				Hermanos
NORWICH ARMS CO	Rev	22/32RF	Norwich Falls	OREA	Rifle	Various	Orechowsky
NOT-NAC MFG CO	Shotgun	Various	Crescent Firearms	ORTGIES	Pistol	Various	Deutsche Werke
NOVELTY	RP	32	Mossberg	OSCILLANT AZUL	Rev	38	Eulogio Arostegui
N.Y.PISTOL CO	Rev	22	Hood Arms Co	O.V.	Rev	32	Ojanguren &
							Vidosa

O

Name	Type	Calibre	Maker	Name	Type	Calibre	Maker
				OWA	Pistol	6.35	Osterreich
OAK LEAF	Shotgun	Various	Stevens	OXFORD ARMS	Shotgun	Various	Stevens
OBREGON	Pistol	.45	Fab de Armas	OXFORD ARMS CO	Shotgun	Various	Crescent Firearms
			Mexico	OYEZ	Pistol	6.35	[Belgium]
OCULTO	Rev	32/38	Orueta Hermanos				
OFF-DUTY	Rev	38	Charter Arms				

P

Name	Type	Calibre	Maker
O.H.	Rev	22/32/38	Orbea Hermanos
OICET	Rev	38	Antonio Errasti
O.K.	SS	22	Marlin
OKZET	Pistol	6.35	Menz
OLD TIMER	Shotgun	Various	Stevens

Name	Type	Calibre	Maker
PADRE	Pistol	7.65	Galesi
P.A.F.	Pistol	6.35	Pretoria Arms
			Factory
PAGE-LEWIS ARMS CO	Shotgun	Various	Stevens
PALMETTO	Shotgun	Various	Stevens

Name	Type	Calibre	Maker	Name	Type	Calibre	Maker
PANTAX	Pistol	22	Woerther	PHOENIX ARMS CO	Pistol	6.35	Lowell
PARAGON	Shotgun	Various	Stevens	PICCOLO	Rev	38	Gabilondo
PARAMOUNT	Pistol	6.35/7.65	Retolaza	PIEDMONT	Shotgun	Various	Crescent
PARKER SAFETY				PILSEN	Pistol	7.65	Zrojovka Plzen
HAMMERLESS	Rev	32	Columbia Armory	PINAFORE	Rev	22	Norwich Falls
PAROLE	Rev	22	Hopkins & Allen	PINKERTON	Pistol	6.35	Gaspar Arizaga
PATENT	Pistol	6.35	[Spain]	PIONEER	Rev	22/38RF	[USA}
PATHFINDER	Rev	22	Charter Arms	PIONEER	Rifle	22	Stevens
PATHFINDER	Pistol	6.35	Echave & Arizmendi	PIONEER ARMS CO	Shotgun	Various	Crescent
				PISTOLET AUTOMATIQUE	Pistol	6.35	Arizmendi
PATRIOT	Rev	32RF	Norwich Falls	PLUS ULTRA	Pistol	7.65	Gabilondo
PEACEKEEPER	Rev	357	Colt	POLICE BULLDOG	Rev	44	Charter Arms]
PEERLESS	Rifle	22	Stevens	POLICE SERVICE SIX	Rev	357	Ruger
PEERLESS	Shotgun	Various	Crescent Firearms	POLICE UNDERCOVER	Rev	32/38	Charter Arms
PEERLESS	Rev	32RF	Hood	POLICEMAN	Pistol	6.35	Manufrance
PENETRATOR	Rev	32RF	Norwich Falls	PONY	Pistol	9S	Iver Johnson
PERFECT	Rev	38	Fochi & Weeks	POPULAIRE	SS	22	Manufrance
PERFECT	Pistol	7.65	Pyrenees	PORTSIDER	Pistol	45	Falcon
PERFECTION	Shotgun	Various	Crescent	POSSE	Rev	22	High Standard
PERFECTION				POWERMASTER	SS	22	Wamo Mfg Co
AUTOMATIC	Rev	32	Forehand Arms	PRAGA	Pistol	7.65	SEAM
PERFECTIONNE	Rev	8mm	Pieper	PRAGA	Pistol	6.35	Novotny
PERFECTO	Rev	32	Orbea Hermanos	PRAIRIE KING	Rev	22	Norwich Falls
				PRATIC	Pistol	6.35	[Spain]
PERLA	Pistol	6.35	Dusek	PRECISION	Pistol	6.357.65	Grand Precision
PETITE	Rev	.22 Short	Iver Johnson	PREMIER	Pistol	6.35/7.65	Urizar
PEUGOT	Pistol	6.35	[France]	PREMIER	Rifle	22	Stevens
PHOENIX	Pistol	6.35	Robar	PREMIER	Rev	22/38RF	Ryan
PHOENIX	Pistol	6.35	Urizar	PREMIER TRAIL BLAZER	Rifle	22	Stevens

505

Name	Type	Calibre	Maker	Name	Type	Calibre	Maker
PRICE J.W.	Shotgun	Various	Stevens	**Q**			
PRIMA	Pistol	6.35	Pyrenees				
PRINCE	SS	.50RF	Iver Johnson	QUAIL	Shotgun	Various	Crescent Firearms
PRINCEPS	Pistol	7.65	Urizar	QUAILS FARGO	Shotgun	Various	Dakin
PRINCESS	Rev	22	[USA]	QUEEN CITY	Shotgun	Various	Crescent Firearms
PRINCIPE	Pistol	6.35	Urizar	**R**			
PROTECTOR	Pistol	6.35	Echave & Arizmendi	RADIUM	Pistol	6.35	Gabilondo
PROTECTOR	Pistol	6.35	Santiago Salaberrin	RANGER	Pistol	22	Pyrenees
				RANGER	Rev	32RF	Dickinson
PROTECTOR	Rev	22/32RF	Norwich Falls	RANGER	Rifle/Shotgun	Various	Stevens
PROTECTOR	Rev	22	Protector	RANGER No 2	Rev	32RF	Dickinson
PUMA	Pistol	22	Bcretta	RANGER No 2	Rev	22/32RF	Hopkins & Allen
PUMA	Pistol	6.35	Urizar	RAPID-MAXIMA	Pistol	7.65	Pyrenees
PUPPET	Pistol	7.65	Ojanguren & Vidosa	RAVEN	Pistol	6.35	Dornheim
				RAYON	Pistol	6.35	[Spain]
PUPPET	Rev	6.35	Ojanguren & Vidosa	R.E.	Pistol	9BB	Republica Espana
PUPPY	Rev	5mm	Crucelegui	RECKY	Rev	22	Reck
PUPPY	Rev	5mm	Retolaza	REDHAWK	Rev	44	Ruger
PUPPY	Rev	5.5mm	Francisco Arizmendi	RECORD	SS	22	Anschutz
				RED CLOUD	Rev	32RF	[USA]
PUPPY	Rev	22	Izidro Gaztanaga	RED JACKET	Rev	22/32RF	Lee Arms
				REFORM	RP	6.35	Schuler
PUPPY	Rev	22	Ojanguren & Marcaido	REFORM	Pistol	6.35	[Spain]
				REGENT	Pistol	6.35/7.65	Bolumburu
PUPPY	Rev	Various	HDH	REGENT	Rev	22	Burgsmuller
PYTHON	Rev	357	Colt	REGENT	Rifle	Various	Kassnar
P.Z.K.	Pistol	6.35	Kohout	REGINA	Pistol	6.35/7.65	Bolumburu
				REGNUM	RP	6.35	Menz

Name	Type	Calibre	Maker
REID PATENT	Rev	22/32/41RF	Irving
REIFGRABER	Pistol	7.65	Union Arms
REIMS	Pistol	6.35/7.65	Azanza y Arrizabalaga
REINA	Pistol	7.65	Pyrenees
RENARD	Pistol	6.35	Echave & Arizmendi
REPUBLIC	Pistol	7.65	Arrizabalaga
RETRIEVER	Rev	32RF	Ryan
REV-O-NOC	Shotgun	Various	Crescent Firearms
REX	Pistol	6.35/7.65/9S	Bolumburu
RG	Rev	Various	Rohm GmbH
RICKARD ARMS	Shotgun	Various	Crescent Firearms
RIGARMI	Pistol	22/6.35/7.65	Galesi
RIVAL	pistol	6.35	Union, Eibar
ROBIN HOOD	Rev	22/32RF	Hood
ROLAND	Pistol	6.35/7.65	Arizmendi
ROME	Rev	22	Rome
ROMO	Rev	22	Rohm
ROWNHNES	Pistol	7.65	[Spain]
ROYAL	Rev	22/32RF	Hopkins & Allen
ROYAL	Rev	38	[Spain]
ROYAL	Pistol	Various	Zulaica
ROYAL NOVELTY	Pistol	6.35/7.65	Zulaica
RUBI	Pistol	22	Venturini
RUBY	Pistol	Various	Gabilondo
RUBY EXTRA	Revolver	Various	Gabilondo
RUMMEL	Shotgun	Various	Crescent Firearms
RURAL	Rev	32	Garantizada

Name	Type	Calibre	Maker

S

Name	Type	Calibre	Maker
S.A.	Pistol	6.35	Societe d'Armes
S & A	Rev	38	Suinaga & Aramperri
SABLE BABY	Rev	22	[Belgium]
S.A.C.M.	Pistol	7.65 Longue	SACM
SAFETY POLICE	Rev	32	Hopkins & Allen
ST HUBERT	Pistol	7.65	Pyrenees
SALSO	Pistol	6.35	Unceta
SALVAJE	Pistol	6.35	Ojanguren & Vidosa
SATA	Pistol	22/6.35	Sabotti & Tanfoglio
SATURN	Rifle	Various	Kind
SCARAB SCORPION	Pistol	9P	Armitage
SCHMEISSER	Pistol	6.35	Haenel
SCHONBERGER	Pistol	8mm	Steyr-Mannlicher
SCHOUBOE	Pistol	7.65	Madsen
SCHUTZMANN	Rifle	Various	Kind
SCORPIO	Rev	38	Gabilondo
SCOTT ARMS CO	Rev	32RF	Norwich Falls
SCOTT REVOLVER-RIFLE	Rev-Rifle	38RF	Hopkins & Allen
SCOUT	Shotgun	Various	Stevens
SCOUT	Rev	32RF	Hood
SECRET SERVICE SPECIAL	Rev	32/38	Iver Johnson
SECURITAS	Pistol	6.35	St Etienne Automatique
SECURITY SIX	Rev	357	Ruger

Name	Type	Calibre	Maker	Name	Type	Calibre	Maker
SELECTA	Pistol	6.35/7.65	Echave & Arizmendi	SPITFIRE	Pistol	9P	Slough
SELECTA	Pistol	7.65	Pyrenees	SPORT KING	Pistol	22	High Standard
SELF	Pistol	6.35/7.65	[Spain]	SPORTSMAN	Shotgun	Various	Stevens
SENTINEL	Rev	22/357	High Standard	SPORTSMAN	Shotgun	Various	Crescent Firearms
SHARP-SHOOTER	Pistol	6.35/7.65/9S	Arrizabalaga	SPORTSMAN BUSH & FIELD	Rifle	Various	Marathon
SHERRY	Pistol	.22	Wilkinson	SPRINGFIELD ARMS	Shotgun	Various	Crescent Firearms
SILESIA	Pistol	6.35	SEAM	SPRINTER	Pistol	6.35	Bolumburu
SILHOUETTE	SS	Various	Wichita Arms	SPY	Rev	22	Norwich Falls
SILHOUETTE	Pistol	.44	Automag	SQUARE DEAL	Shotgun	Various	Crescent Firearms
SIMPLEX	Pistol	8mm	Bergmann	SQUIBMAN	All	Various	Squires., Blngham
SINGER	Pistol	6.35/7.65	Arizmendi & Goenaga	STALLION	Rev	Various	Uberti
SINGER	Pistol	6.35	Dusek	STAR	Pistol	Various	Echeverria
SINGLE SIX	Rev	22	Ruger	STARLET	Pistol	6.35	Echeverria
SIVISPACEM	Pistol	7.65	SEAM	STAR VESTOPKCET	Rev	2?/32RF	Johnson, Bye
SIVISPACEM PARABELLUM	Pistol	6.35	Thieme & Edeler	STATE ARMS CO	Shotgun	Various	Crescent Firearms
SLAVIA	Pistol	6.35	Vilimec	STENDA	Pistol	7.65	Stendawerke
SLOCUM	Rev	32RF	Brooklyn Arms	STERN	SS	22	Buchel
S.M.	Pistol	6.35	[Spain]	STERN-PISTOLE	Pistol	6.35	Wahl
SMITH AMERICANO	Rec	32/38/44	Antonio Errasti	STINGRAY	Rev	22	Rohm
SMOK	Pistol	6.35	Nakulski	STOSEL	Pistol	6.35/7.65	Retolaza
SMOKER	Rev	22/32/38/41RF	Johnson, Bye	SULLIVAN ARMS CO	Shotgun	Various	Crescent Firearms
SNAKE CHARMER	Shotg	410	Sporting	SUPER AZUL	MP	7.63	Eulogio Arostegui
SOUTHERN ARMS CO	Shotgun	Various	Crescent Firearms	SUPER BLACKHAWK	Rev	44	Ruger
SPEED SIX	Rev	357	Ruger	SUPER COMANCHE	Rev	357/44	Gabilondo
SPENCER GUN CO	Shotgun	Various	Crescent Firearms	SUPER DESTROYER	Pistol	7.65	Gaztanaga, Trocaola
SPENCER SAFETY	Rev	38	Columbia Armory	SUPERIOR	Pistol	6.35	[Spain]
				SUPER REDHAWK	Rev	44	Ruger

Name	Type	Calibre	Maker	Name	Type	Calibre	Maker
SUPERMATIC	Pistol	22	High Standard	TEUF-TEUF	Pistol	6.35	Arizmendi & Goenaga
SURETE	Pistol	7.65	Gaztanaga				
SWAMP ANGEL	Rev	41RF	Forehand & Wadsworth	TEUF-TEUF	Pistol	6.35	[Belgium]
				TEXAS LONGHORN	Rev	Various	Texas
SWIFT	Rev	38	Iver Johnson	TEXAS MARSHAL	Rev	45	Sauer
SYMPATHIQUE	Pistol	7.65	Pyrenees	TEXAS RANGER	Rev	38	Unies de Liege
				TEXAS RANGER	Shotgun	12/16	Stevens
T				THALCO	Rev	22	Rohm
T.A.C.	Rev	Various	Trocaola Aranzabal	THAMES AUTOMATIC	Rev	22/32/38	Thames
				THE VICTORY	Pistol	6.35	Zulaica
TANARMI	Pistol	22	Tanfoglio	THOMAS	Pistol	45	James Ordnance
TANKE	Rev	38	Orueta Hermanos				
TANNE	Rifle	Various	Kind	THOMPSON	SMG	.45	Auto-Ordnance
TANQUE	Pistol	6.35	Ojanguren & Vidosa	THUNDER	Pistol	6.35	Bascaran
				THUNDER CHIEF	Rev	22	Squibman
TARGA	Pistol	Various	Tanfoglio	TIGER	Shotgun	Various	Crescent Firearms [USA]
TARGET BULLDOG	Rev	357/44	Charter Arms	TIGER	Rev	32RF	
TARN	Pistol	9P	Swift Rifle Co	TIGRE	Pistol	6.35	Garate Anitua
TATRA	Pistol	6.35	Alkartasuna	TIKKA	Rifle	Various	Tikkakoski
TATRA	Pistol	6.35	SEAM	TIRO AL BLANCO	Rev	38	Ojanguren & Matlade
TAULER	Pistol	Various	Gabilondo				
T.E.	Pistol	7.65	Thieme & Edeler	TISAN	Pistol	6.35	Salaberrin
TED WILLIAMS	Shotguns	Various	Sears Roebuck	TITAN	Pistol	6.35	Armigas
TELL	SS	22	Buchel	TITAN	Pistol	7.65	Retolaza
TERRIBLE	Pistol	6.35	Arrizabalaga	TITAN	Pistol	6.35	Tanfoglio
TERRIER	Rev	22/32/38/41RF	Rupertus [Germany]	TITANIC	Pistol	6.35/7.65	Retolaza
TERRIER ONE	Rev	32		TIWA	Pistol	6.35	[Spain]
TERROR	Rev	32RF	Forehand & Wadsworth	TOKAGYPT	Pistol	9P	Femaru
				TOMPKINS	SS	22	Varsity Mfg Co

509

Name	Type	Calibre	Maker	Name	Type	Calibre	Maker
TORPILLE	Pistol	7.65	[Spain]	UNCLE SAM	SS	.50RF	Iver Johnson
TOURISTE	Pistol	7.65	Pyrenees	UNDERCOVER	Rev	38	Charter Arms
TOWERS POLICE SAFETY	Rev	38RF	Hopkins & Allen]	UNDERCOVERETTE	Rev	32	Charter Arms
TOZ	Pistol	6.34	Tulskii	UNION	Pistol	7.65	Fabrique Francaise
TRAILSMAN	Rev	22	Iver Johnson				
TRAMP'S TERROR	Rev	22	Hopkins & Allen	UNION	Pistol	6.35/7.65	Seytres
TRIDENT	Rev	38	Renato Gamba	UNION	Pistol	6.35/7.65	Unceta
TRIFIRE	Pistol	45	Arminex	UNION	Pistol	6.35	Tomas de Urizar
TRIOMPHE	Pistol	6.35	Apaolozo Hermanos	UNION ARMERA	Pistol	6.35	Union Armera Eibarens
TRIOMPHE FRANCAISE	Pistol	7.65	Pyrenees	UNION JACK	Rev	22/32RF	Hood
TRIPLEX	Pistol	6.35	Domingo Acha	UNION SALES CO	Rev	9RF	[Germany]
TRIUMPH	Pistol	7.65	Garate Anitua	UNIQUE	Rev/RP	32/38RF	Shattuck
TROOPER	Rev	22/357	Colt	UNIQUE	Pistol	Various	Pyrenees
TRUE BLUE	Rev	32RF	Norwich Falls	UNIQUE CORSAIR	Pistol	22	Echeverria
TRUST	Pistol	6.35/7.65	Grand Precision	UNIQUE ESCORT	Pistol	22	Echeverria
TRUST SUPRA	Pistol	6.35	Grand Precision	UNIS	Pistol	7.65	Pyrenees
TTIBAR	Pistol	22	S.R.L.	UNIS	Pistol	6.35	Santiago Salaberrin
TUE-TUE	Rev	Various	Galand				
TURNER & ROSS	Rev	22	Hood	UNIVERSAL	Rev	32	Hopkins & Allen
TWO-BIT	Pistol	6.35	Steel City	U.S.ARMS CO	Shotgun	Various	Crescent Firearms
TYCOON	Rev	All RF	Johnson, Bye	U.S.ARMS CO	Rev	22/32/38/41RF	US Arms
				U.S.REVOLVER CO	Rev	22/32/38	Iver Johnson

U

Name	Type	Calibre	Maker
U.A.E.	Pistol	6.35	Union Armera Eibarens
U.A.Z.	SS	22	Anschutz
U.C.	Pistol	6.35	Urrejola & Co
U.M.C.ARMS CO	Rev	32RF	Norwich Falls

V

Name	Type	Calibre	Maker
VAINQUER	Pistol	6.35	Aurelio Mendiola
VALIANT	Rifle	22	Stevens
VALOR	Rev	22	Rohm
VELO-BROM	Rev	6mm/8mm	Retolaza

Name	Type	Calibre	Maker
VELO-DOG	Rev	5mm	Galand (and many others)
VELO-MITH	Rev	6.35	Crucelegui
VELO-MITH	Rev	6.35	Ojanguren & Marcaido
VELO-MITH	Rev	7.65	Retolaza
VELO-MITH ARTIAN	Rev	6.35	Arizmendi
VELO-SMITH	Rev	6.35	[Spain]
VELO-STARK	Rev	6/6.35	Garate Hermanos
VENCEDOR	Pistol	6.35	Casimir Santos
VENUS	Pistol	7.65	Urizar
VENUS	Pistol	7.65	Venus Waffenwerke
VER-CAR	Pistol	6.35	Verney-Carron
VESTA	Pistol	6.35/7.65	Hijos de A Echeverria
VESTPOCKET	Rev	22	Rohm
VETERAN	Rev	32RF	Norwich Falls [USA]
VETO	Rev	32RF	[Belgium]
VICI	Pistol	6.35	Francisco Arizmendi
VICTOR	Pistol	6.35/7.65	Marlin
VICTOR	SS	38RF	Harrrington & Richardson
VICTOR	Rev	22/32	Crescent Firearms
VICTOR	Shotgun	Various	High Standard
VICTOR, THE	Pistol	22	Harrington & Richardson
VICTOR No 1	Rev	22/32	

Name	Type	Calibre	Maker
VICTOR SPECIAL	Shotgun	Various	Crescent
VICTORIA	Rev	32RF	Hood
VICTORIA	Pistol	6.35/7.65	Esperanza & Unceta
VICTORY	Pistol	6.35	Zulaica
VIKING	Pistol	45	ODI
VILAR	Pistol	7.65	[Spain]56
VINCITOR	Pistol	6.35/7.65	Zulaica
VINDEX	Pistol	7.65	Pyrenees
VIRGINIA ARMS CO	Shotgun	Various	Crescent Firearms
VIRGINIAN DRAGOON	Rev	Various	Interarms
VITE	Pistol	6.35/7.65	Echave & Arizmendi
VOLUNTEER	Shotgun	Various	Stevens
VULCAN ARMS CO	Shotgun	Various	Crescent Firearms
VULCAIN	Pistol	6.35	[Spain]
VULKAN	Pistol	6.35	Pfannl

W

Name	Type	Calibre	Maker
WACO	Pistol	6.35	SEAM
WALAM	Pistol	7.65	Femaru
WALDMAN	Pistol	6.35/7.65	Arizmendi & Goenaga
WALKY	Pistol	6.35	[Spain]
WALMAN	Pistol	6.35/7.65/9S	Arizmendi & Goenaga
WARWINCK	Pistol	7.65	Arizaga
WEGRIA-CHARLIER	Pistol	6.35	Charlier
WELTWAFFEN	Pistol	7.65	MKEK

Name	Type	Calibre	Maker	Name	Type	Calibre	Maker
WESTERN BULLDOG	Rev	44	[Belgium]				Arizmendi
WESTERN FIELD NO 5	SS	22	Pyrenees	YOU BET	Rev	22	Hopkins & Allen
WESTERN SIX-SHOOTER	Rev	Various	Weirauch	YOUNG AMERICA	Rev	Various	Harrington &
WESTERN STYLE	Rev	22	Rohm				Richardson
WHEELER	RP	41RF	American	YOVANOVITCH	Pistol	6.35/7.65/9S	Kragujevac
			Arms Co				
WHITE STAR	Rev	32	[USA]				

Z

Name	Type	Calibre	Maker
Z	Pistol	6.35	Ceska Zbrojovka
ZALDUN	Pistol	6.35	[Spain]
ZB	Rifle/MG	Various	Zbrojovka Brno
ZENTRUM	SS	.22	VEB
ZEPHYR	Shotgun	Various	Stoeger
ZEPHYR	Rev	22	Rohm
ZOLI	Pistol	6.35	Tanfoglio
ZONDA	SS	22	Hafdasa

Name	Type	Calibre	Maker
WICKLIFFE	Rifle	Various	Triple-S
WIDE AWAKE	Rev	32RF	Hood
WINFIELD	Pistol	9S/9P	Bayonne
WINFIELD ARMS CO	Rev	32RF	Norwich Falls
WINOCA ARMS CO	Shotgun	Various	Crescent Firearms
WITTES HARDWARE CO	Shotgun	Various	Stevens
W.L.GRANT	Rev	22/32RF	Lower
WOLF PATENT	Pistol	7.65	[Spain]
WOLVERINE	Pistol	22	Whitney Firearms
WOLVERINE ARMS CO	Shotgun	Various	Crescent Firearms
WOODSMAN	Pistol	22	Colt
WORTHINGTON ARMS	Shotgun	Various	Stevens
WORTHINGTON, GEORGE	Shotgun	Various	Stevens

X

Name	Type	Calibre	Maker
XL	Rev	22/32/38	Hopkins & Allen
XL BULLDOG	Rev	38	Hopkins & Allen
XX STANDARD	Rev	22/32/38	Marlin

Y

Name	Type	Calibre	Maker
YATO	Pistol	7.65	Hamada Arsenal
YDEAL	Pistol	6.35/7.65	Francisco